Cabins, Cottages & Mansions

Homes of the Presidents of the United States

by
Nancy D. Myers Benbow
and
Christopher H. Benbow

THOMAS PUBLICATIONS
Gettysburg PA 17325

W9-BEO-002

Copyright © 1995, 1998 Nancy D. Myers Benbow and Christopher H. Benbow

Printed and bound in the United States of America

Published by THOMAS PUBLICATIONS
        P.O. Box 3031
        Gettysburg, Pa. 17325

All rights reserved. No part of this book may be used or reproduced
without written permission of the author and the publisher, except in the
case of brief quotations embodied in critical essays and reviews.

ISBN-0-939631-61-X

Cover design by Ryan C. Stouch

For Our Families,
Whose Aid and Encouragement
Helped to Make This Book Possible
And
For All Who Love American History.

TABLE OF CONTENTS

FOREWORD

In the years surrounding World War II—the late 30s through the early 50s—a classic American education included at least one course, and frequently several, in which one "learned" American history. Sometimes it was well taught; sometimes it was not. For me, isolated pieces of that education come to mind decades later, when called up by current events or other memory stimulants. I can still, with difficulty, remember the names of most of the presidents of the United States in some semblance of the order of their presidencies. Looking back I can appreciate that this was instilled in me as something basic—a prerequisite to comprehension of the sweep of the history of our country.

Reading *Cabins, Cottages and Mansions* by Chris and Nancy Benbow revives that early learning, and reminds me that the presidency of the United States is a matter of historical sweep. Indeed, it is impossible to comprehend the debate and dilemma of the 1992 presidential campaign without having some reference to where it all came from and what it is all about. This, of course, is not the purpose of the Benbows' book, which is about the physical cabins, cottages and mansions that the forty-one presidents from Washington to Clinton have inhabited. The book is a masterful compendium of information that any amateur historian, or just plain-tourist, should have in traveling about the country and visiting the seventy-five or so historical sites and buildings that have been preserved (or reconstructed) from presidential history. Here are myriad details and elaborate descriptions of what to expect and see, from the colonial grandeur of Washington's Mount Vernon, to Lincoln's reconstructed log cabin birthplace, to midwestern mansions, to the White House itself.

Visiting these historic places, even through the pages of the book alone, can provide students of American history, or any interested reader, insight into the development of each president's personal qualities, as well as a better understanding of day-to-day life in America during the periods that many of the dwelling places represent. Beyond this, the book provides an opportunity to learn about the lives of our past and present leaders, to provide clues about their strengths and comprehension of their weaknesses. While focusing on the physical environment in which the life of each president is played out, the Benbows' presentation lets us see how these men lived, and how they created or took advantage of their opportunities to achieve the measure of greatness to which they became entitled. These are the highest chosen leaders of our country. Their influence on progress and change in our system has been profound. We owe many of them great debts of gratitude, and can appropriately both learn from and appreciate their lives. How better to do this than by actually seeing where they lived and how they lived.

The book, however, is more than this. It makes a statement about the role of the presidency itself. Progressing through its pages, we see the presidents heading a nation that comes into being from its colonial origins, grows from an agricultural to an industrialized economy, is almost wiped out by a civil war but survives to become a world power, and is then beset by economic and social problems that would have been beyond the imagination of its founders. Accordingly, it is profoundly significant to see these men in the context of their own environments in terms of time as well as place.

This is the service provided by the Benbows' book. Every president except McKinley is represented by at least one dwelling place. The Benbows have done a masterful job of assembling all of this information, much of it from private sources since so many of these places are in private hands. (It could be an incidental benefit of the Benbows' work to have the federal government take a more concerted interest in funding, or taking actual custody of, some of the privately held places.)

Many men have a keen sense of place, such that the place defines the man, as the man defines the place. So it is with the presidents. Many of them exhibit a devotion to land and dwellings. Many either built or acquired substantial residences, or maintained significant existing residences through their years in office. Some created dwelling places where they chose to live out their years following their presidential terms. For some of these, in their retirements they may seem to have defined themselves, perhaps with a greater precision than in their terms of office. This may be observed of President Washington, who returned to Mount Vernon after his second term and died there two and a half years later. Washington was, after all he did to get this country started and as its first president, a southern aristocrat, and Mount Vernon reflects his life-time values.

Jefferson is another president whose ultimate dwelling place expresses much of the inner nature of the man. As the Benbows suggest, a visit to Monticello, where Jefferson spent his last sixteen years after his presidency, is a journey into the mind of one of the greatest thinkers of his time. Monticello is filled not only with Jefferson's library, but with the furnishings and inventions that he created.

There are other houses that express both the president and his time. Buchanan's Wheatland in Lancaster, Pennsylvania, a little known but well-maintained example of Federal architecture where Buchanan lived for seven years after his presidency, shows an American version of Victorian elegance. Others are Hayes' Spiegel Grove in Fremont, Ohio, and Benjamin Harrison's home in Indianapolis, both of which are truly fine examples of midwestern elegance in the last half of the 19th century.

My own great grandfather, James Abram Garfield, also showed a keen sense of place, although he did not live to enjoy a retirement from the presidency. Garfield was the twentieth president of the United States. He served only from his inauguration in March 1881 until his death in September of that year. The cause of death was blood poisoning resulting from a bullet wound inflicted two months earlier by Charles Guiteau, a religious fanatic and disappointed office seeker who was shunned by Garfield and the new administration. President Garfield didn't live long enough in the office to have been a good president, but he wasn't a bad one either. In a sense Garfield did make an enduring contribution as president, because his death was the impetus for major civil service reform that eliminated the "spoils system" and changed the federal bureaucracy for all time. In addition, Garfield's prolonged last illness pointed up the need for constitutional changes to permit the vice president, or others in the line of succession, to fulfill the functions of the president in the event of incapacity.

Before he became president, Garfield acquired and developed a substantial farm in Mentor, Ohio, to which he certainly would have retired, had he lived. As it was, the farm, which is known as "Lawnfield," was maintained by Garfield's widow, and was the site of extended family activity for several decades. Lawnfield has now been extensively restored by the Western Reserve Historical Society and is described in some detail in Chapter 19 of *Cabins, Cottages and Mansions.*

There is something to be learned too from the physical places where presidents were born. An amazing number of them in the last century were born in log cabins. In addition to Lincoln there were Jackson, Fillmore, Buchanan and Garfield, to name a few. That was a politically "right thing" in the last century, although humble origins of a physical nature have been politically appealing at other times. On the other hand, there does not appear to have been anything of a disqualifying nature in being born in pretty elegant surroundings. Most of the early presidents were well-born in that sense, as were the Roosevelts and some others who have served in this century. It is also interesting to note that the only two presidents who were born in a hospital were Jimmy Carter and Bill Clinton. Of course that in itself is of no merit in the context of presidential dwelling places since there is nothing either historically or commercially worth preserving about a president's hospital birthplace.

Many of the places that are described in the book are effective in conveying something of the essence of the particular president. An outstanding example is found in the Benbows' description of Sagamore Hill, President Theodore Roosevelt's magnificent home in Oyster Bay, New York. Sagamore Hill was a special place in the life of that president. It was the site of much presidential business, but even more, it was the place where numerous members of Roosevelt's extended family gathered and grew up. The description in the Benbows' book rings with the sound of children at play.

The dwellings of the second Roosevelt, FDR, also have stories to tell about the man. FDR was born amid the comforts of the Roosevelt family estate at Hyde Park, New York,

which has now been fully restored following a devastating fire in 1982. FDR's career was truly that of the Wilsonian "public man." Before he became president in 1933, he held a series of public offices, including the governorship of New York. Prior to 1921, when he contracted polio, much of FDR's private life focused on the family's summer compound at Campobello Island, New Brunswick, Canada, off the easternmost coast of Maine. This is another place whose description rings with the sounds of children. Reading it, one cannot fail to reflect on the extraordinary qualities of a man whose promising career as a public servant might have been wiped out by a crippling disease. Roosevelt returned to Campobello only three times for brief visits after 1921.

Despite his physical handicap FDR went on to become one of the most important of the presidents, the office that he held for more than twelve years, until close to the end of World War II. While the White House in Washington was FDR's residence for those years, he died at the "Little White House" in Warm Springs, Georgia, which is described as a simple "cottage." It is obvious from the description that the cottage and its contents were expressions of the man. Particularly notable is the nautical motif that pervades this land-locked environment, which is clearly reminiscent of FDR and the younger years he spent in better health off the coast of Maine.

The houses associated with President Truman present a sharp contrast. Truman came from a simple rural life in Missouri. Most of his boyhood years were spent on a farm in Grandview. Truman was certainly a president who was not "born to greatness." Indeed there were many who considered that, as successor to FDR, it was unlikely that he would achieve greatness. Nevertheless, in the words of Shakespeare, there are those "whom greatness is thrust upon." Many view Truman as one of the latter.

President Truman owned only one house, a plain but comfortable house by the side of a street in Independence, Missouri, to which he returned after his presidency, and where he died. Still, there was another abode that Truman must have found comfortable during his presidency. This was his "Little White House" in Key West, Florida. The recent restoration of this beach house gives prominent place to the president's poker table and his piano.

The Eisenhower farm in Gettysburg was also a defining environment for the post-presidential years of one of the recent presidents. Because of the wandering nature of Eisenhower's military career he never had any permanent home until purchasing the Gettysburg farm in 1950. This actually occurred in contemplation of Eisenhower's retirement, not only from the military but as president of Columbia University. Then in 1952, the former Army chief of staff was elected president. His real retirement was postponed for the eight years that he served in that office. The Benbows' description emphasizes the great pleasure that the president and his wife took in the Gettysburg property once the time for retirement did arrive.

Except for his Brookline, Massachusetts birthplace, there are no dwelling places for President Kennedy that are open to the public. This is also true for the most part as to the later presidents, some of whom (or their families) continue to live in homes and houses that may some day be open to the public. Presumably a later edition of the Benbows' book will have more on these presidents.

The American presidents, all forty-one of them, have a lot in common, in addition to the fact that (with the exception of George Washington) they all lived in one house—the White House—for part of their lives. For one thing, they all were, or are, mortal men. They were all born natural citizens of the United States, as they must be under the Constitution. They were educated and matured in some segment of American society—whether amid privilege, or in modest circumstances. Almost all of them married and produced children. All but the last five have died. Some were great presidents, some were near great, and some were not so great. But all of them took their turns in personifying an institution that forms one of the fundamental pillars of our form of government. The presidency of the United States is the highest office that mortal man can hold or aspire to in our democratic system. But it is emphatically an office that is held by mortals. Here there can be no pretense to a "divine right of kings"; no acceptance that birth or privilege provides a destiny that is predetermined. Each incumbent holds the office because the democratic process has chosen that individual, and each incumbent will have the office only so long as that process will sustain that choice (and currently not for more than two full terms in any event).

The Benbows' book will not help you decide how to vote in any election. In fact, it is studiously dispassionate when it comes to taking political positions on the events of the presidencies, fairly stating the highlights of the facts of each administration and acknowledging the existence of controversy where appropriate. However, the book may help some voters by confirming that there is a reason to vote. In presidential elections we are not choosing a king. We are not asked to endorse a candidate as perfectly suited. Rather, we are trying to select, from among those that the political system has to offer, the best candidate to carry on the institution of the presidency of the United States—an individual whom we can call upon to cope with the problems of the times, but of whom we have no right to expect perfection.

Cambridge, Massachusetts   Harry A. Garfield II
November 4, 1992

ACKNOWLEDGEMENTS

We owe a great debt of gratitude to our families and friends who supported us over the six years of research, travel, and preparation of the text of this book, especially: A. Louise Myers, who located our publisher; Gloria M. Benbow, who suggested contacting Harry Garfield to prepare the foreword, Terence H. Benbow, for his advice, editing and financial support; Shawn Benbow, for her assistance in marketing; and Johnette Willa Myers, who took some of the photographs, supplied information, and provided so much moral support. For the photograph of the Eisenhower Birthplace in Denison, Texas, that illustrates the proximity of General Eisenhower's father's residence to his workplace, we thank David Michael Wood. We are also very grateful to Dean S. Thomas of Thomas Publications, whose patience and advice helped to see our project to its conclusion.

We also owe a very special thanks to the late Harry A. Garfield, II, the great-grandson of President James A. Garfield, for his contribution of the foreword.

We gratefully acknowledge the contribution of many sources, including not only published works, but also property owners, site personnel and volunteers who reviewed and commented on the accuracy of the text of this book. In many cases, review of the text involved an effort on the part of many members of the staff of a site or library, and the authors apologize to those who assisted us but were unnamed in the responses we received from the sites. For their contribution and work in the furtherance of American presidential and architectural history, we gratefully acknowledge:

— Jean Stroughton, Washington's Birthplace National Historic Site, Washington's Birthplace, Virginia;
— Ann M. Rauscher, manager of media relations, The Mount Vernon Ladies' Association, Mount Vernon, Virginia;
— Dorothy Fischer, Deshler-Morris House, Philadelphia, Pennsylvania;
— David F. Krantz, supervisory park ranger, Adams National Historic Site, Quincy, Massachusetts;
— Mr. and Mrs. Addison Thompson, Jr., Tuckahoe Plantation, Richmond, Virginia;
— Cinder Stanton, director of research, and Mindy Black, communications officer, Monticello, Charlottesville, Virginia;
— Sheryl Kingery, director of interpretation, Thomas Jefferson's Poplar Forest, Forest, Virginia;
— Ann Miller, research director, Montpelier Research Center, Montpelier Station, Virginia;
— James E. Wootton, curator, Ash Lawn-Highland, Charlottesville, Virginia;

— Wilma B. Le Van, administrative assistant, Monroe Hill College, University of Virginia, Charlottesville, Virginia;
— Mr. Thomas H. DeLashmutt;
— Michael Davidson, South Carolina Department of Parks, Recreation & Tourism, Columbia, South Carolina;
— Sharon Macpherson, deputy director for programs, The Hermitage, Hermitage, Tennessee;
— Michael Henderson, Martin Van Buren National Historic Site, Kinderhook, New York;
— Malcolm Jamieson, Berkeley Plantation, Charles City, Virginia;
— Mrs. Charles Hamke, curator, Grouseland, Vincennes, Indiana;
— Mrs. Harrison Tyler, Sherwood Forest Plantation, Charles City, Virginia;
— Joyce White, manager, James K. Polk State Memorial Site, Pineville, North Carolina;
— Kim Finley, curator of collections, James K. Polk Ancestral Home, Columbia, Tennessee;
— Dr. and the late Mrs. William C. Gist, Springfield, Louisville, Kentucky;
— Thomas Noble, park manager, Fillmore Glen State Park, Moravia, New York;
— Ruth A. Schmidt, co-curator, Millard Fillmore House Museum, East Aurora, New York;
— James A. Marvin, curator, Franklin Pierce Homestead, Hillsboro, New Hampshire;
— Anna Avery, curator, Pierce Manse, Concord, New Hampshire;
— Steven Behe, park manager, Buchanan's Birthplace State Historical Park, Mercersburg, Pennsylvania;
— Walter Burgin, headmaster, Mercersburg Academy, Mercersburg, Pennsylvania;
— Sally Cohalan, The James Buchanan Foundation for the Preservation of Wheatland, Lancaster, Pennsylvania;
— Karren Brown, acting superintendent, Abraham Lincoln Birthplace National Historical Site, Hodgenville, Kentucky;
— Martha Greenwell, manager, Lincoln's Boyhood Home, Hodgenville, Kentucky;
— Paul D. Guraedy, superintendent, and Jerry Sanders, chief of interpretation, Lincoln Boyhood National Memorial, Lincoln City, Indiana;
— Brock A. Mayo, Lincoln State Park, Lincoln City, Indiana;
— David Hedrick, manager, Lincoln's New Salem State Historic Site, Petersburg, Illinois;
— Sally A. Poland, executive director, Mordecai Historic Park, Raleigh, North Carolina;
— Jim Small, Andrew Johnson National Historic Site, Greeneville, Tennessee;

- Loretta Fuhrman, Grant Birthplace State Historic Site, Point Pleasant, Ohio;
- Judy and John Ruthven, Grant Boyhood Home, Georgetown, Ohio;
- Chris Eckard, Chief of Interpretation, Pam Sanfilippo, Park Historian, and Karen Miller, Park Ranger, U.S. Grant National Historic Site, St. Louis, Missouri;
- Dan Decker, manager, Grant's Farm, Anheuser-Busch Companies, Inc., St. Louis, Missouri;
- Thomas A. Campbell, Jr., site manager, Galena State Historic Site, Galena, Illinois;
- David R. Mitchell, executive director, Saratoga County Historical Society, Ballston Spa, New York;
- Roger B. Bridges, Rutherford B. Hayes Presidential Center, Fremont, Ohio;
- Suzanne Miller, curator, James A. Garfield National Historic Site, Mentor, Ohio;
- John Damville, historic sites operations chief, Vermont Division of Historic Presentation, Montpelier, Vermont;
- Sharon Farrell, Grover Cleveland Birthplace State Historic Site, Caldwell, New Jersey;
- Matilda Cuomo, New York, New York;
- Lorraine L. Butler, coordinator of visitor assistance, State of New York Office of General Services, Albany, New York;
- Martha Thomas, curator, President Benjamin Harrison Memorial Foundation, Inc., Indianapolis, Indiana;
- William Wyss and Sally Donze, Stark County Historical Society, Canton, Ohio;
- Charles Markis, site manager, Theodore Roosevelt Birthplace National Historic Site, New York, New York;
- Bruce M. Kaye, chief of interpretation, Theodore Roosevelt National Park, Medora, North Dakota;
- Amy Verone, curator, Sagamore Hill National Historic Site, Oyster Bay, New York;
- Robert J. Moore, Jr., chief of interpretation, William Howard Taft National Historic Site, Cincinnati, Ohio;
- Patricia A. Hobbs, curator of collections, Woodrow Wilson Birthplace, Staunton, Virginia;
- Patsy Lee Shulko, Meybohm Realty, Augusta, Georgia;
- Eric Montgomery, executive director, Historic Augusta, Inc., Augusta, Georgia;
- Nancy Vodry, interim director, and Scott Morris, education administrator, Historic Columbia Foundation, Columbia, South Carolina;
- Michael Sheehan and Frank J. Aneilla, Woodrow Wilson House, Washington, D.C.;
- Kelley Gagni, Warren G. Harding Home, Marion, Ohio;
- William W. Jenney, regional historic site administrator, Plymouth Notch Historic District, Plymouth, Vermont;
- Carol Cohan, superintendent, Herbert Hoover National Historic Site, West Branch, Iowa;
- Eileen Jette, curator, and Susan Campbell, publicity chair, Hoover-Minthorn House, Newberg, Oregon;
- Christine Beckman, house manager, and Kathryn A. Kershner, former house manager, The Lou Henry Hoover House, Stanford, California;
- Duane Pearson, superintendent, Home of Franklin D. Roosevelt National Historic Site, Hyde Park, New York;
- Anne Neuman, administrative assistant, Roosevelt Campobello International Park Commission, Lubee, Maine;
- Charles Barnes, The Little White House and Museum, Warm Springs, Georgia;
- Rita Embry, administrator, Harry S Truman Birthplace State Historic Site, Lamar, Missouri;
- David Schafer, Harry S Truman National Historic Site, Independence, Missouri;
- Hal Walsh, The Little White House Museum, Key West, Florida;
- Donna Hunt, park manager, Eisenhower Birthplace State Historic Site, Denison, Texas;
- Colleen Cearley, public affairs specialist, Dwight D. Eisenhower Library, Abilene, Kansas;
- John Latschar, superintendent, Eisenhower National Historic Site, Gettysburg, Pennsylvania;
- Leslie Obleschuk and Peter Terzian, John Fitzgerald Kennedy National Historic Site, Brookline, Massachusetts;
- Melody Webb, superintendent, Lyndon B. Johnson National Historical Park, Johnson City, Texas;
- Leslie Star-Hart, park superintendent, Lyndon B. Johnson State Historical Park, Stonewall Texas;
- Susan Naulty, John M. Olin Archivist, The Richard Nixon Library & Birthplace, Yorba Linda, California;
- Fred Boyles, superintendent, and Bonnie Blaford, park ranger, Jimmy Carter National Historic Site, Plains, Georgia;
- David J. Stanhope, archivist, Jimmy Carter Library, Atlanta, Georgia;
- Beverly Messer, executive assistant to the First Lady, The Georgia Governor's Mansion, Atlanta, Georgia;
- Rod Soubers, supervisory archivist, Ronald Reagan Library, Sima Valley, California;
- Helen Lawton and Dannette Dempsey, Ronald Reagan Home Preservation Foundation, Dixon, Illinois;
- Bob Basura, chief ranger, Sacramento District/Historic Sites, Sacramento, California;
- Jim McGrath, press aide, office of George Bush, Houston, Texas;
- Elaine Johnson and George Wright, Hope, Arkansas;
- Paul David Leopoulos and Carolyn Staley, Little Rock, Arkansas.

GEORGE WASHINGTON

George Washington Birthplace
National Monument
RR. 1, Box 717
Washington's Birthplace, Virginia 22443
(804) 224-1732

Administered by the National Park Service.

Directions: From I-95, take Exit 45 A through Fredericksburg and stay on Va. Route 3 East. Continue on Route 3 for about 38 miles. There will be a sign for the birthplace on the left side of the road. Follow signs to the visitor center.

Open: Daily (except Christmas Day and New Year's Day).

Admission: Fee charged.

Features: Birthplace site, memorial house, visitor center with exhibits and brief film, gift shop, rest rooms, colonial herb and flower garden, colonial living farm, walking trail, burying ground, and picnic area. Handicapped accessible. Educational packets are available for use by teachers.

Special Events: Sheep shearing demonstrations take place on the second, third, and fourth Sundays in May. Candlelight tours of the site are available during a yearly Christmas open house.

The birthplace of the first president of the United States is a lovely setting overlooking Popes Creek and situated just to the south of the Potomac River. Nothing remains of the U-shaped house in which George Washington was born on February 22, 1732—it was destroyed by fire on December 25, 1779. However, the pastoral setting in which George Washington spent the first three and one-half years of his life remains intact. Looking out over the shimmering waters of Popes Creek (named for Nathaniel Pope, the President's great-great-grandfather), it is not hard to see what drew George Washington's ancestors to this Tidewater region. Aside from the natural beauty of the area, the region was also a fertile growing place for vegetables, corn, wheat and, perhaps most importantly, tobacco, which in seventeenth and eighteenth-century colonial America served as a substitute for currency. Here George Washington, who earned his reputation as a soldier and statesman, spent his early years learning the virtues and hardships of life on a farm. Throughout his life, his love of farming was never to diminish.

George Washington's father, Augustine Washington, was a native of the Tidewater area. Augustine Washington's grandfather, John Washington, arrived in America in 1657 and established himself as a prosperous plantation owner with an active interest in public affairs. The family tradition of prosperity and civic-mindedness was passed to John Washington's son, Lawrence Washington, and his son, Augustine Washington. In 1718, Augustine Washington expanded the family estate which was started by his grandfather's purchase of land at Bridges Creek in 1664. He bought from Joseph Abbington an additional 150 acres of land on Popes Creek. It was on this land, Popes Creek Plantation, that Augustine Washington most likely contracted local carpenter David Jones to expand the home already on site. The additions were probably completed around 1726. Jane Butler Washington, Augustine Washington's first wife, died in November 1729. Augustine remarried two years later and his union with Mary Ball resulted in six children, including the eldest, George Washington.

The first world that young George Washington ever knew was that of the farm, where he became familiar with the sight of the harvesting and drying of tobacco, and the sounds of sheep and pigs. In 1735, however, Augustine Washington moved his family to a new location: Little Hunting Creek Plantation, later known as Mount Vernon. Four years later, the family moved again, this time to Ferry Farm, which was on the Rappahannock River just outside Fredericksburg. The site of Ferry Farm is today a county-owned park, and may be seen by driving from the birthplace site on Va. Route 3 west towards Fredericksburg, which is one mile west of the Ferry Farm site.

When George Washington was eleven years old, his father died and young Washington inherited the Ferry Farm estate. Because of his youth, his mother, Mary Ball Washington, managed Ferry Farm, and lived in the Fredericksburg area the rest of her life. After George Washington's half-brother, Augustine Washington, Jr., inherited Popes Creek Plantation, the future president returned to his birthplace for extended stays. Young George Washington came to regard his half-brother with a respect similar to that he had for his late father.

Later, the plantation was passed on to George Washington's nephew, William Augustine Washington. On Christmas Day, 1779, the house was lost to a fire and William Augustine moved away from the plantation. The house was never rebuilt.

Today, through the archaeological efforts of the National Park Service, the federal agency which administers the 538-acre park, the outline of the house in which George Washington was born has been established and may be viewed by visitors. The outline is traced on the lawn of the property by crushed oyster shells. Near the birthplace site is the Memorial House, which was completed in 1931. The house is furnished in a manner which suggests the type of surroundings to which George Washington was accustomed while living in the Tidewater region. It also contains a tea table which, traditionally, belonged to the family during their tenure at Popes Creek. Visitors are greeted at the house by tour guides in eighteenth-century costume and guides conduct half-hour tours of the colonial kitchen and Memorial House.

The entrance to the site is marked by an obelisk which is a one-tenth sized replica of the Washington Monument. The site includes a picnic area overlooking the Potomac River, hiking trails, and a Washington ancestral burying ground. The visitor center offers a display of artifacts which were used by the Washington family and were discovered through archaeological digs which have been conducted at the site. A fourteen minute film on the early life of George Washington is shown at the visitor center on the half-hour during visiting hours, and is available for use by teachers upon request. Many visitors take the short drive to a beach which is on the Potomac and is also a part of the site. The beach, in addition to affording a splendid view of the river, is a place where visitors may go to search for sharks' teeth.

The site also includes a working colonial farm, staffed by National Park Service personnel, in which crops and vegetables are grown. Authenticity, down to the use of oxen to pull a plow, is admirably maintained. The farm features a kitchen house, as well as a weaving room, barns for animals, crop fields, and an herb and flower garden.

Mount Vernon
Mount Vernon, Virginia 22121
(703) 780-2000

Administered by the Mount Vernon Ladies' Association.

Directions: From Washington, D.C., take the Arlington Memorial Bridge to the George Washington Memorial Parkway. Signs indicating the direction to Mount Vernon will be visible on the bridge. Proceed on the Parkway south past Washington National Airport. The Parkway becomes Washington Street in Alexandria, about eight miles south of downtown Washington, D.C. Proceed straight on Washington Street; the road becomes a parkway again when you leave Alexandria. Proceed around the traffic circle to the parking lots.

Mount Vernon is also accessible by bus. Contact Metro Bus and Rail ((202) 637-2437) or Tourmobile Sightseeing Tours ((202) 554-7950). A boat cruise on the Potomac River to Mount Vernon from Washington, D.C. is also available on the Spirit of Mount Vernon between mid-March and October. Call (202) 554-8000.

Open: Daily — call for seasonal hours.

Admission: Fee charged. Discounts for children and senior citizens.

Features: Mansion, outbuildings, gardens, tomb of George and Martha Washington, slave burial ground, Mount Vernon Museum, snack bar, Mount Vernon Inn (restaurant), Museum Shop, Inn Gift Shop, post office, rest rooms, Greenhouse shop, information kiosk, first aid center, and historical trail to be used for hikes by scouting organizations. Second floor of mansion is not accessible to the handicapped, but the museum, the museum annex, gift shops, and rest rooms are handicapped accessible.

Special Events: On the third Monday of February each year, the federal holiday in observance

3

of George Washington's birthday, a ceremony takes place at George Washington's tomb, during which the commanding general of the Military District of Washington, representing the current President of the United States, lays a wreath in memory of the first President. A fife and drum corps is on hand at this ceremony. Also on this day, Mount Vernon becomes an "open house" and all visitors are admitted free of charge. From December 1 to January 6, Mount Vernon sponsors "Holidays at Mount Vernon." During this period, special tours of the Mansion, focusing on entertainment at Mount Vernon in George Washington's day, are conducted.

After leaving his birthplace at Popes Creek Plantation, three-year-old George Washington moved with his parents and family to Hunting Creek Plantation, a property which had been owned by the Washington family since 1674, when it was granted to George Washington's great-grandfather John. The farm, which was also located on the banks of the Potomac River but farther to the north, was purchased by George Washington's father, Augustine Washington, from his sister in 1726. Augustine Washington built a small farmhouse on the site for himself and his family. They remained there from 1735 until 1738, when the Washingtons changed their residence to Ferry Farm, located about one mile east of Fredericksburg; George Washington lived here until his father's death in 1743. Augustine Washington had deeded the Hunting Creek Plantation to his oldest son, Lawrence Washington, who renamed the plantation Mount Vernon in honor of his commander in the British Navy, Admiral Edward Vernon. As young George Washington grew into adolescence, he lived alternately with his half-brother Augustine, Jr., who had inherited Popes Creek Plantation, and his other half-brother, Lawrence Washington, at Mount Vernon.

Two years after Lawrence Washington's death in 1752, George Washington, who had reached the age of 22 and was at that time commander of the Virginia Militia, leased the property from Lawrence Washington's widow. He made drastic structural changes to the property, including raising the roof and adding another floor to the house around 1758, thus doubling its size and enabling the future President to refer to his home, appropriately, as the Mansion House. The changes were made in preparation for his taking up residence at Mount Vernon with his new bride, the former Martha Dandridge Custis, who settled into the house with her new husband and her children, John Parke and Martha Parke Custis, in 1759. From that time onward, George Washington was to occupy many other dwellings as Commander-in-Chief of the Continental Army and as the first president of the United States, but throughout his long career, Mount Vernon was the only place which George Washington truly regarded as home.

Upon the death of Lawrence Washington's widow in 1761, George Washington inherited Mount Vernon, and in the years that followed, arranged to expand his Mansion House even more dramatically than before. He proposed to add rooms to both sides of the house and to expand the outbuildings and the gardens. He also envisioned the addition of a magnificent front porch, or piazza, to the side of the house facing the Potomac River. The completed piazza affords an excellent vantage point from which visitors can, to this day, gaze upon the majestic waters of the Potomac. Most of the process of implementing the plans for improvement and expansion of the Mansion House and grounds went forward in the absence of a busy General Washington, whose military duties kept him away from Mount Vernon from 1775 to 1783, when he resigned his commission and "retired" to Mount Vernon. In 1787, the completion of the expansion of Mount Vernon was marked by the placing of a weather vane in the shape of a dove of peace at the top of the cupola of the Mansion House. The expanded house was then two and one-half stories high and remains one of the most outstanding examples of colonial architecture in America.

More than likely, George Washington had less time than he would have liked to enjoy his expanded new residence. He felt that he could not ignore the need for the new nation to devise a government which reflected the principles of independence and representation of the people for which he had fought so long and so hard. Consequently, he presided over the Constitutional Convention in Philadelphia in 1787. Two years later, at the behest of other figures who played a prominent role in the shaping of the republic, he served as the first president of the United States and moved to New York, the first capital of the young nation. His first residence as president was a Georgian style house on Cherry Street, which was demolished long after the Washingtons left in preparation for the construction of the Brooklyn Bridge. Later, the Washingtons relocated to a four story house at 39 Broadway, which also fell victim to the wrecker's ball. After it was decided, in 1790, that Philadelphia would become the new capital of the United States, the presidential family moved to a house owned by Robert Morris, which was situated at the corner of High and Sixth Streets. Except for certain periods of time in 1793 and 1794, George Washington lived in that Georgian style home for the remainder of his presidency. Today, the house is gone and the property on which the house stood is part of the Independence Park National Historic Site. In November 1793 and again during the summer of 1794, the Washingtons took up temporary residence at what is now known as the Deshler-Morris House, which is still located in the Germantown section of Philadelphia and is open to the public. At the time, the house was owned by Colonel Isaac Franks.

During his presidency, George Washington managed to visit Mount Vernon on 15 occasions, and yearned for the time when he could return to his beloved home and the tranquility of life as a private citizen. The time came for him in 1797, when, after completing his second term as President, he was able to turn his high office over to John Adams and to return to life as a private citizen and gentleman farmer. He spent the two and one-half years that remained to him at Mount Vernon, and died there, in his own bedroom, on December 14, 1799. Two and one-half years later, his wife Martha Washington also died and was entombed in the old family vault beside her husband. George Washington's will directed that a new brick tomb be built at a specified location at Mount Vernon to replace the old vault, which badly needed repairs. It was not until 1831 that the new tomb was completed and the bodies of George and Martha Washington were moved there, along with the remains of other family members. The tomb is surrounded by a brick wall and the bodies of George and Martha Washington are each encased in marble sarcophagi presented in 1837. The graves of other family members, as well as the Mount Vernon slave burial ground, are close by. The tomb, the restored vault, and the slave burial ground may be viewed by visitors to Mount Vernon today.

At the time of George Washington's passing, Mount Vernon had expanded from the 2,126 acres originally leased to him in 1754 to approximately 8,000 acres. After Martha Washington's death, Mount Vernon was divided into five parcels, each of which passed to a different Washington heir. 4,000 acres of the estate, including the Mansion House and the outbuildings, became the property of George Washington's nephew, Bushrod Washington. That property passed from Bushrod Washington to his heirs until 1858, when the Mansion House, the outbuildings, and 200 acres of the surrounding property were purchased by the Mount Vernon Ladies' Association. The Association was formed in 1853, after both the federal government and the Commonwealth of Virginia declined to purchase the property from the Washington family. It mounted a national campaign which raised $200,000 toward the purchase of the property.

Deshler-Morris House
5442 Germantown Avenue
Philadelphia, Pennsylvania 19144
(215) 596-1748

Administered by Deshler-Morris House, Inc., in cooperation with the National Park Service.

Directions:	**From downtown Philadelphia, take Kelly Drive north, turning right onto Midvale. Turn left onto Wissahickon. Turn right at School House Lane, and right again onto Germantown Avenue. Site is third house on the right opposite Market Square.**
Open:	**Seasonal hours. Closed Mondays and holidays. Call for information.**
Admission:	**Fee charged.**
Features:	**House and gardens. First floor of the house and grounds are handicapped accessible, and a book of color photographs is available for those who cannot tour the second floor. Guided tour of site normally lasts about three-quarters of an hour. Educational program and materials are in the process of being developed.**
Special Events:	**In early December, the house is open for special holiday tours. One day during that time every year, a candlelight tour is offered in the evening hours. The house also hosts an annual Christmas tea.**

In the summer of 1793, while Philadelphia was the capital of the United States, yellow fever struck the city. The pestilence was so virulent that most of the executive branch of the government, including President Washington himself, was forced to leave the city after having stayed in town only during the first days of September of that year. President Washington spent most of the next two months of the year at Mount Vernon, and, by late October, made plans to return as close to the seat of his government as he could manage. He rented the home of Colonel Isaac Franks, situated in Germantown, which was approximately seven miles north of Philadelphia. The arrangements to rent the house had been made by Attorney General Edmund Randolph, and of the three houses suggested by Randolph, President Washington chose Colonel Franks' house because it was "more commodious for myself and the entertainment of company."

President Washington arrived in Germantown on November 1 for a scheduled Cabinet meeting, only to find that the arrangements to occupy the Franks' house had not been completed, resulting in his acceptance of other accommodations for a short period. He occupied the house as of November 16, 1793, staying there for the balance of the month. During this time, President Washington held four Cabinet meetings in the house. Much of the focus of these meetings was upon the war between Great Britain and France; the impending convening of Congress in December was also a matter of

concern to the Cabinet. By November 30, the yellow fever epidemic had subsided, and the Washingtons moved back into Philadelphia.

However, this was not to be the only period in which the Washingtons occupied this house. Because the duties of his office would not allow the president to make a long-term visit to his beloved Mount Vernon, he elected to return to the home he so enjoyed the previous year, writing: "...I have taken a house in Germantown to avoid the heat of the City in the months of July and August." On July 30, 1794, the Washingtons returned to the house in Germantown together with their adopted children, Eleanor Parke Custis and George Washington Parke Custis. They took two loads of furniture from the Philadelphia presidential mansion, and remained in the house until September 20 of that year, returning to Philadelphia when the seasonal change of weather permitted them to do so.

During his second stay at Colonel Franks' home, President Washington commuted between Philadelphia and Germantown, attending to his executive duties while in Philadelphia, but leaving affairs of state behind him, to the extent possible, while at the Germantown house. However, while at the house in Germantown, the President learned of the Whiskey Rebellion, in which a group of backwoods farmers engaged in a protest against the enforcement of certain excise taxes in western Pennsylvania. He was forced to issue a Proclamation on August 7, 1794, ordering the insurgents to disperse and put an end to the matter.

Today, this house, named Deshler-Morris House in honor of its first and last private owners, stands as the earliest "White House" still in existence today. This is so because the other houses occupied by President Washington while in office have since been demolished. The first owner of this house was David Deshler, a Philadelphia Quaker merchant, who purchased the site in 1752, when Germantown was still a small village populated by German-speaking people. The original house, built in 1752, was a modest but handsome stone structure with two rooms on each of its two floors. Deshler intended the home to be a summer home suitable for his growing children. It is in this section of the house that the tour begins, and visitors may look at one room on the first floor, which apparently was used for storage, and a kitchen with a large fireplace. The more formal rooms in the house are contained in the second section, which was built by Deshler in 1772 in the Georgian style. Visitors enter the dining room on the first floor of the house and see a long, pleasant room which includes a fireplace made of Valley Forge marble. On the walls of this room are Rembrandt Peale's painting of six-year-old Samuel Morris, a member of the last family to occupy this house as private owners. The Morris family acquired the house in 1834 from the Perot family of Philadelphia merchants, who had purchased the house from Colonel Franks in 1802. The green wooden blinds on the windows in this room were owned by the Morris family, and a set of Trotter chairs with horsehair covers can also be seen here.

Crossing the front hallway, visitors come to the front parlor, where President Washington held four Cabinet meetings during his first stay in the house. The first items that catch one's eye when entering this room are the four Derby porcelain figures sitting on the mantel, which represent the continents of America, Africa, Europe and Asia. Also on display here is a red upholstered sofa, which was transported by the Washingtons from Philadelphia to Germantown to be used during their stay in this house. A small English child's chair has been positioned by the fireplace, and one may see a set of Prince of Wales chairs upholstered in horsehair. A gaming table is on display in a corner of this room, representing George Washington's fondness for card games. The room also features a small collection of eighteenth-century calling cards, which were used to announce the arrival of guests.

Behind the parlor is a small tea room, in which Mrs. Washington would serve tea to her female guests, who could enjoy the beauty of the gardens behind the house visible through the windows of this room. The fireplace is framed in a set of English tiles, each of which depicts an animal. In the center of this room is a round Chippendale mahogany table, which was originally owned by James Smith, a signer of the Declaration of Independence. Also on display here are a set of Windsor chairs and a salmon-colored cabinet, which is built into the corner of the room.

Visitors then step back into the hallway, noting the eighteenth century grandfather clock designed by Frederic Domenick of Philadelphia. A candle lamp hangs from the ceiling of the hallway, and one may also see a row of wooden hooks on the wall close to the ceiling. These hooks were used to hang the long cloaks that eighteenth century visitors typically wore.

Next, visitors ascend the staircase, which was plain-painted and feathered in George Washington's time. In the hallway on the second floor, visitors see a hand painted picture of the city of Philadelphia. The hallway leads to a series of bedrooms, each of which is the same size. The first of these rooms was used by Nelly Custis, President Washington's adopted granddaughter. Among the items to be seen in this room are a washing table with pitcher and a wooden commode. This room also features a fireplace adorned with English tiles and finger vases which rest on the mantel.

Across the hallway is the room used by President and Mrs. Washington during their stays here. Among the features of this room are: a looking glass which was designed using two individual pieces of mirrored glass in order to avoid the higher tax assessment that a single sheet of glass of comparable size would have incurred, a trapunto bedspread which was made by hand in the early 1770s, a drop-leaf bird cage table, a potty chair that belonged to the Morris family, and another fireplace adorned with English tiles.

Behind the Washingtons' bedroom, and above the first floor tea room, is the room used by President Washington as his office. Here, the president would dictate correspondence to his secretary. A device which was used to affix sealing wax to envelopes can be found on the desk in this room.

Returning to the hallway, visitors then walk through a doorway into the 1752 section of the house, where one may see the rooms which were occupied by Mrs. Emerson, the Washingtons' housekeeper, and Mr. Germaine, the president's valet. Among the period pieces featured in these rooms are a shaving bowl and wig curler, which would have been used by an eighteenth-century gentleman, and a trunk which was used by the Morris family in the early 1800s.

Behind the servants' rooms is a toy room. Here, one may see a display of toy animal figures made in 1811 and 1812, as well as a large dollhouse. The dollhouse is an impressive replica of a home situated in downtown Philadelphia and contains fine examples of doll furniture. Also on display here is a primitive painting of Martha Washington saying goodbye to the children: Nelly and Custis. Custis, as he was then called, attended Germantown Academy while living in this house. His room, as well as the rooms used by his tutor and other Washington family servants, is on the third floor of the house, which is not open to the public.

Visitors would be well-advised to complete a tour of Deshler-Morris House with a stroll through the gardens behind the house, to enjoy the same pleasant surroundings which enticed the Washingtons to return to this beautiful home in the summer of 1794.

JOHN ADAMS and JOHN QUINCY ADAMS

Adams National Historic Site
John Adams and John Quincy Adams Birthplaces
133-141 Franklin Street
Quincy, Massachusetts 02269
(617) 770-1175

Administered by the National Park Service.

Directions: From I-93, take Exit 8 (Quincy) to Furnace Brook Parkway. Turn right onto Adams Street. Proceed to Hancock Street, turn right, and proceed to Granite Street. Turn right again and proceed to Franklin Street. Turn left. The houses will be on the right side of the street.

Open: Daily, April through November.

Admission: Fee charged. Children and senior citizens free.

Features: Two houses, visitor center (in downtown Quincy), and United First Parish Church (where both Presidents are buried). Houses and grounds are handicapped accessible. A trolley bus provides transportation between sites.

Special Events: Call site for current special events.

President John Adams was born on October 30, 1735, on a site which was originally part of a 140-acre plot. The house, which today has 133 Franklin Street as its address, was built circa 1681 and, like the adjacent birthplace of John Ouincy Adams, is a saltbox structure with a central chimney. It is framed with huge beams which are joined and secured by wood pegs, and has two-foot-wide planks in its floor and brick-filled walls. It originally had two lower and two upper rooms, but John Adams' father, Deacon John Adams, added a rear lean-to onto the house in 1744, expanding the space to include two more downstairs rooms and two small upstairs rooms, as well as a large attic. It was in this attic that the Deacon practiced his trade of cordwaining (shoemaking). During the day, while John's father tilled the fields, his mother, Susanna Boylston Adams, set about the dangerous business of preparing meals, utilizing the large fireplace which leads to the central chimney. In addition to its usefulness for hearth-cooking, the central chimney provided fireplaces which heated two other lower rooms in the house. This house was the home of President John Adams throughout his formative years, during his period of study at Harvard (he graduated in 1755), and during his early adult life while he taught school at Worcester, Massachusetts and then studied law.

The adjacent house at 141 Franklin Street, where John Quincy Adams was born on July 11, 1767, was purchased by Deacon John Adams in 1744 and inherited by the Deacon's son, John Adams, in 1761. Built in 1663, this saltbox structure was the place in which the Deacon's son, John Adams, began married life with his wife, the former Abigail Smith. Like the birthplace of his father, John Quincy Adams' birthplace was originally a structure with a central chimney and two upper and two lower rooms to which a lean-to was added for a new kitchen. John Adams came to use the original kitchen of this house as his law office. Abigail and John Adams lived in this house, which was their farm home, for brief, interrupted periods between 1764, the year they married, and 1784, during which time they also resided in Boston, where John maintained a successful law practice.

Their Boston homes included a rented house on Brattle Square, where they lived in 1768; a home on Cole Lane; and a house on Queen Street, which was theirs from 1772 to 1774.

John Adams traveled to Paris to serve on a peace commission for eighteen months, and, while there, stayed at the Hotel de Valentinois. He also participated in negotiations with Holland and England. While in Holland, he stayed in Agterburgune by deHoogstraat, Leyden, then in a row house on the Keizesgracht in Amsterdam. Upon returning to Massachusetts, he served as a delegate for the Commonwealth of Massachusetts, and in 1779, John Adams and two fellow delegates drafted the Massachusetts Constitution in the law office of his farm house. Later, John Adams made another sojourn to Europe and his family joined him in Auteuil. After returning to France for a time, he became Minister to Great Britain, and established a legation on Grosvenor Square in London. After John Adams participated in concluding the Definitive Treaty with Great Britain, the Adamses returned home, not to the house on Franklin Street, but to their new home on what is now known as Adams Street.

John Quincy Adams accompanied his parents on their travels. In 1781, he matriculated at the University of Leyden, and later accompanied Francis Dana to Russia as his private secretary. In 1785, after returning from London, the last place he visited while traveling in Europe, he attended Harvard. Upon graduation, he studied law at the offices of Theophilus Parsons in Newburyport, Massachusetts.

In 1774, John Adams purchased his birthplace from his brother, who had acquired its ownership, and sold both it and the birthplace of John Quincy Adams to his son in 1803. John Quincy Adams, his wife, Louisa Catherine Adams, and two of their children resided there until 1806. Both homes are now administered by the National Park Service, having been owned alternately by the Adams family and the city of Quincy previously. Both houses were completely restored in 1982. They are the oldest surviving presidential birthplaces, and the only birthplaces where two presidents were born 75 feet apart!

Adams National Historic Site
(The Old House)
135 Adams Street
Quincy, Massachusetts 02269
(617) 770-1175

Administered by the National Park Service.

Directions:	From I-93, take Exit 8 (Quincy) to Furnace Brook Parkway. Turn right onto Adams Street. House and grounds are on the left side of Adams Street at the intersection with Hancock Street.

Open:	Daily in season — call for hours.
Admission:	Fee charged. Children and senior citizens free.

Features: Home, library, garden, and carriage house. Second floor of house is not handicapped accessible. Visitor center (in downtown Quincy) with gift shop, exhibits, and restrooms.

Special Events: In the early summer there is a week-long annual lecture series about the Adams family. The site also participates in the Christmas celebration, "Holidays in Quincy," every two years.

This gracious home, which was once situated upon approximately forty acres of land at the time it was acquired by John and Abigail Adams in 1787 for 600 pounds, was the homestead of one of America's most prominent and influential families for four generations. Originally named "Peacefield" by John Adams, and later known as "The Old House," the structure was built by Major Leonard Vassall, a West Indian sugar planter. Originally, the house contained a panelled room, west entry, and dining room on the first floor, two bedrooms on the second floor, and three smaller rooms in the attic. The servants' quarters and kitchen were housed in separate buildings, as was typical in the New England of John and Abigail Adams.

In the 12 years following the Adams' purchase of the house, John Adams had little time for anything other than the pressures of affairs of state, although he dearly wished to leave them behind and to settle down to the life of a private farmer. But the duties of public office, first as vice president and then as president, prevailed upon the public-spirited John Adams. While vice president, he first lived on Manhattan Island in an area known as Richmond Hill in a manor house overlooking the Hudson River. The house was demolished in 1849, and the site is at the corner of Varick and Charleston Streets in Greenwich Village. When the nation's capital moved to Philadelphia, Vice President Adams also moved, to "Bush Hill," a three-story box-like structure which was about two miles outside of the city. Upon becoming president in 1797, Mr. Adams lived in a house owned by Robert Morris at High (now Market) and Sixth Streets in Philadelphia which had been occupied by his predecessor, George Washington. Because of the yellow fever epidemic in Philadelphia in 1797, President Adams spent two months with his daughter in Mt. Vernon, New York, which is north of New York City. In 1800, by which time the capital had moved to Washington, D.C., President Adams lived at the Union Tavern in Georgetown while awaiting completion of the White House. The Adams family moved to the unfinished White House later in 1800, using the only six rooms in the residence which were habitable, albeit uncompleted. Abigail Adams later made a statement about hanging her laundry in the East Room. Water had to be carried to the White House from springs located a mile and a half away.

Because John Adams was often away on official duties, it was left to Abigail Adams to make the necessary home repairs and manage the farm in Massachusetts in her husband's absence. Under her supervision and guidance, and often without her husband's knowledge, Abigail Adams expanded the size of the house and improved its efficiency.

She joined the kitchen to the rest of the house and enlarged the "farm building" at the rear of the house to accommodate her husband's library.

In the closing years of her husband's presidency, Abigail Adams virtually doubled the house's capacity by completing its west wing, which included a second entry into a wide hallway, a Long Room which was used to entertain guests (including the Marquis de Lafayette, who visited in 1824), a hallway and study (in which John Adams died in 1826) on the second floor, and bedrooms on the third floor. She also made extensive alterations in the western or kitchen ell. It was to this expanded homestead that John Adams, defeated in a bid for a second term as President, returned in 1801.

Later in 1801, John and Abigail Adams' son, John Quincy Adams, returned from Berlin after completing a series of diplomatic assignments. Eleven years earlier, John Quincy Adams had opened his law office. He became Minister to the Netherlands in 1794 and also served as an envoy to Prussia. In 1797, he married Louisa Catherine Johnson, a British native who had spent some of her formative years in France, whom he had met while on a mission to England. Louisa Catherine Adams spent relatively few years with her husband in rural New England, which seemed to her to be bleak, but during those few years, she and her husband lived at the birthplace homes, while John Quincy Adams served in the Massachusetts senate and later as a United States senator. He later served as a minister to Russia and to England, and while in England, John Quincy and Louisa Catherine Adams lived in "Boston House," a small country house in Ealing, about eight miles from London.

Having been asked to serve as secretary of state in the administration of James Monroe, John Quincy Adams returned briefly to Quincy in 1817. It was the year after his return to America that his beloved mother, Abigail Adams, died. John Quincy Adams moved to Washington to serve on President Monroe's cabinet, and while secretary of state, lived at 1333 F Street in Washington, a home which had formerly been occupied by James Madison. This home, where John Quincy Adams lived until becoming president in 1825, no longer exists.

During his years as a widower, the elder John Adams consoled himself by inviting many of his relatives to share his home with him. He lived long enough to see his son, John Quincy Adams, become president, but was stricken while in the study on the second floor of the house and died on July 4, 1826, only hours after his one-time political adversary, and later friend, Thomas Jefferson, had died at his home in Monticello, Virginia. Unaware of the fate of his erstwhile rival, Adams murmured, "The Union survives; Jefferson still lives," just before his death.

John Quincy Adams served as secretary of state for a full eight years prior to becoming a "minority" president in an election in which no candidate could muster a majority of votes in the Electoral College, and the constitutional responsibility of the House of Representatives was exercised in selecting him as president. John Quincy Adams' single four year term was marred by a coalition of his political adversaries, so as his father had before him, John Quincy Adams completed only one term as president. While John Quincy Adams was president, the White House grounds were enclosed along the boundaries established in 1800, and he enjoyed working with exotic plants found on the grounds for relaxation. In 1829, Andrew Jackson succeeded John Quincy Adams, who, upon leaving the White House, leased the Porter House at Meridian Hill Park on Sixteenth Street in Washington before returning to Massachusetts.

As with his father, John Quincy Adams' political activity had left him little time to attend to his beloved Old House prior to leaving the presidency. When he finally did return, he found that the house had been sadly neglected, and so he planted trees on the grounds and added a second story passageway between the ells of the house. He also classified his library, tramped the fields, and took daily swims in the nearby creek.

The end of John Quincy Adams' presidency was far from the end of his political career, for after he returned to his beloved home, Peacefield, he was elected to the House of Representatives in 1831. He remained a representative until 1848, when he collapsed on the House floor and died a few days later. The duty of caring for the house resided, as it had for many years, with his son, Charles Francis Adams.

The financial burden of keeping the house in good repair nearly tempted Charles Francis Adams to demolish The Old House and to build anew, but his perseverance resulted in his addition of thirty feet to the kitchen ell and to the erection of a stone library next to the house. The library, which overlooks Abigail Adams' garden, was built in 1870, and accords with the specifications in John Quincy Adams' will that it be quiet and fireproof. It houses the impressive library of Charles Francis Adams, whose father and grandfather, the former presidents, were both avid readers. The garden in front of the library includes flowers planted by Charles Francis Adams' wife, Abigail Brooks Adams, whose wealth was important to the preservation of The Old House and grounds. Also here are dwarf English boxwood hedges planted in the eighteenth century.

The house remained in the hands of the Adams family until 1927, when Brooks Adams, a writer who acted as family custodian for the house and lived in it during the summer, died. It was he who added the ornamental front gates to the property. The Adams Memorial Society then took custody of the house and maintained it until 1946, when all the Adams family descendants jointly conveyed the property to the American people. Today, the sites of The Old House and of the Adams birthplace comprise the Adams National Historic Site, which is administered by the National Park Service.

THOMAS JEFFERSON

Tuckahoe Plantation
12601 River Road
Richmond, Virginia 23233
(804) 784-5736

Owned and operated by Mr. and Mrs. Addison Thompson, Jr.

Directions: Tuckahoe Plantation fronts on River Road 7 miles west of Richmond city limits. Enter country lane through white pillars 4.6 miles west of Parham Road south and River Road (or 2.8 miles west of intersection of Gaskins and River Roads); just west of end of Blair Road (Route 649) south of Patterson Avenue, Route 6.

Open: By appointment. Call the site to arrange tours.

Admission: Fee charged.

Features: House, Plantation Street and grounds. A one-room schoolhouse designed by Peter Jefferson, father of Thomas Jefferson, is on the site and is currently used as a gift shop.

Special Events: None.

Thomas Jefferson began his remarkable life on April 13, 1743 at Shadwell, located near Charlottesville, Virginia. He was the son of Peter Jefferson, a surveyor, and the former Jane Randolph, whose family was one of the most prominent families of colonial Virginia. Young Thomas Jefferson spent the first two years of his life at Shadwell when word reached Peter Jefferson that William Randolph, first cousin of Jane Randolph Jefferson and master of Tuckahoe Plantation, had met an untimely death at the age of thirty-two. As provided in a codicil to William Randolph's will, Peter Jefferson and his family, including two-year-old Thomas, journeyed to Tuckahoe to care for William Randolph's two daughters and one son. Thus, Thomas Jefferson came to spend his formative years at Tuckahoe, living there with his family from 1745 to 1752.

Located seven miles west of Richmond, Virginia, Tuckahoe Plantation is the only surviving estate among the five established by the sons of William Randolph of Turkey Island, the first of the Randolphs to settle in colonial Virginia. Just when Tuckahoe was founded is subject to debate, with dates ranging from 1674 to 1730. However, there is no doubt that Tuckahoe is one of America's earliest architecturally significant frame houses, and incorporates some of the finest examples of early Georgian architecture. Such features of the home include: a two room and central hall plan, so named because each floor of each wing of the house contains two large rooms separated by a stair hall. The "H" shape of the home, the product of adding wings to the original house, was popular in colonial Virginia, and similar to the shape of the Capitol in Williamsburg and of Stratford Hall, the Lee family home in the Tidewater region of Virginia. However, the fact that Tuckahoe is of frame construction, rather than brick or stone, makes Tuckahoe a truly unusual colonial-era home. The house also features four chimneys, each placed at the end of the large rooms, thus allowing for heat in the colder months, while parallel doors in the central hallway allow for cross-ventilation in the warmer months. It is said that Thomas Jefferson's interest in Palladian architecture, evidenced at his later homes at Monticello and Poplar Forest, was quite possibly sparked by his childhood admiration of the architectural features of his early surroundings at Tuckahoe.

Of special significance is the magnificently carved stairway located in the north entrance hall of the house, the handiwork of an indentured servant. At one time, the stairway was so coveted by the duPont family that they expressed an interest in purchasing Tuckahoe for the sole purpose of razing the house, salvaging the stairway, and moving it to the duPont family estate at Winterthur. Luckily for modern visitors, these intentions were never realized.

The magnificent grounds of Tuckahoe, which overlook the beautiful James River, include a pair of outbuildings on either side of the mansion, one of which was an office building in Thomas Jefferson's time, and the other of which was the schoolhouse designed by Jefferson's father, which features a rounded ceiling. Here, Jefferson received his earliest education along with other children in the Jefferson and Randolph families. The grounds also feature Plantation Street, a row of servants' quarters now individually used as private homes. Visitors are welcome to walk about the grounds and to view the structures on Plantation Street from a respectful distance.

Tuckahoe remained in Randolph family descendants' hands long after Thomas Jefferson and his family departed from Tuckahoe in 1752 to return to Shadwell. Title to Tuckahoe passed to Randolph descendants Thomas Mann I, then Thomas Mann II, and later was acquired by the Coolidge family, who also descended from the Randolphs. Today, Tuckahoe is owned by Mr. and Mrs. Addison Thompson, and through their efforts it remains a working farm and a magnificent home and grounds. The Thompsons have maintained Tuckahoe in a manner faithful to its colonial origins, making it an essential stop for any historian, architect, or interested visitor who wishes to learn more about the history of early America and one of its most prominent families, or to get a sense of the influences that shaped the mind and character of Thomas Jefferson.

Monticello
P.O. Box 316
Charlottesville, Virginia 22902
(804) 984-9800

Administered by the Thomas Jefferson Memorial Foundation, Inc.

Directions:	From I-64, take Charlottesville exit 121 to State Route 20 South. Turn left onto State Route 53. Follow Route 53 1.6 miles to Monticello. The entrance is on the left side of the road.
Open:	Daily (except Christmas Day) — call for seasonal hours.
Admission:	Fee charged. Discounts for children and senior citizens.

Features: Main house, walking trail, flower and vegetable gardens, plant and museum shops, orchards, ruins of joinery, grave site, picnic area, rest rooms, "Little Mountain Luncheonette." A nearby visitors center, located on State Route 20, includes an exhibition called "Thomas Jefferson at Monticello," which includes family memorabilia, architectural models and drawings and other items related to Thomas Jefferson's gardening, farming and manufacturing activities while at Monticello.

Special Events: On April 13th (Thomas Jefferson's Birthday), a grave site ceremony is held at 11:00 a.m. at which a brief memorial speech is offered. Government representatives present memorial wreaths.

On July 4th, a naturalization ceremony takes place on the east lawn. The ceremony is attended by judges and other dignitaries. A fife and drum corps performs. Remarks are made by a distinguished speaker. In 1994 the speaker was author David McCullough. In early December, a Christmas candlelight tour is given.

A visit to Monticello is more than a discovery of the life and times of an important historical figure. It is a journey into the mind of one of the greatest thinkers of his time. Monticello is a testament to Thomas Jefferson's cleverness and diversity of interests. His myriad of talents and interests encompassed a range far beyond his gifts as a politician and statesman. At Monticello, whose name is taken from an Italian word meaning "little mountain," we see the work of Thomas Jefferson the architect, Thomas Jefferson the innovator, Thomas Jefferson the aesthete and Thomas Jefferson the farmer.

Thomas Jefferson chose this site himself. At an elevation of 867 feet, the view from Monticello encompasses Shadwell, the home where he was born on April 13, 1743. He chose the location as a lad, across the Rivanna River, because at the age of 14, he inherited approximately 3,000 acres from his father, Peter Jefferson, a farmer and surveyor. The elder Mr. Jefferson purchased the farm land in 1736, and one thousand acres of that land became Monticello.

From 1745 to 1752, young Thomas Jefferson lived at "Tuckahoe," which is thirteen miles west of Richmond, Virginia. It is a rare "H" shaped Georgian, two-story frame structure with weatherboard walls except for two solid brick ends on its south wing. Its north wing, which was built circa 1712, has an original marble fireplace. It is privately owned today. (See previous section.)

Thomas Jefferson returned to Shadwell in 1752 and lived there until 1770, when the home was destroyed by fire. However, in 1769, when Mr. Jefferson was 26, construction of his home at Monticello had already begun based on his architectural plans. In 1770, Monticello became Thomas Jefferson's home.

Rather than choosing the Georgian style of architecture so popular in his day, Thomas Jefferson chose a formal classical style exemplified by the work of Andrea Palladio, a sixteenth-century architect. His original design for Monticello consisted of eight rooms. Mr. Jefferson lived in a tiny brick structure with his bride, Martha Wayles Jefferson, while construction of the main house took place. The tiny house is now the south pavilion of Monticello. Construction was so slow, however, that the house was still unfinished at the time of his wife's death in 1782 and his departure for France in 1784.

Politics kept Thomas Jefferson away from Monticello for long periods. In 1776, while serving in the Continental Congress and drafting the Declaration of Independence, Mr. Jefferson lived in the second floor parlor and bedroom of the Jacob Graff, Jr. House, a two and one-half story brick building at the southwest corner of Seventh and Market Streets in Philadelphia. Today, a reconstruction of that building is a unit of the Independence Park National Historic Site, located two blocks from Independence Hall. The first floor is used as a museum and the second floor is decorated with period furnishings.

Thomas Jefferson lived at Monticello in 1779 and 1780 while Governor of Virginia, but was forced to flee for a time to escape capture by the British. In 1789, he lived on Maiden Lane in New York City, which was the nation's first capital. He served as secretary of state and later as vice president under John Adams, and during part of that period, he boarded with Thomas Conrad on the south side of Capitol Hill in Washington. He is also believed to have built and lived at 1047 Jefferson Street in Georgetown, which no longer remains.

It was not until 1796 that Thomas Jefferson was finally able to turn his attention to rebuilding and completing his Monticello home. He redesigned it, expanding the structure to twenty-one rooms, and the new design required demolition of the entrance walls to make room for a series of new rooms. The resulting structure has three stories, with nine upstairs bedrooms and a dome room, all reached by steep, narrow steps. These narrow stairs are so designed because of Mr. Jefferson's aversion to wasting space, but their danger to modern visitors has resulted in the marking of the second and third floors as off-limits to the public. The low window and skylight used to allow daylight into the upstairs rooms, combined with bedrooms located under the eaves, give the impression of a one-story structure from the exterior of the house.

The exception to the otherwise streamlined look of this brick structure is its dome, modeled after that of the ancient Temple of Vesta in Rome. It is reminiscent of the dome of another structure designed by Thomas Jefferson, the rotunda of the University of Virginia, which can be viewed from the grounds of Monticello.

It was at Monticello that Thomas Jefferson spent his post-presidential years (1810-1826) in the company of his daughter, Martha, and his twelve grandchildren. Due to a complex combination of factors, including his neglect of his plantations while in public service, national economic conditions beyond his control, poor financial management and a love of building, books and wine, Jefferson left an estate which was $100,000.00 in debt upon his death on July 4, 1826. To help retire the debt, Jefferson's daughter, Martha Jefferson Randolph, along with one of her sons, sold Monticello to James Barclay in 1831. It was next purchased by then Captain (later Commodore) Uriah P. Levy of the United States Navy in 1836. After Commodore Levy's death, the title to Monticello was tied up in litigation for 17 years. Jefferson Monroe Levy, Commodore Levy's heir, eventually gained clear title to Monticello and made badly-needed repairs. The house and 662 surrounding acres were sold by Levy in 1923 to the Thomas Jefferson Memorial Foundation, Inc., which has remained owner and administrator of Monticello to this day.

A shuttle bus brings visitors to the house. Upon arriving at the entrance hall, visitors first notice the seven-day calendar clock, which has both an indoor and an outdoor face. The day of the week is indicated by the proximity of the clock weights to markers that descend along the south wall. This entrance hall, in which Thomas Jefferson's visitors were received, is filled with natural and scientific curiosities. Moose and elk antlers are on the north wall, and, on the south wall, one sees a concave mirror reflecting images upside down. Mastodon bones, a portrait of Thomas Jefferson and busts of Mr. Jefferson, Voltaire, Turgot and Alexander Hamilton also fill the room.

The South Square Room, which is to the side of the entrance hall, contains a fireplace, above which is a portrait of Martha Jefferson Randolph, the President's daughter, and a bed alcove space which was later used to house books.

Next, visitors enter the Library (or "Book Room," as Thomas Jefferson called it), where a few volumes originally owned by Mr. Jefferson have been placed on display along with other books, which, while not originally owned by Mr. Jefferson, bear the same titles and are the same editions as those books he had in his collection of almost 7,000 volumes. Here visitors also see an architect's table, a six-sided filing table, and a high-backed red leather chair. The library reflects the variety of interests of this remarkable man, who was able to read and speak six languages.

From the Library, visitors can see the South Piazza, which was used by Thomas Jefferson as a greenhouse. They then move to Mr. Jefferson's Cabinet, or study, where he studied and wrote. His study reveals his love of gadgetry and inventions, and included are: a polygraph which makes duplicates of letters (over 19,000 were written by Mr. Jefferson in his lifetime) by a complicated series of mechanisms connecting two pens, a revolving book stand, and a bench upon which Mr. Jefferson propped his rheumatic legs. A reproduction of the lap desk he used to write the Declaration of Independence is also on display here.

Visitors then enter Thomas Jefferson's bedroom. His alcove bed opens on both sides. Above this is a narrow storage space, accessible by stepladder, and yet another example of Mr. Jefferson's efficient use of space. The bedroom is illuminated by a skylight, one of 13 at Monticello.

Leaving the bedroom via a pinewood door grained to look like mahogany, visitors continue on through the entrance hall and the two glass doors that open together when only one is moved. Just ahead is the parlor, where weddings, christenings and other family events were held. Here visitors may see a cherry and beechwood parquet floor, one of the first in America. Over fifty-five works of art once hung in this room and today, many Italian religious paintings hang on one wall. On the other wall, several portraits are displayed, including a portrait of Thomas Jefferson by Gilbert Stuart and an 1858 copy of the Rembrandt Peale portrait of Mr. Jefferson. Roman cornices adorn the doors leading to the outside of the house. In this room, Mr. Jefferson's daughter and granddaughter played the harpsichord and guitar, while Jefferson played his beloved violin.

Walking through a side door, visitors next see the dining room and adjoining tea room, which feature large glass windows and busts of George Washington, Benjamin Franklin, and other contemporaries of Thomas Jefferson. The dining room itself again evidences Mr. Jefferson's flair for adapting clever ideas to his own use. On the sides of the fireplace are small doors which open to reveal dumbwaiters used to bring wine upstairs from the cellar. A revolving serving door allowed slaves to bring food upstairs from the kitchen and then turn the door so that the food would be easily accessible to Mr. Jefferson and his guests. Dinner, which was served between 3:00 p.m. and 4:00 p.m., would include fresh vegetables from among 250 varieties grown in Monticello's 1,000-foot long vegetable garden. Tea would be taken in the tea room at about 9:00 p.m. During the winter, double doors closed off the tea room, which was too cold to use during that season.

Finally, visitors see the North Octagonal Room, or "best guest" room, where favored guests such as James and Dolley Madison and the Marquis de Lafayette stayed. The room includes an alcove bed and a clothes press wardrobe, which was used to keep clothes wrinkle-free in Thomas Jefferson's time.

Visitors who explore the grounds also note the innovative all-weather passageway under the house, in which the wine cellar, kitchen and other dependencies are located. In an era when most estates had such rooms housed in separate buildings, the innovation and utility of Thomas Jefferson's design is undeniable. To complete a tour of the grounds, visitors should stop by Jefferson's grave site, which is contained within a family burial ground. Here many of Mr. Jefferson's immediate relatives and descendants are buried in graves surrounding that of the master of Monticello. After touring the grounds, visitors may either walk back to the east side of the house to catch a shuttle bus or walk down a descending woodland path back to the parking area.

Before leaving the Monticello area, visitors are also strongly advised to stop at the nearby Visitors Center, where an exhibition entitled "Thomas Jefferson at Monticello" provides further insight into daily life on the "Little Mountain" and further information on Thomas Jefferson himself.

It is difficult to imagine a visitor who would not be delighted, or would fail to be impressed, by the beauty of this entire site, or the ingenuity of its principal architect and first owner. It is, indeed, a unique and memorable experience not to be missed.

Thomas Jefferson's Poplar Forest
Forest, Virginia 24551-0419
(804) 525-1806

Administered by The Corporation for Jefferson's Poplar Forest.

Directions:	Poplar Forest is located southwest of Lynchburg, VA. Take U.S. Route 221 or U.S. Route 460 to Route 811, then turn onto Route 661 and go one mile to the main entrance.
Open:	Seasonal hours — call for hours of operation.
Admission:	Fee charged. Discounts for children, students, and senior citizens.
Features:	Main house, original privies, and post-Jefferson dependencies (kitchen, and smokehouse). The visitor center has a museum shop and restrooms. There are archaeological and restoration exhibits as well as archaeological excavations.
Special Events:	Group tours offered. An annual Independence Day celebration featuring craftsmen, interpreters, and musicians.

Poplar Forest was the home of a well-known President, yet remains virtually unknown to the public. Thankfully, it has escaped the threat of destruction. Although Poplar Forest was, in its heyday, a triumph of Thomas Jefferson's architectural skill, its history has been spotted with misfortunes. Despite the toll the years have taken on Mr. Jefferson's beloved retreat, the architectural beauty of this Palladian-style structure endures, as does the genius of Mr. Jefferson's concept.

The site of Poplar Forest, located southwest of Lynchburg, Virginia, was originally a 5,000-acre parcel owned by Mr. Jefferson's wife, the former Martha Wayles Skelton, who was a young widow when they married in 1772. She was the daughter of English-born John Wayles, owner of Poplar Forest, a plantation which Martha Jefferson inherited. (Thomas Jefferson subsequently inherited the property when his wife died at the age of 33.)

The idea of an octagonal house had intrigued Thomas Jefferson possibly after reading a depiction of such a house in William Kent's *Indigo Jones*. He seized upon the notion of building such a house for his younger daughter, Maria ("Polly") Eppes at Pantops, located near Monticello. His elder daughter, Martha Randolph, was already situated on the other side of Mr. Jefferson's "little mountain." However, with the early death of Polly Eppes, the Pantops home was never constructed. But, after Polly Eppes' death, Mr.

Jefferson suggested such a home for his grandson, Francis Wayles Eppes, but this idea also failed to materialize.

Thomas Jefferson, however, may have used many of the concepts he had envisioned for the Pantops house in his design for Poplar Forest at Bedford. Poplar Forest became one of the earliest octagonal homes in America. Its central room, a dining room, was originally a 20 foot cube. To illuminate the central room, Mr. Jefferson proposed a skylight stretching across the roof from east to west to measure 16 panes long by 2 panes across, or 16 feet 4 inches long by 3 feet 6 inches wide. Today, a low ceiling, installed to create additional space, has blocked the skylight. An original fireplace still stands, supported by a brick arch reaching down into the wine cellar directly under the dining area.

Thomas Jefferson's love of symmetry in architectural design is also reflected by the four elongated, octagonal rooms he placed to the north, south, east and west of the square-shaped central room. The north room is divided by a hallway with doors leading to either side of the segmented room, permitting easy access to the central room. The resulting segmented rooms, called chambers, have been used as small bedrooms or storage rooms.

The rooms to the east and west were bedrooms. The west bedroom, with its magnificent view of the Peaks of Otter, was Thomas Jefferson's. The east room was for family members, including his granddaughters and perhaps his grandson, Francis Wayles Eppes, when they visited. The central portion of each room had an alcove bed, which allowed its user access to either side of the room and virtually divided a long bedroom into two smaller rooms.

The south room was Thomas Jefferson's parlor. Here he kept a library of about 650 books, many of them Greek and Latin classics. Two of the four triple-hung windows opened to create doorways to the south portico. The entablature in this room includes a frieze modeled after the original from Palladio's Temple of Fortuna Virilis.

Extending from the octagonal frame of the house on the east and west sides are small rectangular pavilions which contained entrances to narrow staircases. Thomas Jefferson, a believer in the economy of space, designed them to provide access to the lower level. Fan-shaped windows called lunettes facing to the east and west grace these small extensions of the house.

On the north and south faces of the house are Palladian-style porticos. The columns of each portico are Tuscan style, unlike the Doric style columns at Monticello. However, as with Monticello, the portico of the "private" (south) side of the house is more spectacular than that of the public entrance on the north side. These columns, made of brick, are stucco-covered.

The bulk of the exterior of the house is composed of brick, laid by Hugh Chisholm, a skilled brick mason who worked extensively on Monticello. While still president, Thomas Jefferson lent his professional assistance in laying out the foundation of Poplar Forest. Mr. Jefferson, who insisted on strict adherence to his architectural plans, would ask that a wall be moved if it was even a fraction of an inch in variation with his drawings.

Thomas Jefferson's passion for proportion and symmetry is even more evident at Poplar Forest than at Monticello. From the front, the house appears to be a one-story structure. The lower level floor, however, can be entered from the south side of the house. To facilitate entry, Mr. Jefferson contoured the south lawn with gentle slopes leading downward so that the lower portion of the lawn is level with the ground floor. On either side of the house are "privies" (toilets) which, like the main house, are brick octagonal structures. These rooms are capped with domed roofs so that they resemble small temples.

Today, a straight entranceway points about eight-tenths of a mile outward from the front of the house. Were it not for the obscuring effect of the boxwoods planted on the north lawn after Jefferson's time, this entranceway would provide a clear view of the north portico of the house to arriving visitors. A portion of this road is the original entrance to Poplar Forest.

Two structures directly to the east of the main house, the kitchen and the smokehouse, are inconsistent with the overall design of the property. These are post-Jefferson structures, built in the mid-nineteenth century. They are traditional in appearance, and are constructed of the same brick as the other buildings. These buildings were constructed directly above the remains of the "wing of offices" added to the house by Jefferson in 1814, which included a kitchen, a smokehouse, a cook's room, and perhaps a dairy. The wing of offices was covered by a flat roof that could be used for strolling and was fronted on the south side by a covered walkway. Two other brick buildings, which now stand to the east of a mound, are also post-Jefferson structures.

Thomas Jefferson's increasing financial difficulties made his hold on his Poplar Forest retreat tenuous. But the homestead did generate a good share of his income, for the land proved an excellent source of marketable crops such as tobacco and wheat.

In 1822, Thomas Jefferson's grandson, Francis Wayles Eppes, married Elizabeth Cleland Randolph. Although Mr. Jefferson had reservations about his grandson's marriage at such a young age, he approved of the bride and wanted to see the only surviving child of his beloved daughter, Polly Eppes, properly settled. Therefore, he turned Poplar Forest over to Francis Eppes. Three years later, as a result of an attempt to burn soot out of a fireplace, Poplar Forest suffered a fire in which the balustrade, platform and many shingles of the house were lost.

Thomas Jefferson accepted news of the destruction philosophically, and offered assistance in repairing the damage and in designing improvements. However, Francis Eppes soon reported another problem to his grandfather: water leakage. The leaks were so severe that, according to Mr. Eppes' letters, the central room was the only dry room in the house. The necessary repairs were apparently made.

In 1828, two years after the death of Thomas Jefferson, Francis Eppes sold Poplar Forest to William Cobbs of Bedford County. The estate has had several subsequent owners. In 1845, another serious fire occurred at Poplar Forest, and from that time forward, the house has not conformed with Mr. Jefferson's original vision in several respects. Most significantly, the subsequent rebuilding of the house brought about a dramatic change in the exterior roofline of the house. Also, the addition of an attic and dormer windows, as well as the elimination of the balustrade, Chinese railing and the pediments give the house a non-Jeffersonian appearance. Poplar Forest, however, remains a small masterpiece, and may well owe its existence today to the Corporation for Jefferson's Poplar Forest, which purchased the house and 50 surrounding acres of land in 1984 and subsequently acquired an additional 430 acres.

Today, the home remains unfurnished and all of its interior walls have been stripped in an effort to determine their original appearance. The aim of these efforts is to restore Poplar Forest in as accurate a fashion as possible. Much remains to be discovered, but the Corporation for Jefferson's Poplar Forest appears determined to achieve its goal of a restoration which is faithful to the appearance of the home in Thomas Jefferson's time.

At present, imaginative visitors may come to Poplar Forest and enjoy Thomas Jefferson's small masterpiece, and may, someday, have the opportunity to see the octagonal home as a fully restored house museum.

JAMES MADISON

Montpelier
P.O. Box 67
Montpelier Station, Virginia 22957
(540) 672-2728

Administered by the National Trust for Historic Preservation.

Directions: From Washington, D.C., take U.S. 66 to U.S. 29 to Culpeper, Va., then south on U.S.15 to Orange, Va. An alternate route is south on I-95 to Fredericksburg, then west on Route 3 to Route 20 west toward Orange, Va. Montpelier is four miles southwest of (after) Orange.

From Richmond, take I-64 west to Route 15 north to Orange.

From Charlottesville, take Route 20 northeast to Montpelier (located four miles before Orange).

Open: Seasonal — call for hours.

Admission: Fee charged. Discounts for children, students, AAA, and senior citizens. Free admission to National Trust for Historic Preservation and Friends of Montpelier members.

Features: Mansion, garden temple, gardens, James and Dolley Madison grave sites, picnic area. A train station, general store, racetrack/steeplechase, horse graves, and a bowling alley later used as an office were added by the du Pont family, who purchased the property in 1900. Over forty species of trees may be viewed on the grounds of Montpelier, and visitors may obtain a "tree walk" map which indicates the location of each species. The tour of the site begins with a ten minute narrated slide show at the visitor center, and a shuttle bus transports visitors to the mansion. The tour lasts approximately one and one-half hours.

Disabled persons are encouraged to call before visiting the site.

Visitors to Montpelier may also wish to view the nearby James Madison Museum, located at 129 Caroline Street in Orange, Virginia. Call (540) 672-1776.

Special Events: On March 16, President Madison's birthday, a ceremony takes place at which wreaths are presented by representatives of the Marine Corps and the Daughters of the American Revolution. Virginia Historic Garden Week tours take place at the site in April or May.

The site also hosts the Montpelier Hunt Races, which take place on the first Saturday in early November. The mansion is closed on that day.

After many years of private ownership, the principal home of President James Madison is now open to the public. The original estate was the result of a patent obtained by Thomas Chew and Ambrose Madison, James Madison's grandfather, for 4,675 acres of land in what is currently known as Orange County, Virginia. It was divided into equal shares for Mr. Madison and Mr. Chew. The original house was Georgian in design, and was built by James Madison, Sr., the President's father, who served as a justice of the peace and sheriff in Orange County in addition to being a successful planter, building contractor, and ironworks proprietor. The house was completed around 1765, but was to undergo significant renovations.

James Madison, Sr. was operating the farm with his mother, Frances Taylor Madison, at the time he married Nelly Conway in 1749. It was on March 16, 1751 that Nelly Madison, while visiting her mother's home at Port Conway, King William County, Virginia, gave birth to her son, James Madison, Jr.

The Georgian brick mansion that was to become James Madison's home for most of his eighty-five years was still incomplete when the Madisons began to occupy it around 1760. The exact configuration of the original house and its rooms is in the process of being determined through research. Later substantial changes were made to the mansion by both the Madisons and subsequent owners. Modern visitors to the mansion will view artist's renderings of the house as it may have appeared originally and during subsequent periods of remodeling and expansion. Vivid descriptions by the tour guide, as well as information about significant architectural features of the house and on-site presentations by the research staff, help visitors visualize the appearance of the mansion during the period that the president and his wife, the former Dolley Payne Todd, were in residence here. President Madison's mother also lived at Montpelier at that time, and remained there until her death at the age of 97.

To be sure, James Madison's long career brought him to other locales and residences. He was educated at Donald Robertson's school at Inves Plantation in King and Queen County, Virginia. He later attended and graduated from the College of New Jersey (which became Princeton University many years later). While serving in the government in Philadelphia, Mr. Madison frequently stayed at the House-Trist Home at Fifth and Market Streets. When the seat of government moved to Washington, D.C., Mr. Madison moved to the "Six Buildings" row house at 2107-2117 Pennsylvania Avenue, where he remained until 1797. "Six Buildings" was constructed in 1794, and razed in the 1930s. During the Jefferson administration (1801-1809), he stayed at 1333 F Street, a three-story brick home with cupolas for fire escapes, four bedrooms on its third floor, a coach house and stables. This house no longer exists.

When James Madison, Sr., passed away in 1801, his son inherited the Montpelier estate. The younger James Madison's knowledge of architecture had already led him to add Tuscan columns and a portico to the house in 1800. The bases of the Tuscan columns originally began at the level of the first floor of the mansion, which is above ground level at the front of the mansion, where a stairway leads to the entrance. (A subsequent owner, Frank Carson, had the Tuscan columns extended to the ground.) From 1809 to 1812, major additions were made to the house, including one story wings with basement kitchens on either side of the house, as well as a Tuscan colonnade to the rear of the house, extending outward from a porch which features three triple-hung windows.

These windows reach to the floor and are designed to permit a person inside the mansion to raise the two lower sashes and to step through the opening as though walking through a door. Other renovations also contributed to the transformation of the mansion from its previous Georgian style appearance into a Neoclassical style.

The renovation of 1809-12 was no doubt due to James Madison's election to the presidency in 1808. His election, together with the popularity of First Lady Dolley Madison as a social hostess, meant that Montpelier became a favored spot for many social occasions. Visitors to Montpelier were never disappointed with its hospitality or with the success of the parties ably hosted by Mrs. Madison. Her outgoing, charming personality and her skills as a hostess complemented her husband's shy, diffident personality. He was, however, greatly respected as a political thinker and statesman, especially by his close friends and political allies Thomas Jefferson and James Monroe, who preceded and succeeded James Madison, respectively, as president.

One other important addition was made on the grounds of Montpelier around 1810 when a garden temple was added to the north front lawn. It is a domed structure with ten columns extending to its base. Today it is considered one of the finest examples of garden architecture. A small door at its base led to Madison's icehouse. To the north and rear of the house is the site of Madison's formal gardens. Renovated in the twentieth century during the du Pont ownership, and still blooming to this day, the garden celebrates the four seasons. Equally impressive is the view from the front portico of Montpelier, from which one may look straight down the sloping lawn and see a commanding view of the Blue Ridge Mountains. It is said that from the portico, Dolley Madison, with the aid of a spyglass, could observe how many guests were arriving at the mansion and would see to it that the appropriate number of places were set for dinner.

As noted above, Madison's public career had left him little time to spend at Montpelier between 1794 and 1797 and from 1801 through 1817. During the War of 1812, Madison's stay at the White House was interrupted by the burning of the structure in 1814, and the Madisons relocated to a suite on the east side of Octagon House, which is actually a hexagonal structure built in 1800 for Colonel John Tayloe and his family. (The structure still stands at 1799 New York Avenue in Washington and serves as the headquarters of the American Institute of Architects.) Afterward, from 1815 to 1817, the Madisons lived in the corner house of "Seven Buildings," a series of row houses at 1901-1913 Pennsylvania Avenue which were built circa 1800 and were the only buildings which remained standing between the White House and Georgetown after the burning of Washington.

After James Madison's retirement from the presidency, he seldom left Montpelier. He lived there until his death in 1836. Accumulated debts would not allow Dolley Madison, his widow, to maintain Montpelier, therefore, she auctioned its furnishings and sold Montpelier to Henry Moncure of Richmond in 1844. In 1849, the once vivacious Dolley Madison died in poverty at the age of 81.

Ownership of Montpelier had changed six times before it was purchased by William du Pont, Sr., in 1901. Under du Pont's ownership, the mansion and surrounding property was drastically reshaped. Mr. du Pont enlarged the mansion still further and added barns, greenhouses, a saw mill, a blacksmith shop, and staff houses to Montpelier. He oversaw construction of a train station near the property, which was installed by special arrangement with the Southern Pacific Railroad for his commute to and from Wilmington, Delaware. He also had built a general store for supplies and installed a bowling alley for his own enjoyment. Upon his death in 1928, his daughter, Mrs. Marion du Pont Scott, inherited the property. As a person who shared her father's fondness for horses, she was responsible for the addition of two racetracks, a steeplechase course, and stables to the property. She also initiated the Montpelier Hunt Races, which are still run on the first Saturday of November each year. The graves of three of Mrs. Scott's favorite horses, two of which were sired by Man O' War, are also located on the grounds. One room seen by a modern visitor to Montpelier is a room designed by Mrs. Scott which features many photos of race horses and racing events in which she participated. The room also includes a wind directional device installed in the ceiling. It is one room of the mansion which will retain its present appearance; many other rooms in the mansion will eventually be interpreted to their appearance during James Madison's time.

Mrs. Scott, who died in 1983, devised the 2,700-acre estate to the National Trust for Historic Preservation, which, after a concerted effort to prepare the site for tours, opened Montpelier to the public in 1987, thus allowing interested visitors to view the site of the principal home of the author of the Bill of Rights.

JAMES MONROE

Ash Lawn-Highland
James Monroe Parkway
Charlottesville, Virginia 22902-8722

Administered by the College of William and Mary.

Directions: From I-64, take Charlottesville exit to State Route 20 south. Turn left at State Route 53 and drive for three miles, passing Monticello entrance. Take a right turn onto County Route 795 and drive for one-half mile to the entrance of Ash Lawn-Highland, which is on your right.

Open: Daily (except New Year's Day, Thanksgiving Day and Christmas Day) — call for seasonal hours.

Admission: Fee charged. Discounts for children and senior citizens. Group and special rates available. A combination ticket including a visit to Monticello and Michie's Tavern is also available.

Features: House, gardens, slave quarters, gift shop, rest rooms, bus and picnic facilities. Lunch and Virginia wine tasting are both available by reservation.

Special Events: Call for a complete list of special events which include a champagne and candlelight tour in April.

The site celebrates President Monroe's birthday on April 28.

In May, the site sponsors a Kite Day and awards prizes for the best design and best flight.

A Summer Opera Festival takes place on the grounds from June to August. Also taking place during the summer are a "Music at Twilight" series, "Plantation Days at Highland," and

"Summer Saturdays" family programs of music, dance, drama and puppetry.

In November, an Open House takes place in which residents of Charlottesville and nearby counties are invited to tour the site free of charge.

In December, the fields of Ash Lawn-Highland are opened for Christ-

mas tree cutting. Donations are requested. Other Christmas season events include: Christmas by Candlelight; Gingerbread and Lace: A Christmas Celebration; Winter Shopping Spree; and Sounds of the Season: A Holiday Concert. Each of these events features music of the season and refreshments.

James Monroe, the fifth president of the United States, was born in Westmoreland County, Virginia on April 28, 1758 in a small, wooden structure situated not far from George Washington's birthplace on Pope's Creek. The house was subsequently destroyed. Today, all that remains of the site is a state marker on a road off Virginia State Route 3, behind which are wooden boards marking the foundation of the house. Contained within these boards is a tree stump on which an American flag has been placed. President Monroe's other extant American homes include the home of his uncle, Judge Joseph Jones, at 301 Caroline Street, Fredericksburg, where he lived from 1786 to 1789 while practicing law in that community (a Fredericksburg property James Monroe once owned is now a museum open to the public). Today, that home is privately owned. During the early 1790s, James Monroe bought a farm in Charlottesville and built or reconstructed a house on a hill on that site. Today, the farm is the site of the University of Virginia and the farmhouse, now known as Monroe Hill House, is used by Monroe Hill College, a division of the University. From 1811 to 1817, Mr. Monroe leased a late Georgian style, red brick white stone trim, three and a half-story home at 2017 I Street in Washington, where he stayed until the White House restoration was complete. The interior of the house on I Street was altered for utilitarian purposes and in part as the result of a fire in 1963. Today, that home is occupied by the Washington Arts Club and is normally not open to the public. In 1811, Mr. Monroe inherited land in Leesburg, Loudon County, Virginia from Judge Jones, and he lived on that land in a frame house known as "Monroe Cottage." This structure still stands and is privately owned. In 1821, Mr. Monroe made "Oak Hill" his official residence. Oak Hill was built during James Monroe's first term as president (1817-21) on the same Loudon County property on which Monroe Cottage is situated, and was designed by Thomas Jefferson and built by Hoban. It is a Palladian style plantation home with Doric columns, and James Monroe planted oaks on the property for every state in the Union. He retired to Oak Hill at the completion of his second term in office, and in 1823, enlarged and changed the house. The house now features a double flight of stairs with an iron railing leading to its entrance and a huge Roman-Doric portico overlooking its garden faces southward to the Bull Run Mountains. Today, the house is privately owned and rarely open to the public. James

Monroe's wife died at Oak Hill in 1830, and Mr. Monroe, who was reportedly heavily in debt and forced to leave Virginia, sold Oak Hill and moved to New York City in 1831 to live with his daughter and son-in-law in a three-story, dutch-roofed row house at 63 Prince Street, on the corner of Marion Street, until his own death on July 4, 1831. Today, the Prince Street house is a mixed-use building with a luncheonette on the first floor and residential units on the upper floors.

With the exception of the White House, Ash Lawn-Highland, which was known in James Monroe's day as Highland, is the only one of President Monroe's various residences which is both extant and usually open to the public. The house and grounds appear to maintain the simple charm that they must have had under James Monroe's ownership. James Monroe, never a wealthy man, had fought alongside George Washington in the Revolutionary War (the famous painting of the crossing of the Delaware includes a depiction of young Lieutenant James Monroe holding the American flag), and had held numerous public offices (more than any other President before or since) when he purchased the 1,000-acre farm and estate in 1793 for a cost of $1.00 per acre. He had two significant reasons for purchasing the farm: his aspiration to purchase an income-generating property he believed could produce 20,000 pounds of tobacco a year, and the mutual desire of James Monroe and his friend Thomas Jefferson to become neighbors in Albemarle County.

Mr. Monroe met Mr. Jefferson while the latter was serving as Governor of Virginia, and the two men quickly became friends. Mr. Monroe then began to study law under Mr. Jefferson.

Thomas Jefferson assisted his friend, James Monroe, by selecting the site for the house and loaning his gardener to plant the orchard. Mr. Jefferson, however, played no role in drafting the architectural plans for the house, which is evident when one views the property. The house is a simple frame structure, which has been remodeled and enlarged over the years. Today, the house is a two-story frame structure with a one-story wing extending from the rear of the house. Beneath the wing is a kitchen and porch. Even as remodeled, the house maintains a character which stands in stark contrast to the Palladian classicism of Monticello or the Georgian splendor of Mount Vernon. It retains the rectitude of its original owner, who wanted a "cabin-castle" befitting the life of a farmer.

James Monroe and his wife, the former Elizabeth Kortright of New York, moved to Highland from Charlottesville in 1799 and lived there until 1823. During this period, the farm grew to 3,500 acres and included as its residents 30-40 slaves, various managers and overseers, and a blacksmith. A reconstruction of the slaves' quarters can be seen on the site today. Despite the crop growing and wood gathering activities on the plantation, it was never as financially successful as Mr. Monroe had originally hoped. In 1826, he sold the farm for $18,107.

In 1974, a subsequent owner, wealthy industrialist Jay Winston Johns, who had opened the plantation to the public, bequeathed the plantation (renamed "Ash Lawn") to the College of William and Mary, James Monroe's alma mater. The College maintains Ash Lawn-Highland as a site open to the public and has collected both originals and replicas of Mr. Monroe's furnishings and other household items which are on display throughout the house.

The house's entrance hall (not part of the original home, but added circa 1880 by James Massey, a subsequent owner) includes a large mirror, in front of which is placed a drop leaf "tribute table," so named because its top is formed from a single section of blond Honduras mahogany given to President Monroe by the Republic of Santo Domingo (now the Dominican Republic) circa 1825 in gratitude for his support for the Latin American independence movement.

Past the entrance hall lies the original section of the house. The drawing room is lined with wallpaper depicting French pastoral scenes. It also includes a set of French Empire chairs, a bust of Napoleon presented by the French Emperor himself to Monroe while the latter was serving as Minister to France, and a pianoforte built by Thomas Gibson of New York circa 1820. Monroe's French clock sits on the fireplace mantel.

Through an enclosed passageway (thought to have been a porch at one time because of its sloping floors) visitors enter the study. Here hangs a portrait of Maria Monroe, the President's younger daughter and the first daughter of a president to be married in the White House, and smaller portraits of the president's elder daughter, Eliza Monroe, and her friend and schoolmate Hortense de Bechatnais, who later became Queen of Holland. The Louis XVII desk in the study is similar to that on which the Monroe Doctrine was written (at Oak Hill). A canvas floor cloth in the study is not original, but was quite common in James Monroe's time.

In the dining room are other, larger portraits of Queen Hortense and Eliza Monroe, as well as one of Madame Compan, the headmistress of the French school they attended. In the center of the room is an American Hepplewhite dining table, which folds out to seat 12 to 14 people. Also in the room is a set of Federal chairs used by the Monroes. A French mirror was used for reflecting candlelight in the room.

The bedchamber includes a high post bed, designed to provide extra warmth, underneath which is a trundle bed. A Sheridan cabinet and writing desk which belonged to President Madison are also in this room, along with a Sheridan wash stand. Additionally, there are four gondola chairs, which belonged to President Monroe's granddaughter, and an all-wood working clock, designed by Eli Terry circa 1815. This amazing clock required the application of baking grease and animal fat to its inner workings in order to perpetuate its use!

The Monroe daughters' bedroom contains the family crib and a cradle. Also in this chamber is a replica of a king's crown canopy bed which belonged to the Monroes.

Finally, a guide demonstrates the spinning of wool taken from Merino sheep. At Highland, women would spin wool constantly in the basement rooms adjoining the kitchen. In the kitchen itself, food was stewed, boiled, or toasted in an open hearth. Toasting was accomplished with the aid of a "toe-toaster," an appliance in which bread or other food would sit with one side exposed to the flame of the open hearth. When one side was toasted, the device could be spun with a covered foot, permitting the other side to be toasted. (Because of the potential for fire hazards associated with open hearth cooking, cooks and kitchen help always wore shoes, while many of the other slaves and servants did not.) Spices were hung from a shelf to dry. The ground floor level windows were covered from the outside by "cow bars," to prevent the animals from entering the kitchen.

A visit to Ash Lawn-Highland is a revealing study of the private life of a public servant who, through most of his life, lived modestly. Although he left the presidency $75,000 in debt, James Monroe ended his life solvent. James Monroe was a man who preferred practicality to extravagance, and the simplicity of his character, as well as the basic values in which he believed, are reflected by this home.

Oak Hill Farm
Aldie, Virginia
(703) 777-1246

Owned by Mr. and Mrs. Thomas H. De Lashmutt.

Directions: Oak Hill Farm is located just to the west of Route 15 and several miles south of Leesburg, just northwest of the intersection of Routes 15 and 50.

Open: For special events only. Please call the site for further information.

Admission: Please call the site concerning admission fees.

Features: House and grounds.

Special Events: Please call the site for information.

During his second term as president, James Monroe decided to make Loudoun County, where he, together with his uncle, Judge Joseph Jones of Fredericksburg, had purchased property in 1794, the site of his permanent seat. A man of modest origins who came to believe firmly that one's home should reflect one's station in life, President Monroe determined to build a home for himself and his family that would reflect his well-earned stature in society. On Monroe's orders, construction of that home, a stately brick structure that came to be known as Oak Hill, began in 1822 and was completed in 1823. It is said that the name was derived from thirteen trees, a gift from Congress representing the thirteen states, which Monroe planted on the property. At first, it served as a convenient summer home for President Monroe and his family because of its proximity to Washington, but after President Monroe left office it became his retirement home. He resided there from March 1825 until October 1830, when he departed Oak Hill shortly after the death of his beloved wife, Elizabeth Kortwright Monroe.

President Monroe's decision to make his Loudoun County property the site of his new home was motivated both by its proximity to Washington and, perhaps more significantly, by financial considerations. A man who often dipped into his own pockets to pay for living and entertainment expenses related to his roles as foreign minister and, later, as president, James Monroe incurred a substantial debt to the Bank of the United States, which reached $75,000.00 by 1825. As early as 1816, he had attempted to sell his Loudoun County property but was unable to obtain what he considered a reasonable price. Ultimately, he resorted to selling his Albemarle County land (Highland) to settle his accounts. In 1826, President Monroe turned all but 707 acres of the Albemarle property over to the bank in full satisfaction of his debt. With regret, he relocated away from his close friends and neighbors, Thomas Jefferson and James Madison. President Monroe envisioned his new home as both a retirement home and a financially profitable farm where he could plant crops and raise sheep.

A grand three-part brick structure with a stone foundation, Oak Hill reflects the transition from the Federal architectural style to the Greek Revival style that was occurring at the time of its construction, as well as the influence of Monroe's friend and mentor, Thomas Jefferson. The three-part winged house form, used by Jefferson in his earliest version of Monticello, was long used in Virginia as a symbol of wealth and status. The south elevation (rear) of the house features a Roman Revival-style pedimented portico with Doric columns. In keeping with the Federal style, the house is basically symmetrical, and the unusual odd number of columns on the portico lend to that symmetry. Extending through the interior length of the house is an east-west transverse passage, accessible from Oak Hill's central doorway, by which all rooms in the house can be reached. The house also features a gabled central pavilion that advances approximately four and a half inches from the wings, indicating that this is the most important part of the house. It is said that the stones paving the cellar floor of Oak Hill were salvaged by James Hoban from the president's house (the White House) after it burned in 1814. The overall impression conveyed by the house is a dignified grandeur, indicative of Monroe's desire to convey to his visitors a sense of his status as the preeminent resident of Loudoun County in his day.

Events of historical significance during President Monroe's residence at Oak Hill include the August 1825 visit of the Marquis de Lafayette and President John Quincy Adams to Oak Hill, where they spent two nights prior to calling upon Thomas Jefferson at Monticello. In gratitude for Monroe's friendship and assistance over the years, Lafayette made a gift of two Grecian marble mantels, each of which is the centerpiece of one of the two double parlors in the house. The two mantels differ slightly and are far more ornate than the wooden mantels found throughout the rest of the house. Dolley Madison is also reported to have visited the house. Most significantly, it was in his office at Oak Hill that President Monroe drafted his best-known achievement as president--the Monroe Doctrine. This famous document became the cornerstone of American foreign policy, and established an enduring precedent in the role of the president in setting American foreign policy.

After President Monroe's death, his younger daughter, Maria Gouverneur, became owner of Oak Hill. His older daughter Elizabeth had been given Monroe's Ashfield estate on the Chickahominy River near Richmond in 1809, and it was Monroe's intention, as stated in his will, to treat Maria equitably by having her receive $6,000.00, the price he had originally paid for Ashfield, from his estate. However, the lack of liquid assets in Monroe's estate resulted in Maria obtaining outright ownership of Oak Hill. She resided there with her husband, Samuel L. Gouverneur, until her death in 1850. Subsequently, Samuel Gouverneur remarried and moved to Maryland, taking the original Oak Hill furnishings with him. The Gouverneur family began to sell parcels of Oak Hill in 1840 and by 1870 had sold the entire farm.

The main tract, house and outbuildings were sold by Samuel Gouverneur, Jr., grandson of President Monroe, to John Walter Fairfax, who later became a Confederate Army colonel. During the Battle of Bull Run, the house was occupied by Union General George Meade, which probably saved Oak Hill from destruction by Yankee soldiers who burned almost every farm they encountered in Virginia. It is said that one day while General Meade was relaxing on the portico at Oak Hill, he spotted a horseman galloping across the field. Meade asked Mrs. Fairfax who the rider was and, waiting until the rider had passed out of sight, she replied, "Why, that, General Meade, was Colonel John Mosby." Meade was clearly rankled by his missed opportunity to capture the evasive and daring "Gray Ghost" who was regarded by the Confederacy as a hero and by the occupying Yankee forces as a scourge for his many successful raids. Colonel Fairfax's son Henry bred carriage horses, as well as a stallion named "Matchless" which won top honors at the New York Horse Show, bringing the highest price ever for a hackney. Throughout the history of Oak Hill, its owners have continued to use the property as a working farm and to raise livestock.

In 1948, Mr. and Mrs. Thomas N. De Lashmutt bought the Oak Hill property at auction; their son and his family currently reside in the house and open it to the public for special occasions. The owner's mother has helped to restore Oak Hill to its historical roots by collecting furnishings that once belonged to Presidents Monroe, Washington, Adams, and Madison. Adding to modifications to the house made between 1922 and 1927 by architect Henry Davis Whitfield of New York, who enlarged the length and height of the wings of the house, the De Lashmutt family hired Frank Almirall of the Washington firm of Almirall and Coughlin to make further refinements to the structure of the house. The result is a structure that maintains the grandeur that its originator, James Monroe, intended, and is therefore a "presidential" home in the true sense of the word.

ANDREW JACKSON

Andrew Jackson Birthplace Marker
Waxhaw, North Carolina
(704) 843-1832

Administered by the Division Of Archives and History, Department of Cultural Resources, State of North Carolina.

Andrew Jackson State Park
Lancaster, South Carolina
(803) 285-3344

Administered by the South Carolina Department of Parks, Recreation and Tourism.

Directions: To marker in North Carolina: From Charlotte, take U.S. 521 South about 20 miles, crossing the state line into South Carolina. Turn left onto State Route 75 East. Proceed about four miles, crossing the state line into North Carolina. At Waxhaw, a sign indicates a right turn towards the site. Turn right onto Rehobeth Street. After four miles, bear right onto Old Charlotte Road, which will terminate at an intersection located just past the state line in South Carolina. Turn left onto Andrew Jackson Road and proceed to the end of the road. The marker is located in the center of a circular drive.

To State Park in South Carolina: Park is located nine miles north of Lancaster, South Carolina on U.S. 521.

Open: North Carolina marker: All times. South Carolina State Park: Daily — call for seasonal hours.

Admission: Free to both sites.

Features: Historic stone marker in North Carolina. Andrew Jackson State Park, located in South Carolina, features trails, 25 camp sites (with showers), and boat rentals available for fishing only.

Special Events: None.

It is a little-known fact that President Andrew Jackson is responsible for a great conflict which has divided the South and the North. The North fired the opening salvo, with the South retaliating by using all the resources at its disposal. The North felt that it had no choice but to defend its claim over the territory in question. It did so by invading the South in an attempt to legitimate its claim.

The controversy, which still rages in the Carolinas, is over the question: where was President Andrew Jackson born?

North Carolina and South Carolina each claim to contain the site of the birthplace of the hero of the Battle of New Orleans, and America's seventh chief executive, within its borders. Both states also have stone markers commemorating President Jackson's birth. The South Carolina marker cites a letter, written by Andrew Jackson himself, stating that he was born on "Barnes Crawford's plantation," historically shown as having been located in Lancaster County, South Carolina. The North Carolina marker, the older of the two stone markers, includes a carved depiction of a log cabin and a declaration that it marks the actual site of Andrew Jackson's birth. South Carolina's marker makes no such claim, but in apparently intentional contradiction of the North Carolina marker, stresses that Andrew Jackson "himself" stated that he was born "on South Carolina soil."

In order to ensure that interested passers-by can locate the North Carolina marker, a sign at the entrance to Andrew Jackson Road provides directions. The sign, which was evidently placed by the government of the State of North Carolina, appears to constitute a territorial invasion and an act of taunting defiance. The sign at the entrance of Andrew Jackson Road is placed just to the south of the state line. . .in South Carolina.

It is agreed, however, that Andrew Jackson was born in the region near Waxhaw Creek in a log cabin. His father died a week before he was born on March 15, 1767. Andrew Jackson's early life, between 1767 and 1781, was spent almost exclusively in the Waxhaw area. At the age of 14, Andrew Jackson, who must have learned self-reliance almost from the beginning of his life, was left truly on his own when his mother died. Later, the Revolutionary War claimed the lives of two of his brothers in addition to nearly costing him his own. (He had signed up for the Revolutionary militia, was captured by the British, and almost died of smallpox while in prison. He also received a near fatal wound from a British officer.)

The controversy over the place of Andrew Jackson's birth stems from both confusion over what the colonial boundaries were in 1767, and disagreement concerning the home in which Andrew Jackson's mother was staying at the time of his birth. Some believe that Andrew Jackson's mother was visiting a sister's home in North Carolina. She appears to have worked at James Crawford's plantation about the time Andrew Jackson was born. Those who do not give credence to Andrew Jackson's letter on the subject of his birthplace think that his description was based only upon sincere beliefs, and not on accurate information.

While North Carolina has no memorial to Jackson's birthplace other than its stone marker, South Carolina has devoted a state park, located in the Waxhaw area, to Andrew Jackson. Among the features devoted to President Jackson are: an equestrian statue of Mr. Jackson in his youth; a museum depicting a kitchen, bedroom, and a tool room (which houses artifacts) as they might have looked in the Waxhaw area at the time of Mr. Jackson's birth; a representation of an early nineteenth century Waxhaw schoolhouse, and a meeting facility.

The park also has such traditional features as camp sites, picnic tables, nature trails, a playground, and a fishing lake.

The Hermitage
4580 Rachel's Lane
Hermitage, Tennessee 37076
(615) 889-2941

Administered by the Ladies' Hermitage Association

Directions:	**From Nashville, take I-40 east (12 miles) to exit 221 (Hermitage exit). Turn left onto Old Hickory Boulevard (State Route 45) and drive north three miles. Follow signs.**
Open:	**Daily (except Thanksgiving Day, Christmas Day and the third week in January) — call for hours.**
Admission:	**Fee charged. Discounts for children, senior citizens, and groups.**
Features:	**Audio tour of mansion and grounds. Sign language tours for the deaf are also available, and much of the mansion tour is handicapped accessible (non-motorized wheelchairs preferred, three wheel variety are forbidden because they are too unstable). The Visitor Center includes a museum, museum store, res-**

taurant (Rachel's Garden Cafe), and a theater which shows a film presentation about the Jacksons and the Hermitage. The grounds also include a smokehouse, garden, cemetery, the "Original Hermitage," Tulip Grove Mansion, church, and a Confederate cemetery.

Special Events: Grave site services are held at Andrew Jackson's tomb on or near January 8 (the anniversary of the Battle of New Orleans) and March 15 (Andrew Jackson's Birthday).

After he and his brother were freed from captivity by the British, Andrew Jackson did not return to his boyhood home at the Waxhaw settlement. In 1784, he decided to study law, and after three years was admitted to the North Carolina Bar. He then acted as a public prosecutor for North Carolina's Western District, whose boundaries were similar to those of the current state of Tennessee, although the North Carolina legislature questioned whether he was formally appointed to the post and therefore refused to pay him. Andrew Jackson then journeyed across the Appalachian Mountains to begin his new career.

Once in Nashville, Andrew Jackson's position in his new community rose rapidly. After three years he married Rachel Donelson Robards, a divorcee whose family was quite prominent and influential. Their union was a love match and enhanced his social standing, due to the new family and exten-

sive contacts he acquired. Jackson went on to attain such public offices as: member of the Tennessee Constitutional Convention, member of the United States House of Representatives (Jackson was Tennessee's first U.S. representative), and United States senator. He also spent six years as a superior court judge, riding circuit among several Tennessee cities.

After living at two other Tennessee plantations (Poplar Grove and Hunter's Hill), Andrew Jackson purchased the land which was to become the Hermitage in 1804. It was a 425-acre tract within two miles of Andrew and Rachel Jackson's previous plantation at Hunter's Hill. By February of 1805, the Jacksons were occupying their home on this tract. It was a square block home with three rooms, a large room downstairs and two bedrooms upstairs. The downstairs room was used as a parlor and sitting room. Nearby were three smaller log homes, each one story in height, which may have been used to accommodate guests. The log home was to remain the home of Andrew and Rachel Jackson for 16 years.

It appears to have been a happy home, where the couple lived together with Rachel Jackson's nephew (whom the Jacksons adopted and renamed Andrew Jackson, Jr.) and, from 1817 onward, a ward, A.J. Hutchings. The senior Andrew Jackson's duties as general of the U.S. Army during the War of 1812 meant prolonged absences from his home, during which time the farm was operated by one or more of Rachel Jackson's brothers with the aid of overseers and slave labor.

In 1818, Andrew Jackson, now a prominent political figure and military hero, decided to build a larger house. Construction of the first Hermitage mansion commenced in 1819. After a stint as governor of the Florida territory, during which time the Jackson family lived in Pensacola, the Jacksons returned to Tennessee in October 1821 to occupy their new home. It was a red-brick structure typical of southern plantation homes of the day. The two-story mansion's bricks were made in a kiln located on the farm itself. The first floor had four rooms connected by a central hall, as did the second floor. The ground floor rooms consisted of two parlors, a dining room, and the Jacksons' bedroom. The larger parlor had a doorway leading to Mrs. Jackson's garden on the side of the house.

Andrew Jackson's military successes, combined with his political experience, made him an attractive candidate for the presidency in the eyes of his political associates. The core of Jackson's support was a group of influential political figures known as the Nashville Junta. By 1823, Andrew Jackson was again serving in the U.S. Senate, and his partisans persuaded the Tennessee General Assembly to nominate him for President. In the election of 1824, he ran against a large field of candidates, notably William Crawford and John Quincy Adams. As no candidate achieved an electoral college majority, the election had to be decided by the U.S. House of Representatives. In the end, John Quincy Adams was chosen to become the sixth president of the United States.

Immediately after John Quincy Adams' inauguration, Andrew Jackson left the U.S. Senate and did not return. His partisans, upon learning of President Adams' appointment of Henry Clay as Secretary of State, accused President Adams and Mr. Clay of corruption. They made immediate preparations for the campaign of 1828 by again persuading the Tennessee General Assembly to nominate Andrew Jackson for President, and by using many of the same grassroots campaign tactics that are still in use today, such as slogans, parades and buttons. Many partisan newspapers were also printed and distributed by the Jacksonians.

The Andrew Jackson campaign of 1828 was perhaps the single most important mechanism leading to the formation of the Democratic Party. In an election which had four times the voter turnout of the 1824 election due to the changes in many state constitutions which opened up the voting franchise to thousands more men, Jackson was an easy victor in both the popular and electoral vote.

Andrew Jackson's joy in his election victory was shortlived, however, for on December 22, 1828, his beloved wife, Rachel, died. Her death so affected President-elect Jackson that he could not begin his journey to Washington until mid-January of 1829. When he finally did make the trip, he was accompanied by his niece, Emily T. Donelson, and her husband (and cousin), Andrew Jackson Donelson. (The Donelsons had married in 1824.) Emily acted as First Lady at the White House, and Andrew Jackson Donelson became the President's personal secretary.

In 1831, during President Jackson's first term in office, a major remodeling of the Hermitage mansion took place. Two wings were added to the house, one containing the dining room and the other housing the library. Colonnades with Doric columns were also added to the front of the house. Andrew Jackson, Jr. and his wife, Sarah Jackson, were visited by the president in both 1832 and 1834 at the Hermitage, for which Andrew, Jr. and Sarah Jackson acted as master and mistress in President Jackson's absence. Later that year, the President was informed that a fire had gutted the entire house with the exception of the dining room area.

In 1835, Andrew Jackson contracted with Joseph Reiff and William Hume, who were building the Tulip Grove Mansion for the Andrew Jackson Donelsons, to rebuild the Hermitage mansion. They did so, using plans similar to those of the 1831 design, but added a back portico, a large front portico with Corinthian columns and a passage between the library and the farm office. The white-painted front portico with its six columns altered the typical plantation look of the mansion, transforming it into a Greek Revival house,

Upon his retirement from high office, President Jackson lived at the Hermitage for the remaining eight years of his life. His interest in political matters continued, especially concerning the annexation of Texas and the Oregon territory. Never having been formally affiliated with a religious denomination before his retirement, President Jackson joined the Presbyterian Church during his retirement. On June 8, 1845, Andrew Jackson died at the Hermitage.

After President Jackson's death the 1,050-acre Hermitage property was inherited by his adopted son, Andrew Jackson, Jr., who lived in the mansion with his wife, Sarah Jackson, for eleven years before financial difficulties forced them to sell the property. In keeping with his father's wishes, Andrew Jackson, Jr. first offered the property to the state of Tennessee. The state purchased the mansion and five hundred acres for $48,000.00. The Jacksons left the Hermitage in 1858, but, two years later, they returned from their Mississippi plantation to the Hermitage to live as tenants at will. During the Civil War, the Jacksons lost one son, and the surviving son, Andrew Jackson III, returned to live at the Hermitage. His father, Andrew Jackson, Jr., died in a hunting accident in 1865, but the state permitted Andrew Jackson III's mother, Sarah Jackson, to remain at the Hermitage. She lived there with her sister, Marion Adams and, for a time, Andrew Jackson III and his wife. Sarah Jackson's daughter, Rachel Jackson Lawrence, also lived nearby. Sarah Jackson died in 1887, and Andrew Jackson III remained at the Hermitage until 1893.

In 1889, a movement to preserve the Hermitage began, resulting in the formation of the Ladies' Hermitage Association that same year. A charter member was Rachel Jackson Lawrence, who had oversight of 25 acres of the Hermitage property, including the mansion. In 1960, the Association purchased an additional 125 acres of property abutting the north boundary of the tract to prevent nonconforming future development. Since then, additional acreage has been added, so that 625 acres of property are now under the jurisdiction of the Ladies' Hermitage Association. The property has been open to the public since 1889, the year that the Ladies' Hermitage Association was incorporated. In 1989, the Association marked its centennial year by undertaking an ambitious, multimillion dollar project whose aim is to restore the mansion to its appearance during the eight years prior to President Jackson's death in 1845.

The continuing vitality of the Association is also marked by the unveiling of a Visitor Center, at which an introductory film on the Hermitage and its first occupants, Andrew and Rachel Jackson, is shown. It is also here that visitors are furnished with audio tape players and headsets for the newly-established audio tour of the mansion and grounds.

The tour begins on the grounds of the Hermitage, where visitors note the guitar-shaped carriageway leading to the front entrance of the house. Visitors then enter the mansion by crossing the front portico and passing through the main entrance. The first room visitors see is the entry hall, which is quite spacious and was illuminated in Andrew Jackson's era by a whale oil-burning chandelier. Its Greek revival transoms, facing north and south, provided ventilation when opened during the summer. The entry hall is decorated with French scenic wallpaper depicting the story of Telemachus searching for his father Odysseus. A circular staircase curves into the entry hall.

To the left of the hallway are twin entrances to the double parlors, used in the past for after-dinner entertainment. The back parlor served as a family room when its sliding doors were closed. The chandeliers in these rooms were illuminated by candles. Visitors then cross the entry hall to a door on the right and enter a narrow hallway. To the right, at the front of the house, is President Jackson's bedroom. Above the mantel in this room is a portrait of Rachel Jackson at age 52, which the President had placed there so that it would be the first and last object he would see each day. The bed and window hangings are replicas of those Andrew Jackson used in the winters he lived at the Hermitage. President Jackson's huge bed measures 6 feet 9 inches from post to post. Andrew Jackson died in this bed in 1845.

Across the narrow hallway is the bedroom of Sarah Jackson and Andrew Jackson, Jr. Hanging on the wall in this room is a portrait by artist George P.A. Healy of the 39-year-old Sarah Jackson, painted in 1845 at the dying president's request.

The narrow hallway leads to a larger hall with a side entrance. Visitors are now in the library wing of the mansion. To the right, as visitors face the side entrance, is the library, where Jackson and his colleagues often mapped political strategy. This room was also the center of Andrew Jackson's daily activities in the last eight years of his life. In this room, Andrew Jackson spent his mornings reviewing his correspondence while sitting in a leather and wood chair presented to him by Chief Justice Roger B. Taney. On the other side of this wing of the mansion is the farm office.

A stairway from the hallway in the library wing leads upstairs to another hallway. The room to the right was Little Rachel's room, which is closed. Across the hall is the room used for a brief period beginning in 1837 by painter E.W. Earl who, in 1818, married Rachel Jackson's niece, Jane Caffery. He painted at least 34 portraits of President Jackson, and many of other family members and friends of the Jacksons.

Outside Mr. Earl's room begins a hallway located directly above the entrance hall of the house. A platform leads to a large rear window in the back of this hallway. Two doorways on the left wall (as one faces the back of the house) lead to the family rooms. The baseboards in both rooms are wood, painted to resemble marble.

By going down the stairs, exiting the mansion through the rear, turning left on the back portico and left again, visitors see the dining room in the wing of the mansion behind the parlors. In this room, dinner would be served at 3:00 p.m. Perhaps the most interesting feature of this room, however, is the "Eighth of January" mantel, so named to mark the date on which Andrew Jackson commanded his troops in the Battle of New Orleans: January 8, 1815.

The kitchen is housed in a building which is attached to the mansion by a covered passage. Its proximity to the dining room, which was accessible by walking on the covered passage and through the dining room back door, ensured easy transportation of food. The remnants of a bell system, which no longer functions, can be seen on the outside mansion wall nearby.

A tour of the grounds also includes visits to the smokehouse and other dependencies. Another point of interest is the cabin of "Uncle Alfred," a one-time slave who, upon receiving freedom, remained a caretaker at the Hermitage for the rest of his life, and is buried near President Jackson. In addition, visitors may also view the two surviving log cabins of the "original" Hermitage, the gardens, the cemetery, the Hermitage Church and nearby Tulip Grove Mansion (home of the Andrew Jackson Donelsons). A visit to the Hermitage offers an experience rich in both history and beauty, and is well worth making.

MARTIN VAN BUREN

**Martin Van Buren National Historic Site
(Lindenwald)
P.O. Box # 545
Kinderhook, New York 12106
(518) 758-9689**

Administered by the National Park Service.

Directions:	From Albany, take I-90 east to Route 9 (exit 12) and take Route 9 south to Route 9H. The site is five miles south of the junction of Routes 9 and 9H on the right side of the road.
Open:	Daily in season — call for hours.
Admission:	Fee charged. No charge for children and senior citizens.
Features:	Mansion and 22-acre estate. The mansion is now a restored house museum, which includes exhibits, a gift concession, and a ten minute video presentation on Martin Van Buren. Tours are offered every half hour. Arrangements can be made for those requiring special assistance. Comfort stations are outside of the mansion.
Special Events:	On December 5, a grave site ceremony takes place in honor of Martin Van Buren's birthday. (Note that neither Martin Van Buren's birthplace nor his grave site are located on the Lindenwald grounds.)

The man who came to be known as the "Red Fox of Kinderhook" was born in a tavern on December 5, 1782. The tavern, which was demolished in the late 1800s, was a clapboard building with a small kitchen annex and was owned by Martin Van Buren's father, Abraham, a respected landowner and farmer in the small town of Kinderhook, located about 25 miles south of Albany on the east side of the Hudson River. Martin Van Buren's great-grandfather was a native of Holland who settled in the Hudson Valley in 1631. Like his father, Martin Van Buren's mother, the former Maria Hoes, was also of a prosperous family which was among the first to settle in the Kinderhook area. Thus, Martin Van Buren's roots were deeply embedded in Hudson Valley soil, and, despite the journeys on which his political career took him, it is small wonder that he chose to retire in the land of his forebears and near the place of his birth.

In 1796, Martin Van Buren began to pursue a legal career at the age of 14 by clerking in a Kinderhook law office, and later in New York City. He was admitted to the bar in 1803 and joined his half-brother's practice in Kinderhook in 1804. By this time, he had already become aligned with the Jeffersonian Republicans. He married his childhood sweetheart, the former Hannah Hoes, in 1807 and moved to Hudson, New York where he became a surrogate (probate judge). His rising political career, which took him from the New York state senate to state attorney general and then to the leadership of the Jeffersonian Republicans in New York, brought him to Albany, the state capital, which was his home through 1820. It was during this period, 1819, that his wife, Hannah Van Buren, with whom he had had four sons, died. In 1821, he became a United States senator. During this period, Martin Van Buren stayed in a boarding house in Georgetown. By 1828, he became manager of Andrew Jackson's presidential campaign and was, thereby, instrumental in the founding of the Democratic Party. That same year, Senator Van Buren became Governor Van Buren, but only held that office for 71 days because President Jackson appointed him secretary of state.

While secretary of state from 1829 to 1831, Van Buren was a tenant in the Stephen Decatur House, a red brick Federal style home designed by Benjamin Henry Latrobe and built in 1819 for Commodore Stephen Decatur, who was renowned for his victories in the War of 1812 and in the Barbary Wars. After Commodore Decatur was killed in a duel in 1820, Mrs. Susan Decatur rented the elegant town house to Van Buren and a host of other distinguished men, including Secretaries of State Henry Clay and Edward Livingston. It is said that during Mr. Van Buren's residence there that he cut a window in the wall on the garden side of the house so that he could relay signals to President Jackson at the nearby White House. Today, Decatur House, located at 748 Jackson Place, N.W., Washington, D.C., is a property of the National Trust for Historic Preservation and is open to the public.

In 1831, Martin Van Buren left Decatur House upon his appointment as Minister to Great Britain. However, the Senate never confirmed this appointment. As President Jackson's ally, however, the political career of the "Little Magician" was hardly over. He was Andrew Jackson's running mate in the re-election campaign of 1832, and spent a term as vice president of the United States. During this period, Martin Van Buren lived in a corner of the row houses on 1901-1913 Pennsylvania Avenue known as the "Seven Buildings." These buildings, constructed circa 1800, were the only buildings between the White House and Georgetown to survive the burning of Washington.

In 1837, Martin Van Buren succeeded Andrew Jackson to the presidency. (Until George Bush's election in 1988, Mr. Van Buren was the last sitting vice president to have been elected president.) After two years in the White House, President Van Buren, looking ahead to his retirement, purchased the 220-acre Lindenwald estate for $14,000.00. However, his retirement was to come sooner than President Van Buren expected, for he was defeated in his re-election bid by his Whig opponent, William Henry Harrison. While at the White House, President Van Buren installed stables, fountains, stone walls, and iron railings in the White House gardens.

Martin Van Buren's love of renovation carried over to his post-presidential years at Lindenwald. The Lindenwald mansion had already undergone extensive changes since the time of its original construction in 1797 as a simple, rectangular Georgian style home for Judge Peter Van Ness. It stayed in the Van Ness family until 1824, when it was sold to help retire family debts, by President Van Buren's friend and one time employer, William Van Ness. By the time President Van Buren purchased the property, a classical ballroom had been added. Mr. Van Buren was not content with such modest changes to the structure because he wanted to convert his estate to a working farm. By 1845, it was so, complete with flower gardens, ornamental fish ponds, wooden fences and outbuildings.

Martin Van Buren's changes to the mansion itself were even more dramatic. He removed its central stairway and expanded the rooms on both floors of the house. He added 51 French wallpaper panels, depicting a hunting scene, to the expanded downstairs hall. These panels were removed in 1977 and rehung in 1987. He also purchased fine early Empire and late Classical furnishings and Brussels carpets. Ninety percent of the furnishings on display in the mansion today belonged to Mr. Van Buren and/or his family.

Martin Van Buren's son, Smith Thomson Van Buren, agreed to move into Lindenwald in 1849 to help manage the estate. Mr. Van Buren gave his son license to redesign the house as he saw fit, for himself and his family. Consequently, Smith Thomson Van Buren sought out architect Richard Upjohn, who designed Trinity Church in lower Manhattan. Mr. Upjohn's architectural changes were profound: he added 18 rooms to the house, a front porch and other exterior features reflecting the Gothic and Romanesque styles and a four-story Italianate tower at the rear of the house. Smith Thomson Van Buren added the crowning touch by having the house painted yellow, resulting in an eclectic looking structure with three stories and 36 rooms.

The house also has many other notable features. For example, Martin Van Buren's library contains a collection of original political cartoons, a picture of Henry Clay, a friend and political rival of Martin Van Buren's, and a bust of Martin Van Buren fashioned by Hiram Powers. Mr. Van Buren also had indoor plumbing installed in the house, including a flush toilet and bath tub in which he bathed every day. The kitchen wing also includes pumps and plumbing, a coal range and a brick oven.

Martin Van Buren had bedrooms on the second floor for himself and his children, including: Abraham, whose wife, Angelina, acted as hostess in the Van Buren White House and was a cousin of Dolley Madison; Martin, Jr.; John; and Smith Thomson. These rooms have low ceilings and feature sleigh beds of Empire or Classical design. The President's room contains the bed in which he died of bronchial asthma in 1862.

After the president's death, the house went through a variety of uses, including: a tea house, a nursing home, an antique shop, and theatrical quarters before the purchase of the mansion and 22 of the surrounding acres by the United States government in 1976. Today, visitors to the mansion can view Lindenwald as the home of a man who, like his political idol, Thomas Jefferson, was fond of architectural innovation and remained active in the American public realm until his death.

WILLIAM HENRY HARRISON

Berkeley Plantation
Charles City, Virginia 23030
(804) 829-6018

Privately owned by Malcolm and Grace Jamieson.

Directions: From I-95 south, take Hopewell exit and follow State Route 10 east, turning left onto the Benjamin Harrison Bridge. From I-295 north, follow "James River Plantations" signs. Berkeley is three miles from the bridge road following Route 5 east. Entrance is off Route 5 and is clearly marked.

Open: Daily (except Christmas Day) — call for hours.

Admission: Fee charged. Discounts for children and senior citizens.

Features: Mansion, gardens and grounds, gift shop, rest rooms. Luncheon may be purchased on the plantation grounds between 11:00 a.m. and 3:00 p.m. daily.

Special Events: In September, the site hosts a Scottish Festival. On the first Sunday in November, a Thanksgiving Festival is held. The site is also available for wedding receptions.

35

This historic plantation was the scene of many "firsts," including the celebration by Virginia of the first official Thanksgiving in 1619 and the composition of the military anthem "Taps" by General Daniel Butterfield of the Army of the Potomac in 1862. The ninth president of the United States, William Henry Harrison was born here on February 9, 1773. His grandfather, Benjamin Harrison, had constructed the early Georgian mansion in 1726. His father, Benjamin Harrison V, was a signer of the Declaration of Independence and was also born at Berkeley.

The plantation house is a symmetrically shaped, three-story brick structure with a hallway surrounded by two rooms on each side on the first floor and a full basement where a brief slide presentation on the history of Berkeley is shown. The basement also has a museum which includes an exhibit on the Civil War occupation of Berkeley, as well as paintings, Civil War relics and Native American artifacts, all open to the public. The second and third floors, the private residence of Malcolm and Grace Jamieson, are not open to the public. The plantation house, a treasure almost lost as an historical landmark, was occupied by 140,000 Union troops under General McClellan of the Army of the Potomac. In 1862 the plantation house became Union Army headquarters and was also used as a Civil War hospital. The Union Army cut many trees on the plantation, and used the Harrison family furniture as firewood. The Harrisons, who had lost the plantation prior to the Civil War because of financial reversals, were not present to protect their former home. Although General McClellan was subsequently dismissed by President Lincoln, who visited Berkeley twice to review the Union troops, Berkeley's pattern of decline had already begun and was to continue for the following forty years. At one point during this period, the house was even painted red and used as a storage barn for hay and grain.

It was in 1907 that John Jamieson of Scotland, a former drummer boy in General McClellan's army during the occupation of Berkeley, discovered that the plantation was for sale. Needing a valuable source of timber to be used in constructing New York Harbor, he purchased the 1,400-acre plantation for $28,000. The plantation house, thought valueless, was included as part of the sale at no additional cost.

Mr. Jamieson's son, Malcolm Jamieson, has endeavored, quite successfully, to restore the plantation home and grounds to the glorious style of its days as the Harrison family seat. The furnishings collected by the Jamieson family are antiques: most are original from the Harrison era and are the products of Virginia craftsmen. The house itself retains its original window frames, floors and masonry, as well as the first pediment roof in Virginia. Among the furnishings of special interest are: a Chippendale settee whose original stitched covering took three women eight years to complete and an English gentlemen's secretary whose diamond-back mirrors have not lost their reflective quality in almost two hundred years. Glancing up the set of stairs leading from a small hallway adjoining the dining room, visitors may see the musicians' gallery, where musicians played unobtrusively for party guests on the main floor. Also on display here is a framed handkerchief used as a campaign souvenir of William Henry Harrison's Whig presidential campaign, with a picture of the hero of the Battle of Tippecanoe and the campaign slogan: "Tippecanoe and Tyler too."

It was to Berkeley that William Henry Harrison, the first president to campaign actively for his high office, returned in 1841 to write his lengthy inaugural address. He delivered the speech outdoors in a freezing rain on March 4, 1841, and within one month he was dead. (At 69, he was our second oldest president.) Forty-seven years later, however, his grandson, Benjamin Harrison, was elected as the 23rd president of the United States, making Berkeley Plantation the ancestral home of two American presidents. It is fortunate that, unlike the birthplaces of other former chief executives, Berkeley remains preserved and, indeed, flourishes thanks to the efforts of Malcolm and Grace Jamieson and their family.

Grouseland
3 West Scott Street
Vincennes, Indiana 47591
(812) 882-2096

Administered by the Francis Vigo Chapter of the National Society of Daughters of the American Revolution.

Directions:	From Chicago, take U.S. 41 south to Vincennes. Turn right at Harrison Street, and left at West Scott Street, which is five blocks up Harrison Street on the left.	**Open:**	Daily (except Thanksgiving Day, Christmas Day and New Year's Day) — call for seasonal hours.
		Admission:	Fee charged. Discounts for children, students, and senior citizens.

Features: Mansion. Log cabin visitor center next door has gift shop and book shop. Not handicapped accessible.

Special Events: On the Saturday evening of Memorial Day weekend, the site holds candlelight tours guided by volunteer docents in period costume.

After his departure from Berkeley Plantation in 1787, William Henry Harrison did not return to his birthplace until 1841. Then, as president-elect, he returned to the room where he was born to write his inaugural address.

After attending Hampden-Sydney College, Virginia, followed by a brief period studying medicine, William Henry Harrison joined the army, beginning with a regiment at Fort Washington in Cincinnati, Ohio in 1791. In 1795, he married Anna Symmes, whose father owned vast tracts of land in Ohio, and the couple settled in North Bend, Ohio, where William Henry Harrison built a five-room log home. By 1797, this log home, which was known as "The Cabin," had been enlarged to what became known as the "Big House," a sixteen-room mansion with clapboard siding and wainscoting on the interior walls. The house was the birthplace of Mr. Harrison's grandson, Benjamin Harrison, who became

the 23rd president of the United States. The house burned in 1878 while Anna Harrison was still living there.

In 1800, William Henry Harrison was appointed the first governor of the Indiana Territory, covering a land mass now divided by all or part of various Midwestern states. With his military background, Mr. Harrison appeared to the government to be well-suited to this appointment because of the many problems settlers in the territory had with Native American tribes residing in or near the territory. Upon receiving his appointment, Mr. Harrison and his family moved to the territorial capital in Vincennes.

In 1801, William Henry Harrison, desirous of building a home reminiscent of his birthplace at Berkeley Plantation, purchased 300 acres of cleared land on the banks of the Wabash. During the years 1803 and 1804, Governor Harrison built a hand-made brick home in the modified Federal style.

His love of hunting grouse (a small game bird about the size of a quail) inspired the name of his new home—Grouseland.

Grouseland mansion was the Harrison abode from 1804 to 1812. William Henry Harrison left Grouseland in 1812 to become Commander-in-Chief of the Northwest Territory, during which time he fought in Canada in the Battle of the Thames. His military successes during this time, as well as his career in Indiana when he led the territorial forces in the famous Battle of Tippecanoe, made him a military hero throughout the United States and provided impetus for his subsequent career in politics. He served briefly as a member of the U.S. House of Representatives, as an Ohio state senator, and a United States senator. He also served during the late 1820s as United States Minister to Columbia, South America.

As his notoriety grew, and his military successes (particularly the Battle of Tippecanoe) became famous, William Henry Harrison was viewed as a potentially strong presidential candidate. He received the nomination of the Whig Party in 1840 and selected as his running mate a man who was born just a few miles from Mr. Harrison's birthplace at Berkeley Plantation, John Tyler of Virginia. (See next section.)

William Henry Harrison won the presidency in a campaign that was noteworthy for propaganda and exaggeration on both sides. The fictitious story that Mr. Harrison was born in a log cabin and drank hard cider was an example of the excesses of the campaign. Mr. Harrison went on to win this hard fought campaign and, a few months after his election, returned to his birthplace at Berkeley Plantation to write his inaugural address. Sitting at a writing desk in his mother's bedroom, the room in which he was born, President-elect Harrison wrote an inaugural speech of such length that it took two hours to deliver. He rode a horse in the inaugural parade, taking off his hat and exposing his head to the dampness and freezing rain. The prolonged exposure to the weather resulted in his catching a cold that later became pneumonia. On April 4, 1841, thirty-one days after his inauguration, William Henry Harrison died, and John Tyler became the first vice president to succeed to the presidency due to the death of his predecessor while still in office.

Today, Grouseland stands as the only surviving home in which William Henry Harrison lived during his adult life, with the exception of the White House. The home cost Mr. Harrison $20,000.00 to build, certainly a large sum for its time. In design, the home diverges from the traditional Federal style of his Berkeley Plantation birthplace in that one of the side walls of the house is bowed, as are many of the interior walls, including the staircase wall and some of the second-floor walls. Excavations on the site uncovered the remains of the sandstone foundation of the house's original porch, which was removed sometime between 1836 and 1850. By 1850, the house was being used as the Harrison House Hotel and, in place of the original porch, a long hotel porch extended along the front of the property. By about 1860, the long porch had also been removed and two small porches, one at the front entrance of the house and one at the side entrance, were added. By 1900, a bay and porch were added to one end of the house's service passage and a closet and bathroom were added to the other end. These "improvements" were removed during the 1949-1950 restoration of Grouseland, which took place due to the efforts of the Francis Vigo Chapter of the N.S.D.A.R., which had acquired the house by that time. In 1984, the Chapter undertook the project of reconstructing a front porch similar to that used in William Henry Harrison's time, using what had been learned in the excavation as partial guidance. Today, the house has a Greek Revival-style two story front porch. It consists of four white columns on the first and second floor levels, and forms a balcony reached through a double-dutch door at the front of the second-floor hallway. The first floor landing of the porch is accessible by means of a set of stairs on three sides of the porch.

The walls of the house are twelve to fourteen inches thick and are insulated with clay and straw, making the structure very strong and durable. Another distinctive feature of this house is the door at its entrance, which establishes a theme that is repeated on many of the other doors in the mansion. The design on the upper part of these doors forms a cross, and the pattern on the lower part suggests an open Bible. Above the front and back doors are fan-shaped windows, a common design in the elegant homes of William Henry Harrison's time.

Originally, the main house was separated from the service wing behind the progeny. This service wing was a dependency, with a warming kitchen and a wine cellar. Presumably, the dependency was also used for the household chores such as weaving, sewing, and candlemaking. It is believed that the Harrison boys slept in the upstairs rooms of the dependency. Because the winters in Vincennes were more severe than the Harrisons originally thought, they added a passageway using bricks and mortar, thus uniting the two buildings into one. The passageway was used by servants or slaves transporting food from the warming kitchen to the dining room, and for other purposes.

Through the front door of the home, visitors see a large hallway leading to a distinctive cherrywood stairway. The stairway ascends directly along the left-hand wall of the home and then curves upwards to face the front of the house. An 1813 portrait of William Henry Harrison, painted by John Wesley Jarvis, hangs near the front door in this hallway.

Turning to the left, visitors then enter the parlor. This room was sometimes referred to as the Counsel Room since it was also used by the Harrisons not only for entertainment, but to conduct government meetings. Most of the furniture in this room, as in the other rooms, was not owned by the Harrisons, but was nonetheless manufactured in their time. A notable exception is the English Waterford crystal chandelier, a gift to the Harrisons from one of their grandsons. The chandelier's rope is decoratively wrapped in blue velvet matching the hand silk screen pattern of the wallpaper. The wallpaper is yellow with a blue design stretching along the top of the four walls, and, like the paper in the dining room, is not original to this house. Another distinctive feature of this room is the third wall with its three large windows that afforded the Harrisons a commanding view of the Wabash River, no longer visible due to new buildings and tree growth. Other features worthy of note are: a 200-year-old desk, still bearing a large scratch it received in transit; a pianoforte made in 1800 by John Geid Company of New York; and a silver tea service dated 1790. A relatively small, round wooden table in the center of this room belonged to the Harrisons. On the floor, as in the hallway and dining room, is an oriental rug (again, like the floor, not original to the house). The rugs are, however, of a kind that was commonly used during the Harrisons' time.

Crossing the hallway, one enters the dining room. This room features an original Hepplewhite sideboard belonging to the Harrisons, given to them as a wedding gift by Mrs. Harrison's parents. On one of the wooden shutters on the left-hand window is a bullet hole made by a native American's rifle in an apparent attempt to kill William Henry Harrison. Near the fireplace is a cloth and wood frame fire screen used to protect peoples' faces from the heat of the fire and stray cinders. The place settings on the dining room table are English Royal Crown Derby, with the exception of the knives at the table, which were not used in the Indiana territory of the early 1800s. Across the room from the fireplace mantel is a bull's-eye mirror used to reflect the candlelight and provide more illumination. Near the fireplace is a high chair whose bottom section may be unscrewed from the base to form a footstool. An early 1800 barometer hangs on a wall near one of the windows in this room.

Next, visitors ascend the winding stairway at the front of the house, noting the bowed walls of the second floor hallway. This section contains four bedrooms. The large bedroom to the left is thought to have been William Henry Harrison's. It contains two high rope beds, each of which has a canopy. One of these beds has posts with leaf carvings, reflective of the growing trend in Victorian furniture to include symbols of nature. A portable writing desk is situated on a dresser to the side of one of the beds. Across the hall is another bed with a canopy, possibly intended for guests. Behind it is yet another, smaller bedroom, used for children or guests.

Walking through what is believed to have been the master bedroom and turning to the left, visitors come to another small room. It contains child-sized furniture, a column of narrow shelves concealed within the walls by a narrow door near the mantel, a cradle, and a group of dolls dating back to the early 1800s. The proximity of this room to what appears to be the master bedroom supports the idea that this room was once a nursery or child's bedroom. The Harrisons had three children when they arrived at Grouseland, and eight by the time they left. (They had two more children before William Henry Harrison's death in 1841.)

A door near the nursery leads to two large rooms in the dependency wing of the house. As noted above, these are thought to be the Harrison boys' bedrooms. To the rear is a narrow winding stairway leading to the first floor. It is thought that this part of the house was used for food preparation or storage. One of the rooms here still contains the original floorboards and is currently used as the morning room. The other room is now the gift shop.

Adjacent to the gift shop is yet another room in the service passage. This room is now a small museum documenting highlights of William Henry Harrison's military and political careers, notably the hat, sword and spurs he wore at the Battle of Tippecanoe, various newspapers documenting his military successes, prints and illustrations of those battles, and campaign paraphernalia from the 1840 presidential campaign.

The basement is also open to visitors and includes an arts and crafts room with a fireplace, a loom, a spinning wheel and other crafts equipment used for candlemaking. Another room, containing a cistern, the chief source of water for the home, contains more Harrison artifacts: one of William Henry Harrison's walking canes, articles of dishware, and family photographs. In the rear portion of the basement is a room depicting an old warming kitchen and includes a large hearth with metal pots and pans and a wooden table in the center used for slicing vegetables. A large bowl of popcorn (a popular snack of the era) is on the kitchen table.

After the family left Grouseland in 1814, the mansion and property had a series of subsequent owners. One of those owners was a farmer who used Grouseland as a storage barn, filling its rooms with hay and grain and allowing pigs and other animals to trample through its hallways. Miraculously, little damage appears to have been done to the woodwork in the house. In 1909, the house was slated for demolition. When a leading member of the Francis Vigo Chapter of the Daughters of the American Revolution noticed a man walking down the street with a wooden shutter that she later learned belonged to the mansion, she initiated a fund-raising drive, raising sufficient funds for the local D.A.R. Chapter to purchase the property. After a two-year restoration campaign, Grouseland was opened to the public as a house museum and has remained opened on that basis to this day.

Although the size of the property that this magnificent mansion stands on has shrunken considerably from its original 300 acres, and although some of the dependencies which originally existed on the property are now lost, the mansion itself thankfully survives and is preserved for visitors who will enjoy immensely a visit to this glorious home.

JOHN TYLER

Sherwood Forest Plantation
14501 John Tyler Memorial Parkway
Charles City, Virginia 23030
(804) 829-5377

Privately owned and maintained by President Tyler's grandson and his family.

Directions: From Richmond and points South, West, and North: From I-64 or I-95, take I-295 South, exit 22A to Rt. 5 East, Charles City. Follow Rt. 5 approx. 20 miles.

From Williamsburg and I-64 West: Exit 242 to Williamsburg and Rt. 199. Follow Rt. 199 to Rt. 5 (John Tyler Hwy). Turn left on Rt. 5. Proceed approx. 20 miles. The entrance is on the left side of the road.

Open: Open to the public daily, except Thanksgiving Day and Christmas Day.

Admission: Fee charged. Discounts for children, senior citizens, and AAA.

Features: Guided tours of main rooms of Big House, self-guided tour of plantation grounds with marked points of interest.

Special Events: President Tyler's birthday celebration, March 29. Fresh flower arrangements for Historic Garden Week in Virginia, last week in April. Tyler family Christmas traditions tour in December.

This beautiful mansion and grounds are unique among the homes featured in this book because they are still owned and ably managed by the descendants of a former president of the United States. Sherwood Forest was so named by President John Tyler because of his treatment as an "outlaw" by the Whig Party. The mansion, which was built circa 1730 on a 1,200-acre estate, had fallen into disrepair when President Tyler purchased it in 1842 at a price of $10,000.00. By 1844, President Tyler had the Georgian clapboard structure renovated. The property was renovated by connecting the central structure to two smaller buildings on either side.

The resulting structure, some 301 feet long, is the longest frame house in America.

Before purchasing Sherwood Forest, the future president attended the College of William and Mary, and boarded with his brother-in-law, Judge James Semple, while a student there. While his father was governor of Virginia, John Tyler apprenticed at the law office of Edmund Randolph. In 1809, he began practicing law in Charles City County. He married Letitia Christian in 1813, and honeymooned at the Greenbrier Cottage in White Sulphur Springs (now in West Virginia). The couple settled at Mons-Sacer, a five-hundred acre section of Greenway, the estate on which President Tyler was born on March 29, 1790. The home on this 1,200-acre estate, which President Tyler later inherited, is a story and a half frame house which has a brick basement, dormers and outside chimneys. Today, the house is privately owned.

Between 1811 and 1834, John Tyler served intermittent terms in the Virginia House of Delegates. He also served in the United States House of Representatives beginning at age twenty-six, and lived in a boarding house while in government service. In 1821, he lived either at Woodburn, which he built in 1811, or at Greenway in Charles City. He was governor of Virginia from 1825 to 1827, residing in the executive mansion. He became a United States senator in 1828, serving in that capacity until 1836. During this period, he lived on a six hundred acre farm on the York River in Gloucester County, Virginia. In 1837, he moved to a home on Francis Street in Williamsburg, Virginia. This home, which was his until 1841, was later demolished.

In 1841, John Tyler became president. While in office, he used "Woodley" at 3000 Cathedral Avenue in Washington as a summer home (as had his predecessor Martin Van Buren) and also summered at the Greenbrier Cottage, in White Sulphur Springs, Virginia (now West Virginia). From 1853 to 1858, years after President Tyler left office, he summered at "Villa Margaret," at the beach at Old Point Comfort, Hampton, Virginia. He first rented, and then bought, this beach home.

Tragically, President Tyler's wife of 29 years, Letitia Christian Tyler, died in 1842, the year that President Tyler purchased Sherwood Forest. President Tyler made Sherwood Forest home for himself and his new bride, the former Julia Gardiner of Gardiner's Island, New York, whom he married while in office, thus becoming the first president to do so. In purchasing this Charles City plantation as his new home, President Tyler selected a location very close to his birthplace at Greenway. His enjoyment of the plantation began in earnest in 1845 at the end of his term of office, as he became an active supporter of the secessionist movement. He also served in the ill-fated Peace Convention of 1861 and, at the time of his death on January 18, 1862, as a member of the Confederate Congress. The Confederate Congress met in Richmond, and, while serving there, the former president stayed at the Ballard House and later at the Exchange Hotel.

President Tyler's quieter years at Sherwood Forest were earned by a turbulent term in office. He became the first vice president to clearly establish the precedent of presidential succession upon the death of his former running mate, President William Henry Harrison, in 1841. (President Harrison was a previous owner of the Sherwood Forest property.) Because the Constitution makes reference to the authority of a vice president to act as the president should the president be unable to perform his duties, it was, at the time, arguable whether the vice president had clear constitutional authority to succeed a deceased president. President Tyler, however, did indeed take the oath of office and succeed the late president, a source of outrage to Senator Henry Clay, whose presidential ambitions were undisguised, and other Whig Party leaders. This dispute created a rift between President Tyler and the Whig Party which never healed, and led to the resignation of Tyler's entire "inherited" cabinet, except Daniel Webster. President Tyler filled the vacuum of this mass resignation by appointing John C. Calhoun and several other talented statesmen. Despite such political strife, President Tyler was not prevented from achieving the annexation of Texas by the end of his administration.

After President Tyler's death, Sherwood Forest was occupied by Union forces under the command of General McClellan. These troops burned many valuable possessions of the Tyler family, including papers belonging to the former president. An attempt by Union soldiers to set fire to the house by burning hay under a table (now situated in the hallway, its charred surface evidencing this incident) was foiled by General McClellan, a former beau of Julia Gardiner Tyler. His intervention protected Sherwood Forest from total destruction.

Julia Tyler, after weathering the Union occupation of her plantation, soon learned of the impending arrival of still another Union general known to the Confederacy as "Beast" Butler. Believing the plantation would not survive more destruction, she devised a daring means of escape. By auctioning off her possessions, she raised funds to purchase cotton, selling it to pay for passage for herself and her children to Bermuda from Wilmington, North Carolina. She successfully ran a blockade of ships traveling to Bermuda and made good her escape. A small silk flag, resembling a Confederate flag, was flown from the ship that ran the blockade. It is framed above a side door in the sitting room of the house today. After a stay on Gardiner's Island until the end of the war, Julia Tyler returned to Sherwood Forest, discovering the mark (which remains today) of General Butler's sword in her front door, trees and boxwood shrubs removed and other damage to Sherwood Forest. Hiring immigrant laborers from Sweden, Julia Tyler set about the business of restoring Sherwood Forest as a working plantation and a charming home. She succeeded admirably. Her son, Dr. Lyon Gardiner Tyler, president of the College of William and Mary for 31 years, inherited the plantation. Today it is owned by the family of Dr. Tyler's youngest son, Harrison Tyler, and remains in appearance much as it did during the days of President Tyler.

The house's central portion is connected to the former kitchen building by a long hallway, and to President Tyler's law office on the other side by a private ballroom which is 68 feet in length. The room was designed by John and Julia Tyler for dancing the Virginia Reel. The house has 24 rooms, 7 sets of stairs, and 18 fireplaces. One-third of the furniture is original. (The dining room wallpaper is an exact reproduction replaced by a private concern in 1976.) President Tyler's porcelain, china, silver, mirrors, and girondoles are still in use at the plantation. All of the hardware in the home (including an 1845 heat register) is original. The Tyler family opened the plantation for public tours in an effort to share its rich history with visitors.

JAMES KNOX POLK

James K. Polk Memorial State Historic Site (Birthplace)
Box 475
Pineville, North Carolina 28134
(704) 889-7145

Administered by the Division of Archives And History, Department of Cultural Resources, State of North Carolina.

Directions:	From Charlotte, take U.S. 521 South to Pineville. Site is 1/2 mile south of Pineville on the left side of the road.
Open:	Daily — call for seasonal hours.
Admission:	Free.
Features:	Marker commemorating the birthplace of James K. Polk, replicas of President Polk's birthplace and a kitchen house, a visitor center with museum, gift shop and rest rooms. Guided tours and a 25-minute movie depicting President Polk's life are included. Picnicking on grounds. (Groups interested in visiting the site are requested to make advance reservations.)

Special Events: On the first Saturday in November, to mark President Polk's birthday, the site hosts a celebration at which people dressed in period costume demonstrate eighteenth-century crafts and chores, including cooking, spinning, weaving, and woodworking. At Christmas time, the site hosts a dramatic presentation depicting late eighteenth-century Christmas traditions and a special tour at which customs of the period are observed and the interior of the birthplace replica is illuminated by candlelight. (Note that although the Christmas tour takes place during the day, candlelight is appropriate due to the darkness of the interior of the birthplace replica.) Both the November and Christmas events are free.

The eleventh president of the United States, James Knox Polk, was born of Scottish Presbyterian stock, in what is now known as Pineville, in Mecklenburg County, North Carolina. His great uncle, Thomas Polk, was the first of the Polk family to come to the area from Pennsylvania, and was a founder of Mecklenburg. Thomas Polk's father, William Polk, followed his son to North Carolina from Pennsylvania, together with the rest of the Polk family. William Polk's other son, Ezekiel Polk, was the father of Samuel Polk, who married Jane Knox. On November 2, 1795, Jane Knox Polk gave birth to a son, James Knox Polk.

Young James Polk lived at the Polk plantation with his three siblings until he reached the age of 11. During that time, Samuel Polk became prosperous as a land surveyor, and ran a successful cotton and corn plantation on 250 acres of land. There we can imagine that young James learned much about farming life. Although the Polks lived in a log home, it was a spacious, two-story structure with a separate kitchen house. Fenced enclosures for cows and other animals were situated nearby. Sugar Creek was a ready source of water, and about five slaves lived on the plantation, carrying on the day-to-day work. Living under these conditions, the Polks were considered a prosperous family in their community.

James Polk's restless grandfather, Ezekiel Polk, was responsible for the departure of Samuel Polk and his family from Mecklenburg County. Motivated by a desire for available land and by religious differences with his North Carolina neighbors, Ezekiel Polk managed to acquire title to land in Tennessee through surveying activities. He settled in central Tennessee with some members of his immediate family in 1803. It was not until 1806 that Samuel Polk's family followed him to Tennessee. Jane Knox Polk, mother of four, was not eager to undertake a five hundred mile journey through wilderness and mountains to settle in unknown territory. When they finally made the journey, it took a month and a half to reach their destination.

Samuel Polk's father bestowed upon his son a substantial parcel of land in Tennessee, and it was there, six miles north of the Duck River, that the Samuel Polk family lived for ten years. They cleared their new land, developed a farm, and, in time, established themselves as a prominent family in the community. During their decade at the farm, the Polks saw an influx of new settlers in the area sufficient to form a new county in Tennessee. Maury County was created in the region, and its county seat, Columbia, south of the Polk farm, was established. The Polk family moved to Columbia in 1816.

Today, twenty-one acres of the Polk birthplace have been acquired by the state of North Carolina. A marker in the shape of a pyramid, erected in 1904, commemorates the birthplace. Replicas of the Polk birthplace and kitchen house, both of which are filled with furnishings of the early 1800s, stand on the site, which also includes a visitors center including a Polk museum where a 25-minute film on Polk's life is shown. The site is also ideal for picnics and nature hikes.

James K. Polk Ancestral Home
301 West 7th Street
Columbia, Tennessee 38401
(913) 388-4913

Administered by the James K. Polk Memorial Association.

Directions:	From I-65 (south of Nashville), take exit 46 and proceed 9 miles west toward U.S. 31. Take U.S. 31 south and drive toward U.S. 43. The house is 2 blocks west of the square on U.S. 43.
Open:	Daily (except Thanksgiving Day, Christmas Eve, Christmas Day and New Year's Day) — call for seasonal hours.
Admission:	Fee charged. Discounts for children and senior citizens. Special rates for other groups of 10 or more with advance reservations.
Features:	Main house, kitchen house, gardens, and adjacent Walker house (which includes museum, video presentation, gift shop, and rest rooms). Not handicapped accessible.
Special Events:	None.

The James K. Polk Ancestral Home is the only home President Polk ever lived in, besides the White House, which remains extant. It was built in 1816, while James Polk was attending the University of North Carolina at Chapel Hill, by James Polk's father, Samuel Polk, whose entrepreneurial and surveying activities drew him to move into Columbia and away from the farm which had been his home for the past ten years. The James K. Polk Ancestral Home is a two-story brick structure of the Federal style popular in Tennessee in 1816. This modest home, like others of its time and location, is built of hand-made brick and has a large stair hall, a parlor and dining room downstairs and three bedrooms upstairs. The house's large windows and high ceilings made the house suitable for summer weather. Winters were relatively mild, but each major room is equipped with a fireplace for heat.

Behind the house, a separate kitchen building was constructed. It is a short walk away from the back door leading into the dining room of the main house. In 1820, James and Sarah Polk's oldest daughter, Jane Maria Polk Walker, and her husband built a hand-made brick house of similar style next door to the Polk home. Today, the two houses share a common courtyard and garden, and the Walker house is used as a reception area, gift shop, and museum. A video presentation on President Polk's life is shown there.

James K. Polk was plagued with health problems as a youth. At the age of 17, he required a serious urinary bladder stone operation and his father had to carry him 250 miles to a noted Kentucky doctor, who performed the surgery. Although James Polk's health improved at that point, his physical problems were not over. He graduated with top honors from the University of North Carolina in 1818, but when his father came to take him home, his health was too poor to make the trip back to central Tennessee. After a few weeks, he had recovered sufficiently to make the trip and returned to live in his parents' new home for the first time.

James Polk, for a short time, lived with his parents and seven younger siblings. However, it was not long before Mr. Polk left home at the age of twenty-three to apprentice in the law under Felix Grundy, a noted Nashville attorney and friend of Andrew Jackson. While there, Mr. Polk was chosen to become clerk of the Tennessee state senate, which meant periodic stays in Murfreesboro, the state capital at that time. Upon admission to the bar in 1820, Mr. Polk set up a law practice in Columbia, living in his parents' house. His duties at the State Senate took him to Murfreesboro for another short time, and in 1823 he was elected to the state legislature in his own right.

While in Murfreesboro, James Polk met and courted Sarah Childress, a young woman who, although from a small frontier town, had an educational background remarkable for a woman of her day. On January 1, 1824, she and James Knox Polk were married in Murfreesboro. After several days of celebration in Murfreesboro and Columbia, the Polks settled into a cottage in Columbia, just down the road from Mr. Polk's parents' home.

In 1825, James Polk's political career began in earnest. He was elected to the U.S. House of Representatives that year, and soon rose to the position of speaker of the house (the only president ever to have held that office). In the House, he became an ardent spokesperson for the policies of Andrew Jackson at a time when the Democratic Party was beginning to emerge, and during which Andrew Jackson, in 1829, had become president. He remained in Congress through 1838, the year in which the emergence of the rival Whig Party as a potent force in Tennessee prompted Mr. Polk to run for governor of that state. He held that office for one two-year term, only to be defeated in a re-election bid at the hands of his Whig opponent, James C. Jones.

A defeat by Governor Jones of James Polk's comeback election effort in 1842 threatened to end Mr. Polk's political career. Mr. Polk, however, did not resign himself to political obscurity. He actively sought the Democratic vice presidential nomination in the spring of 1844, at a time when the Democratic convention was deadlocked among several contenders for the presidential nomination, the principal candidates being former president Martin Van Buren of New York and Lewis Cass of Michigan. The party leadership had agreed that, in the event of a deadlock, the compromise Democratic ticket would be Silas Wright of New York for president and Mr. Polk for vice president. At the key moment, however, Mr. Wright refused the presidential nomination, prompting the Democratic leaders to turn to James Knox Polk as their presidential nominee.

James K. Polk's positions on key issues, especially his strong support for the annexation of Texas (which was appealing to southern voters) and the expansion of the United States into the Oregon Territory (appealing to Northerners) gave him the potential for a broad national constituency. The problem was that Mr. Polk, the first "dark horse" to achieve the presidency, was virtually unknown to the overwhelming majority of the electorate. In addition, his Whig opponent, Henry Clay, was well-known and a formidable political adversary. These circumstances led to the invention of the taunting Whig campaign slogan of 1844: "Who is James K. Polk?" Mr. Polk's unswerving support of the policies of Andrew Jackson, combined with the similarity in background of Polk and his mentor, caused James K. Polk to be called (perhaps with derisive intent) by the nickname "Young Hickory." Despite the obvious political handicaps of the Polk candidacy, and Mr. Polk's loss to Henry Clay in Polk's home state of Tennessee, New York provided James K. Polk with a victory by the narrowest Electoral College majority in history: a two vote margin. James K.

Polk's accomplishments in his four-year term as president were many (including the founding of the U.S. Naval Academy and the Smithsonian Institution, and the issuance of the first U.S. postage stamp in 1847). Arguably, the most important and lasting contribution made by the Polk administration was the addition of 800,000 square miles of territory to the United States via the annexation of Texas (which, technically, occurred on the final day of the Tyler administration, although the state of Texas was admitted to the Union during the Polk administration) and the acquisition of California and the Oregon Territory.

James K. Polk did not seek re-election as president. Instead, he retired to Nashville upon completion of his term of office. His health had been shattered by the strain of office. (Two portraits of President Polk made within three years of each other, currently hanging close to each other in a corner of the parlor of the James K. Polk Ancestral Home, reveal the effects of the pressures of office upon him.) The former president and his wife established residence at the former home of Felix Grundy. That house came to be known as Polk Place. It was demolished in 1900, but a photograph of the Nashville residence shows a large two-story structure with Federal style windows and a Greek Revival colonnade.

James Knox Polk visited his mother at her Columbia home one last time, in April 1849. On June 15, 1849, the eleventh president of the United States died of cholera.

Sarah Polk, a charming, attractive hostess during the White House years, also had a very rigid aspect to her character, and never permitted dancing or hard liquor at White House functions. This aspect of her character manifested itself in self-discipline after her husband's death. She never remarried, spending her 42 remaining years of life living at Polk Place. She was seldom seen in other than black clothing, mourning her husband's death until her own in 1891. She was, however, quite active in civic matters, and, during the Civil War, was a mediating influence in the conflict due to her extensive contacts and acquaintances with members of both sides. Polk Place became "neutral territory" during the war, and was spared from the ravages of battle because of the respect accorded Mrs. Polk by leaders on both sides. Mrs. Polk had an adopted daughter: her niece, Sarah Jetton Fall, who lived with her mother at Polk Place.

After Sarah Polk's death, Mrs. Fall and her daughter, Mrs. Saidee Fall Grant, took steps to preserve the most valuable possessions of the Polk family. Although Polk Place was lost to the wrecking ball by 1900, Mrs. Grant managed to organize the James K. Polk Memorial Association in 1924, which purchased the James K. Polk Ancestral Home using a combination of state and private funds.

Today, the Association has acquired both the James K. Polk Ancestral Home and the home next door, in which Polk's sister, Jane Walker, had lived. The James K. Polk

Ancestral Home houses a combination of furnishings and other possessions belonging to Samuel Polk and his wife and to James K. Polk and his wife. Most of the president's extant furnishings on display in this house were actually used in Polk Place or at the White House.

There are shelves of law books remaining from James K. Polk's law practice, and a print of the signing of the Declaration of Independence hangs on the wall. A chair with a writing arm, which once belonged to Sarah Polk, is also kept in this room.

A side doorway takes visitors to the adjoining bedroom of President Polk's sister Jane, where they see a four-poster bed designed with acorns atop each post. Sarah Polk's folding, portable writing desk (used by her in her capacity as "secretary" to the president) is also in the room. A portrait of 45-year-old Sarah Polk, wearing her widow's black mourning garb, hangs in this room.

Next, visitors see a trunk room on the left, which contains a travel trunk used by Sarah Polk for Washington trips. Some of Mrs. Polk's clothing, including a Parisian-made black cape, is also on display in this room.

Visitors then walk across the hall to the south bedroom, containing the four-poster bed of Saidee Grant, Mrs. Polk's great niece. A chest of drawers, with a "wig compartment" concealed on either side of a mirror, is to the left side of the room.

Behind the house is a reconstructed two-room kitchen house containing period kitchen implements, including a biscuit board used by Ophelia Polk Hays, another of the president's sisters. The building was reconstructed in 1945, following an archaeological probe for the foundations of the original building.

The garden in the courtyard is probably more elaborate than the original. It includes an iron fountain taken from the garden at Polk Place.

Next door is the Walker house, built in 1820 and used by Polk relatives, which remained in the family until 1870. It currently houses other mementoes of Polk's life, including an exhibit tracing his career, and rotating exhibits from the Polk Association's collection. The site provides a revealing view of the life and times of an influential president.

ZACHARY TAYLOR

Springfield
5608 Apache Road
Louisville, Kentucky 40207
(502) 897-9990

Privately owned by Dr. William C. Gist.

This section is dedicated to the memory of Betty Gist, whose devotion to American history and support for this book will not be forgotten.

If contacted in advance, Dr. Gist will permit interested persons to tour his house.

As an infant, Zachary Taylor first came with his family to "Springfield," the 400-acre Taylor family farm, in the Beargrass Creek region near Louisville, Kentucky, in the spring of 1785. His father, Colonel Richard Taylor, originally came to this region in the late fall of 1784. The Springfield property was located in Jefferson County, Kentucky, and was east of the Louisville city limits. A prominent and well-to-do family, the

Taylors had lived at Hare Forest, a plantation in Orange County, which is near Culpeper, Virginia. Col. Taylor sold Hare Forest in 1784, and set forth with his family and slaves to find a new home. While on their journey, a case of the measles broke out in the party with which the Taylors were traveling, and the Taylor party had to be quarantined immediately. The Taylors managed to secure temporary lodgings on a plantation called

47

Montebello, located near Barbourville, in Orange County, Virginia. It was at Montebello that Zachary Taylor, the third son and third child of Col. Taylor and Sarah Dabney Strother Taylor (who had nine children in all, the first six of whom were sons and the others daughters) was born on November 24, 1784. It is thought that the Taylors lived in log outbuildings while at Montebello but the original buildings no longer exist. Leaving his wife and three young sons at Montebello, Col. Taylor journeyed on to Kentucky with his slaves in order to establish the new Taylor home at Springfield. In 1785, Col. Taylor brought his family to Kentucky to make the Springfield farm their new home. The Taylor family, a well established and respected family in Virginia, continued to be well regarded and successful in Kentucky. The Springfield property later expanded to as much as 700 acres, and, according to early nineteenth-century tax records, Col. Taylor came to own about 10,000 acres of property in seven Kentucky counties. Of the nine children of Col. and Mrs. Taylor, eight, including Zachary Taylor, survived into adulthood.

Zachary Taylor spent most of the first 23 years of his life at Springfield. The original home on this site, built by Colonel Richard Taylor and his slaves, was a log home, which was later moved to the back of the property for slave quarters. It was replaced by the current structure, a large two and a half story Georgian Colonial red brick, Flemish bond house, constructed in a style similar to that of a Virginia plantation home sometime between 1785 and 1790. The bricks used to build the home were fired on the Springfield property. The resulting house was a comfortable manor home for the Taylor family, who lived and prospered here. The home had two rooms on each floor and featured walnut wood and ash flooring. Sometime between 1810 and 1820, a second side of the house was built. It also had two rooms on each floor and featured ash flooring, but had wider mantels and larger fireplaces, and the wood on the newer side of the house was painted, rather than walnut stained, as was the older side of the house.

While not formally educated during his youth, Zachary Taylor was raised by parents who were well educated and conversant in the customs of formal society, and who passed along their knowledge and social graces to their son. Years later, when Zachary Taylor had children of his own, he resolved that they would receive the formal education that he did not experience as a child, and enrolled his children in private boarding schools. Zachary Taylor's son, Richard, enrolled at Yale University at the age of 14, and, after leaving Yale, faced an uncertain future. Fatherly concern motivated Zachary Taylor to turn over to his young son management of Fashion Plantation, a property that the elder Taylor had acquired in Mississippi. Richard Taylor went on to make Fashion Plantation a very successful operation indeed, and he later went on to become a Confederate general. It is poignant that Zachary Taylor never lived to see how successful his son became, for Zachary Taylor died in 1850, when his son Richard was only 24 years old.

In 1808, Zachary Taylor, who had lived with his family in the original Springfield house, left Springfield to pursue a career in the U.S. Army. Over the course of the next forty years, Zachary Taylor resigned from the Army on several occasions,

but always re-enlisted. He returned to Kentucky while on leave in 1810 to be married, on June 21st, to Margaret Smith. Margaret Smith Taylor was a genteel woman from Maryland who proved to be a loving and supportive military wife. Together, Zachary and Margaret Taylor had six children, five daughters (three of whom lived into adulthood) and one son. With the exception of Sarah Knox Taylor, who was born in Vincennes, Indiana, the Taylor children were probably born at Springfield. Zachary and Margaret Taylor were married in Louisville, not on the Springfield farm but at the home of Zachary Taylor's sister-in-law, which was a log cabin a few miles away. The future president rose to the rank of major general and became famous for his victorious battles in the Blackhawk War in Indiana, in Florida against the Seminoles, and in the Mexican War. His long military career took him to a variety of places, including Fort Snelling, in Minnesota; Forts Howard, Crawford and Winnebago, in Wisconsin; Forts Armstrong and Dearborn, in Illinois; and Vincennes, Indiana. He also spent time in St. Louis, Louisville, Cincinnati and New Orleans. Other places that he visited include Fort Gibson, Oklahoma; Fort Smith, Arkansas; Fort Washita, Texas; Florida; and Jesup, Baton Rouge, and Pass Christian, in Louisiana. During some of this period, Mrs. Taylor returned to Springfield to live while her husband pursued his military career. From these travels to most of the regions of the territorial United States, Zachary Taylor acquired a national perspective that later served him well as president, and a major goal of his administration was to hold together a nation whose regions were divided over the question of slavery and other important regional concerns of the day.

Throughout his life, Zachary Taylor, who had been raised by a father who was successful both as a military man and as a farmer, also sought success in both of those roles. For this reason, Zachary Taylor resigned from military service from time to time to work as a plantation farmer. For example, in 1815, Zachary Taylor retired from the Army for a year to farm on a three-hundred acre tract on Beargrass Creek. References have been found to a "cabbin" in which he may have lived during this period, or he may have lived at Springfield. There is also a reference to a home on the east side of First Street in Louisville in which he may have lived. It is known that he moved to Bayou Sara, Louisiana in 1820. He also purchased three hundred acres in Feliciana Parish, Louisiana in 1823 and, in 1830, bought one hundred thirty-seven adjoining acres of property over the state line in Wilkinson County, Mississippi. In 1841, he bought, at a cost of $95,000.00, Cypress Grove Plantation, a one thousand nine hundred-acre property located near Rodney in Jefferson County, Mississippi. The property included a modest wooden house with a colonnaded veranda. At the end of the Mexican War, he also bought for his "retirement" a four-room "Spanish cottage" at 727 Lafayette Street in Baton Rouge, Louisiana. Today, the site is located on the grounds of the Louisiana State Capitol, but the cottage no longer stands.

After the annexation of Texas in 1845, Zachary Taylor received orders to defend the territory against any Mexican attempts to reconquer it, and Major General Taylor did so, invading the northeastern states of Mexico. Stories of General Taylor's compassion for his troops, his willingness to fight together with them in the front lines, and his orders to his troops to bind up the wounds of fallen Mexican soldiers after battles, made Zachary Taylor a popular hero nationally, and the potential political significance of this phenomenon was not lost on leaders of the Whig Party. Concerned about the increasing political popularity of Major General Taylor, President James K. Polk withdrew many of Taylor's troops and assigned them to the command of General Winfield Scott. Left with a small force of about 5,000 men, Major General Taylor and his troops nonetheless withstood an attack led by Mexican leader Santa Ana at Buena Vista in February 1847. It was shortly after this time that Zachary Taylor "retired" to Baton Rouge, Louisiana. By then, however, the legend of Zachary Taylor, nicknamed "Old Rough and Ready" because of his disregard of formalities in dress and personal style and his preparedness for battle, was clearly established in the minds of many Americans. He was regarded as a man who cared greatly about his troops, a leader without an inflated ego, and a general who won battles against overwhelming odds despite a lack of formal military training.

As a result of the fame he gained from his military victories, and especially the incident at Buena Vista, all of which appealed to an American public overwhelmingly desirous of territorial expansion, the Whig Party nominated Zachary Taylor to run as its presidential candidate in the election of 1848. In doing so, the Whigs offered a candidate who was a political outsider, carried none of the negative baggage of politicians with a record, and yet was regarded as a leader. The Taylor nomination angered such Whig politicians as Senator Henry Clay, who had long aspired to the presidency and believed that, as an experienced politician, he was far more qualified for the presidency than Zachary Taylor, a political neophyte. The Democratic candidate in 1848 was Louis Cass of Michigan, and former President Martin Van Buren tried for a political comeback as the candidate of the anti-slavery Free Soil Party. Mr. Van Buren's presence on the ballot split the Democratic vote in Mr. Van Buren's home state, New York, thus throwing New York, and the election, to Zachary Taylor, who became the twelfth president of the United States.

Some of the Whig leadership that nominated Zachary Taylor did so with the expectation that once in office, President Taylor would be a docile figurehead who would appear at public ceremonies, provide patronage to loyal Whigs, and follow the will of Whig leaders on matters of policy. However, these Whig leaders were disappointed. For example, on the question of patronage, President Taylor resisted pressure to appoint Whigs to certain government offices, using as his guiding principle that any person, Democrat or Whig, who is performing ably in his present post ought to be retained. On the divisive slavery question, President Taylor rejected the federally-imposed compromise sought by Senator Henry Clay, and preferred to let individual states and territories decide the question for themselves. The Taylor view came to be known as

"popular sovereignty." An alienated state of Texas, which had only been admitted to the Union a few years before, threatened to secede in 1849.

President Taylor's actions and views on such issues as patronage, slavery and other important questions made him an anathema, not only to Democrats but, perhaps more significantly, to members of his own party, including Senator Clay, patronage-hungry Whig leaders, and many Southern Whigs (who thought that, as a slave owner himself, President Taylor would take a position more consistent with his own practice). For them, President Taylor's term of office came to a convenient and sudden end due to a long illness resulting in his death on July 9, 1850. Indeed, upon learning of President Taylor's death, Senator Clay remarked, "Now my compromise will go through." (Senator Clay's prediction proved to be correct.) The political enmity faced by President Taylor during his term in office provided strong circumstantial evidence for a theory that he had been poisoned while in office, possibly by eating deliberately tainted fruit. Due to Mrs. Taylor's refusal to permit an autopsy at the time of the president's death, the cause of death had never been conclusively established. In 1991, a team of experts, all of whom donated their time and proceeded with the permission of President Taylor's descendants, attempted to prove the theory by exhuming President Taylor's body for an autopsy. The autopsy results proved conclusively that President Taylor was not poisoned by arsenic. However, the autopsy did not eliminate the possibility that the president was murdered by some other means, such as an untraceable poison.

Coincidentally, the date that President Taylor's body was exhumed was June 17, 1991, exactly one hundred fifty-six years after the day that President Taylor's daughter, Sarah Knox Taylor, became the first wife of Jefferson Davis, a military man who later became president of the Confederate States of America. Their 1835 wedding took place in Louisville over the objections of Zachary Taylor, who did not want his daughter to suffer the same hardships and loneliness of a military wife that Sarah's mother had endured. Mr. Davis overcame these objections by resigning from the military, and the wedding took place. However, Sarah Taylor Davis died tragically of malaria eighty-seven days after the ceremony. Zachary Taylor and Jefferson Davis did not reconcile until twelve years later at Buena Vista, where Jefferson Davis, a colonel, distinguished himself in battle. Reportedly, General Taylor approached Col. Davis and told him that his daughter was clearly a better judge of character than he, Zachary Taylor, was. From that time forward, Zachary Taylor and Jefferson Davis were good friends.

Zachary Taylor was succeeded as president by vice president Millard Fillmore of New York, who served as chief executive for the remainder of President Taylor's unexpired term. After the Fillmores moved into the White House, Mrs. Fillmore ordered the removal and replacement of some of the White House rugs, which bore stains from tobacco chewed by President Taylor. Tobacco chewing, which is not currently regarded as the habit of a gentleman, was a socially acceptable practice in the early nineteenth century, even among men in society.

After the death of Zachary Taylor's father, Colonel Richard Taylor, in 1829, the Springfield property was owned jointly by Zachary Taylor and his surviving siblings (three sisters and four brothers). The surviving Taylor siblings decided that Zachary Taylor's older brother, Hancock Taylor, would live at Springfield with his wife and children. Thus, Springfield remained the property of the Taylor family until 1867, when Hancock Taylor's widow sold the property. Like many Southern plantations, Springfield had fallen upon hard times after the abolition of slavery made it far more difficult to maintain a work force sufficient to operate a working farm. Since the period of residence of the Taylor family, the size of the Springfield property has decreased considerably, and some changes have been made. The wing of the house containing its large dining room and kitchen dates back to circa 1790, and is notable for the unpainted wooden wainscoting on the lower portion of its walls. On either side of the hallway, also part of the older wing, are its original doorways. The front and back doorways are parallel, allowing for cross ventilation to cool the house.

The newer side of the Springfield house dates to 1820 and did not exist at the time Zachary Taylor lived at Springfield, although he did visit the property from time to time after the new wing was built. It features a double parlor on the first floor. The front parlor appears to have been used for entertaining, and the rear to have been a library. It still has its original bookshelves along the wall and cabinet spaces underneath for storage.

Springfield had a succession of owners after the Taylor family sold it in 1867. The person to whom Mrs. Taylor sold the house wanted to alter its appearance to that of a Victorian farmhouse, and did so by installing a wraparound porch, gingerbread trim and other "improvements." The new owner also painted the house pea green and yellow. For many years, the appearance of Springfield was not at all as it had been while the Taylors owned the house.

The first major restoration of the interior of the Springfield house took place in the 1930s. In 1962, while a Mr. and Mrs. Davis were owners of Springfield, some of the Victorian "improvements" to the house were removed. That same year, the property was designated a National Historic Landmark. On April 3, 1974, exactly two hundred thirty years after the birth of Zachary Taylor's father, a tornado caused severe damage to the property. In the aftermath of the tornado, it was decided that the house would be restored to the Georgian Colonial look it had in the Taylors' time. The wraparound porch and tin roof were removed and the house began to look more as it did in the early nineteenth century.

A recent past owner of the home, Mr. Hugh S. Haynie, a nationally syndicated cartoonist, renovated the home and made various improvements to the property, including the installation of a driveway on the side of the house. Under his ownership, the house was modernized while still retaining many of the features of the original home. Throughout the twentieth century, the federal government had made attempts to acquire the property for use as a National Historic Site and/or a Zachary Taylor house museum, but these proposals never succeeded because the demolition of neighboring homes would have been necessary in order to provide the amount of land suitable for a National Historic Site. Fortunately, however, the house is in excellent condition due to the caring nature of its series of private owners.

The house was acquired as a private residence by Dr. William Gist, a past president of the National Society of the Sons of the American Revolution, active in historical and genealogical organizations, and noted researcher on the history of the house and on the life of Zachary Taylor. He has acquired a number of furnishings and articles dating to the period in which the Taylors lived in the house, and occasionally discovers artifacts on the property that appear to have been used by the Taylors, including a spoon that seems to be made of nickel alloy or coin silver made circa 1800-1810. Other artifacts include nineteenth century coins and animal teeth. Dr. Gist is particularly proud of a circa 1810 white upholstered Sheridan sofa. He has also acquired an early American secretary dating to roughly the same time period. A 1793 Pennsylvania tall case clock stands in the hall. In the dining room are an 1807 cherry sideboard and dining table that were owned by friends of the Taylors, so that it is likely that Zachary Taylor himself once sat at this table. Dr. Gist also owns a square grand piano made in Louisville in 1848; the piano is still in playable condition. Upstairs are seven rope beds made of either cherry or walnut with overshot coverlets which are navy and white or red and white. These beds, which lend to the informal "country" look of the upstairs rooms, are similar to the beds the Taylors owned in the early nineteenth century. One piece of furniture at Springfield is original—a simple rocking chair made of poplar, a yellowish wood. The chair, which documents establish was owned and used by the Taylors at Springfield, was donated to the house and will always remain there. In November 1984, the Gists promoted the bicentennial of President Taylor's birth, and hosted a birthday party at Springfield in honor of Zachary Taylor, complete with cake and spice. Their efforts in promoting Zachary Taylor's 200th birthday earned them a letter of commendation from President Ronald Reagan in July 1985.

President Taylor, buried a short distance from Springfield at Zachary Taylor National Cemetery, would certainly be pleased to see how well this home has been maintained. Although no longer the scene of a 700-acre plantation requiring the services of 52 slaves (in 1841), the house is nevertheless a fine example of early American plantation architecture. It is good to know that the only extant building in which Zachary Taylor once lived has survived in such excellent condition. President Taylor would also have been pleased to know that his boyhood home was the first building in Louisville and Jefferson County to be designated a historic landmark. His dying words, "I have endeavored to do my duty; my only regret is the friends I leave behind," sums up his life well, for his sense of duty and moral obligation, to his family, to his troops, and to his country, was the significant trait that made this otherwise modest man a great leader.

MILLARD FILLMORE

Millard Fillmore Birthplace (replica)
Fillmore Glen State Park
Route 38
Moravia, New York 13118
(315) 497-0130

Administered by the State of New York Office of Parks, Recreation and Historic Preservation.

Directions:	Fillmore Glen State Park is located one mile south of Moravia, N.Y. on Route 38. The park entrance is on the left. The birthplace replica is in front of a parking area on the left side of the entrance road.
Open:	Daily — dawn to dusk.
Admission:	Fee charged per car.
Features:	Log cabin replica. Park is 938 acres and includes 70 campsites and 3 camping cabins open in season, swimming, hiking trails, playground, playing fields, picnic areas, showers, comfort stations and fishing. Cabin is handicapped accessible.
Special Events:	Park facilities can be rented for special events, e.g., wedding receptions.

Millard Fillmore was a man of humble beginnings whose father had come from Vermont to settle in Locke Township, Cayuga County, New York. President Fillmore was born on January 7, 1800 in a modest log cabin built circa 1795. After a brief stay in this cabin, the Fillmores moved to a 100-acre leased farm in Sempronius, New York. Young Millard Fillmore grew up in relative isolation on that farm, where there were no neighbors less than four miles away. The small farm cabin housed not only his immediate family, but also his aunt and uncle.

Millard Fillmore's years of isolation ended when his father decided that his son should not live the life of a farmer. In 1815, young Millard Fillmore was sent to Sparta, New York to apprentice for a clothmaker. Over the course of the following three years, he worked at a sawmill and did a brief stint teaching school in Scott, New York, until he earned enough money to buy his release from his apprenticeship. In 1819, he began to study law with Judge Wood of Monteville. By 1821, he had moved to Aurora (now East Aurora), New York with his parents and clerked for a Buffalo law firm. By age 23, Mr. Fillmore had been admitted to the New York bar and began a law practice in Aurora.

The original birthplace cabin, whose location is marked on Skinner Hill Road in what is now known as Summerhill, was destroyed in the 1840s. 5.7 miles west of that site, in Fillmore Glen State Park, a replica of the birthplace cabin, based on descriptions of the original, stands. It is a "Swedish-style" 21 by 16 foot cabin chinked with mortar mixed with animal and human hair. The cabin, which dates back to the 1840s, formerly stood on the John H. Rouse farm. In 1963, the Rouses donated the cabin to the Millard Fillmore Memorial Association, which restored the cabin in as authentic a manner as possible, largely through volunteer efforts. Its logs, which are ash, birch, elm and white pine, are the original cabin logs. The log rafters are held together with wooden pegs. The iron cut nails, hinges, door latch and fireplace crane were hand forged. Its chimney is made of fieldstone taken from the Fillmore birthplace site. Its roof is hand-split red cedar from British Columbia.

The completed cabin was dedicated on May 23, 1965. It is a two-room structure which visitors may enter and view the rooms through large glass windows. In the cabin, visitors see items used by people of Millard Fillmore's time and circumstances, such as nineteenth-century farm machinery, a delft blue dining set, a high box bed, a small cradle, and a mirror to reflect light. A stone chimney and hearth was used for cooking and heating, and a bellows and candle molds are also found here. This cabin, and its simple furnishings, suggest the modest origins of the man who became the thirteenth president of the United States.

The Millard Fillmore House Museum
24 Shearer Avenue
East Aurora, New York 14052
(716) 652-4228

Administered by the Aurora Historical Society, Inc.

Directions:	From Buffalo, take Route 400 south to East Aurora. Turn right on Main Street (Route 20A). Proceed over the railroad tracks and turn right after four blocks at Shearer Avenue. House is on right side of the road.
Open:	June to October, Wednesdays, Saturdays, and Sundays. Also open by appointment for groups.
Admission:	Fee charged. Children under 12 are free.
Features:	Guided tour of house by docents in period costume. Rest rooms. First floor is handicapped accessible.
Special Events:	The site hosts a Christmas Sale in December, and permits wedding pictures to be taken in the garden.

In 1826, Millard Fillmore, who had moved to Aurora (now East Aurora), New York and had set up a law practice, married the former Abigail Powers. The Fillmores moved into a new home, built in part by Mr. Fillmore's own hands, across from his law office on Main Street. Mr. Fillmore quickly became one of Aurora's most influential citizens, and was elected to the New York State Assembly in 1828. After his first term, during which he spent much of his time in Albany and lived in Temperance House, he left the house in Aurora and moved to 180 Franklin Avenue in Buffalo. In 1832, Mr. Fillmore was elected to Congress, staying at Gadsby's and the Willard Hotel while in Washington, D.C. He was an unsuccessful candidate for governor of New York in 1844, and by 1846, became the first chancellor of the University of Buffalo. He assumed the office of state comptroller of New York in 1848, and, while at this post, was nominated as the Whig candidate for vice president, running on a ticket with Zachary Taylor. The Whig ticket was elected and after President Taylor died in 1850, Millard Fillmore succeeded Zachary Taylor as President.

While in the White House, President Fillmore, like his fellow New Yorker and predecessor Martin Van Buren, made improvements, including installing the first White House kitchen range. While First Lady, Mrs. Fillmore established the White House Library. As President Van Buren had, President Fillmore summered at the president's cottage at Greenbrier, in White Sulphur Springs, Virginia (now West Virginia). As president, Millard Fillmore urged passage of the Compromise of 1850, which had been opposed by his predecessor, President Taylor. The compromise abolished slave trading in Washington D.C., permitted California to enter the Union as a free state, organized the Utah and New Mexico territories without reference to slavery, settled a Texas boundary dispute, and established a stricter fugitive slave law. The last provision cost President Fillmore political support in the North, and as a result he was not nominated for president in 1852. The Democrats regained the White House in 1852 when Franklin Pierce became president.

Millard Fillmore made another unsuccessful bid for the Presidency in 1856 as the candidate of the "Know-Nothing" Party, so-called because its platform was reportedly so anti-immigrant and anti-Catholic that, when asked about specific platform planks, party members supposedly refused to divulge the party philosophy, and instead declared, "I know nothing." Millard Fillmore's ties with the Know-Nothings were probably based more on the desire for a spot on the ballot than on a shared philosophy.

Millard Fillmore's term as president ended on March 4, 1853, and he and Mrs. Fillmore attended the inauguration of his successor, Franklin Pierce. Afterward, the Fillmores stayed at the Willard Hotel in Washington, D.C., where Mrs. Fillmore, who had been exposed to the cold March weather during the inaugural, died on March 30th. The former president returned to Buffalo, living in the house on Franklin Street until 1858, when he was remarried to Caroline

Carmichael McIntosh, a wealthy widow. They lived in Hollister House at 52 Niagara Square in Buffalo, a Gothic structure of baronial proportions. The Fillmores hosted magnificent parties there, but maintained a strict personal lifestyle, forbidding consumption of alcohol and tobacco and use of foul language in their home. After Millard Fillmore's death in 1874, the house was sold and became the Castle Inn, which was later razed and replaced by the Hotel Statler. President Fillmore ended his life as a prominent citizen and active philanthropist in Buffalo.

The house in East Aurora, in which Millard Fillmore's career began in earnest, was moved to the back of its lot on Main Street to make way for a theater. After many years in disrepair, it caught the eye of Mrs. Margaret Price, an artist and wife of Irving Price of Fisher-Price Toys. Fascinated with the house and its history, she purchased it in 1930 and moved it to its present location on Shearer Avenue, where she remodeled it and used it as an art studio. In 1975, the house came to the attention of the Aurora Historical Society, which organized a fund raising campaign and bought the house. The Society then set about restoring the house to its 1826-30 appearance, drawing upon recollections of older persons who remembered the interior of the house from childhood. A 1910 newspaper photo story was also a valuable source of information.

Today, the house stands as a fine example of a Federal period frame dwelling. It is constructed of wood, probably pine, and its exterior is now painted with colors typical of the period which were selected based upon careful research. It retains its original floorboards, which rest on hand-hewn joists with bark possibly installed by Millard Fillmore. Its present interior colors were, to the extent possible, matched with colors uncovered during the restoration of the house. Visitors go up three steps and pass through a six-paneled Federal door, where they first see the living room. Its walls are stenciled red and green in patterns traced from those used in another Aurora home of the same period, and the room is decorated with authentic period furniture. The front windows are twelve over eight and have their original panes. The fireplace mantel is copied from the front doorway frame.

A passageway leads to the kitchen, which has a brick fireplace and a bee hive oven. Because the original kitchen wing, woodshed and outbuildings were not moved with the house in 1930, the kitchen was recreated based on the 1910 news photo article. Hearth cooking demonstrations take place here during the summer using the large chimney and fireplace, which occupy their original positions. An iron pot hangs from a crane made circa 1829 which was originally used in a nearby home of the same period. The kitchen also has hand wrought iron hardware, and the adjoining pantry features authentic tinware and pottery. Visitors then climb a narrow staircase to see the bedrooms, which retain their wide pine floor boards. These rooms contain period pieces, including antique dolls and toys, and Millard Fillmore's own bed. Another room, which features a stand-up desk, is set up to depict a law office.

Finally, the house has a library, which was added to the original house as a room for the display of furnishings, books and artifacts of Millard Fillmore's presidential and post-presidential years. The library serves as a reminder that Abigail Powers Fillmore established the first White House Library, and the admittedly ostentatious decor of the room is intended to reflect the splendor of Hollister House, where most of the Empire and Victorian pieces in the library were originally used. Also in this room is a bookcase used by President Fillmore in the White House, a large square rosewood piano used by Abigail Powers Fillmore, and a harp played by the Fillmores' daughter, Mary Abigail. Both instruments were played in the White House.

Next to the house is a carriage barn, which was recently built to house Millard Fillmore's sleigh and a period tool collection which belongs to the Aurora Historical Society. The barn was constructed using wood from the site of the recently dismantled Fillmore family barn on nearby Olean Road. It is believed that the barn's hand-hewn beams were those used for the barn built by Millard Fillmore's father, Nathaniel Fillmore.

The East Aurora Garden Club designed two gardens for the grounds: the Presidential Rose Garden and Abigail's Dooryard Herb Garden, which features varieties used before 1840. The latter garden is free-flowing in design and includes aromatic, medicinal, dyeing and culinary herbs.

A visit to this house provides insight into the rise of an ambitious young man from humble beginnings to the highest office in the land, and to prosperity in his later years.

FRANKLIN PIERCE

Franklin Pierce Homestead
Hillsboro, New Hampshire 03244
(603) 478-3165

Administered by the Hillsborough Historical Society.

Directions:	The site is three miles west of Hillsboro, New Hampshire, at the junction of Routes 9 and 31.
Open:	Daily in season. Call for hours.
Admission:	Fee charged. Children under 18 are free. Bus and large group tours available by appointment only.

Features: 45 minute guided tour of house, rest rooms. Not handicapped accessible.

Special Events: None.

Franklin Pierce was born on November 23, 1804 in the vicinity of Hillsboro, New Hampshire. His father, Benjamin Pierce, had bought a log cabin and approximately 50 acres of land about a half a mile outside of Lower Village, and later constructed a small wood frame house on that site. It is unclear precisely where Franklin Pierce's birth took place; however, sometime shortly after his birth, he moved into his father's new home. The house was a 10-room structure, painted on only three sides to save money and, after twenty or more years went by, was painted red in back. Today, a two-story ell has been added to the structure. The ell was added sometime within the twenty-year period after the house was first built, and it is believed that a one story ell may have been added prior to its expansion to two stories. For the first few years at the home, Benjamin Pierce, who had a liquor license, operated the home as a tavern. He later ceased operation of the tavern, perhaps because of his acquisition of a 200-acre site which became a full working farm.

Benjamin Pierce enlisted as a private in the Revolutionary War effort the day after the war began. He was promoted to the rank of ensign as the result of his bravery at Saratoga and, by the time the British were evacuating New York, he had risen to the rank of lieutenant. When he returned to Hillsboro, Benjamin Pierce was recruited into the state militia as a major and, by the time he retired in 1807, he had become a brigadier general. The president's father later became governor of New Hampshire. Benjamin Pierce's first wife died after bearing one daughter, and he remarried and had eight children by his second wife, of whom Franklin Pierce was the sixth.

After studying at schools in Hancock and Francestown, Franklin Pierce went on to higher education at Bowdoin College in Brunswick, Maine, where he met Jane Means Appleton, daughter of a former president of the college. Jane Appleton, who married Franklin Pierce, had family ties to Boston aristocracy, thereby assuring Mr. Pierce of his own place in society. In 1825, Mr. Pierce came to Portsmouth, New Hampshire, where he studied law. After attending law school in Northampton, Massachusetts, Mr. Pierce returned to New Hampshire and was elected to the state legislature at age 29. After two terms, he was elected to the United States House of Representatives in 1833. While in Washington, he boarded at a four-story brick house on Pennsylvania Avenue near Third. Throughout this period, however, Franklin Pierce considered the mansion built by his father his own home, and although he also bought another house in Hillsboro about a quarter of a mile from the mansion, he spent little time there. His wife did not care much for Hillsboro and, after the death of his first son, Franklin Pierce sold the house to his youngest brother and moved to Concord. He never lived in Hillsboro after that time, but always thought of his place of birth as his true home. The mansion was inherited by Franklin Pierce's oldest sister, and Mr. Pierce continued to visit her there, as well as call upon his brother and other friends and relatives in the area.

The Franklin Pierce Homestead was purchased by the state of New Hampshire in 1930. The state leases the site to the Hillsboro Historical Society, which makes the site available to visitors today. Modern visitors realize that the Franklin Pierce Homestead is a mansion fitting for a sizeable family. It is now white on three sides with green blinds, its back wall is red, and it has two large fireplace chimneys and a two-story ell.

Visitors to the Franklin Pierce Homestead start their tour either at the front door of the house or in the nearby barn. The first room visitors see is the parlor, whose walls are adorned with 1823 Dufour wallpaper. One panel is removed, revealing the original colorful wall and stenciling underneath. A woodwork clock sits on the mantel in this room. The names of those who worked on manufacturing the clock are inscribed on it.

Visitors next see a sitting room, which was originally the taproom of Benjamin Pierce's tavern. They then view the kitchen/dining room, which has a beehive baking oven and a reflector or "spit" oven. Visitors also see a boot jack and a Revolutionary War soldier's diary here. This room was recently restored and now has, once again, the brightly colored walls, woodwork and stenciling it possessed in Franklin Pierce's time. The adjoining pantry has high windows which allow light into the kitchen and pantry to make it easier to see when the door is closed. At one time, it provided light for the bartender when it extended into the taproom.

The next room visitors see is the master bedroom, which features a canopied rope bed with rope tighteners, a spinning wheel, a hitchcock chair and a spool chair. Visitors next view the second or "new" kitchen, which features a cheese press, a hearth with a stew pot on a fireplace crane, and a flax wheel. Next to the new kitchen is a pantry/workroom. A "set kettle" is only a few small steps from the "new" kitchen past a sliding panel which served as the principal source of hot water for the mansion, and was used to do the laundry.

Next, visitors come to the barn, which contains a sleigh that belonged to Franklin Pierce. Visitors also see a winnowing machine used to separate grain from chaff, a flax loom, and a rocking churn. From there, the tour comes to what is perhaps the grandest place in the mansion, the second floor ballroom, which features reproduced stenciling on its walls. Benjamin Pierce once drilled the state militia here. The room also features a semi-circular senate desk from Concord and door latches with seals.

Visitors next see a bedroom, which features an Empire mirror, and a fireplace with a device called a "pig." The "pig" resembles a jug, and was filled with warm water and used as a foot warmer. The next room on the tour is the Franklin Pierce Room, which contains a sideboard and a sofa and chairs used by the Pierces in the White House. The sofa and chairs have been reupholstered using authentic period cloth, and a quill pen portrait of Franklin Pierce is also seen here. Jane Pierce's parasol, shoes, and a series of the

Pierces' letters are also here. Visitors also see a silk handkerchief inscribed "E Pluribus Unum" given to Mrs. Pierce by the Swiss government and a donation card used in the fund-raising drive for construction of the Washington Monument. A corset on display in this room was worn by Franklin Pierce under his uniform in parades.

Another part of the mansion is used as a Hillsboro town museum, and is the last stop on the tour.

The Franklin Pierce Homestead is currently undergoing restoration, and will once again feature the brightly colored and stenciled walls that were once displayed. Guides, who are prepared to discuss topics ranging from the political life of Benjamin and Franklin Pierce to life in the nineteenth century, convey to visitors to this house a sense of the period from 1804-1839, and the growth of the house from a farmhouse/tavern to a mansion. The weary travelers, tradesmen and militiamen who once visited this house gave way to a more gentile and distinguished group, notably neighbors and politicians. Celebrated personalities, such as Daniel Webster and Nathaniel Hawthorne, were visitors. Benjamin Pierce's godson, Benjamin Pierce Cheney, who lived three houses down, was probably a frequent visitor and later went on to found the American Express Company. A young boarder staying at the mansion wrote enthusiastic letters about Franklin Pierce and the house to his sister, Harriet Beecher (later Harriet Beecher Stowe). As this house was in transition from its construction until 1839, the year Benjamin Pierce died, so America itself was changing, from the simpler lifestyle of the eighteenth century to the more complex society of the Industrial Revolution. A visit to the Franklin Pierce Homestead gives visitors a taste of the life of a prominent early American family in transition, as well as of the early life of an American president.

Pierce Manse
14 Penacook Street
Concord, New Hampshire 00301
(603) 224-9620
(603) 224-7668

Administered by the Pierce Brigade.

Directions:	From I-93, take exit 15 west, and turn right onto North Main Street. The site is located at the end of North Main Street, where it intersects with Penacook Street.
Open:	Mid-June to mid-September, Monday to Friday. Closed on Independence Day and Labor Day.
Admission:	Fee charged.
Features:	Home, gift shop, rest room. Lecture and meeting room in basement, available for rent.
Special Events:	On or about the 23rd of November, a wreath-laying ceremony commemorating all U.S. presidents takes place at President Pierce's grave site. This is followed by coffee at the home. The site hosts a tea for Pierce Brigade members and tour guides in September.

Having resigned from the United States Senate in order to resume his law practice in Concord, New Hampshire, Franklin Pierce purchased a modest, two-story, Federal-style house in 1842. He moved in with his wife, Jane Means Appleton Pierce, and their two small sons, Franky and Benny Pierce. Franklin Pierce's sojourn at this home was a mixture of success and tragedy. Before moving in, the Pierces lost their first son, Franklin Pierce, Jr., a three-day-old infant. In 1843, one year later, their second son, Franky Pierce, was born, but he succumbed to typhus at the age of four in the Pierce home. Two months before Franklin Pierce's inauguration as president in 1853, his third son, Benny Pierce, was killed in a railroad accident. Due to this series of tragedies, when President Pierce died in 1869 he left no heirs and no direct descendants.

In Concord, Franklin Pierce's successful legal and political careers flourished. A strong proponent of the Jacksonian Democrats, Mr. Pierce became widely respected in his party, largely because of his oratorical skills. His successful career in Concord was interrupted by the outbreak of the war with Mexico in 1848. A strong supporter of the territorial expansion of the United States, Mr. Pierce enlisted as a private in order to participate in the Mexican conflict. He quickly received a commission as brigadier general and acquired the reputation of a military hero as a result of his role in the war.

His combined legal, political, and military experiences made him an attractive potential candidate for the presidency, and he received the nomination of the Democratic Party for president in 1852.

During his successful candidacy, Franklin Pierce was plagued by accusations emanating from Northern Abolitionist Forces to the effect that, despite his northern origins, Mr. Pierce sympathized with the pro-slavery position which predominated in the South. As evidence of his southern sympathies, his political opponents produced a letter written by Mr. Pierce to Jefferson Davis, who later became president of the Confederacy. Today, the letter is framed and hangs in the Pierce Manse.

During his administration, Franklin Pierce continued to be a strong advocate of territorial expansion. During his first year in office, he sent an emissary (James Gadsden of South Carolina) to negotiate a purchase of 29,500 acres of land, stretching from the southern border of California to the Rio Grande River. This land acquisition became known as the Gadsden Purchase, and resolved a dispute over the boundary between Mexico and the United States.

By the time Franklin Pierce returned from his service in the Mexican War in 1848, he had determined to sell the Pierce Manse, probably because of the grief he and his wife shared over the loss of their son, Franky Pierce. For the next four years, the Pierces boarded at the home of a friend and were still there when Franklin Pierce received word of his nomination to the presidency. The Pierce Manse remained in private ownership long after Franklin Pierce's death in 1869, and was slated for demolition as part of an urban renewal project in 1966. In response to the threatened destruction, a group of citizens known as the Pierce Brigade was formed for the express purpose of preserving the building. The Brigade acquired the building itself, but was required to move the house from its original location at 18 Montgomery Street, in Concord's Historic District.

The Pierce Manse is currently administered by the Pierce Brigade, which has filled the home with furnishings and decor typical of Franklin Pierce's time. The home still has its original pine floors, but the Victorian-like wallpaper has been manufactured recently. Among the notable architectural features of this house are gun stock corners, with wooden posts of tapering shape, narrowing as they reach the floor. Another noteworthy feature is the reproduced door latches, manufactured after a style popular in the early 1840s in New England and originally used in the house. There are several closets built into the house, including a small one to the right of the front door which was originally a gun cabinet and was common in many homes of the period. The widespread use of gun cabinets may have been due to fear of tribal Indian attacks, a holdover from old wars.

To the left of the front entrance hall is a double parlor, divided by sliding doors. The front parlor appears to be the living and sitting area, containing several furnishings of interest: an early Victorian bookcase with shelves covered by drapes which belonged to the Pierces; a wooden Victorian table used as a dressing table by the President's grandniece, Mary; and a center table belonging to Mrs. Pierce's sister, Mary, which was later known as "The White House Table." In another corner of this room there is a sofa which was given to Jane Pierce as a part of her wedding dowry. Two black wooden chairs in the room belonged to the Pierces, and leaning beside the fireplace is the president's walking stick; the silver band around the ivory handle is inscribed "General Frank Pierce." The cane later belonged to President Pierce's grand-niece, who apparently sawed off part of its wooden shaft to accommodate her smaller size.

The back parlor of the house was the dining room. Here, there is a small side table which belonged to the Pierces, and a steel engraving above. Framed on the wall is a lithograph of George Washington, presented to Franklin Pierce in gratitude for his monetary contribution to the construction of the Washington Monument. Also on the wall are photographs made from daguerreotypes; one photograph depicts the Pierces' third son, Benny Pierce, and was reproduced and enlarged from a daguerreotype the size of a thumbnail and apparently meant to be contained in a locket. The other photo is a rare picture of Jane Pierce with her son, Benny Pierce. The photographs suggest that Jane Pierce had a pale complexion, and it is suspected that she suffered from consumption. Her early death in 1863, six years before her husband,

is further evidence of her apparent poor health.

Behind the dining area is the kitchen, currently a souvenir shop. The reconstructed hearth includes a crane used to swing the large pots and kettles in and out of the fire, Franklin Pierce's fire tongs, a small box for carrying embers to warm one's feet in church during winter, and a small beehive oven. The kitchen's walls are not wallpapered but are painted and include a stencil design, painted in 1976, modeled after a similar design found in the Franklin Pierce Homestead in Hillsboro. A series of silver spoons, which were also part of Jane Pierce's dowry, are displayed in a cabinet. Two Shaker chairs are kept in the house as a reminder of Franklin Pierce's eloquent oratory in opposition to proposed legislation calling for the ouster of the Shakers from New Hampshire, which was debated in the New Hampshite State Legislature during his term of office. Pierce was a fervent advocate of religious tolerance, and aroused some controversy to due his friendly dealings with the Catholic Church in his Protestant dominated community. He was baptized in the Baptist Church, but associated himself with various denominations during his life, including Presbyterian, Congregational and Episcopalian.

A staircase leads from the entrance hall to the second floor, which has two large bedrooms and a small room which was used as a nursery. The hallway includes a lithograph of Franklin Pierce and Nathaniel Hawthorne, who were friends throughout much of their adult lives. At the front of the house is the master bedroom, including a shaving stand President Pierce used at the White House, and an export Chinese lacquer sewing chest possibly used by Jane Pierce. Near one wall is a knotty-pine chest with a painted Pierce coat of arms inside the cover. Near the fireplace is the cowhide hatbox with Franklin Pierce's monogram inscribed on it and inside it is Franklin Pierce's beaver top hat, which he wore at his inauguration as president. Above the mantel in the room is a portrait of the Pierces' second son, Franky Pierce. Beside the bed hangs a slipper rack made of soft wood, and grospoint. The furniture in the other large room on the second floor includes Benny Pierce's little bed and a painting of the little boy, plus a steel engraving of Czar Nicholas I of Russia and a drawing of Franklin Pierce and his horse.

Coming back down the stairs to the entrance hall, visitors will see several items of interest, including a campaign chest used by Pierce during his service as brigadier general in the Mexican War. On the wall hangs a program of the graduation of Franklin Pierce's class from Bowdoin College. A wooden sofa upholstered in red cloth also appears in the hallway and was taken from the room at the Eagle Hotel in Concord where Franklin Pierce stayed before taking the train to Washington to be inaugurated as president.

Stylistically, this large, white frame house is a blend of Federal-style features and aspects of the early Victorian era. Its modest style and relatively simple furnishings suggest a man of humble character who, despite personal tragedy, served as the nation's chief executive during a turbulent period in American history.

JAMES BUCHANAN

Buchanan's Birthplace State
Historical Park
U.S. 16
Mercersburg, Pennsylvania

(c/o Cowans Gap State Park
H.C. 17266
Fort Loudon, Pennsylvania 17224)
(717) 485-3948

Administered by the Commonwealth of Pennsylvania.

Buchanan's Log Cabin Birthplace
Mercersburg Academy
Mercersburg, Pennsylvania 17236
(717) 328-2151

Administered by Mercersburg Academy.

Directions: To Log Cabin: Located on the campus of Mercersburg Academy, which is 10 miles from the intersection of I-81 and U.S. 16 (Greencastle, PA). From I-81, take Baltimore Street Exit #3 and take U.S. 16 west. Turn right into the Academy campus and follow signs for Nolde Gymnasium and service building. The log cabin birthplace will be on your left before the gymnasium.

To State Park: From the Mercersburg Academy campus, turn right onto U.S. 16 west, which will take you through Mercersburg. Continue on U.S. 16 for five miles. The state park entrance will be on your right.

Open: Log Cabin is available for viewing at all times. However, visitors do not enter the one-room cabin. Rather, they look through the windows into the cabin's interior.

State park is open daily from 8:00 a.m. to dusk.

Admission: Free to both sites.

Features: At cabin: parking and handicapped accessible rest rooms available at nearby

Fort Hall, and picnic benches are nearby.

At state park: Stone pyramid marking birthplace, picnicking, rest rooms. Handicapped accessible.

Special Events: At cabin, Mercersburg Academy faculty member in period dress discusses history of cabin on occasional basis.

At state park, none.

James Buchanan, the fifteenth president of the United States, was born at Stony Batter, near Mercersburg, Pennsylvania, on a site marked by a stone pyramid. The stone pyramid was conceived by Harriet Lane, the president's niece who served as White House hostess for the bachelor president. Today, the site upon which the Buchanan log cabin was originally located is an 18-acre state park. The cabin itself was moved to Fayette Street, Mercersburg, in 1850 and was used as a weaver shop. In 1925, the cabin was moved again to nearby Chambersburg and served as a gift shop and later as a Democratic headquarters. The cabin was purchased by the headmaster of Mercersburg Academy in 1953 and brought to its cam-

pus. Its present early American furnishings, while not original, suggest President Buchanan's humble origins in a one-room home.

From 1794 to 1796, young James Buchanan lived at Dunwoodie Farm, a three hundred-acre property along the West Conococheague Creek, near Mercersburg. In 1796, he moved to a two-story brick house in Mercersburg, and while there he helped his father, who ran a country store. From 1807 to 1809, he attended Dickinson College in Carlisle, Pennsylvania, while staying at the Widow Duchman's inn on East King Street. He later spent a year in Elizabethtown, Kentucky (a location very close to the birthplace of his successor, Abraham Lincoln) doing title work on land belonging to his father. He returned to Lancaster, Pennsylvania to become a county prosecutor, and then served in the Pennsylvania legislature. In 1815, he and a partner purchased a tavern on East King Street in Lancaster. This property had already been used by Mr. Buchanan as an office and living quarters. He was elected to the U.S. House of Representatives in 1820, and while in Washington from 1821 to 1831, shared board with Senator Barnard at Mrs. Peyton's, and then boarded at Mrs. Cottinger's. In 1831, Mr. Buchanan became minister to Russia and he rented a legation headquarters, Ville Dame Brockhauser at Wassilioshoff on the Grand Neva #65. It was furnished and had a courtyard, stables, carriage and sleigh house. At home in Lancaster, managers of Mr. Buchanan's estate purchased a home at 42 East King Street, formerly owned by Robert Coleman.

From 1834 to 1844, James Buchanan served as a United States senator. In 1845, he served as secretary of state under President Polk, and rented a furnished residence (including chinaware) on F Street next to John Quincy Adams for $2,000.00 a year. In 1849, he purchased Wheatland in Lancaster. From 1853 to 1855, while serving as minister to Great Britain, he lived at 56 Harley Street, in London.

From 1857 to 1861, James Buchanan served as the fifteenth president of the United States. While living at the White House, he had a conservatory, designed by Edward Clark, added to the White House grounds. He summered at the "Old Soldier's Home" at Rock Creek Church Road and Upshur Street N.W. in Washington. A gray stucco, two and one-half story brick structure with a gabled roof, it is today a guesthouse and supervisors' lounge for the United States Soldiers' and Airmen's Home. It has a five-bay porch bordered with a wrought-iron railing. The home was also known as "Corn Rigs" because of the nearby cornfield and the ridge ("rigs" is the Scottish word for "ridges) on which the home stood. It was also named Anderson House for General Robert Anderson, who played a key role in creating the home.

After leaving office in 1861, President Buchanan returned to Wheatland, which was his home for the rest of his life.

Wheatland
1120 Marietta Avenue
Lancaster, Pennsylvania 17603
(717) 392-8721

Administered by the James Buchanan Foundation for the Preservation of Wheatland.

Directions:	From Pennsylvania Turnpike take exit #20 (Lebanon) or exit#21 (Reading) and bear south toward Lancaster. Turn right on Orange Street and bear right on Marietta Avenue (PA Route #23). Wheatland is on the left side of the street.
Open:	Daily (except Thanksgiving Day) — April 1 through November 30.
Admission:	Fee charged. Discounts for seniors, students, and children.
Features:	Mansion, 8 minute audio-visual presentation, museum exhibition, 2 gift shops, refreshments, rest rooms, picnic tables. Not handicapped accessible. Allow one hour for presentation and tour.
Special Events:	Special Victorian Christmas candlelight tours are held for one week in early December. The mansion house is specially decorated for these tours. (See text for other special events.)

This lovely brick, Federal-style home is situated on 4 acres of land dominated by large, old trees and graced by a spacious lawn. When James Buchanan purchased the property in 1848, it was a 22-acre parcel with a house which was built in 1828 for William Jenkins, a lawyer and banker. Wheatland is considered a fine example of Federal architecture.

James Buchanan, who began his residency at Wheatland while secretary of state, was a lifelong bachelor and shared his residence with his nephew, James Buchanan Henry, who served as his personal secretary during the first two years of his administration, and his niece, Harriet Lane, who acted as the mistress of Wheatland and as First Lady during her bachelor uncle's administration. Harriet Lane resided at Wheatland from the time her uncle left office in 1861 until 1866, when she married Harry Elliott Johnston and moved to Baltimore. When President Buchanan died in 1868, Harriet Lane Johnston inherited Wheatland and spent summers there until she sold the property in 1884. The house and estate remained in private hands until 1935, when it was sold to the James Buchanan Foundation for the Preservation of Wheatland. Wheatland was designated a National Historic Landmark in 1961.

Approaching the house, one notes its sturdy, red-bricked facade, adorned with white trim and shutters on the first floor and green shutters on the second floor. A rectangular center section is abutted by east and west wings. Three white gables may be seen on the roof of the central portion of the house from either its north or south side.

Inside, the home is decorated with Federal and American Empire furnishings, most of which are either original or a product of the time period (1848-1868) in which President Buchanan lived in the house. One is first struck by the T-shaped hallway of the first floor of the house. Symmetry is marred only by the staircase at the eastern side of the house. The staircase features a smooth, mahogany banister with a crystal "peacestone." Identical fan-shaped windows are seen over both the front and rear doors of the house. One may also see, on the western side of the hallway, a tall-case clock which was made by Martin Shreiner in the early 1800s. Also notable are hand-stenciled linoleum floors and deeply gouged, symmetrical shapes found in the woodwork around the doors. The wooden baseboards in the hallway are painted to resemble marble. Servants greeted callers at the front door and acted as a buffer to the outside world by insisting that guests present calling cards so that the residents of the home could determine whether to receive them. In 1868, President Buchanan was laid out in his coffin in this hallway as multitudes of Lancaster citizens came to pay their final respects to the president.

The dining room contains two long sideboards, above which hang portraits of the master of the house and his nephew. This area also served as a sitting room on occasion.

Harriet Lane's parlor, located across the hall from the dining room, is noted for its still-operable Chickering piano and its American-made, rococo revival furniture. A small writing desk is adorned with carved floral patterns. Portraits of Queen Victoria and her husband, Prince Albert, decorate the parlor wall. The small, armless sofas, or tete-a-tetes, were designed to accommodate the hoopskirts worn by women of the period. Both the parlor and dining room are illuminated by gas chandeliers.

From the library, James Buchanan ran his 1856 campaign for the presidency. Its separate doorway permitted political visitors to enter the house from the outside without using the front entrance. The room has been restored to conform to its appearance in Frank Leslie's *Illustrated Newspaper* in 1857. Noteworthy are the heavy, mahogany library table, oak bookcase, and geometrically patterned rug.

Upstairs, visitors see a tin footbath (which resembles an upside-down, wide-brimmed hat) in the president's bedroom. Several mahogany beds, and a series of window blinds which date from 1828 (the year Wheatland was built) are also of interest.

In the Visitor's Center, visitors see a large bowl which was a gift to President Buchanan from the Japanese government given during the Japanese visit to Washington, D.C. in 1860. It is one of the largest pieces of porcelain known to exist.

Tour guides are dressed in period-style clothing, lending an early Victorian aura to the home. For a special treat, candlelight tours are conducted during Victorian Christmas Week in early December.

ABRAHAM LINCOLN

Abraham Lincoln Birthplace
National Historic Site
2995 Lincoln Farm Road
Hodgenville, Kentucky 42748
(502) 358-3137

Administered by the National Park Service.

Lincoln's Boyhood Home
U.S. 31E
Hodgenville, Kentucky 42748
(502) 549-3741

Administered by Lincoln's Boyhood Home, Inc.

Directions: To birthplace: From Louisville, take I-65 south to Route 61 south. Follow signs at Hodgenville to the site, which is three miles south.

To boyhood home: Return to Hodgenville and continue on Route 31E for six miles. Log cabin home and visitor center are on the left.

Open: Birthplace: Daily (except Christmas Day)—call for seasonal hours.

Boyhood home: Daily from April 1 through October 31. Call for seasonal hours.

Admission: Birthplace: Free.

Boyhood Home: Fee charged.

Features: Birthplace: Visitor Center with exhibits shows the film "Lincoln: The Kentucky Years" on an hourly basis. Memorial building contains a reconstructed "birthplace" cabin. Sinking Spring, hiking trails, picnic area, rest rooms. Provisions can be made for the handicapped.

Boyhood Home: Reconstructed log cabin, gift shop/museum, picnic grounds, log pavilion, rest rooms. Handicapped accessible.

Special Events: Birthplace: Musical tribute to Martin Luther King, Jr. on the Sunday before King Day. Wreath laying at Memorial Building on President Lincoln's Birthday, February 12th. In mid-July, a Founder's Day musical drama about the pioneers is staged at the site. On the second Thursday in December, a "Christmas in the Park" celebration takes place, with music, refreshments and decorations.

Boyhood Home: Available for private parties, family reunions, weddings, company picnics and other events.

Abraham Lincoln Birthplace NHS (top), and Abraham Lincoln's Boyhood Home (below).

It was on December 12, 1808, that Thomas Lincoln, a former militia man, carpenter and general laborer, bought a 300-acre farm located on the south fork of the Nolin River for $200.00 cash. At the time, Thomas Lincoln and his young wife, Nancy Hanks Lincoln, had been married over two years and had a one-year-old daughter, Sarah Lincoln. Thomas Lincoln's ancestors had come from England by way of Virginia. Thomas Lincoln's father, Abraham Lincoln, first made the journey to the Kentucky wilderness but was killed by a native American during a raid in May, 1786. This left ten-year-old Thomas Lincoln to fend for himself and his family, and he was to quickly learn self-reliance in the rugged, Kentucky frontier. His reckless nature led him through much of Kentucky, until he finally settled at what later became known as the Sinking Spring Farm. The limestone springs, from which the farm took its name, lie within a crevice in the earth and may still be seen today. It was at the Sinking Spring Farm, on February 12, 1809, that Nancy Hanks Lincoln gave birth to a son, Abraham Lincoln.

Like George Washington and many other men who grew up to become chief executive, Abraham Lincoln spent the first years of his life on a farm. Thomas Lincoln's farm, however, differed in operation from the plantations in Virginia since Mr. Lincoln had no slaves. It was he who stood behind the plough, wielded the tools and did so much of the work necessary to feed the family on whatever crops the red clay could yield. Nancy Lincoln would prepare all of the meals for her husband and their two children using Dutch and clay ovens.

Young Abraham Lincoln and his sister Sarah Lincoln probably learned their lessons listening to their parents reading from the Bible. When he was old enough, Abraham Lincoln played near the large boundary oak tree on the Sinking Spring Farm. The oak, which died in 1976, was found to be 195 years old at the time of its death.

In 1811, the Lincolns decided to leave Sinking Spring Farm to live at Knob Creek Farm, only a few miles away. Their hope was that they might have better luck farming on the land of Knob Creek which they believed was better for raising crops. It was here that Abraham Lincoln spent five formative childhood years, and in manhood he claimed that his earliest childhood memories were of Knob Creek Farm.

Because Abraham Lincoln was unusually tall and strong for his years, he was put to work doing various chores around the farm, such as carrying water and gathering firewood. While living at Knob Creek Farm, he received his first formal education in a basic ABC school. Often, travelers using the road between Louisville and Nashville that ran directly in front of the cabin, would stop by and tell their stories. This is how young Abraham Lincoln received some of his earliest knowledge. Other significant events in his young life include the birth and death of his baby brother, Thomas Lincoln, Jr., believed to have been born in 1811

and to have died four years later, and Abraham Lincoln's own brush with death, averted when a schoolmate, Austin Gollaher, using a long pole, saved him from drowning in the creek.

The Lincolns' stay in Kentucky was ended by a series of lawsuits concerning the title to the Sinking Spring and Knob Creek Farms. In each case, the suit was brought by alleged debtors or former owners claiming title to at least a portion of each of the properties. Faced with these legal entanglements, and the possibility of better farmland in Indiana, the Lincolns crossed the Ohio River in 1816 to search for their new home.

After the Lincolns left Kentucky, about two-thirds of the original Sinking Spring Farm tract was sold to various buyers or traders. The Creal family settled upon the remaining core of the farm. The remains of a log cabin, believed to have been Abraham Lincoln's birthplace home, were removed from the site in 1860 and placed at a nearby farm. A New York businessman, interested in Abraham Lincoln's birthplace, purchased the farm in 1894 and had the cabin moved back to its original site. Shortly thereafter, the cabin was once again moved, this time to be taken on a nationwide exposition tour. This required dismantling it, moving it, and reassembling it for each exposition.

Around the turn of the century, a group of distinguished Americans formed the Lincoln Farm Association, whose goal was to preserve the Abraham Lincoln birthplace and establish a memorial at the birthplace site. The Association bought the remainder of the Lincoln farmland in 1905, and purchased the cabin in 1906. Using over $350,000.00 in small contributions, a marble and granite memorial was constructed to house the cabin, and was dedicated in 1911 by President Taft. The birthplace site became a national park in 1916, and a national historic site in 1959.

The reconstructed "birthplace" cabin is a 16 by 18 foot structure with one door. Its windows did not use glass, but were instead covered with grease paper. On the side of the one-room cabin is a stone hearth, and a wooden chimney extends up the side wall. The walls are made of oak and chestnut logs, chinked with clay and horse hair.

The reconstructed "boyhood home" log cabin sits on the original farm site. It is similar in design and construction to the birthplace cabin and consists of the remains of the original logs taken from Austin Gollaher's cabin. The reconstruction took place in 1931. Today, it houses antique furnishings and other historic items depicting the cabin as it might have appeared during Abraham Lincoln's boyhood.

Taken together, the two sites illustrate what life was like for Abraham Lincoln during his youth. They are the places in which a great leader first became conscious of life, and where he learned his basic values. Those who are interested in the influences which formed the character of one the most notable Americans who ever lived will be fascinated by what they find here.

Lincoln Boyhood National Memorial
Box 1816
Lincoln City, Indiana 47552
(812) 937-4541

Administered by the National Park Service.

Lincoln State Park
Box 216
Lincoln City, Indiana 47552
(812) 937-4710

Administered by the Indiana Department of Natural Resources.

Directions: From Louisville, Kentucky, Take I-64 west to Santa Claus exit 63. Take Indiana State Road 162 west to Lincoln Boyhood National Memorial and adjacent Lincoln State Park.

Open: Lincoln Boyhood National Memorial: Daily (except Thanksgiving Day, Christmas Day and New Year's Day) Lincoln State Park: Daily.

Admission: Lincoln Boyhood National Memorial: Fee charged. Under 17 free. Lincoln State Park: Fee charged.

Features: Lincoln Boyhood National Memorial: Visitors should stop first at the Memorial Visitor Center, where information is available on the park, nearby attractions, camping, accommodations, and restaurants. Rest rooms, a water fountain, and a public telephone are located here. Park Rangers are on duty to orient visitors to the Memorial's major features, including the Memorial Visitor Center itself, the grave site of Nancy Hanks Lincoln (Abraham Lincoln's mother) and the Lincoln Living Historical Farm. Lincoln and park theme books, postcards and slides for sale. Parking. Handicapped accessible.

The Visitor Center features two memorial halls, exhibits, a museum, and an auditorium, where a 24-minute film, "Where I Grew Up," is shown every hour.

The Living Historical Farm features the log buildings, animals and crops of a pioneer farm. Costumed "pioneers" carry out family living and farming activities from mid-April through late-September.

Lincoln State Park: Crawford School site (unmarked), a lake and facilities for boating, swimming, camping, hiking, picnicking, nature center. Park surrounds Little Pigeon Creek Baptist Church, whose graveyard includes grave of Sarah Lincoln Grigsby. Church is still active and not under park jurisdiction.

Special Events: Lincoln Boyhood National Memorial: In February on or near Lincoln's Birthday, the park honors Abraham Lincoln and his family with special programs, speakers and events. Annually in mid-June the Indiana Lincoln Festival is conducted, featuring special events, exhibits, tours, talks and displays whose aim is to let the world know that Lincoln was a Hoosier!

Lincoln State Park: Amphitheater features "Young Abraham Lincoln," a musical outdoor drama, nightly (except Monday) from mid-June to late-August. The musical "Big River" is also performed. Seating for 1500.

*** This section was written by members of the staff of the Lincoln Boyhood National Memorial. ***

Abraham Lincoln lived a quarter of his life in Indiana, having moved there with his parents in the autumn of 1816, when he was seven years old. Years later, Mr. Lincoln recalled that his father came to Indiana "chiefly on account of the difficulty in land titles in K[entuck]y" and "partly on account of slavery." The Land Ordinance of 1785 subdivided Indiana nearly into sections by government survey, and the Northwest Ordinance of 1787 outlawed slavery there. The Lincolns settled near Little Pigeon Creek in western Perry (now Spencer) County.

At first, Mr. Lincoln's mother, Nancy Hanks Lincoln, cared for her family in a rough shelter called a half-faced camp. By early 1817, a sturdy log cabin housed the family. Autumn frosts of 1818 had already colored the foliage of the huge trees of oak, hickory, and walnut when Nancy Lincoln became desperately ill. She was stricken with milk sickness, a poisoning caused by the white snakeroot plant. Cows that ate this abundant weed passed the poison on in their milk and people who drank this poisoned milk or ate its products faced death. On October 5, 1818, Nancy Hanks Lincoln died. She was taken to her final resting place overlooking the Indiana farm she so dearly loved.

Widower Thomas Lincoln set out for Elizabethtown, Kentucky in late 1819. He married a widow by the name of Sarah Bush Johnston and returned to Indiana with her and her three children. These two hardy pioneers, Thomas and Sarah Lincoln, united their two families. Sarah's three children— Elizabeth, Matilda and John—joined Abraham and Sarah Lincoln and Dennis Hanks to make a new family of eight. Sarah Bush Johnston repeatedly asserted that "Abe was a good boy," and she grew to love him a great deal. Abraham Lincoln said of his stepmother that "she proved to be a good and kind mother" to him, and he referred to her as "Mother" in his letters. By all reports their relationship was excellent, and the new Mrs. Lincoln considered her stepson a model child who was always honest, witty, "diligent for knowledge," and never uttered "a cross word."

By 1827, Thomas Lincoln realized his dream by becoming the outright owner of 100 acres of Indiana land. On August 2, 1826, Lincoln's sister, Sarah, married her childhood sweetheart, Aaron Grigsby. But after only 18 months of marriage, Sarah Lincoln Grigsby died in childbirth at the age of 21 on January 20, 1828.

Abraham Lincoln was a boy "raised to farm work," and, since he was "large for his age," he "had an axe put into his hands at once; and...he was almost constantly handling that most useful instrument—less, of course, in plowing and harvesting seasons." He remembered Indiana as "a wild region, with many bears and other wild animals still in the woods," and his life in the "unbroken wilderness" was a fight with the "trees and logs and grubs."

There were other influences on this frontier lad as well, such as talk and story-telling at Gentry's store, and sexton duties at the Little Pigeon Baptist Church. Abraham Lincoln's first glimpse of a wider world came when he was 16 and went to work on a farm on the banks of the Ohio River. In 1829, he floated down the Ohio and Mississippi Rivers to New Orleans with a cargo of produce. After selling the cargo and flatboat, he rode a steamer back home.

Back in Indiana, Abraham Lincoln must have contrasted the rich, bustling life of New Orleans with the routine of farm life. He returned to the familiar chores, but added clerking, more reading, and attendance in court to his routine. It was during this time that he read his first law book, *The Revised Laws of Indiana.*

Abraham Lincoln lived to regret the lack of opportunity for education in the crude frontier state. There was absolutely nothing to excite ambition for education," he remembered, and he belittled the "schools, so called," in which no qualification was ever required of a teacher, beyond reading writin' and cipherin' to the Rule of Three." In his youth, Mr. Lincoln attended ABC schools "by littles." He later expressed amazement that, when he left Indiana, "somehow, I could read, write, and cipher to the Rule of Three." But "that was all," and he admitted that "when I came of age I did not know much." In 1860, Mr. Lincoln felt that what he had "in the way of education" he had "picked up" since his Indiana years.

When Abraham Lincoln returned to the state in 1844 to campaign for Henry Clay, he visited his old home and over a year later wrote a poem which began this way:

My childhood-home I see again,
And gladden with the view:
And still as mem'ries crowd my brain,
There's sadness in it too.

The stanzas that followed referred "[t]o woods, and fields, and scenes of play and school-mates loved so well," but dwelled mainly on the madness of Matthew Gentry, a "fortune favored child," three years older than Abraham Lincoln, who went berserk before young Lincoln's eyes. Mr. Lincoln could not help but complain that death tore "more blest ones hence" but left poor Matthew "ling'ring here." He doubtless also had in mind the death of his mother from "milk sickness" in 1818 and the death of his sister in childbirth in 1828. He experienced his own brush with death at age 10, when a horse kicked him in the head and left him unconscious for a time. Still, he could recall the rough good times on the frontier and wrote at about the same time a humorous poem about a boisterous "Bear Hunt" that put the "woods...in a roar" with a "merry corps of hunters; it made the usually quiet and solitary forest alive with fun."

Fear of white snakeroot poisoning, news of the fertile Illinois soil, and the possible break-up of his family lured Thomas Lincoln westward in March 1830. Thomas sold his Indiana farm and the Lincoln family—now grown to 13 persons—pulled away from the homestead. With them went Abraham Lincoln, who had just turned 21.

So within the boundaries of the Lincoln Boyhood National Memorial and the adjacent Lincoln State Park, one of America's greatest men grew from childhood into early manhood. Here are the grave of his mother, the farm where he grew up, the site of the cabin in which he lived, the site of a spring from which he drew water, the school and church which he attended, the fields he helped clear and cultivate--indeed, as he himself said, "the very spot where grew the bread that formed my bones."

Lincoln's New Salem State Historic Site
R. R. 1, Box 244A
Petersburg, Illinois 62675
(217) 632-4000

Administered by the State of Illinois Historic Preservation Agency.

Directions:	**Located south of Petersburg, Illinois on Route 97.**
Open:	**Daily (except New Year's Day, Martin Luther King Day, Presidents Day, Veterans Day, Election Day, Thanksgiving Day, and Christmas Day). Call for seasonal hours.**
Admission:	**Free.**
Features:	**Restored nineteenth century village, including shops, Rutledge Tavern (where Abraham Lincoln worked and lived), self-guided tours, campgrounds, showers, toilets, picnicking, Talisman Riverboat scenic rides, gifts, refreshments, rest rooms. Handicapped accessible.**
Special Events:	**Craft festivals, Candlelight Tour, The Great American People Show nightly except Mondays during the summer.**

In March 1830, Thomas Lincoln gave up his 100-acre farm at Little Pigeon Creek, Indiana, to move westward to Macon County, Illinois. Spurred by stories of the fertile Illinois soil, combined with a fear of the "milk sickness" which claimed the life of his first wife, Nancy, Thomas Lincoln sold his Indiana property. He settled on a plot of land north of the Sangamon River and tried to raise a corn crop, but his sojourn to this area was brief. In March 1831, Thomas Lincoln moved on to Coles County, Illinois.

By this time, Thomas Lincoln's son, Abraham Lincoln, had grown to young adulthood. At the age of 22, Abraham Lincoln decided to part from his father to make his own way in the world. Today, a commemorative stone marker indicates Abraham Lincoln's first home in the state of Illinois. Near the stone is a memorial cabin representing the original home, the last that Thomas Lincoln and his son lived in together. This site, which until recently was called the Lincoln Trail Homestead State Park, is now closed to the public.

It was shortly after Abraham Lincoln left his father that he met Denton Offutt, who hired him to take his goods by flatboat from Springfield to New Orleans. An unexpected delay, caused by a mill dam, forced Mr. Lincoln and Mr. Offutt to stay temporarily in the small settlement of New Salem. Upon discovering this settlement, Offutt decided that it would be profitable to set up a store. He hired Abraham Lincoln to run it for him, thus giving Mr. Lincoln his first exposure to merchandising.

Abraham Lincoln stayed in New Salem for seven years, working at a number of jobs, including postmaster and store operator. During this time, he had no permanent place of residence, but it is known that he did live in the community, presumably with residents in their lofts. Mr. Lincoln's years in New Salem were marked at first with uncertainty and with no definite plans for his future, and then later with an increasing sense of direction and purpose.

His first opportunity to serve his country came during the Blackhawk War of 1832. Mr. Lincoln joined a volunteer company in order to participate in the combat effort, and, in April 1832, he was chosen captain of his company. Upon returning to New Salem at the conclusion of the war, Mr. Lincoln's life and career goals began to take shape. He made his first foray into electoral politics by running for the Illinois state legislature (the only election he ever lost by popular vote). It was also around this time that he began to study law.

Two years later, in 1834, Mr. Lincoln was elected to the state legislature as a Whig, and served three terms in that office. During that time, he was instrumental in the decision to move the Illinois state capital from Vandalia to Springfield. When the new location of the state capital became official, Mr. Lincoln, a member of the Illinois Bar, left New Salem to establish a law practice in Springfield.

Today, all of the buildings on the original New Salem site are reproductions, with the exception of the Onstot Cooper's Shop. In 1839 (two years after Mr. Lincoln left) the local county seat was moved to nearby Petersburg. As the local commercial activity increased at the new county seat, it declined in New Salem, leading to the city's demise. In the early 1900s, an organization known as the Old Salem Chautauqua Association aroused interest in reconstructing the old village, and in 1906, received aid from newspaper publisher William Randolph Hearst, who agreed to purchase the site and to convey it in trust to the Association.

In 1919, the Association conveyed the title to the property to the state of Illinois. In 1932, reconstruction began due to the combined efforts of private contractors for the state and the Civilian Conservation Corps. The cooper's shop had already been restored to its original site in 1922. Authentic 1830s furnishings were collected for use in the reconstructed cabins where, today, guides dressed in period costume explain what life was like in New Salem.

The details of Mr. Lincoln's life during his New Salem years must be left to oral tradition and speculation since there are few documented facts. Perhaps the most familiar tale concerning Mr. Lincoln's life there is his purported romance with Ann Rutledge, the daughter of a taverner instrumental in founding the settlement. It is thought that Mr. Lincoln did odd jobs at the tavern while he courted Miss Rutledge. It is also said that the two intended to marry, but she died a tragic early death.

A walk through this site (free to the public) is both instructive and pleasant, especially so on a sunny day with a picnic lunch. This site tells the story of how a talented young man found his own way and took his first steps toward greatness. It also provides further clues as to what influences shaped Mr. Lincoln's life.

Lincoln Home National Historic Site
413 South 8th Street
Springfield, IL 62701-1905
(217) 492-4150

Administered by the National Park Service.

Directions:
> From Chicago, take I-55 south to Springfield. Exit at Peoria Road and proceed past State Fair Grounds. Turn right at North Grand Avenue and left at 7th Street. Proceed six blocks to the Visitor Center and parking, which are on the left.

Open:
> Open daily. Call for seasonal hours. After 10:00 a.m. on holidays and during the summer, expect a one to two hour wait to view the interior of the Home. Free tickets for admission to the Home for a tour are issued at the Visitor Center on a first-come, first-served basis.

Admission:
> Free. A parking fee is charged April through October.

Features:
> Visitor center which includes book store, orientation film, exhibits and rest rooms. The first floor of the House is handicapped accessible. Other Lincoln sites which are located nearby include the Old State Capitol State Historic Site, where Abraham Lincoln gave his "House Divided" address; the Lincoln Herndon Law Offices State Historic Site; and the Great Western Depot, where Abraham Lincoln delivered his Farewell Address to the people of Springfield in 1861.

Special Events:
> The site sponsors an annual Lincoln Colloquium in October, and President Lincoln's Birthday activities on February 12. Dramatizations, slide presentations and other programs are presented on a regular basis during the summer. Interested persons can call the site for up-to-date information regarding these and other special events.

When a young state legislator named Abraham Lincoln first came to Springfield, Illinois in 1837, the town was a relatively small community with a population of about 3,000. Springfield was, in many respects, not unlike a farming village in that its streets were still unpaved and pigs, cows and horses wandered its thoroughfares. It was in this town that Abraham Lincoln made his final transition from frontiersman to lawyer and statesman.

While living in Springfield, Abraham Lincoln drew upon the education that he had begun "by littles," as he referred to it. He had spent much of his time in New Salem, Illinois, studying law and pursuing a political career. In Springfield, both of these careers blossomed, thanks to Mr. Lincoln's own innate skills with the English language and the network of friends and associates he established. He acquired a reputation as one of the best trial lawyers in the state, successfully arguing some major cases in which the decisions became landmarks. Here he also met and married Mary Todd, a member of a wealthy and influential family.

Abraham and Mary Todd Lincoln began their married life in 1842, living in the Globe Tavern in Springfield, paying rent of $4 a week. After their first son, Robert Todd Lincoln, was born, they realized that they would need a larger, more prominent place to live.

The Reverend Charles Dresser of St. Paul's Episcopal Church in Springfield owned a home on the corner of 8th and Jackson Streets. He had been trying to sell the house since 1841 as he wanted a larger home himself, and in late 1843, looking for a prospective buyer, he approached Abraham Lincoln. Mr. Lincoln bought the home on January 16, 1844 by paying $1,200.00 in cash and by surrendering title to a lot he owned worth a further $300.00. Thus Abraham Lincoln acquired the only home he ever owned.

The house, originally constructed in 1839 for Rev. Dresser, was a one and one-half story, Greek-revival style home built four feet above street level and reached by a set of wooden stairs. It was painted white and had green shutters, and included a kitchen, dining room and two large front rooms. The frame of the house consisted of roughsawed oak, the siding was made of wood hickory, and the doors and interior were made of black walnut. The house was assembled using hand-made nails and wooden pegs. The stairway to the second floor is made of walnut and still survives today.

Because of the demands of an expanding family, Abraham Lincoln ordered several improvements to be made to the property. In 1850, he contracted for the construction of a brick retaining wall and a white picket fence to be built along the 8th Street boundary of the house. Lincoln decided to replace the paving at the front of the house with concrete because the animals had torn the old wooden planks. In 1855, the retaining wall and picket fence extended to the Jackson Street side of the property.

The house underwent a series of remodelings and expansions during the Lincoln family's years here. For the last of these expansions, which took place in 1856, a Springfield firm was contracted by the Lincoln family to do the necessary work. The contractors cut the roof eaves just above the window line and raised them nine feet, making the front portion a full two-story structure. A second floor was also added to the rear of the house, creating room for four new bedrooms, a sewing room, and a storage room. Stoves were installed in the front bedrooms which burned wood and helped keep the house warmer in the winter. The Lincolns had earlier sealed off the fireplaces on the first floor and placed a large stove in the fireplace in the front parlor as a heat source. This remodeling cost $1,300.00. Most of it took place while Abraham Lincoln was busy with his law practice, traveling to other communities throughout the state, and it was left to Mrs. Lincoln to supervise the work. As she was brought up in larger, more fashionable homes, the increase in size of the house was no doubt to her liking.

The National Park Service, which currently administers the property, recently completed a two-year restoration program designed to reinforce the structure of the home. It has been open to the public since 1887 and, in recent times, has had an average of 3,000 visitors a day. In a previous restoration, which took place in 1987 and 1988, a climate control system was installed to protect the furnishings on exhibit. A significant portion of the structural material of the house is original, and the furnishings were either owned by the Lincolns or, at least, were made around the time the Lincolns lived in the home.

Turning to the left upon entering the home, visitors see the double parlors, which are divided by a large folding door. The front parlor was used for parties and political receptions. It was in this room, in 1860, that Abraham Lincoln received official notification that he had been nominated by the Republican Party to run for president. Visitors notice immediately that this is not the home of a frontier backwoodsman, but is a rather fashionable residence with lovely furnishings. One notable feature is the ornate, wood-burning stove which provided heat for the entire first floor. Also in the room is a rosewood furniture set, originally upholstered with black horsehair. The wallpaper and rugs are reproductions of period patterns. The predominant form of lighting in the house was by candles. Although gas-lighting was introduced to Springfield while the Lincolns were in residence, it did not reach the Lincoln Home neighborhood until after the family had departed for Washington. The cornices above the windows are all made of brass. Parties held by such renowned or popular couples as the Lincolns were commonly referred to as "squeezers" because

of the number of people that would crowd into the parlors. (And these parlors were by no means small!) The printed sketches of these rooms recorded in Frank Leslie's *Illustrated Newspaper* in 1861 were used as a guide for the present-day restoration of the parlors.

Across the hallway is the sitting room, the Lincolns' every day room. The fireplace was sealed off when the Franklin stoves were installed. The modest furnishings here include a set of cane-back chairs. Sitting on a table is a stereoscope of the type used for entertainment by the Lincoln family. A popular subject for stereoscope viewing was Niagara Falls, where Abraham and Mary Todd Lincoln had visited. The family took their meals in the dining room directly behind the sitting room.

A stairway in the central hallway leads up to the second floor, which includes four bedrooms, a servant's room and a storage room. The ceilings on the front portion of this floor are eleven feet high, although the low overhead on the front stairwell must have been a source of discomfort to Abraham Lincoln, who was 6-feet, 4-inches tall! The bed on display in Mr. Lincoln's bedroom would not have represented such a problem, however, because here, visitors see a nearly seven foot long, four-poster bed of the period. Across the hall is a guest room, featuring a French mahogany sleighbed which is 6-feet 6-inches long. The polished brass cornices over the window are similar to those on the first floor. Behind Mr. Lincoln's room is his wife's room, featuring rocking chairs, and behind that is the servant's room, which is the only room on the second floor that does not have wallpaper. However, the room does contain a small wooden bed. Across from this room is the entrance to the rear stairwell, leading back downstairs to the kitchen.

In the kitchen, visitors see a large, wood-burning stove, a dry sink, a dough table with a chute and a storage compartment for flour. To the rear of the kitchen is a small pantry, and on the other side a door leading to the outside porch.

On February 6, 1861, President-elect Lincoln and his wife held a farewell reception in their home. On February 8, the Lincoln family vacated their home and moved into a Springfield hotel. On the morning of February 11, Abraham Lincoln delivered his Farewell Address and left Springfield with his son, Robert Todd Lincoln. On the following day, Mrs. Lincoln left with her two other sons, and joined Mr. Lincoln in Indianapolis. After their departure, the furnishings in their Springfield home were sold or given away to friends. Title to the house remained in the family, even after the president's assassination, and the house was rented out to a series of tenants, the last of which was a Civil War veteran named Osborn H. Oldroyd, a collector of Civil War and Lincoln mementos.

Throughout his presidential years, and until he met his tragic death on April 15, 1865 after having been shot by assassin John Wilkes Booth, Abraham Lincoln's home was, of course, the White House. Mrs. Lincoln refurbished the interior of the White House ostentatiously, but the decor was marred by office seekers and celebrators of battle victories. Like his predecessor, James Buchanan, Abraham Lincoln also used "Corn Rigs" as a summer home while president. (See page 62.) But in the turmoil of his years as president, Abraham Lincoln probably longed for happier times at his home in Springfield.

Beginning in 1883, Mr. Oldroyd suggested that the Lincoln Home be deeded to the state of Illinois as a historical site. On May 25, 1887, a bill was introduced in the Illinois state legislature which provided for state acquisition of the property. The bill passed both houses of the legislature and was signed into law by Governor Richard J. Oglesby on June 16, 1887. Mr. Oldroyd became the first of nine custodians who occupied the home between 1887 to 1972. Sometime after 1887, the appearance of the home was altered slightly, with the addition of a kitchen and laundry room at the rear. For a time, the paint colors used on the exterior were also changed.

In 1950, a decision was made to restore the house to its 1860 appearance. The addition to the rear was removed, and the outside was repainted to approximately the same shade it had been during the later years of the Lincolns' residence.

From 1887 to 1955, only four of the first floor rooms were open to the public. By 1955, the entire house, except for the second floor trunk room, was open to visitors. On August 18, 1971, the house and four surrounding blocks were designated a National Historic Site. The sidewalks surrounding the property are now paved in wood, and the exteriors of the buildings have been restored to their 1860 appearance. The net effect is to create an atmosphere similar to that with which Abraham Lincoln was familiar during his pre-presidential years. It is easy to imagine how painful it must have been for him and his family to leave this warm, friendly setting for the awesome responsibilities facing him. The seventeen years he spent in Springfield, nurturing his talents and raising his family, were perhaps the best of his life.

ANDREW JOHNSON

Andrew Johnson Birthplace
(Mordecai Historic Park)
One Mimosa Street
Raleigh, North Carolina 27604
(919) 834-4844

Administered by Capitol Area Preservation, Inc.

Directions: From I-85, take U.S. 70 south into Glenwood Avenue. Turn left at Peace Street, and left again at Pearson Street, which becomes Wake Forest Road. Mordecai Historic Park is on the left side of the road.

Open: Daily, except Christmas Eve, Christmas Day, New Year's Eve, and New Year's Day. Call for hours.

Admission: Fee charged. Discounts for seniors, AAA, and students. Children under 6 free.

Features: The site offers one-hour tours beginning every half-hour. The park includes the restored birthplace, the original Mordecai plantation house and several other examples of 18th and 19th century architecture. It also includes a gift shop (open during tour hours and special events) and the Mordecai Herb Garden.

75

The small, gambrel-roofed structure which is generally recognized as the house in which President Andrew Johnson was born is sometimes referred to in jest as "the wandering birthplace of Andrew Johnson." It is believed that the birthplace was originally a kitchen building located in the courtyard of Peter Casso's Inn, which was located on the corner of Fayetteville and Morgan Streets, directly across from the North Carolina State House in Raleigh. Sometime after 1867, the house was moved to 118 East Cabarms Street, where it was rented. On July 1, 1904, it was sold for $100.00 to the Wake County Committee of the Colonial Dames of America, who in turn presented it to the city of Raleigh. The city had the house moved to two different locations in Pullen Park, which is across from the campus of North Carolina State University in Raleigh. On July 9, 1975, the house was moved to its present location at Mordecai Historic Park, and was restored and opened to the public two years later.

It is believed that this small kitchen building was built in the 1790s, shortly after the city of Raleigh had been planned and laid out. Peter Casso's Inn, as it existed in 1808, stood at the crossroads of two major highways across from the State House, one of two brick buildings sitting in the midst of a small frame structure. Perhaps because of its location, Casso's Inn gained a measure of notoriety in the area. It was a hotel which was located in what was then a relatively small country village with a population of about one thousand people. It was behind this inn that Jacob Johnson and his wife, the former Mary McDonough, lived in the small kitchen house in which Andrew Johnson was born on December 29, 1808. Jacob Johnson was hostler at Casso's Inn and janitor at the State House, while Mary, who was known as "Polly the Weaver," did weaving for the inn. Andrew Johnson's origin was humble and his parents were uneducated, but is it believed that they instilled the positive values of integrity and industriousness in their son.

When Andrew Johnson was barely three years old, his father died as a result of over-exertion in the rescue from drowning of two friends who were prominent members of the community. This heroic act is evidence of the character of Jacob Johnson, who, in addition to being honest, was well liked by the townspeople. This was the legacy which he passed on to young Andrew Johnson.

Little is known of Andrew Johnson's later childhood. Presumably, Mary Johnson cared for him and his only brother, William, until Andrew Johnson was old enough to take up a trade. He was apprenticed to a tailor, James J. Selby, at the age of fourteen. Among Mr. Selby's customers, some of whom were the leading figures in the county, was a patron who would stop by and read to all of the boy apprentices while they were working with clothing. Andrew Johnson thus developed the desire to learn to read himself.

Roughly two years after he began his apprenticeship, Andrew Johnson's life was marred by an incident involving himself and his young friends. Up to this time, Andrew Johnson had developed a reputation for leadership among his young companions and a penchant for the rough and tumble

activities of a young adolescent, but had never been known to behave in a less than honorable manner. However, one night he and some friends were caught throwing stones at the home of a tradesman. The tradesman's wife threatened to have the boys arrested, causing the young friends to flee town in fear. All except Andrew Johnson, who had taken his tailor's tools with him, quickly returned home. Andrew Johnson, however, fled to the town of Carthage, about sixty miles southwest of Raleigh. His tailoring skills enabled him to support himself by making suits for the local gentlemen. Because Raleigh was a relatively short distance from Carthage, Andrew Johnson, still in fear of discovery, journeyed farther south to Laurens, South Carolina. After a year of working at tailoring and making new friends in Laurens, Andrew Johnson decided to return to Raleigh to work out the apprenticeship with Mr. Selby. Mr. Selby had sold his tailor shop and had no work for his former apprentice, so Johnson felt that his only option was to journey over the mountains to a new life in Tennessee. He took responsibility for his family, and, obtaining a small wagon and an old horse, left Raleigh with his mother, stepfather and brother in September 1826. After a month's journey, the family arrived in Greeneville, Tennessee, which became Andrew Johnson's hometown for the rest of his life. The next time he visited Raleigh was at the invitation of the mayor of Raleigh (to dedicate a monument on his father's grave) in June 1867, when Andrew Johnson had become president of the United States.

The birthplace structure itself has two stories. Inside on the ground floor is a single room, which was originally a kitchen with a large hearth. Above the kitchen is a loft space, which is reached by a set of steep steps. It was in this loft that Andrew Johnson was probably born. The house has a nineteenth-century Wake County style brick chimney, which has been reconstructed. The house was apparently moved piece by piece the first time it was relocated, and the bisection marking in the floor shows where the whole structure was divided in two for the move to Mordecai Park. Some new material and some taken from another old building was apparently used in restoring the house. In the latest restoration of the house, which took place in the 1970s, cypress boards were used to replace the original pine siding.

The house had been used as a kitchen for about 75 years. Its wide fireplace contains a trammel or adjustable pothook, and many pots and kitchen implements. It is believed that all of the wooden materials in the structure itself were pine at the time that the Johnsons lived in it. There was no insulation of walls other than siding because of the extreme heat inside the kitchen. The flooring near the stairs of the first floor is original but the stairs themselves are of recent reconstruction. The ground floor has two windows.

Upstairs, the loft room has walls which are plastered using an eighteenth century brushed court finish plaster. It is original, except for the plaster and green paint on the walls, and has four windows. The front and rear windows, which have shed dormers, are double hung and in casements.

The house's wooden furnishings are not original, but are of the period in which Andrew Johnson was born. The previous wooden furnishings in the house while it was located at Pullen Park were destroyed while in storage in 1975. Only the iron and tin items on display at the time still remain.

A state marker now stands not far from where the birthplace originally stood. That marker is the only indication of the simpler times and circumstances in which Andrew Johnson, destined to become the seventeenth president of the United States, was born.

Andrew Johnson National Historic Site
Depot & College Streets
Greeneville, Tennessee 37743
(423) 638-3551

Administered by the National Park Service.

Directions:	From I-81, take Greeneville exit to U.S. Route 11E and follow signs to the National Historic Site. (It is suggested that a tour begin at the Visitor Center.)
Open:	Daily, except Christmas Day.
Admission:	Fee charged. Under 18 and over 61 free.
Features:	Andrew Johnson's two Greeneville homes (1830s and 1851), his tailor shop (enclosed in the Visitor Center), and his

burial site. Rest rooms are at the Visitor Center. Some parts of the 1851 home are not handicapped accessible.

Special Events: Candlelight tours of home during Christmas season. Wreath laying ceremony at grave site on Andrew Johnson's birthday, December 29th. Memorial Day service at grave site. Occasionally, weddings have been held on the grounds of the 1851 home.

In 1826, 17-year-old Andrew Johnson and his family moved to Greeneville. He later married Eliza McCardle, and the pair prospered from his successful tailoring business. His prosperity enabled him to purchase the brick house on the corner of College and Depot Streets, now part of the Andrew Johnson National Historic Site. Andrew Johnson and his wife lived here from the 1830s to 1851. It is a Federal-style, two story structure built in brick with a white trim, and has an ell with an enclosed walkway along its side. Today, two rooms of this house are open to the public and feature exhibits on the Johnson family genealogy. The public is not admitted into the rest of the house, but may look through its ground floor windows for a glimpse of what the rooms may have looked like in the 1830s and 1840s.

In 1851, while a Congressman, Andrew Johnson purchased another home in Greeneville, between Summer and McKee Streets, from James Brennan. Except for his years at the White House (1865-1869), Johnson lived here for the rest of his life. The property sits directly on the street in the Northern Irish tradition. Although built in the Federal style popular in East Tennessee in the 1840s, the house has some Greek Revival features. The doorway, particularly noticeable, is flanked by pilasters housing small side lights. The dentils of the cornice and the transom are also Greek Revival. However, the house also bears a striking resemblance to Mr. Johnson's previous home; it is a Federal red brick house with an ell extending into a half-acre lot. Between 1868 and 1869, a second floor was added to the ell in anticipation of Andrew Johnson's return after his term as president.

A self-guided tour of the house and grounds is available. First, visitors see Andrew Johnson's bedroom, where there are portraits of Mr. Johnson's wife, Eliza Johnson, his only brother, William Johnson, and his son, Robert Johnson. (There is speculation to the effect that Eliza Johnson taught her husband how to read when he was still a tailor in Greeneville.) Andrew Johnson's hat and vest are lying on the bed, his razor is on the washstand, and a horseshoe he used as a paperweight is on the table.

Across the hall on the first floor is the parlor, filled with gifts the president and his wife received. Included is an ivory basket given by Queen Emma of the Hawaiian Islands and a fruit basket donated by a group of Philadelphia school children. Also in the room is a cardstand and inkwell, made from remnants of the Tennessee marble used in the construction of the United States Capitol Building. A large portrait of Andrew Jackson hangs on the wall. An overstuffed chair with original upholstery, used by Andrew Johnson, is also seen. Finally, visitors see a carpet, settee, and matching chairs purchased by the Johnsons when they lived at the White House.

Up the stairs and toward the front of the house is Eliza Johnson's bedroom, containing furnishings of gold oak, an ornate French candy box, a handkerchief embroidered with a picture of the White House, and a cedar bucket given to Mrs. Johnson by prisoners of the Tennessee State Penitentiary while her husband was military governor of that state.

Across the hall is a spare guest room often used by the president's younger daughter, Mary Johnson Stover. Its most prominent feature is its "goose egg" bed, so called because of the ovular shapes carved into the headboard. A side door leads to a room on the second floor ell, known as the children's room. It is believed that Mary Stover's children slept here, and accordingly, a small child's bed is in the room.

Next door is Robert Johnson's room. Robert Johnson, one of Andrew Johnson's sons, never married. He participated with his brother, Dr. Charles Johnson, in the Greeneville Knoxville Convention prior to the Civil War. (Both Robert and Charles Johnson died in their early thirties.) The purpose of the convention was to form a new secessionist state in East Tennessee, but the convention failed to achieve its purpose.

Visitors then walk onto the porch and down an outdoor flight of stairs to the first floor landing of the ell, where they see Andrew Johnson, Jr.'s bedroom, directly below the children's room. Andrew Johnson, Jr. was the president's youngest child, and was 13 when his father was inaugurated. He later ran a painting shop in Greeneville but, like his brother, died at a very early age. His room is furnished in blue and there is a stereoscope in it.

Next to Andrew Johnson, Jr.'s room is the dining room. Thought to have once been the kitchen because of its extended hearth, it has two cherry dining tables, with rectangular drop leaves, pushed together to look like one. A sideboard is against one wall. In addition to the crystal, china, and silverware in the room, there are two silver service sets. One is a silver water set given to Andrew Johnson by the "loyal White Citizens of Nashville" while he was the military governor of the state, and the other was given by the Johnsons to another couple as a wedding present.

Down another flight of stairs to the lowest level is a kitchen. Here there is a cast-iron stove, a wooden mallet used to beat biscuits, and a meal or flour chest.

Behind the ell is a small flower garden and large lawn. Several blocks from the homestead is the Johnsons' burial site. The Visitor Center, located in another part of Greeneville, includes Andrew Johnson's tailor shop and many other exhibits.

ULYSSES SIMPSON GRANT

Grant Birthplace State Historic Site
Point Pleasant, Ohio 45153
(513) 553-4911

Administered by Historic New Richmond.

Directions: To birthplace: From Cincinnati, take U.S. 52 east to Point Pleasant. The site is on left side of the road.

To boyhood home: From Point Pleasant: Continue on Route 52 east of Ripley, then turn left onto "new" Route 68 (a four lane road) north to Georgetown. Turn left onto Route 125 west, continue to Main Street and turn right. Proceed two blocks to Grant Avenue. The site is two blocks up on the left on the corner of Grant Avenue and North Water Street.

Open: Birthplace: open April through October.

Boyhood home: open by appointment only.

Admission: Birthplace: Fee charged. Discounts for Seniors and children.

Boyhood home: Free.

Features: Birthplace: Thirty minute tour of small cottage. No other facilities. Ample parking. Handicapped accessible.
Boyhood home: Guided tour of house. No other facilities. Parking on street. Not handicapped accessible.

Special Events: Decorated Christmas tour of birthplace. Birthplace and boyhood home have a joint celebration of Grant's birthday in late April. Both sites celebrate with a ceremony including bands, veterans, scouts and historians. Cake and punch are served at both homes on that day.

Grant Boyhood Home
219 Grant Avenue
Georgetown, Ohio 45121
(937) 378-4222

Privately owned by Mr. and Mrs. John A. Ruthven.

It was in 1822 that an itinerant tanner, Jesse Root Grant, and his wife, Hannah Simpson Grant, rented a small cottage in the quiet hamlet of Point Pleasant, Ohio, located on the banks of the Ohio River. The availability of work in a nearby tannery had drawn the Grants to this village. Their stay, however, was to be brief and by 1823, Jesse Grant had saved enough for a tannery of his own in nearby Georgetown, 20 miles east of Point Pleasant. Before leaving for Georgetown, a significant event took place in the small cottage: Hannah Grant gave birth to her first son, Hiram Ulysses Grant, on April 27, 1822.

At the time, the Grants' small, rented home was a one-room cottage. The entire structure measured only 16 by 19 feet, its frame was made of Allegheny pine, and the walls were reinforced with brick. The cottage has since been expanded, and now is a soap box structure with three rooms. The original room, now located at the front, is furnished with antiques and period pieces demonstrating the lifestyle of the time. Visitors see a simple rope bed with a quilt, as well as some of the Grants' clothing and a pillowcase on the bed. A small, oilburning lamp (a "beddie lamp") hangs over the mantel of the fireplace. Some evidence of Jesse Grant's tannery work can be found in the room, particularly a pair of boots and a leather enclosed chest with his initials on it, later used at West Point by his oldest son (who, due to an error on his application form, became known as, and retained the name of, Ulysses Simpson Grant).

With the money he earned in tanning, Jesse Grant managed to build a tannery of his own in Georgetown. Across the street from the new tannery, he constructed a brick home for his family. The Grants moved into their new home in the fall of 1823. It was here that the future president spent sixteen and one-half of the first seventeen years of his life. Even as a young boy, the future president assisted his father at the tannery, and had a happy childhood. His five siblings were born while his family lived in Georgetown.

The house, once described as a "half-house," is a two-story, Federal-style brick home. Today, it is painted completely white. When the original section of the house was built in 1823, it was a two-room structure, just 300 feet east of the town square. The first of two additions to the home was made in 1824 when a kitchen wing was added to accommodate the growing family, and in 1828, a parlor and two bedrooms were added. Today, the restored woodworking in the house has been painted three different colors, so that visitors can easily identify which rooms are located in each of the three sections of the house.

Most of the furnishings are not original, but were crafted during, or close to, the time that the Grants lived in the home. The front parlor, however, does contain a set of rocking chairs, a couch, and a cradle owned and used by the Grant family. The parlor is the only room on the first floor of the front section. The second floor is reached by a series of stairs, at the top of which is a large room that appears to have been the master bedroom and a much smaller room that was probably a child's bedroom. Because the small room is in the front, one may speculate that this was General Grant's boyhood bedroom. Towards the back of the master bedroom, two stairs lead down to the 1828 wing and one more bedroom, probably used by General Grant's brothers and sisters.

Beside the back bedroom is a series of stairs leading down to the 1824 kitchen wing of the home. The kitchen contains a large hearth and various furnishings of the time, notable among which is a large pie safe of a size comparable to that of a wardrobe. A porch that was enclosed when the Grants built the three-room addition in 1828 is currently being used as a museum. Among the artifacts displayed here is a field desk used by a Georgetown resident, Colonel James Louden. The desk is essentially a large wooden box with many compartments, and contains ink, pens, stationery, and a variety of other writing implements. Also on display here are Grant's own binoculars, gloves, family Bible, and bed cover. A bonnet belonging to his wife, Julia Dent Grant, can also be seen here.

General Grant's boyhood home is currently owned by Mr. and Mrs. John A. Ruthven, who completed the restoration in 1982. It is now listed on the National Register of Historic Places, and has achieved National Historic Landmark status. In addition to the Grant tannery across the street (currently a privately owned house), visitors can see the two schoolhouses that Grant attended (the first one is on the other side of Grant Avenue and is now privately owned; the second one is owned by the state of Ohio and is closed for anticipated repairs). By visiting both the birthplace and the boyhood home, one may see how the Grant family prospered through hard work, and how the future general and president, despite his modest beginnings and sporadic formal education, grew to become a West Point graduate, a military hero and a holder of the highest office in the land.

Ulysses S. Grant National Historic Site
"White Haven"
7400 Grant Road
St. Louis, MO 63123
(314) 842-3298

Administered by the National Park Service.

Directions:	From downtown St. Louis, travel south on I-55, exiting on Bayless Road. Turn right at the end of the off ramp and turn left at Gravois Road (Route 30). Turn right at Grant Road following the sign for the entrance to the site. The site is marked by a sign on the right-hand side of the road.
Open:	Daily except Thanksgiving Day, Christmas Day and New Year's Day.
Admission:	Free.
Features:	Five historic structures: Main House, Barn/Visitor Center (information desk, sales area offering books and other items, exhibits, public restrooms), Chicken House, Ice House and stone building on 9.65 acres of grounds. The Visitor Center is accessible to persons with disabilities.
Special Events:	The site sponsors special programs on the first Saturday of each month. Please call the site for details.

White Haven circa 1860, looking towards the main house.

After graduating from West Point in 1843 where, due to a clerical error, Hiram Ulysses Grant came to be known as Ulysses Simpson Grant, Lieutenant U. S. Grant began his long army career by reporting to Jefferson Barracks, near St. Louis. Soon after arriving in Missouri, he visited the family of his former West Point roommate, Frederick Dent, at the Dent family plantation known as "White Haven," an 1100-acre plantation located along Gravois Creek. The name appears to originate from the name of the Dent family ancestral home on Mattawoman Creek, Maryland, which possibly was taken, in turn, from the name of a region in England. It was at White Haven that Lt. Grant met Frederick Dent's sister, Julia, and afterward became a regular visitor to White Haven. Spurred by the news that his regiment was about to transfer, Lt. Grant proposed to Julia in 1844 and eventually married her on August 22, 1848, at the Dent family's city home in St. Louis. The Grants' period of engagement was lengthened by Lt. Grant's departure from Missouri to participate in the Mexican War. As a wedding gift, Grant's father-in-law, "Colonel" Frederick Dent, presented the newlyweds with the 80 acres of the White Haven farmland that later came to be known as "Hardscrabble."

Ulysses S. Grant, who had already been assigned to duty at Fort Jessup, Louisiana and Corpus Christi, Texas by the time of his wedding in 1848, spent much of his early married life away from White Haven on military duty in various places, including Madison Barracks and 253 East Fort Street in Sacketts Harbor, New York, as well as Detroit. In 1852, he was assigned to duty at Fort Vancouver, Washington and was later transferred to Fort Humboldt, California where, to earn extra income, he attempted potato farming. It is said that by 1854, Grant's drinking problem became so severe that the Army gave him an ultimatum: give up the bottle or your commission. Reportedly, he did both.

U. S. Grant resigned from the military in 1854 and returned to White Haven, looking forward to a new life with his wife and young children. The Grants came to live in "Wish-ton-wish," the stone home of Louis Dent, one of Julia Dent Grant's brothers. This home was gutted by a fire in 1873 which destroyed all of the Grant family's St. Louis furnishings. In 1855, Grant began to cut, hew and notch the logs that would be used for "Hardscrabble," the log cabin built mostly by Grant himself in 1855 and 1856. After Julia Grant's mother died in January 1857, the Grants returned to White Haven to live at the behest of Mrs. Grant's father, "Colonel" Frederick Dent, and Grant set about managing the plantation, where wheat, oats, potatoes and Indian corn were grown and more than 75 horses, cattle and pigs were tended by slaves (Missouri was a slave state during this period under the terms of the Missouri Compromise). The Grants remained at White Haven until 1860, when Grant, having made unsuccessful ventures into farming and real estate and having applied unsuccessfully for a position as county engineer, relocated with his family to Galena, Illinois to work in his father's leather goods store.

Despite Grant's move to Galena and the subsequent outbreak of the Civil War, which revived Grant's military career, Grant never lost contact with his White Haven home. Rather, he became increasingly involved with White Haven. During the war, he began paying the property taxes on White Haven and in 1865 became its sole owner and manager. During his presidency (1869-1877), Grant had tenants who acted as caretakers for White Haven, and for them he wrote very specific instructions as to what kinds of crops to plant and how to tend to his farm animals. President Grant's original intention was to retire at White Haven after leaving office, and he even arranged for a railway line to be extended toward White Haven, which line was used by Grant, friends and others in visiting the plantation in 1873. However, circumstances compelled Grant to abandon his plans to retire at White Haven, although he did retain ownership of the farm until a few months before his death in 1885.

In 1913, the house at White Haven and a small portion of the surrounding land and improvements were purchased by the Wenzlick family, in whose hands it remained until the 1980s, when a condominium developer expressed interest in the property. Local citizens, fearing the destruction of the house to make way for condominiums, formed the organization "Save Grant's White Haven." Title to the house and the immediately surrounding land (9.65 acres) was transferred to St. Louis County Parks and to the State of Missouri jointly, and in 1990, the National Park Service, pursuant to legislation sponsored by Senator Christopher Bond and Representative Richard Gephardt of Missouri, acquired the site using funding secured by the Jefferson National Expansion Historical Association. The site was renamed the "Ulysses S. Grant National Historic Site" in honor of the president who established the first U. S. National Park on March 1, 1872.

Contrary to its name, the house, which at this writing is being restored to its 1875 appearance, was not white during the nineteenth century, but was originally beige with dark brown trim. Interestingly, during the period that Col. Dent, who sympathized with the Confederacy, was owner, the house was repainted entirely gray. In 1874-5, by which time President Grant had become owner, the house was again repainted, this time predominantly green. The oldest portion of the house, including the front "piazza," is a two-story structure of French frame construction, to which a vertical log wing, possibly used as a parlor, was added circa 1830. A second wing, possibly used for bedrooms, was added sometime in the 1830s or 1840s.

A stone building at the rear of the house served as the summer kitchen, while the winter kitchen was located in the basement below the west wing of the house. Behind the house stand two structures: a triangular-shaped ice house, which is part of the original Dent plantation, and the chicken house, which housed the hens and roosters which Julia Grant loved to name according to their personalities and may also have housed her favorite ornamental birds, including the Shanghai, Brahma, and Bantam breeds. A stone springhouse, a hay barn, livestock stables and pens and 18 slave cabins were all once part of this farm but have now all been demolished.

A very dedicated Park Service staff and volunteers are available to answer questions, conduct special events such as "living history" presentations, storytelling for children, panel discussions and farming demonstrations. Visitors to the site may also enjoy exhibits on Grant's life at White Haven and the history of the plantation itself at the barn/visitor center, originally built in accordance with instructions made by Grant in an 1868 letter and moved to its current location in 1962. Archaeologists continue to unearth additional clues as to what life was like for the Dent and Grant families at White Haven while the ambitious project of restoration of the main house to its 1875 appearance continues. Once completed, visitors will have an even clearer idea of what the one place that Grant could call home throughout his military and political career was like during his lifetime.

Grant's Farm ("Hardscrabble")
10501 Gravois Road
St. Louis, Missouri 63123
(314) 843-1700

Administered by the Anheuser-Busch Companies, Inc.

Directions:	See directions from previous section. The site is just past Grant Road on the right.
Open:	By appointment only from April 15 through October 29.
Admission:	Free. Reservations are required and should be made well in advance.
Features:	General Grant's restored log cabin home. A trackless train, which is handicapped accessible, takes visitors past the cabin, and Bauernhof courtyard, which

houses stables. The Tier Garten, also on the site, has a large collection of various species of animals. Visitors also see Deer Park, a 160-acre game preserve housing 30 different exotic species. Visitors end the tour by viewing the Budweiser Clydesdale horses. Across from Gen. Grant's cabin is a fence built from 2,563 rifle barrels used by Union and Confederate troops in the Civil War.

Special Events: Please call the site for details.

When U.S. Grant resolved to return to St. Louis, site of his first tour of military duty, he wrote, "Whoever hears of me in ten years will hear of a well-to-do old Missouri farmer." He established a farm on an 80-acre property received by his wife as a dowry, and called it Hardscrabble. While building a log cabin home on the site, U.S. Grant and his family stayed at his father-in-law's estate, White Haven, and at "Wish-ton-Wish."

The completed cabin is a story and a half structure. Grant cut its oak and elm logs himself, and also split its shingles and hauled the stones used for its cellar and foundation. He finished up by shingling the roof, completing the floors and stairs, and had carpenters work on the white window frames, doors and sashes. Grant observed the tradition of having a cabin-raising, a party in which neighbors ostensibly assist in building the cabin. The neighbors were served hard cider and ginger cakes, but did little to help complete the cabin. Thus, the cabin was largely the product of U.S. Grant's own handiwork.

The ensuing years were difficult for Grant, who by this time had to support a wife, two sons and a daughter. He found that farming did not earn an income adequate to support his family. It is also possible that he was suffering from malaria during this period.

The Grants lived at Hardscrabble until 1860, when U. S. Grant's mother-in-law died, and the Grant family moved back to White Haven to assist Mrs. Grant's father, Colonel Frederick Dent. The Grants never returned to Hardscrabble; rather, they moved to a two-story brick cottage at 121 High Street in Galena, Illinois. Grant worked in his brother's tannery business until the Civil War, which brought him back into military service.

U.S. Grant leased Hardscrabble to tenant farmers beginning in 1860. He retained title to the property until 1884, when financial trouble forced him to surrender title to a mortgage holder, William H. Vanderbilt of New York. Mr. Vanderbilt sold the property to Luther H. Conn in 1888. Mr. Conn, a former Confederate soldier, had made lucrative real estate deals in St. Louis, and in 1891 sold the property and cabin to Edward Joy, who moved the cabin to another location nearby. The cabin's next owner, C.F. Blanke, a coffee merchant, moved the cabin to St. Louis as a World's Fair attraction in 1904. After the fair, Adolphus Busch, founder of Anheuser-Busch, Inc., the brewing company, purchased the cabin. Mr. Busch had, by coincidence, recently purchased an estate which included some of the former White Haven acreage. He had the cabin dismantled and moved, one more time, to a site about one mile from its original location.

Today, the cabin remains the property of the Busch family. Anheuser-Busch officials had the deteriorating cabin completely restored in 1977. Furnishings typical of the period were located and an effort was made to restore the cabin as nearly as possible to descriptions of the home as it was in General Grant's time there. Most visitors to the site see only the exterior of the cabin while passing it on a trackless train ride. However, visitors can view the interior of the cabin by special advance arrangement or during Grant's birthday celebration in April.

Today, the cabin is a memorial to a man who overcame many setbacks and went on to become both a military hero and holder of the nation's highest office.

U.S. Grant Home State Historical Site
511 Bouthillier Street
Galena, Illinois 61036
(815) 777-0248

Administered by the Illinois Historic Preservation Agency.

Directions:	U.S. Route 20 and Illinois Route 84.
Open:	Daily (except some holidays, call ahead).
Admission:	Free, donations accepted.
Features:	The site includes no special features other than the home itself. The park across the road includes picnic tables and a log home with a Grant pictorial exhibit. The site has an overlook area which affords a view of Galena, a historic town which has five other historic homes preserved by the Illinois Historic Preservation Agency. First floor and rest rooms are handicapped accessible.
Special Events:	A Civil War encampment is reenacted on Columbus Day weekend.

In 1865, General Ulysses S. Grant returned in triumph to the town in which he had resided immediately before he re-entered military service at the outbreak of the Civil War. Upon his return to Galena, the citizens decided to honor his military triumphs with special gifts. After a triumphal parade through the streets of Galena, the Grants were escorted to a beautiful Italianate bracketed brick mansion sitting high upon a hill overlooking the town. A small group of local Republicans arranged for the purchase of this house. The official records show that the house was purchased by Thomas B. Hughlett of Galena in consideration of $2,500.00 and that title was subsequently transferred to General Grant. The house had been erected in 1860 as a home for the former city clerk, Alexander J. Jackson.

Although the house remained in General Grant's name from 1865 to 1881, he spent relatively little time at this residence, largely because of his election to the presidency in 1868, his service in that high office for a period of eight years, and his world tour, which lasted from 1877 to 1879. During his long absences from the house, a series of caretakers who lived in the community kept the house in order so that it would be prepared for General Grant and his family whenever they chose to use it.

As visitors face the home from the street, there is a small piazza located at the left front corner of the house. Walking up to the piazza and through the entranceway, visitors enter the hallway extending to the right, and turn right to enter the parlor. This room, like most of the other rooms in the home as it exists today, contains furniture originally used by the Grant family. Visitors note the wooden furniture with its black horsehair upholstery. A large square piano is also situated in this room and at the front wall is a large marble fireplace. It was in this room that General Grant received his friends upon learning that he had been elected president of the United States in 1868. Modern restoration of the room is based upon illustrations appearing in Frank Leslie's *Illustrated Newspaper*, which was published during the time that Grant lived in this home.

Walking toward the rear of the house and turning left, visitors enter the dining room. The furniture here is made of light oak and the seats of the chairs surrounding the dining room table are cane. The place settings consist of English white ironstone, "white wheat" pattern china. In this room, as in other rooms of the house, the wallpaper patterns and carpets are historically documented reproductions.

Turning to the left, visitors emerge into the hallway, then proceed up the narrow, winding stairway to the second floor of the home. Here, visitors see the five bedrooms of General and Mrs. Grant and their three sons and daughter. Each room contains a small woodburning stove and a large wardrobe, as no closets exist in this house. Many of the wooden furnishings on this floor are also made of oak.

Also appearing on the upstairs level is a dressing room, generally associated with Nellie Grant, General Grant's daughter. It contains a sewing machine of the period and a dresser with a mirror placed in an adjustable wishbone frame.

At the rear of the second floor is a second series of stairs winding down to the rear section of the first floor of the house. Turning to the left, visitors see the library, with General Grant's collection of books placed in glass-encased, wood-framed cabinets along the wall, and various oak furnishings which are original to the Grant family. This is the room in which Grant conducted various political conferences during the 1868 presidential campaign and from which, after leaving the White House, he carried on much of his correspondence for the brief period of time he stayed here.

To the rear of the first floor is the large kitchen, which has easy access to the Grants' dining room. A large wood-burning cook stove dominates this room. In front of the stove is a wooden table probably used in the preparation of vegetables and other foods. The kitchen also contains the bellows for the stove, a dry sink, a salt box, and many other kitchen appliances used during the time the Grants were living there. To the rear of the kitchen, and to the right hand side, a doorway leads to a small pantry.

On the other side of the kitchen's rear wall, is a doorway leading to a small side room. Behind the small room is another room originally used as a storeroom. This room's most prominent feature is a large copper tub which is encased by a wooden box. However, the chief source of water at the house was a cistern located at the side of the kitchen. Water was drawn from the cistern using a chain with small cups and a crank to lift the water from below the ground to the surface. A washroom, woodroom and another room were added to the house in 1879, but were removed circa 1932.

Although General Grant spent a relatively short period of his life in Galena, this was his official residence from 1865 to his death; Grant was registered to vote at this address. The house stands today as a fitting tribute to a military hero who attained the nation's highest office, and is a crowning jewel in a community which has done much to preserve buildings with historical significance, making a visit to Galena a very worthwhile experience indeed.

Grant Cottage State Historic Site
Off Route 9
Mount McGregor, Wilton, New York 12866
(518) 587-8277

Administered by the Friends of Ulysses S. Grant Cottage in cooperation with the New York State Dept. of Parks.

Directions:	From the Northway (I-87), take exit 16 west on Ballard Road to intersection at Route 9 and follow historic site markers. From Route 50 in Saratoga, take Route 9 north to the intersection at Ballard Road, take a left and follow historic site markers. Please stop briefly at the entrance of the Mount McGregor Correctional Facility before proceeding to the Grant Cottage.
Open:	Memorial Day to Labor Day, Wednesday to Sunday, 10:00 a.m. to 4:00 p.m.
Admission:	Fee charged.
Features:	Cottage, scenic eastern outlook of the Hudson Valley, small gift shop, rest room. Not handicapped accessible. Tour lasts 20 to 30 minutes.

Special Events: In late June, there is a Civil War reading and musical event.

In late July, there is a reenactment of the arrival of the Grant family at the cottage.

In late August, there is a Victorian picnic at the site.

The site hosts an open house on the second Sunday in October.

After leaving Galena in 1865, General Ulysses S. Grant went on a national tour and settled into a house at 205 I Street in Washington, D.C. During this time, he served as commanding general of the Army and also served, beginning on August 1, 1867, as interim secretary of war until Secretary Stanton was reinstated by Congress on January 14, 1868. In May of that year, General Grant became the Republican presidential nominee, winning election in November.

During his years as president, U.S. Grant authorized the most drastic renovation of the White House since the War of 1812, installing cut glass chandeliers, gilded wallpaper, gilt woodwork and ebony and gold furniture in a so-called "Greek Style." 3238 R Street N.W., also in Washington, was his first "Summer White House." While president, he later summered at 991 Ocean Avenue in Long Branch, New Jersey, a large, two and a half-story cottage of red brick with iron railings and a captain's walk on top. The cottage, which no longer stands, was a combination English villa and Swiss chalet.

After two terms as president, which were marred by the Credit Mobilier scandal and other setbacks, General Grant retired on March 4, 1877. (Credit Mobilier was a dummy corporation set up by principals of the Union Pacific Railroad. It siphoned profits from the railroad and distributed payments to certain federal officeholders. There is no evidence that President Grant was per-

sonally involved in the scandal.) By May 17, General Grant and his family were sailing on the steamship *Indiana*, the start of a two-year world tour. They returned to the United States in 1879, and, for a short time, lived in their house in Galena. The following year, Grant had considerable support for re-nomination as president at the Republican Convention. However, the convention wound up nominating another native Ohioan, James A. Garfield, on the 36th ballot.

In August of the following year, General Grant moved to a new home at 3 East 66th Street in New York City. This brownstone house no longer exists. In June 1884, Grant, heavily in debt, decided to write his memoirs. Several months later, in November, while dictating to his secretary, he felt a terrible pain in his throat. The cause of the pain was throat cancer, and the disease eventually claimed his life.

On February 27, 1885, General Grant signed a contract with his friend, Mark Twain, to publish his memoirs. By May 23, Volume I of the memoirs went to the press. Grant knew, however, that he had to finish his memoirs in order to provide the income his family would desperately need after his death. To complicate matters, summer was approaching, and it would be very difficult for him to concentrate on his writing in the oppressive New York City heat.

Fortunately for the Grant family, Mr. Joseph W. Drexel of New York made a cottage available to the Grants which sat atop Mt. McGregor in Saratoga County, New York. The cottage, which Mr. Drexel had recently purchased, was built by Duncan McGregor and was located near the 300-room Balmoral Hotel in Wilton, N.Y. It is a two-story structure surrounded by a covered porch, and today, after a paint analysis, it has been painted in its original color scheme—dark green with red trim.

The Grants arrived at the cottage on June 16, 1885. For the next several weeks, General Grant battled the disease and the specter of death in a race against time to finish his memoirs. In July, Mark Twain visited Grant to tell him that advance sales of the memoirs would assure royalties of at least $300,000.00 for Mrs. Grant and her family. (The memoirs eventually earned $450,000.00 in royalties.)

General Grant finished his memoirs on July 19, 1885. On July 23, four days after the task was completed in its entirety, the eighteenth president of the United States died of throat cancer.

Today, visitors touring the cottage where General Grant died see it furnished just as it was on that day. The furnishings were arranged by order of Mr. Drexel to accommodate Grant and his family. The first room visitors see is the room which was used by Grant's secretary as an office during his stay here. Today it contains a gift shop and a small exhibit.

In another room adjoining the former office, the so-called "sick room," visitors see the two chairs on which General Grant spent most of his time. His fans, candle and lamp are also in this room. A portion of his wardrobe is here, as well as a large case containing medical appliances that he and his physicians used at the cottage. A smaller case holds his pencil and pads, two messages to friends and the pen he used to do his last writing.

Grant's illness prevented him from lying down, so he slept in the two chairs in this room sitting in one and resting his feet on the other. He was taken to the bed in the reception room on the evening of July 22, 1885, and died there the next morning.

The next room visitors see is the reception room, which features the bed on which General Grant died, his favorite chair, and the original rugs. The clock on the mantel was stopped at 8:08 a.m. on July 23, 1885 by Grant's son, Colonel Fred Grant, to mark the time of his father's death.

The last room visitors see is the dining room which, complete with Dresden china, is virtually as it was during the Grants' stay in the cottage. Only a portion of the table service was removed. Floral arrangements used at General Grant's funeral procession in New York City were shipped to the cottage after the funeral, and were displayed in the dining room during the memorial service held here. They are on display in this room today. The largest one, called "Gates Ajar," was presented by the Leland Stanfords, the founder of Stanford University and his wife. Another piece, a pillow, was presented by the Grand Army Post to which Grant belonged. A third, a small cross with heart and anchor, was presented by Mrs. Amos Bissel of Denver, Colorado.

Outside, the grounds afford a sweeping view of the Hudson Valley, and visitors can see as far as Vermont and New Hampshire from this point.

The story of this cottage is a story of triumph over tragedy, and how General Grant, at the close of his life, demonstrated qualities of courage and tenacity which perhaps surpassed those he demonstrated in the Civil War. His struggle to complete his writings in the face of his approaching death assured that his beloved family was properly provided for.

RUTHERFORD BIRCHARD HAYES

Rutherford B. Hayes Presidental Center ("Spiegel Grove")
1337 Hayes Avenue
Fremont, Ohio 43420-2796
(419) 332-2081

Affiliated with the Ohio Historical Society.

Directions: Fremont is off the Ohio Turnpike (I-80-90) between Toledo and Akron, Ohio. Take Rawson Avenue and follow the signs to the Hayes Presidential Center.

Open: The Presidential Center, which includes the residence and grounds ("Spiegel Grove"), library and museum, is open daily except Thanksgiving, Christmas, and New Year's Day. The Library is closed Sundays and holidays.

Admission: Fee charged. Discounts for Seniors and children.

Features: Residence, Presidential library, museum, 25-acre wooded estate, tomb of President and Mrs. Hayes, trees named for prominent guests, slide presentation. Dillon House, a nineteenth-century home, is located adjacent to Spiegel Grove, but not open to the public for tours. Gifts and books are available for purchase at the museum; restrooms. Limited handicapped accessibility.

Special Events: The site is decorated for the Christmas season in the last week in November. Weddings and meetings are held at the Dillon House and sometimes on the site. Arrangements are made in advance.

The nineteenth president of the United States, Rutherford Birchard Hayes, was born on October 4, 1822, in Delaware, Ohio. Like his predecessor, Andrew Jackson, Mr. Hayes was born after the death of his father. He was the fifth child of his parents, Rutherford Hayes, Jr. and Sophia Birchard Hayes, but he and his sister, Fanny Arabella Hayes, were the only two of those children who survived into adulthood. Rutherford Hayes' parents, who were of Scottish descent, had made the forty-three day journey by wagon from Dummerston, Vermont, to Ohio in 1817. The house in which President Hayes was born was the first brick house in Delaware, Ohio. It was a two story structure with a wooden addition and was located on the corner of William and Winter Streets. It was torn down in the 1930s to make way for a gasoline station, despite an attempt to save the building.

Young "Rud" Hayes and his sister, Fanny Hayes, became the wards of their mother's bachelor brother, Sardis Birchard, a merchant, banker and philanthropist in what was then Lower Sandusky (later Fremont), Ohio. "Rud" Hayes' Uncle Sardis sent him to district school in Delaware, then to Norwalk Seminary in Norwalk, Ohio, and finally to Isaac Webb's Maple Grove Academy in Middletown, Connecticut. In accordance with his mother's wishes and his own, "Rud" Hayes then returned to Ohio to attend Kenyon College. He graduated as class valedictorian in 1842, and studied law at the office of Sparrow & Matthews in Columbus for ten months. During that time, he stayed at his sister's house. On August 28, 1843, he entered Harvard Law School and by 1845, he had graduated and was admitted to the Ohio bar.

Rutherford Hayes decided to establish a law practice in Lower Sandusky. After a quiet first year, Mr. Hayes formed a partnership with Ralph P. Buckland. Mr. Hayes spent time away from his hometown during this period, visiting relatives in West Brattleboro, Vermont, and spending one winter in Texas. After four years of practicing law in Lower Sandusky, in late 1849 Mr. Hayes moved on to Cincinnati, where the prospects for a law practice proved more promising. By 1850, he was sharing an office and living quarters there with John W. Herron, who became a lifelong friend and was later to become the father-in-law of President William Howard Taft.

1850 was also the year that Mr. Hayes became re-acquainted with Lucy Webb, whom he met while on a visit to his birthplace in Delaware in 1847. Lucy Webb was a native of Chillicothe, Ohio, and graduated from Cincinnati Wesleyan Women's College in June 1850. On December 30, 1852, Rutherford Hayes and Lucy Webb were married. Their first home together was the home of Mrs. Hayes' mother at 141 West Sixth Street, Cincinnati, Ohio. Later, in 1854, they moved to 383 Sixth Street in Cincinnati, a narrow three-story house. Neither of the houses on Sixth Street exists today. By this time, their first child, Birchard Austin Hayes, had been born, and was later followed by seven other Hayes children.

On December 26, 1853, Mr. Hayes formed a new law partnership with Richard M. Corwine and William K. Rogers. Mr. Rogers left the partnership in 1856 to go to Minnesota. In December 1858, Mr. Hayes entered politics by his appointment to an interim term as city solicitor of Cincinnati. He later won election to this post in his own right, serving until April 1, 1861. When his term in office ended, Mr. Hayes briefly resumed private practice, but the course of his life took an unexpected direction at the outbreak of the Civil War.

Rutherford Hayes joined the Union Army as an officer. While in the military from 1861 to 1865, he rose from the rank of major to brevet major general. He was wounded in battle on four occasions. While still serving in the Army, Mr. Hayes was elected to Congress as a Republican from Cincinnati. (Interestingly, Mr. Hayes' successor as president, James A. Garfield, a fellow Ohioan, was also elected to Congress in absentia while serving as an Army officer.) During his second term in Congress, Representative Hayes resigned to run successfully for governor of Ohio. He was inaugurated in January 1868, and served in Columbus for two two year terms.

In May 1873, Mr. Hayes left both Columbus and Cincinnati to return to Fremont (Lower Sandusky had been renamed by this time, and Mr. Hayes had played a role in its renaming shortly before leaving for Cincinnati) to make his uncle's home at Spiegel Grove his own permanent home. Spiegel Grove had been so named by Rutherford Hayes' uncle, Sardis Birchard, because after a rain storm, the pools of clear water on the grounds reflect its grove of trees like mirrors ("spiegel" is the German word for mirror). As long ago as November 5, 1845, intending to establish a home to pass along to his nephew, Sardis Birchard had acquired the property from the heirs of Jacques Hulburd, one of the first settlers in the area. The building of the residence at Spiegel Grove began in 1859 and D.L. June, a prominent local contractor, was hired for the job. Sardis Birchard had his wish as his nephew, Rutherford Hayes, and the rest of the Hayes family moved to Spiegel Grove.

Upon his arrival, Rutherford Hayes, who had been given free rein to do as he wished with the property, set about adding two frame buildings to the grounds. In Mr. Hayes' time, these buildings contained a kitchen, office and library for Mr. Hayes' large book collection.

Sardis Birchard died in January 1874, and Rutherford Hayes inherited Spiegel Grove. Mr. Hayes attempted to change the name of the estate to "Birchard Grove" in honor of his beloved uncle, but the name did not stick. Spiegel Grove remains the name of the estate to this day.

In 1875, Ohio Republicans persuaded Rutherford Hayes to run for a third term as governor. He was elected, but did not serve six months before the Republican Convention nominated him for president on June 14, 1876. The ensuing campaign was lively, but neither he nor his Democratic opponent, Governor Samuel J. Tilden of New York, was personally active in it. The results of the election were contested, and because of the uncertainty of the number of electoral votes to which each candidate was entitled, Congress appointed a special election commission to determine who won the election. The commission determined that Mr. Hayes was the winner, and Mr. Hayes, who had resigned the governorship of Ohio before the commission announced its findings, left for Washington on March 1, 1877. He was privately given the presidential oath of office on March 3, and publicly inaugurated on March 5.

While president, Rutherford Hayes had the first telephone installed in the White House. Mrs. Hayes, as first lady, started the traditional White House Easter egg roll, which is held annually to this day. During the White House years, the Hayes family spent their summers at the Soldiers' Home ("Corn Rigs") in Washington, D.C., the same place that had served as a summer home for Presidents Buchanan and Lincoln.

Despite the uncertainty surrounding the manner in which Rutherford Hayes was selected to hold the office, he proved to be a determined and principled president. Among his notable accomplishments were the final withdrawal of troops from occupation duty in the South, and his civil service reforms. In addition, he named his own cabinet, resisted legislative riders, and won the New York Custom House fight. He succeeded in removing a successor as president, Chester A. Arthur, as Collector of Customs. He also resumed specie payments, thus reviving a depressed economy. Under his administration, Native Americans were treated as citizens rather than "aliens" or "wards." He traveled extensively to promote national unity, including, significantly, his Great Western Tour of 1880, which made him the first president to visit the west coast while in office. In all of this, President Hayes followed the maxim: "He serves his party best, who serves his country best."

In spite of President Hayes' belief in the wisdom of his actions, his policies were controversial and cost him some political support in his own party. Nevertheless, Rutherford Hayes received many pleas from Republicans to seek renomination for a second term as president. However, President Hayes stood by his earlier pledge to serve one term only. His decision cleared the way for the nomination and election of President Hayes' successor, James A. Garfield, who became president on March 4, 1881.

President Hayes returned home to Spiegel Grove, where he spent his remaining years as an active private citizen and devoted himself to many worthy causes, including education, prison reform, and veterans' affairs. In addition to participating in public affairs as a speaker and member of various boards, President Hayes also managed to supervise a major expansion of his Spiegel Grove home. In 1880, while still president, Hayes arranged to have a large addition, which mirrored the existing house, placed on the north side of the house, and remodeled the interior. Thus, the house was doubled in size and an eighty-foot veranda joining the new and old wings of the house was added. In 1889, he added a large dining room, a kitchen and several upper chambers. Of the rooms in the original house built for his uncle, Sardis Birchard, only the red parlor and the ancestral room above it survived this renovation without change. A voracious reader, President Hayes also enlarged his library by over 10,000 volumes.

While still in office, President Hayes began the custom of naming trees in Spiegel Grove in honor of prominent guests. When his old regiment gathered at Spiegel Grove on September 14, 1877, the president named five oaks after five of his visitors. These trees became known as the "Reunion Oaks." Some of the names given to trees at Spiegel Grove include: William McKinley, James A. Garfield, and William Tecumseh Sherman.

In 1889, Lucy Hayes died, and President Hayes' remaining few years were lonely. In 1893, the former president became ill in Cleveland while enroute to Fremont. Although urged to remain in Cleveland, he remarked: "I would rather die at Spiegel Grove than to live anywhere else." He continued on his journey, and died quietly at Spiegel Grove on January 17, 1893. President and Mrs. Hayes are both buried in a tomb on the Spiegel Grove property.

Between 1909 and 1914, the president's family, through Colonel Webb C. Hayes, conveyed Spiegel Grove to the state of Ohio (the first 10 acres were deeded to the state on March 30, 1909). The gift was conditioned on the construction of a fireproof library and museum building on the grounds to house the president's papers and effects. Thus, the Hayes library became the first free-standing presidential library. The library is, to this day, open to the public as a research and reference center without cost, although admission is charged for tours of the house and museum visits. In 1928, Congress authorized the donation of several iron gates formerly used at the White House to Spiegel Grove. These were installed at various spots on the perimeter of the grounds.

The Hayes home is large and stately. On guided tours of the interior of the mansion, visitors see many fine antique furnishings and portraits of the president and Mrs. Hayes and other family members. This magnificent estate is unparalleled in beauty and splendor, and must be viewed by anyone who enjoys history, fine architecture and fine furnishings.

JAMES ABRAM GARFIELD

James A. Garfield National Historic Site
("Lawnfield")
8095 Mentor Avenue
Mentor, Ohio 44060
(216) 255-8722

Administered by The Western Reserve Historical Society, which owns the collection on display at the site. The building and grounds are the property of the National Park Service.

Directions: From the east: Take I-90 to the Mentor-Kirtland Route 306 exit. Turn right; take Route 306 for two miles north to Route 20 (Mentor Avenue). Turn right; take Route 20 for two miles east. Lawnfield is on Route 20, on the north side of the road.

From the west: Take I-90 to the Mentor-Kirtland Route 306 exit. Turn left; take Route 306 for two miles north to Route 20 (Mentor Avenue). Turn right; take Route 20 for two miles east. Lawnfield is on Route 20, on the north side of the road.

Open: Tuesday through Sunday. Closed Mondays and major holidays.

Admission: Fee charged.

Features: Home, visitor's center in old carriage house, museum, video presentation.

Special Events: Contact site for information.

The last of the "log cabin" presidents, James A. Garfield, was born in Orange Township (now Moreland Hills), Ohio on November 19,1831. Mr. Garfield's father, an industrious man, had been apprenticed to a farmer but managed to save enough money to buy his own farm in Orange Township. When James Garfield was two years old, his father died, leaving him to be brought up by his mother on the Cuyahoga County farm. He was pampered because he was the youngest and most intelligent child in the family. In 1848, he worked briefly as a muledriver on the canal and later worked as a carpenter in Chester, Ohio. The following year, as the result of his mother's efforts to save money, young James Garfield was sent to Geauga Seminary in Chester. He later became a student at Western Reserve Eclectic Institute (today known as Hiram College) in Hiram, Ohio, and Williams College in Williamstown, Massachusetts. While at Williams, he formed a friendship with the college's president, Mark Hopkins. He also taught penmanship briefly at an academy in North Pownal, Vermont. (This was the same academy at which Garfield's 1880 vice presidential running mate, Chester A. Arthur, was headmaster a few years before Mr. Garfield's stint here.)

The next period of James Garfield's life was eventful. In 1856, he returned to Ohio to teach at Western Reserve Eclectic Institute, and became its president a year later at the age of 26. He also became an ordained minister of the Disciples of Christ denomination, thereby becoming the only minister to serve as president of the United States. He took up the study of law, passed the bar examination and was admitted to the Ohio Bar. He married Lucretia Rudolph, from a well respected family. During this period in his life, Mr. Garfield lived in a two-story white frame house at 6825 Hinsdale Street in Hiram. The house is privately owned today.

In 1859, less than one year after he was married, James A. Garfield became an Ohio state senator. However, the outbreak of the Civil War interrupted Senator Garfield's political career. He entered the service as a lieutenant-colonel, and rose to the rank of major general. Like his fellow Ohio Republican and predecessor as president, Rutherford B. Hayes, Mr. Garfield was also elected to Congress while serving in the military. He served in the House of Representatives for 17 years, staying in furnished rooms in Washington, and later building a three story brick home in Washington, D.C., at Thirteenth and I Streets across from Franklin Square.

In 1876, Representative Garfield purchased a farm with 118 acres of land. He later added an additional 40 acres. The farm house was a dilapidated, one and one-half story structure known as the James Dickey Farm. Garfield set about adding another story and a half to the house to accommodate his wife, five children, and mother.

The following year, Representative Garfield became the house minority leader. In 1880, he was a delegate to the Republican National Convention. The convention was deadlocked for a number of ballots, with no candidate able to muster enough votes for nomination. On the 36th ballot, the convention finally pulled together a majority of delegates behind a candidate: James A. Garfield. Garfield went on to win the election against his Democratic opponent, General Winfield S. Hancock. Throughout the campaign, however, Garfield was dogged by charges that he had accepted a $329 bribe from a railroad construction company. Using his exceptional oratorical skills, he denied the charges and convinced enough voters of his innocence to survive the election.

As president and party leader, one of Mr. Garfield's priorities was to heal the rift between the so-called "Stalwart" and "Half-Breed" factions of his party. He had already taken the first step in this process by running on a ticket with Chester Alan Arthur of New York, who was aligned with the "Stalwart" faction of the Republican Party. The next step was to dispense patronage in a manner that would placate both factions. In this process, a certain number of federal office seekers, who were numerous because of the changes of administration in 1881, were bound to be disappointed. Among them was a man named Charles Guiteau, who very much wanted to become U.S. Consul in Paris. Having been denied the position after two meetings with President Garfield, Mr. Guiteau appeared at the Baldmore and Potomac Station in Washington, where he knew that the president would be on hand to take a train to New England. Mr. Guiteau, armed with a gun, shot President Garfield twice. Reportedly, as he shot the president, the assassin declared, "I am a Stalwart and Arthur is President now!"

President Garfield's life lingered on for over two months after the shooting. He was taken back to the White House. Then in September, he was moved to a large, Queen Anne-style house on the Elberon Hotel grounds in Elberon, New Jersey, in the hope this location would aid his recovery. President Garfield's progress soon reversed due to an infection resulting from dirty hands and instruments used in an attempt to locate the bullet. Due to this infection, President James A. Garfield died in Elberon on September 19, 1881.

The Garfield family returned to the house in Mentor, which had been named "Lawnfield" by a newspaper reporter visiting the house during one of James Garfield's campaign speeches from his front porch in 1880. In 1885, four years after the President's death, Mrs. Garfield added a wing to the house which includes the third floor bedrooms, a laundry room/kitchen and a Memorial Library. The library was built with $400,000.00 worth of private donations sent by a grieving nation to the Garfield family. The Presidential Memorial Library houses President Garfield's book collection.

Lucretia Garfield lived at Lawnfield at various times until her death in 1918. She died while living with her daughter, Mollie Garfield, in Pasadena, California. The house remained the property of the Garfield family until the 1930s, when it was donated to the Western Reserve Historical Society. Lawnfield was opened as a museum in 1936, and on December 28, 1990, it became a National Historic Site.

Today, Lawnfield remains a lovely home and reminds its visitors of a tragic chapter of American history—the death of an American president after only six months in office.

CHESTER ALAN ARTHUR

Chester A. Arthur Historic Site (replica)
North Fairfield, Vermont 05455
(802) 933-8362

Administered by the Vermont Division for Historic Preservation.

Directions: From I-89, take Saint Albans exit. Proceed about 10 miles east on Route 36 to Fairfield. From Fairfield, turn left, proceeding towards Bordoville. The historic site is on the right side of the road.

Open: Memorial Day through Columbus Day, Wednesday through Sunday.

Admission: No fee charged.

Features: Symbolic replica of the home the Arthur family lived in during Chester Arthur's infancy (not exact replica), picnic tables, comfort stations. Handicapped accessibility is possible.

Special Events: None.

Chester Alan Arthur, who spent most of his life in New York State, is generally considered to have been born on October 5, 1829 in North Fairfield, Vermont. However, there is some controversy as to both the exact date and the location of his birth. During the 1880 national campaign, when Chester Arthur was running as the Republican vice presidential candidate, Arthur P. Hinman tried to prove that Mr. Arthur was born outside of the United States, and was therefore ineligible, under the U.S. Constitution, to serve as vice president. The controversy continues due to inconsistent information sources. The Arthur family Bible states that the year of birth is 1829; and the 1850 U.S. Census, completed "as of June 1, 1850," records Chester Arthur's age as 20, meaning that he would have to have been born on or before June 1,1830. However, both an 1880 political biography and President Arthur's tomb indicate that 1830 is the year of birth. Recorded accounts concerning President Arthur's birthplace also conflict. Some sources say that he was born in Waterville, Vermont, and others say that he was born in Dunham, Quebec, Canada. Assuming that President Arthur was born in Fairfield, as is generally considered to be the case, there is even some uncertainty as to where in Fairfield he was actually born. Therefore, it may never be known with absolute certainty where President Arthur was born and whether he was, in fact, constitutionally qualified to hold the office which he held.

It is known that Chester Arthur's father, William Arthur, was an Irish-born Baptist minister who had graduated from Belfast College and came to Vermont by way of Canada. Having been a Presbyterian and, at the time of his marriage, an Episcopalian, Reverend William Arthur was converted to the Baptist faith while attending a revival meeting in Burlington. He moved to the Fairfield area in 1828 with his wife, Malvina Stone Arthur, and four daughters. That year, William Arthur was ordained as a Baptist minister and Fairfield Center was the location of his first church. In 1829, he and his family moved to North Fairfield, and Reverend Arthur became the pastor at the Old Brick Church, which today stands a short distance northwest from the Chester Arthur Historic Site. The Old Brick Church is also open to the public and administered by the Vermont Division for Historic Preservation. It is generally thought that Chester Arthur was born during this period, the fifth child and first son of Reverend and Mrs. Arthur.

The Arthur family later moved to Williston, Vermont, where Reverend Arthur served as an academy principal, and still later to Hinesburg, Vermont. In 1835, when Chester Arthur was less than six years old, the Arthurs left Vermont to live in western New York State. The Arthurs lived briefly in two New York towns—Perry, in Wyoming County, and York, in Livingston County. Later, Chester Arthur studied at the Union Village Academy in Union Village (now Greenwich), a town near Saratoga, New York. While there, the Arthurs lived in a parsonage which is now located at 22 Woodlawn Avenue in Greenwich and is privately owned.

In 1845, Mr. Arthur began his college days at Union College in Schenectady. He lived on campus and, to meet his expenses, taught school at Schaghticoke, New York during his winter vacations. He was elected to Phi Beta Kappa, the honor society, in his senior year. Graduating from Union in 1848, Mr. Arthur traveled to Ballston Spa, New York, for his legal training, and then in 1851, became a principal at an academy in North Pownal, Vermont. (Three years later, the man who later became Mr. Arthur's running mate, James A. Garfield, taught penmanship at the same academy.) In 1852, he traveled to Cohoes, New York, where, as a school principal, he saved enough money to continue his legal studies. He then studied law in Lansingburgh, N.Y. and later used his savings to complete his studies in New York City. In 1854, he was admitted to the New York bar and, a few years later, became a junior partner of a New York City law firm: Culver, Parker and Arthur. While there he took on a case which earned him a reputation as a civil rights advocate: the court held that freed slaves had the right to unimpeded travel through New York State. Chester Arthur entertained the idea of relocating to the Kansas Territory but, after a few months there, returned to New York.

Back in New York, Mr. Arthur became active in Whig politics, and his firm took on many other civil rights cases. He became an active Republican at about the time the party was formed.

On October 29, 1859, Chester Arthur married Ellen Lewis ("Nell") Herndon of Fredericksburg, Virginia. They later had three children and first lived at 34 West 21st Street in New York City, which had been Nell Arthur's home before their marriage. At the outbreak of the Civil War, Mr. Arthur became engineer-in-chief, with the rank of brigadier general, on the staff of Governor Morgan of New York in 1860, and later became acting quartermaster general of the Army in New York City.

In 1861, the Arthurs moved to a two-story family hotel near 22nd Street and Broadway, and spent their summer in Long Branch, New Jersey. While living at the hotel, Mr. Arthur became inspector general for the Army of the Potomac. When Horatio Seymour became the Democratic governor of New York in December 1863, Mr. Arthur lost his position on the Republican governor's staff. He returned to private practice but remained politically active, aligning himself with the so-called "Stalwart" faction of the Republican Party and the New York Republican machine led by U.S. Senator Roscoe Conkling. In 1865, the Arthurs moved to a five-story brownstone row house at 123 Lexington Avenue, where they held musicales and entertained graciously. The flight of stairs leading to the main entrance on the second floor has been removed and today, the structure is a somewhat dilapidated building housing both commercial space (on the ground floor) and residential space (on the upper floors). With the exception of the White House, this was Mr. Arthur's official residence for the rest of his life.

Having been a loyal lieutenant of the Conkling machine, Mr. Arthur was rewarded with political patronage. On November 20, 1871, he was appointed collector of customs for the Port of New York by President Grant. He used that post to dispense further patronage to Republican Stalwarts. Mr. Arthur was removed from that post by President Hayes, who was trying to institute civil service reform, in July 1878, and Mr. Arthur then returned to private practice.

In 1880, Mr. Arthur was a delegate-at-large to the Republican National Convention, where he and other Stalwart forces loyal to Senator Conkling strongly advocated renominating former President Ulysses S. Grant to succeed President Hayes. Delegates supporting James G. Blaine and other anti-Grant delegates mustered enough votes to nominate James A. Garfield for president. After this happened it was clear that a pro-Grant, or "Stalwart," Republican had to be nominated for vice president to ensure support from that faction of the Republican Party for the fall campaign. On that basis, the Convention turned to Senator Conkling's loyal lieutenant: Chester A. Arthur. The triumph of this personal honor for Chester Arthur was counterbalanced by the death of Mrs. Arthur that same year. In the ensuing campaign, Arthur's presence on the ticket, as well as his skilled management of the Conkling machine, was a significant factor in the Republican ticket's victory in 1880.

President Garfield held office until September 19, 1881, when he died 80 days after he was shot by assassin Charles Guiteau. That day, Chester Arthur took the oath of office as president privately in New York City, and was publicly inaugurated in Washington on September 22. As president, Chester Arthur was both conservative and conciliatory, and his cabinet included Robert Todd Lincoln as secretary of war. During his administration, a massive naval improvement program took place, and the U.S. Tariff Commission was established. Ironically, President Arthur, who was such a beneficiary of patronage, is regarded as the father of the federal civil service system. As his biographer, Thomas Reeves, observed, Mr. Arthur's ascent to the presidency had transformed him "from a spoils-hungry, no-holds-barred Conkling henchman into a restrained, dignified Chief Executive."

Unhappy with the condition in which his immediate predecessors had left the White House, President Arthur refused to move there until its renovation and redecoration were complete. Instead, he stayed on the second floor of the residence of Senator John P. Jones of Nevada, located at New Jersey and B Streets in Washington until December 1881. The president auctioned off twenty-four wagonloads of former White House furnishings during this time. The Jones residence, which was one of three stone houses built by General Benjamin F. Butler in 1874, was later demolished to make way for government office buildings.

Once in the White House, President Arthur had art nouveau and Victorian furnishings placed there under the direction of Louis Comfort Tiffany. Afterwards, the president and his sister, who acted as White House hostess while Arthur was in office, entertained lavishly.

In his second year in office, President Arthur learned that he was suffering from Bright's Disease, a potentially fatal inflammation of the kidneys. He was not renominated for president in 1884; the Republican National Convention nominated James G. Blaine as its candidate. On November 18, 1886, almost two years after leaving office, Chester Arthur died of a massive cerebral hemorrhage in New York City. He was buried in the family plot in the Rural Cemetery in Albany, New York.

The house commemorating Chester Arthur is not intended to be an exact replica of the original Arthur home, but is symbolic, because other than an old photograph of the Arthur home, there is no known source which can describe the size and shape of the original house. The replica is unfurnished, and displays pictures relating to President Arthur and his career. The site affords a wonderful view of the mountains, hills and farm land which comprise the pastoral setting where President Arthur once lived.

GROVER CLEVELAND

Grover Cleveland Birthplace
State Historic Site
207 Bloomfield Avenue
Caldwell, New Jersey 07006
(201) 226-1810

Administered by the New Jersey Department of Environmental Protection and Energy, Division of Parks and Forestry.

Directions: From the New Jersey Turnpike, take I-280, exiting at Route 527. Take Route 527 north to Caldwell. Site is at the intersection of Bloomfield and Arlington Avenues, on the north side of Bloomfield Avenue.

Open: Wednesday through Sunday.

Admission: Free.

Features: House, two and one-half acre property, picnic table. Parking is along the street in front of the home. Entrance to the building is gained after travelling along a dirt driveway and path and climbing three steps to a porch and a raised threshold. The entire museum can be viewed from the first floor. Rest room facilities are not provided. The halls and doors are adequate to handle a wheel chair.

Special Events: A local garden club decorates the site at Christmas time.

Grover Cleveland, the only President to serve two non-consecutive terms, was born in Horse Neck (now Caldwell), New Jersey on March 18, 1837. His parents, the Reverend and Mrs. Richard C. Cleveland, lived in the Presbyterian Manse, which served as the parsonage for the minister of the First Presbyterian Society of Horse Neck. Stephen Grover Cleveland, as he was originally named, was named after the Reverend Stephen Grover, the first installed minister of the Society. Rev. Grover had proposed the construction of a church and parsonage in 1793. The church was built while Rev. Grover was minister, but it was not until 1832 that the parsonage was finally completed at a cost of $1,490.00, which was considered a large sum for a house at the time. Two years later, Rev. Cleveland was installed as pastor.

Four years after his son's birth, Rev. Cleveland and his family moved to Fayetteville, New York, where they lived at 109 Academy Street. From there, the Clevelands moved to Clinton, New York, where Rev. Cleveland became the District Secretary of the Central New York Agency of the American Home Missionary Society. Young Grover Cleveland attended school in both Fayetteville and Clinton, but interrupted his formal education at the age of fourteen to help support his family. He became a store clerk for John McVickers, earning one dollar a week.

In 1853, the Cleveland family moved to Holland Patent, New York. Shortly after that, Rev. Cleveland died, and Grover Cleveland decided to join his eldest brother, William Cleveland, who was a teacher at the New York Institution for the Blind. There Grover Cleveland worked as an assistant teacher for a year and sent his small wages home to his mother.

When Grover Cleveland was eighteen, he decided to head west to seek his fortune. On his way, he stopped to visit relatives in Buffalo where his uncle, Lewis F. Allen, had a farm on Grand Island on the Niagara River, and offered him a job helping out there. He decided to accept the offer and live at the farm but before the year was out, Grover Cleveland's uncle had arranged to have his nephew clerk at a Buffalo law firm. There Grover Cleveland studied law while earning five dollars a week.

Grover Cleveland remained in Buffalo from 1855 to 1882. During that time, he first roomed at the old Southern Hotel in downtown Buffalo, then had a suite of rooms in Weed block at Main and Swan Streets. A bachelor throughout this period, he dined at Salem Restaurant, Gerot's French Restaurant, and Tifft House.

Grover Cleveland's legal and political fortunes rose in Buffalo. He was admitted to the bar in 1859. He became chief clerk at his law firm, and used his wages to support his younger brothers and sisters. He became active in the Democratic Party, working for Horatio Seymour's successful New York gubernatorial campaign in 1862. As a reward for his hard work, he was appointed assistant district attorney of Erie County, and held that office throughout the Civil War. In 1865, Mr. Cleveland suffered a setback when he lost his first election, for the office of Erie County District Attorney, to his roommate and Republican opponent, Lyman K. Bass. Five years later, Mr. Cleveland ran for sheriff and won that office and as sheriff, he gained a reputation for honesty, exposing crooked contractors who had delivered short supplies of food and fuel to the county jail. At a hanging of two convicted murders, he sprang the trap himself, explaining that he couldn't ask deputies to do a job just because he didn't want to do it himself. By the end of his term in 1873, Mr. Cleveland had saved enough from his salaries and fees to be out of debt for the first time in his life.

For the following nine years, Grover Cleveland prospered in private practice, and remained active in local politics. In 1881, he ran successfully for Mayor of Buffalo as a reform candidate, and lived up to his campaign image by his veto of many crooked measures sent to him by a corrupt city council.

Western members of the New York Democratic State Committee, who were interested in wresting power from the eastern block of the State Democratic Party, promoted the idea of running Grover Cleveland as the Democratic candidate for governor of New York in 1882. Ironically Mayor Cleveland, who had earned a reputation as a reformer, was nominated with the support of the New York City Tammany machine, but Mayor Cleveland made no promises to Tammany politicians who supported him. Mayor Cleveland's Republican opponent, Charles J. Folger, was President Arthur's secretary of the treasury and known to be the candidate favored by the corrupt millionaire Jay Gould. This brought a number of reform-minded Republicans into the Cleveland camp, and Mr. Cleveland was elected governor by the largest margin of any gubernatorial candidate up to that time.

As Governor, Grover Cleveland resided in the Executive Mansion in Albany (see next section) and, to the chagrin of the Tammany politicians who had backed him, continued to be a reform-minded public official. He refused to sign into law measures he regarded as beneficial to Tammany at the expense of the public, and read every word of every bill before he signed or vetoed it, even if it meant staying up all night to do so.

As Grover Cleveland entered the second year of his term as governor, the presidential election was approaching, and it was clear that the Republican candidate to succeed President Arthur would be James G. Blaine, who, as speaker of the house while Ulysses S. Grant was president, was implicated in the Credit Mobilier scandals. The Democrats realized that they needed a candidate with a reputation for honesty, and Governor Grover Cleveland of New York became the favorite. Despite Tammany's efforts to discredit Governor Cleveland with spurious charges that he was anti-labor, anti-Irish, and anti-Catholic, Grover Cleveland was nominated at the Democratic National Convention on the second ballot. Governor Thomas A. Hendricks of Indiana became the running mate of "Grover the Good."

The ensuing 1884 campaign was one of the most scurrilous in American history. Ten days after the Democratic Convention, a Buffalo newspaper ran a story that Grover Cleveland had fathered an illegitimate son ten years earlier. Governor Cleveland knew that it was possible that the charge was true, and therefore he did not deny it. Governor Cleveland's Democratic partisans, in a move unauthorized by him, charged that James G. Blaine's first son was born only three months after he married his wife. They also aimed charges of corruption at Mr. Blaine. The paternity story gave rise to the chant:

Ma, ma, where's my Pa?
Gone to the White House, ha, ha, ha!

James G. Blaine was the subject of another campaign chant:

Blaine! Blaine! James G. Blaine!
Plum-ed knight from the State of Maine!

and its alternate version (clearly used by the Democrats):

Blaine! Blaine! James G. Blaine!
Continental liar from the State of Maine!

In the end, James G. Blaine was probably undone by the remark of a spokesman for a delegation of Protestant clergymen who came to visit him. The spokesman referred to the Democratic Party as the party of "rum, Romanism and rebellion." Mr. Blaine did not disavow the remark, which Democrats printed and distributed in front of Catholic churches on Sunday. Grover Cleveland narrowly carried New York on Election Day, and with it the election. The national popular vote margin was also narrow: 4,879,507 for Governor Cleveland, 4,850,293 for Mr. Blaine.

Grover Cleveland left Albany for Washington, where he confronted a crowd that didn't really know him but awaited with interest what the first Democrat to occupy the White House in 24 years would say. To them, President Cleveland spoke confidently and without notes in favor of civil service reform and against corruption. President Cleveland carried his reform beliefs into his presidency by vetoing special interest legislation and calling for a reduction in tariffs.

On June 2, 1886, Grover Cleveland became the only president to marry in the White House. The 49 year-old president married 21 year-old Frances Folsum, daughter of one of his former law partners. The Clevelands eventually had five children, and their second daughter, Esther, remains to date the only child of a president born in the White House.

During his first term, President Cleveland spent the summer of 1886 at "Red Top," a twenty-seven acre property located north of Georgetown on Tennalytown Road (now Wisconsin Avenue). The stone house on this property was enlarged in 1886, and called Oak View by Mrs. Cleveland.

Later, the house was demolished. The area is now named Cleveland Park in President Cleveland's honor.

Some of President Cleveland's actions in his first administration cost him political support. For example, the Interstate Commerce Act, passed with Cleveland's approval, represented an attempt to regulate the powerful railroads. He alienated Civil War veterans by vetoing a measure that would have given $12.00 a month to unemployed veterans, calling the measure a fraud and a raid on the public treasury.

Despite these actions, which antagonized many special interests, President Cleveland was renominated by acclamation at the 1888 Democratic Convention. The Republicans nominated Senator Benjamin Harrison of Indiana, a former Civil War general and grandson of President William Henry Harrison. President Cleveland knew that Tammany would oppose him this time, and, without New York, he was a certain loser. True to the president's prediction, he lost New York by 13,000 votes, and subsequently lost the election. By a quirk of the American electoral college system, although President Cleveland polled almost 100,000 more votes than Senator Harrison, Sen. Harrison won the electoral vote by a margin of 233 votes to 168 for President Cleveland. At the end of President Cleveland's term, Frances Cleveland told the White House staff to take good care of the furnishings because they would be back in four years.

The Clevelands moved to New York City, where Grover Cleveland joined a law firm and stayed with his family at the Hotel Victorian. They later moved to 816 Madison Avenue, a red brick town house with an oak paneled interior. The former president rode to work each day on a streetcar. He also bought a small summer home in Buzzards Bay on Cape Cod, Massachusetts. In 1892, the Clevelands moved to 12 West 51st Street. They continued to spend summers on Monument Point in Buzzards Bay in a large two-story cottage they called Grey Gables.

Meanwhile, under President Harrison, the Republican Congress imposed higher tariffs, stepped up on silver coinage, increased veterans' pensions and passed numerous appropriations measures, and thus came to be known as the "Billion-Dollar Congress." All of those actions were publicly opposed by former President Cleveland. The political impact was evident in 1890, as nearly half of the Republicans in the House lost their seats.

The Republicans renominated President Harrison in 1892, and selected Whitelaw Reid, publisher of the New York *Tribune*, as his running mate. The Democrats, despite a concerted effort by Tammany to deny Grover Cleveland the nomination, renominated him on the first ballot. Former Congressman Adlai E. Stevenson of Illinois (grandfather of the 1952 and 1956 Democratic presidential candidate whose son, Adlai Stevenson III, is a former Senator from Illinois) was nominated for vice president. The left-wing Populist Party was a strong third party in the election, so much so that the Democrats did not run electoral slates in several states, and its candidate, James B. Weaver of Iowa, polled over a million votes. Despite this, Grover Cleveland won the election by a surprisingly comfortable margin, and returned to the White House on March 4, 1893.

President Cleveland's second administration was marked by economic crisis. In May, the Panic of 1893 set in. The stock market collapsed, and large companies went bankrupt. The economy continued to plague the nation throughout President Cleveland's second term. During this time, President Cleveland summered at "Woodley," a Georgian style house at 3000 Cathedral Avenue in Washington, which is currently the site of the Maret School. President Cleveland's predecessor and fellow New Yorker, Martin Van Buren, had also summered there while in office.

President Cleveland's conservative economic stance and his support of the gold standard cost him enough political support to remove any possibility of his renomination. Instead, the Democrats nominated William Jennings Bryan, a "free silver" Democrat who electrified the 1896 Democratic convention with his famous "Cross of Gold" speech. In the end, the Republicans prevailed in 1896 with their candidate, William McKinley. President Cleveland, who disliked Mr. Bryan's economic platform, was pleased.

After leaving office, Grover Cleveland settled in Princeton, New Jersey. His home was Westland, at 28 Bayard Lane, now 15 Hodge Road. He bought the home for $30,915.00. It was built by Commodore Robert Field Stockton for his daughter, and is a classic Georgian-style structure with a pillared front porch, palladian windows on the upper level and four squared off chimneys in the center. It was modeled after Morven (which was, until recently, the New Jersey governor's mansion). Mr. Cleveland had the house expanded by adding rooms to the rear of the house. Sometime later, these were separated into another house. Today, the house is privately owned.

Grover Cleveland gained even greater respect in his later years. In 1905, he was asked to serve as one of a board of trustees to reorganize the Equitable Life Assurance Society. He spent that summer at Intermont, near Tamworth, New Hampshire. In 1907, he became head of the Association of Presidents of Life Insurance Companies. By 1908, he was beset with heart and kidney problems as well as gout, and on June 24, 1908, he died in bed at his home in Princeton at the age of 71.

Today, the Grover Cleveland birthplace is a house museum with four rooms on the first floor available for viewing. The tour is conducted by Sharon Farrell, the caretaker for the birthplace home (Sharon and her family use the upper floor as their residence.) She speaks to visitors about the history of the house. It remained a church manse until

1913, when it was opened as a house museum by a private foundation. The site was acquired by the State of New Jersey in 1934.

The first floor rooms are not furnished as they were in Grover Cleveland's time but rather, they are filled with objects and furnishings related to Mr. Cleveland, many of which were donated by members of his family. On a chair in the front parlor rests a cape, made by Frances Folsum Cleveland, who sewed as a hobby. Visitors also see a pastel portrait of Mr. Cleveland and a doll wearing a copy of a dress once worn by Mrs. Cleveland, who scandalized Washington by wearing black to social functions.

Next, visitors see Grover Cleveland's birth room. Here visitors see the Clevelands' cradle, and a quilt made by the president's mother. Rev. Cleveland's shaving stand and mirror, and Mother Cleveland's glasses, are also on display here. Finally, visitors can see the Cleveland family Bible in this room.

The next room is now used as an exhibit room. Here visitors may see the top hat that President Cleveland wore at his second inaugural parade. Also on display here is Mr. Cleveland's smoking pipe collection, which perhaps contributed to the growth of cancer in his upper jaw. Flags used in the Cleveland inaugural parade are on exhibit in this room.

Many items related to President Cleveland's White House wedding are also here. Perhaps the most interesting of these items is the piece of the Cleveland wedding cake saved in a small box covered with handmade lace. Pieces of the cake were distributed to the wedding guests in identical boxes in 1886. Visitors may also see Mrs. Cleveland's bridal wreath, as well as the Clevelands' marriage license and the silver dollar they used to pay for it.

Also in this room are Grover Cleveland's fishing gear and books on fishing, his lifelong hobby. There is also an extensive collection of walking sticks and canes, which were presented to President Cleveland by dignitaries at special events. The room contains both Mr. Cleveland's retirement desk and the desk he used as Mayor of Buffalo. Sheet music of the General March played at President Cleveland's Inaugural and a song about "Baby Ruth" Cleveland is here. (Tragically, Baby Ruth died of diphtheria at the age of twelve and a half.) Finally, Thomas Nast's cartoons of Mr. Cleveland and his 1884 opponent, Mr. Blaine, are on display here.

The tour concludes in the kitchen, which is furnished in a manner evocative of the Clevelands' time here. Overall, a visit to the home provides a fascinating look at the life of a President who, as he said himself in his last words, "tried hard to do right."

The New York State Executive Mansion
138 Eagle Street
Albany, New York 12202
(518) 473-7521

Administered by the New York State Office of General Services.

Directions:	From the Gov. Thomas E. Dewey (New York State) Thruway (I-87), take Exit 23 (Albany) to I-787.	**Admission:**	None.
		Features:	Mansion and grounds.
Open:	By appointment on Thursdays.	**Special Events:**	None.

From the time that Samuel J. Tilden became the first New York governor to occupy the Executive Mansion in 1874, the tie between the occupant of that mansion and national politics has been close. Governor Tilden became the Democratic presidential candidate two years later, and was locked in such a tight contest with Republican former Governor Rutherford B. Hayes of Ohio that it took a special commission to settle the election by determining that Hayes was the winner. Of the 28 successors to Governor Tilden who have lived in the New York Executive Mansion, three went on to become president (Grover Cleveland, Theodore Roosevelt and Franklin Roosevelt), three became vice president (Levi P. Morton, Theodore Roosevelt and Nelson A. Rockefeller), and three were nominated for president but not elected (Charles Evans Hughes, Alfred E. Smith and Thomas E. Dewey).

The story of the mansion begins in the 1850s, when Albany businessman Thomas Olcott decided to build a house on the hill bounded by Eagle and Elm Streets. Shortly after it was built, it was acquired by the Robert L. Johnsons. The Johnsons enlarged the house to the size of a mansion by the 1860s. After Samuel J. Tilden was elected governor in 1874, he rented the Johnson house for approximately $9,000 a year to use as his official residence. There, in 1875, he hosted an impressive reception for his friend William Cullen Bryant, the poet.

Governor Tilden's successor, Governor Lucius Robinson, continued to rent the house on Eagle Street until 1877, when Governor Robinson persuaded the state to purchase it.

By the time Grover Cleveland became governor, some doubts were voiced about the wisdom of the state's action in purchasing the mansion. A Grover Cleveland biographer described it as "not a very imposing house, although there is some attempt at architectural beauty of a rather clumsy sort...." But Governor Cleveland was not particularly affected by these doubts because his occupancy of the mansion only lasted a short time. He was elected governor in 1882, but in November 1884, he was elected president. He was officially notified of his election as president in the same mansion parlor where the Bryant reception took place. On January 6, 1885, Grover Cleveland resigned as governor, and moved to a small house on Willett Street, where he lived until his inauguration as president.

Grover Cleveland's gubernatorial successor, Governor David B. Hill, although a bachelor, thought that the mansion was too small and had it drastically remodeled and expanded. Isaac G. Perry, architect for the state capitol, drew the plans and brought in carpenters, masons and stone cutters from the capitol to work on it. Thus, the original Olcott house design was completely swallowed up and in its place was a morass of balconies, bays, turrets and gables which was later termed "Hudson River helter-skelter" in the *New Yorker* magazine. During this period, Governor Hill stayed at the Hoyt House, next door to the mansion. When the renovation was complete he moved into the expanded mansion, the Hoyt House was razed, and an iron fence was installed around the combined properties.

In 1899, the second New York Governor to become president, Theodore Roosevelt, moved to the mansion. He brought his entire family here from their home at Sagamore Hill, in Oyster Bay, Long Island. Years after their stay in Albany, Roosevelt's daughter, Alice Roosevelt Longworth, recalled the mansion as "a big, ugly, rather shabby house, larger than any house we had heretofore lived in, hideously furnished." Yet the presence of the Roosevelts must have breathed life into the "gloomy abode," for the Roosevelt boys converted the basement into a menagerie of pets, and installed a gymnasium in the top floor hall, where Governor Roosevelt himself refereed boxing matches for his sons and their friends. Their stay here was a brief two years, however, because in 1900 Governor Roosevelt was elected vice president of the United States on the William McKinley ticket, and then moved to Washington.

Years later, in 1915, Governor Charles S. Whitman and his wife began the process of refurbishing the mansion by converting its large veranda into an elegant breakfast room. He also began a tree planting tradition at the mansion by planting a weeping elm in back of the mansion to mark the birth of his son. On April 25, 1958, a sugar maple was planted outside the mansion by President Harry S. Truman and Governor Averell Harriman in observance of Arbor Day. The grove of New York state apple trees on the grounds was planted by Governor Hugh L. Carey, who also began a new tradition on Arbor Day, 1981, by planting a sugar maple in honor of one of his distinguished predecessors, Governor Alfred E. Smith.

When Governor Smith occupied the mansion in the 1920s, its backyard was converted into a zoo containing dogs, donkeys, deer, raccoon, a bear, monkeys and other animals. He also modernized the drawing room but the mansion remained essentially Victorian in appearance, with dark oak woodwork, stained glass windows and a statuette of a dour female in draperies on the newel post.

When Governor Franklin Delano Roosevelt became the next occupant of the mansion, he decided that the mansion should become a gubernatorial museum of sorts. He asked former governors and their families to donate some furnishings or objets d'art used during their stay there. In response, Mrs. Theodore Roosevelt sent an engraving of Christopher Columbus. The daughter of Governor Roswell P. Flower sent a marquetry table, but little else came of this idea. Governor Roosevelt himself, however, converted one of the mansion greenhouses into a swimming pool during his two two-year terms as Governor (1929-32).

On the night of March 23, 1961, while Nelson A. Rockefeller was governor, a flash fire broke out in the mansion, destroying much valuable and irreplaceable art. Resisting pressure to build a new mansion, Governor Rockefeller decided to restore the old one. During his long administration, he made several personal gifts to the mansion and its grounds, including tennis courts. He also decorated the mansion with fine works of modern art by Picasso, Klee, Miro, Nevelson and others.

After Mario Cuomo became Governor in 1983, his wife, Matilda, decided that the mansion should be restored yet again. However, she had no immediate funding source available to her, and Governor Cuomo insisted that no public money be used for the project. Undaunted, Mrs. Cuomo set about organizing the Executive Mansion Preservation Society, which raised more than one million dollars in less than four years. The Society then set about restoring the plumbing and the 65 year-old kitchen. Mark Hampton set to work redecorating the first floor drawing room, the Memorabilia Room, and the formal dining room. New governors have traditionally taken the oath of office by the fireplace in this room. The Memorabilia Room, which is off the foyer, was converted from a governor's office by Mrs. Herbert Lehman, whose husband was governor for ten years and was Governor Franklin Roosevelt's immediate successor in that office. It displays glass and chinaware from previous administrations and it also features antique rose-taffeta and maize-damask fabrics. The formal dining room has a table with 22 side chairs and two arm chairs and dates back to Governor Hill's administration in the 1880s. Presidents Cleveland and Taft, Queens Wilhelmina and Beatrix of the Netherlands, Albert Einstein, Madame Eve Curie, Bob Hope and Hazel Scott have dined here. The dining room is used primarily for official functions. Between the dining room and drawing room is a reception area, featuring Eastlake furnishings from the 1800s. This parlor suite and the dining room table and chairs were in the house when it was acquired.

Upstairs are the redesigned guest rooms. Notable among these is the Princess Suite, so named by Governor Rockefeller for then-Princess Beatrix of the Netherlands. It is used by prominent guests, and was restored by designer Stanley Hura and architect Charles Kaminsh after the 1961 fire. It features a Chinese needlepoint rug, a pair of settees reupholstered in a Schumacher stripe, and walls sheathed in a Schumacher brocade. It also features a fringed sofa and two chairs from Carlyle. Antique pillows on the sofa are from Charlotte Moss. American art on loan from New York museums and private collections is on display throughout the mansion.

Also upstairs is a large room formerly used as a family sitting room, although a few governors have used it for special purposes. For Governor Franklin D. Roosevelt, it was a room used for working on bills and correspondence and holding press conferences. For Governor Rockefeller, it was a trophy and hospitality room used to celebrate outstanding New York athletes and sporting events. Governor Cuomo decided to use the room as a "Family of New York" room, in keeping with a theme of his administration. It featured artworks and representative displays from each of New York's 62 counties on a rotating basis.

The New York Executive Mansion's eclectic look and colorful history, as well as the elegance of its design and grounds today, make it a home rich in history.

BENJAMIN HARRISON

President Benjamin Harrison Home
1230 North Delaware Street
Indianapolis, Indiana 46202
(317) 631-1898

Administered by the President Benjamin Harrison Foundation.

Directions: From southbound I-65, Meridian Street Exit: Proceed east after exiting, cross Meridian Street to Delaware Street, turn left and proceed north on Delaware Street to 1230 North Delaware Street. The site is on your left.

From northbound I-65, Pennsylvania Street exit: turn left onto 11th street, and turn left again onto Delaware. The home is on your left, just beyond the viaduct.

Open: Daily (except the month of January, including New Year's Day, 500 Mile Race Day, Easter Sunday, Thanksgiving Day and Christmas Day). Guided tours begin every 30 minutes.

Admission: Fee charged.

Features: Guided tour of the home (lasting 45 minutes to one hour); bookstore/gift shop, rest rooms. First floor is handicapped

accessible. The third floor (which originally included a ballroom) is now used as a museum of the Harrisons' artifacts and rotating exhibits. The home also offers numerous educational programs for elementary and secondary school students.

Special Events: On July 4th, the home hosts an ice cream social. The lower level of the home can be rented for weddings and receptions. The basement meeting rooms can accommodate up to 70 people.

As a member of a family which had been active in politics for the three generations preceding him, it is hardly surprising that President Benjamin Harrison followed the footsteps of his distinguished ancestors. His great-grandfather, Benjamin Harrison V, was a signer of the Declaration of Independence and a three-term governor of Virginia. President Benjamin Harrison was born at the North Bend, Ohio, home of his grandfather, William Henry Harrison (who served as the ninth president of the United States for one short month) on August 20, 1833. The "Big House," as the birthplace home was called, had sixteen rooms with clapboard siding and had wainscotting on the interior walls. Sadly, the home was destroyed by fire in 1858 while President William Henry Harrison's wife was still living there. Shortly after his birth, Benjamin Harrison's father, John Scott Harrison, an Ohio congressman who was the only man in American history to be both son and father of a president, moved with his family to "The Point," a brick two-story farm house situated on six hundred acres of land in North Bend. This house deteriorated and was razed in 1959, despite attempts by the local chapter of the Daughters of the American Revolution to save it.

It was at The Point that young Benjamin Harrison, along with his brothers and sisters, was educated until he turned 14 and was sent to a private school to prepare for college. Because the family could not afford to send young Benjamin Harrison to one of the prestigious New England colleges they preferred, Benjamin Harrison was sent to Farmers College, in College Hill, Ohio, and later to Miami University in Oxford, Ohio. After graduating in 1852, he lived in the home of a married sister in Cincinnati, paying her $5.00 a week while studying law. On October 20, 1853, he married the former Caroline Lavinia Scott, the daughter of the president of a girl's school in Oxford, Ohio, and the couple moved to The Point, where Benjamin Harrison continued his legal studies. Shortly thereafter, Benjamin Harrison was admitted to the Ohio bar at the age of 21.

In March 1854, Benjamin and Caroline Harrison moved to Indianapolis, Indiana, where they rented the first floor of a two story frame house on North Pennsylvania Avenue for $7.00 a week. Benjamin Harrison got his first job as a crier at the Federal court and became acquainted with town lawyers. Mrs. Harrison, who was expecting her first child, was ill and weak during her pregnancy. On doctor's orders, she stayed with her family for a time, and, during the autumn, of 1854, lived at The Point.

In 1855, after the birth of their first child, the Harrisons moved to a one-story frame house, which had three rooms with an open shed for summer cooking, and cost them $6.00 a month in rent. That same year, an Indianapolis lawyer, William Wallace, brother of Ben-Hur author Lew Wallace, invited Benjamin Harrison into partnership with him. The Harrisons moved again, this time to a two-story house on North New Jersey Street.

At the age of twenty-seven, Benjamin Harrison entered politics and became the Republican candidate for the office of reporter to the Supreme Court of Indiana. This created friction between Benjamin Harrison and his father, a Whig, who refused to visit him during his candidacy. John Scott Harrison and his son reconciled their differences after the elder Harrison left Congress, and the two maintained an affectionate and mutually respectful relationship until John Scott Harrison's death in 1878. An able speaker, Benjamin Harrison won the election handily, and he and his family moved yet again to a two-story frame house on the southeast corner of North and Alabama Streets. None of the homes mentioned above are extant.

In 1862, Benjamin Harrison was offered the command of a regiment of Indiana volunteers, which he was to recruit himself. Second Lieutenant Harrison vigorously pursued this task, organizing the men who comprised his regiment, the 70th Indiana Volunteers, and received a commission as colonel. The regiment saw action in the Civil War, particularly in Atlanta, Georgia in 1864, where "Little Ben" Harrison led several infantry charges against Confederate positions. He also distinguished himself at Nashville, Peachtree Creek, and Kennesaw Mountain. Upon the recommendation of General Hooker, Benjamin Harrison was promoted to brigadier general in March 1865.

After the war ended, Benjamin Harrison resumed his office at the Indiana Supreme Court, to which he had been re-elected while in the service in 1864. He declined re-nomination to this office at the end of his term, and formed a law partnership with a man who later went on to become Indiana's Governor Porter. Because of his oratorical and intellectual skills, his war record, and his political contacts, Benjamin Harrison became one of Indiana's leading legal and political figures.

Benjamin Harrison also took steps to build a grander home for himself and his family. In 1867, he bought two building lots at 1230 North Delaware Street at auction for $4,200.00. Later, in 1872, he made an unsuccessful bid for the Republican nomination for governor, but continued to prosper as a lawyer. In 1874, he commissioned architect Herman T. Brandt to build a grand 16-room brick Italianate home on the North Delaware Street property at a cost of approximately $28,000.00. The design of the home was originally conceived by Benjamin and Caroline Harrison, and construction was completed in 1875. The Harrisons moved into their new home in 1875 with their 20 year-old son, Russell Harrison, and their teenage daughter, Mary Harrison. This was Benjamin Harrison's permanent home until his death in 1901.

In 1876, Benjamin Harrison reluctantly accepted the Republican gubernatorial nomination, losing the election by 5,000 votes out of 434,000 cast to his Democratic opponent, Jimmy "Blue Jeans" Williams, a farmer who resembled Abraham Lincoln and wore overalls at all occasions. Undaunted, Mr. Harrison continued his political involvement by leading the Indiana delegation at the 1880 Republican National Convention. He supported James G. Blaine through thirty ballots, but in the end, shifted to James A. Garfield, thus helping to secure the nomination for Mr. Garfield. Mr. Harrison declined the offer of a Cabinet post in the Garfield administration, and instead became a United States senator from Indiana after the state legislature elected him to that post.

During his term in the Senate from 1881 to 1887, Benjamin Harrison sided with the party leadership on most issues. He favored increases in tariff duties, voted for civil service reform, urged an increase in the size of the U.S. Navy, and opposed President Cleveland's vetoes of pension bills. He served on the Committee for Indian Affairs and supported statehood for the Dakota Territory and veteran's benefits measures passed during his term.

Benjamin Harrison's political career suffered an apparent setback when the voters failed to return him to the Senate in 1886. (By this time, U.S. Senators were elected by popular vote.) However, his political fortunes rebounded in 1888 when the Republican National Convention, meeting in Chicago, deadlocked between John Shemlan of Ohio and Walter Q. Gresham of Indiana. James Blaine, who was in Scotland at the time, cabled: "Take Harrison." Benjamin Harrison won the nomination on the eighth ballot. Levi P. Morton of New York, who later served as governor of that state, became Mr. Harrison's running mate.

Not surprisingly, Benjamin Harrison's campaign against President Grover Cleveland drew public and press comparisons to the presidential campaign of Mr. Harrison's grandfather, William Henry Harrison. The slogan "Tippecanoe and Morton, too" was popular, and the log cabin symbol of the old Harrison campaign was dusted off and used in the 1888 effort. A network of clubs, including the Tippecanoe Club and the Harrison Marching Society, rallied popular support for the Republican candidate. Mr. Harrison himself campaigned from the small porch of his home on Delaware Street, relying on his supporters to spread the word. (The porch was later expanded.) In the end, President Cleveland was the popular vote winner, but Mr. Harrison received 65 more electoral votes than Mr. Cleveland and thus won the presidency.

President Harrison began his term on a cold and rainy day, March 4, 1889. With Republicans finally in control of both houses of Congress, several significant pieces of legislation were enacted, notably the Sherman Antitrust Act, which forbade the formation of trusts, business combinations, conspiracies or monopolies in restraint of trade. The McKinley Tariff Act raised import duties to new highs. Congress also voted for pensions for any Civil War veteran who could not work, regardless of whether the disability was service-related. The Republican Congress paid the price for passage of the McKinley Tariff Act in 1890, when farmers and laborers, angry at merchants who used the tariff increase as a pretext to mark up prices on goods, voted into office a House of Representatives with a majority of 235 Democrats to 88 Republicans.

Significantly, the Harrison administration saw the admission of six new states: Washington, Idaho, Montana, Wyoming, North Dakota and South Dakota. President Harrison proclaimed that the flag be flown over public buildings. At home in the White House, Mrs. Harrison had drawn plans to enlarge the presidential residence, but the bill did not pass in the House. Yet the White House was improved in many respects, including the rebuilding of the engine room, the laying of new floors, the modernization of the kitchens and the expansion of the greenhouse. Most importantly, electric lights and bells were installed. Mrs. Harrison also started the White House china collection and set up the first White House Christmas tree. The Harrisons spent their summers in Cape May, New Jersey while President Harrison was in office.

When President Harrison faced Grover Cleveland for the second time in 1892, voters were still annoyed over high prices brought about by the McKinley Tariff Act and had the Populist Party available as a ballot alternative. Thus, despite a first ballot nomination at the Republican Convention, President Harrison lost the 1892 election to Mr. Cleveland.

In October 1892, a few days before the election, Mrs. Caroline Scott Harrison, who had been elected the first president general of the Daughters of the American Revolution the previous year, died of tuberculosis. President Harrison left the White House as a widower, accepting an invitation to deliver a series of law lectures at Stanford University in 1893-94. He then returned to Indianapolis to practice law.

In 1895, President Harrison had the Delaware Street house completely remodeled, replacing the natural gas lighting of the chandeliers and fireplaces and the old coal-fed gravity furnace heating system with electricity. Prior to this time, household staff lit and extinguished the old gas lights using a special tool. But even after the installation of electricity, the Harrison family was still averse to turning lights on and off, probably because early electrical systems often gave people a shock. Therefore, they retained Ike Hoover, the man who had installed the wiring, to operate the lighting. Mr. Hoover went on to become a White House usher for 42 years. President Harrison also had a complete plumbing system installed and added a large Ionic columned, Colonial Revival porch to the front of the house.

In 1896, President Harrison married for the second time. His second wife was Mary Scott Lord Dimmick, niece of his first wife, Caroline Scott Harrison. The marriage was so opposed by President Harrison's own children, Mary and Russell Harrison, that they refused to attend the ceremony. Nonetheless the marriage took place, and the Harrisons had one child, a daughter, Elizabeth Harrison.

In 1897, the former President wrote a book on American government: *This Country of Ours*. He later acted as counsel for the Venezuelan government in a boundary dispute and argued his case before an international arbitration tribunal.

On March 13, 1901, President Harrison died in his Indianapolis home. His wife and their daughter moved to New York and rented the house as a boarding house. In 1937, the house was sold to the Arthur Jordan Foundation. Restoration work began almost immediately, and much of the original furniture, which had been stored in the third floor ballroom, was returned to its original place. Following a second renovation in 1974, the entire house was opened to the public for the first time.

Today, visitors to the house enter through a door with reproductions of the original 1874 French glass. The glass bears the Harrisons' initials. Visitors then come into the entry hall, and learn that the house is a fine example of Italianate architecture and uses beechwood inlay throughout. The paint color in the front hall is the same as that used in the 1890s, as is the color of the crown molding and medallion. A newspaper of the period states that the original wallpaper was of a dark figured design mixed with gold. Here sits the Harrisons' leather sofa, in its original position, as verified by an 1888 campaign photograph. Visitors also see a hall tree of the period, which was used to store umbrellas, hats and wraps. A tall case clock in the entry hall was made about 1800 by George Waltz of Hagerstown, Maryland. It was probably purchased by Benjamin Harrison during his presidency.

Visitors then see the front parlor, located on the south side of the first floor. This was the formal parlor where important guests were entertained and where significant events, including political meetings and social functions, were held. When President Harrison's daughter, Mary, had her wedding reception here in 1884, the front parlor was elaborately decorated with flowers and the bride and groom greeted the wedding guests under a canopy of greens. Here the windows are adorned with puddle drapes and have their original shutters. The carpet in this room, which belonged to the Harrisons, is the only original carpet in the house today. Pier mirrors are set on marble stands. The vases and humidifier on the mantel were gifts of the Hungarian ambassador to President Harrison and his first wife, Caroline. On the curio cabinet is a Tiffany favrile hand blown glass vase, which was a wedding gift from the president to his second wife, Mary Lord Dimmick Harrison, in 1896. On the wall to the left of the back parlor doors is a seascape painting given by President Harrison to his daughter, Elizabeth, on her first birthday, February 21, 1898.

The parlor is decorated with gold Rococo Revival furniture, including chairs and a settee which, while not original, reflect the decorative style of the period. An original gaslight chandelier hangs here. The high transoms here allow smoke and heat to rise.

In the portals between the front and back parlor, Benjamin Harrison accepted the Republican nomination for president on July 4, 1888.

Next, visitors see the back parlor, which was used in a fashion comparable to today's family room. A view of Peasant Run Parkway in Indianapolis painted by Indiana painter Jacob Cox hangs over a square rosewood grand piano with pearl inlay and ivory keys. While not original to the house, the piano is similar to the one that was once in this room. Caroline Harrison, who taught music before her marriage, was an accomplished pianist who used to play for her Sunday School class at the Harrison's church, the First Presbyterian Church in Indianapolis. An 1889 T.C. Steele oil portrait of Benjamin Harrison commissioned by John Wanamaker (who served in President Harrison's cabinet) hangs over the fireplace. In front of the fireplace is a peacock and floral patterned needlework piece. To the right of the fireplace hangs a landscape painting which was a gift to Mary Lord Harrison. Also on display here is a Regina phone, which plays music in a manner similar to a nickelodeon using changeable copper discs.

Walking toward the west side of the house, visitors next see the library, where the 1888 campaign was planned and many important political meetings took place. This was also the room Benjamin Harrison often used when he worked at home. Because a telegraph line fed firsthand election returns to this room, it was here that Benjamin Harrison learned of his 1888 Electoral College victory. 1888 campaign photographs document the appearance of this room better than any of the other rooms in the house. Here, visitors see a number of family portraits, including portraits of Benjamin Harrison V, a signer of the Declaration of Independence, President William Henry Harrison, John Scott Harrison and Benjamin Harrison. Also here is a portrait of Abraham Lincoln by Jacob Cox. It was hung over President Lincoln's casket when he lay in state at the Old State House Rotunda on April 30, 1865. Visitors also see a large walnut case made especially for Benjamin Harrison by a German cabinetmaker in gratitude for Mr. Harrison's successful defense of the cabinetmaker in a legal matter. A horn chair, made of Texas longhorns and upholstered with Texas bobcat fur, was given to Mr. Harrison on the day of his presidential inauguration by a wealthy Texas rancher named O'Conner. This room contains a fragment of Indiana limestone from the U.S. Capitol. Benjamin Harrison collected walking sticks, which were considered a status symbol of his period. Included in his collection is a "centennial" cane (Benjamin Harrison served in the centennial year of the presidency), which can be seen on the table in the center of the room. On this cane are hand carved faces of presidents from George Washington to Benjamin Harrison. The cane was probably a gift of the New York Centennial celebration. The wallpaper in this room, an oriental influenced design similar to the motif of Mrs. Harrison's desk, which is also in this room, was reproduced using fragments of the original wallpaper found behind the bookcase when the bookcase was restored in 1986. The design matched that shown in an 1888 photograph. The wallpaper colors are metallic gold, green and salmon.

Crossing the back hallway, where visitors see one of the 500 original Indiana Bell telephones still in existence, visitors next come to the dining room, which is decorated with Eastlake furnishings, including the original walnut table and chairs. The carpet in this room is inlaid into the floor. A sideboard and side table, both late Empire pieces dating from the 1840s, are here, as is a bronze statue by the French artist Charpetier, which was probably a gift to President Harrison at the White House. On the side table is a silverplated icewater pitcher given to Caroline Harrison, whose oil portrait hangs over the table, by the Iowa Women's Republican Club. On the sideboard is a silverplate coffee and tea service used by the Harrisons in the White House. A high chair used by Elizabeth Harrison is also in this room. On the second and fifth shelves of a cabinet in this room are china designed and painted by Caroline Harrison, who was especially interested in ceramics and china painting. On the third shelf is the White House china designed by Caroline Harrison, who initiated the concept of the White House China Collection. The 44 stars in its border represent the 44 states admitted to the Union by the end of President Harrison's term, including six admitted while Benjamin Harrison was in office (a record for any president). The design also includes corn (which was chosen by Caroline Harrison because it was, in her words, "a crop indigenous to the North American continent") and goldenrod (a favorite wildflower of President Harrison).

Ascending the stairway to the second floor, one sees the winding rail Elizabeth Harrison liked to slide down as a child and floral, watercolor paintings by Caroline Harrison. In the second floor hall is a portrait of Benjamin Harrison in his Civil War uniform, made from a photograph from the studio of Civil War photographer Mathew Brady. In the northeast corner is the nursery, featuring Benjamin Harrison's cradle, made for him in 1833. It has a crown-top which would have supported mosquito netting, which was useful in the days before houses had window screens. The bed was shipped to Indianapolis by John Scott Harrison so that it could be used by Benjamin Harrison's daughter Mary, who was born in 1858. It was later used by Mary Harrison McKee's daughter, Mary Lodge McKee, who lived in the White House along with her mother while Benjamin Harrison was president. Also in the nursery is a portrait of Mary McKee's older brother Benjamin Harrison (fondly nicknamed

"Baby") McKee, which was painted after his grandfather left the White House. ("Baby" McKee, who was two years old when Benjamin Harrison became president, was a favorite subject of the press, who liked to report his antics with his grandfather.) Also here are floral watercolors by Caroline Harrison and one of President Harrison's favorite rocking chairs. The nursery, which has a closet, was originally Mary Harrison's dressing room.

Adjacent to the nursery is the front bedroom, which was Mary Harrison's bedroom when she was a teenager. It features a half tester (2 poster) bed with a large headboard. It may have had decorative draperies hanging from its top to the floor at one time. Several items which belonged to William Henry Harrison are also here, including a cradle, bookcase, bootjack and walking stick. Over the cradle hangs a portrait of Anna Symmes Harrison, wife of William Henry Harrison. Also here are hand-colored Currier lithographs of William Henry Harrison, including one to the left of the dresser which shows him dying in the White House after his one month in office. On the mantel is an ostrich plume fan, which was a Christmas gift to Caroline Harrison at the White House from Ida Honore Grant, daughter-in-law of General Ulysses S. Grant. President Harrison appointed General Grant's son (Ida Grant's husband), Frederick Dent Grant, as a representative of the United States to the Court of Vienna.

Just west of the front bedroom is the upstairs sitting room, which was used as a private parlor and connects with the master bedroom. It features a walnut bombe desk with inlaid floral design from Nuremburg, Germany, a large floor vase made by Rookwood Pottery of Cincinnati, a late nineteenth century Swiss music box, and upholstered pieces of Eastlake furniture once used by the Harrisons in the front parlor (according to a 1902 photograph). Visitors see a large portrait of Caroline Scott Harrison which was commissioned by the National Society of the Daughters of the American Revolution, of which Caroline Harrison was the first president general.

The next room is the master bedroom, which contains the bed in which President Harrison died on March 4, 1901 at the age of 67. Elizabeth Harrison, daughter of the President and Mary Lord Harrison, was born in this room. On the table in the alcove and beside the fireplace are photographs of Elizabeth Harrison and her father. Above the fireplace is an oval framed portrait of President Harrison's first two children, Mary and Russell Harrison. The bedroom suite is made of rosewood and satinwood in the Renaissance Revival style. On the headboard is a carving of Cleopatra's head, and many other carvings adorn this splendid furnishing. Also here is a "Whitney Home Gymnasium," patented in 1882 and used by the President for exercise both here and in the White House. A Caroline Harrison water color seascape depicting Cape May Point, New Jersey, a favorite Harrison vacation spot, hangs on the wall here. On the dresser is Caroline Harrison's sterling silver vanity. Behind the bed is a door that originally led to a dressing room, thus making that room, the bedroom and the sitting room a three-room master suite. According to Mary Lord Harrison, the dressing room was later used as a bathroom.

Moving across the hallway, visitors see watercolors by Caroline Harrison and by Mrs. W.H. Harrison Miller, wife of Benjamin Harrison's law partner. Visitors then come to the side room, which is set up as a law office. This room was originally Russell Harrison's bedroom, and later became Elizabeth Harrison's nursery and bedroom. The room now contains furnishings from Benjamin Harrison's law office, which was on Market Street in downtown Indianapolis. The desk, made by the John Moore Company of Indianapolis, is a patented folding desk, which opens up in the manner of a Wooten desk. Over the desk is a photograph of the Harrison law office taken for the 1888 campaign. There are two filing cabinets: a large one for rolled documents and a small one for flat paper filing. In the small filing cabinet, in a drawer marked "K," is a letter written by Helen Keller to Caroline Harrison in October 1892, the month Caroline Harrison died in the White House. Mr. Harrison's military tactics books are here, as well as the Mathew Brady photograph from which the portrait in the hall was copied. Over the filing drawers is another photograph. This photo depicts President Harrison with his cabinet. On the far right of the photograph is William Henry Harrison Miller (not related to the Harrisons), who was Benjamin Harrison's law partner and attorney general in the Harrison administration. Mr. Miller is also depicted in the T.C. Steele portrait over the desk. Also here is a charcoal drawing of the "Big House," where Benjamin Harrison was born, as well as a model for the Charles Niehaus bronze statue of Benjamin Harrison which now stands facing New York Street in University Park, Indianapolis.

Upstairs on the third floor, a ballroom originally extended from the front to the back stairs. Today, the third floor is largely used as a museum. Here one sees President Harrison's "one horse open sleigh" used at his Adirondack Mountain hunting lodge. To the left of the front stairs are Harrison-Morton 1888 campaign posters. Also in the museum are campaign medals donated by New York city attorney Benjamin Harrison Walker, grandson of Benjamin Harrison, and handpainted campaign posters from William Henry Harrison's 1840 presidential campaign. The museum also has a statue made of dimes, which was done to honor President Harrison for his handling of the Chilean Incident of 1891. The incident, which began as a saloon brawl, escalated into an international conflict and could have led to war had President Harrison not intervened. A diorama in the museum depicts the Battle of Resaca, a major battle in the Confederate Georgia campaign during the Civil War. A large exhibit case to the right of the diorama contains Civil War artifacts, including Benjamin Harrison's sword, cup and Bible; a drum used by Benjamin Harrison's regiment during the Civil War, authentic Union uniforms and a reproduction of a Confederate uniform.

Downstairs on the first floor is the kitchen, complete with a wood burning stove, pie safe, ice box, Hoosier cupboard and a dry sink with a hand pump. None of these items are original, although they do reflect the appearance of many kitchens of the late nineteenth century. The kitchen was also the servants' dining room and was occasionally used by small children of the Harrison family. Reflecting that fact, "Baby" McKee's signed Thonet Bentwood high chair is here, as well as a silver tray engraved with his name and birthdate. Hanging on the kitchen wall is the Harrisons' grocery bill from Cape May, New Jersey, dated 1891. Caroline Harrison's bundt pan and cookie cutters are also in the kitchen.

Next to the kitchen is a room which was once the butler's pantry, but is now a gift shop. Servants took food through this room to the dining room. In addition to a butler and other servants who lived in the house, the Harrisons hired staff as needed, including a seamstress named Josephine, a pastry chef and a laundress. Besides the conversion of the pantry into a gift shop, another part of the house is now used for a modern purpose; the original dirt floor cellar of the house has been replaced by a series of community meeting rooms.

For its architectural and decorative splendor as well as its historical significance, the Harrison home offers its visitors a fascinating exhibit of a man who continued the public-spirited tradition of his distinguished family.

WILLIAM MCKINLEY

The Saxton House
331 Market Avenue South
Canton, Ohio 44702-2107
(330) 454-3426

Owned by the National Park Service. Occupied and managed by the Stark County Foundation.

Directions: From Cleveland, take I-77 south for 58 miles. Take exit for U.S. 62 east. Take Market Avenue exit and proceed south into downtown Canton. Pass Tuscarawas Street. Site is three blocks south on the right side, at the intersection of Market Street and 4th.

Features: This site was renovated by the Stark County Foundation which uses the site for office space. The third floor conference room is available to the public for meetings.

Special Events: Open house in May.

President William McKinley is the only president for whom there is not a single extant private residence, other than the White House, that he once called home. He was born in Niles, Ohio on January 29, 1843. He was the seventh in a family of nine children born to his parents, William and Nancy, who were of Scots-Irish ancestry. His father owned an iron making business and his mother was active in the local Methodist church.

The house in which he was born was a two-story colonial style structure with lap siding. The McKinleys remained in Niles, where young William attended school across the street from his home until he was nine and the family moved to Poland, Ohio. The subsequent history of the birthplace is tragic. By 1875, the building was owned by J. Benedict and part of the building was used as a grocery store. By 1893, the City National Bank had been built on part of the site, and the birthplace had been moved to the back of the lot, on Franklin Alley, where it was used as an undertaker's storage space. After William McKinley's election as president in 1896, an effort was made to preserve the birthplace. The house was divided in half, and the half in which William McKinley was born was moved to Riverside Park, a resort in Evansville, Ohio. Riverside Park proved to be unprofitable, and closed in 1901. The house was occupied by tenants until 1908, when it was vacated and vandals and souvenir hunters severely damaged the abandoned building. In 1909, Lula Mackey, an attorney and admirer of President McKinley, purchased the dilapidated structure, along with the other half of the house, which remained in Franklin Alley and was also in poor condition. She moved both halves to her 200 acre estate at Tibbets Corners. The two halves were joined there and completely restored and given the name "McKinley Heights" by Mackey. The house was then filled with McKinley relics and pictures, and for years it attracted many visitors. Its operator, Lula Mackey Weiss, died in 1934. Three years later, a tragic fire, probably set by prowlers, struck the restored birthplace, and destroyed it. Most of the relics and pictures were salvaged, but the structure burned to the ground. Today, the McKinley Savings and Loan Association stands on the original birthplace site and across the street, on a site including the spot where the little white schoolhouse that William McKinley attended once stood, is the McKinley National Birthplace Memorial. The site of the memorial was provided by the City of Niles.

The McKinley family moved to Poland, Ohio in 1852 to take advantage of the better educational opportunities. There young William attended the Poland Seminary. The family lived in a brick house, and later a frame house on Main Street. Neither house stands today.

In 1860, William McKinley entered Allegheny College in Meadville, Pennsylvania, but left college that same year because of poor health. He returned to Poland and taught at the nearby Kerr District School. In 1861, after the school closed, he became an assistant postmaster in Poland. He was working at the post office when the Civil War broke out. Like his great-grandfather, who fought in the Revolu-

tionary War, and his grandfather, who fought in the War of 1812, William McKinley enlisted as a private in the service on June 11, 1861. He served in the 23rd Ohio Volunteer Infantry, which was also the regiment of Lieutenant Colonel Rutherford B. Hayes (who became a major general by the end of the war). In April 1862, nineteen-year old William McKinley became a commissary (mess) sergeant. His display of bravery at Antietam led to a battlefield commission as second lieutenant in September 1862, and he became brigade quartermaster on Major Hayes' staff. He was promoted to First Lieutenant in February 1863, and then to Captain on July 25, 1864. He was transferred to the staff of Generals George Crook and Winfield Scott Hancock. In March 1865, he was promoted to brevet major.

When the war ended, Major McKinley, only twenty-two years old, declined an offer to remain in the army, and decided to study law. He spent a year at the law office of Charles E. Glidden in Youngstown, Ohio, where he roomed with George F. Arrel at 36 Joy Street. In 1866, he enrolled in Albany Law School, in New York State. In March 1867, William McKinley was admitted to the Ohio Bar.

William McKinley decided to practice law in Canton, where his elder sister, Anna, was teaching school. They shared a small frame house on the corner of Shorb and Tuscarawas Streets in Canton. Mr. McKinley lost no time entering the political fray. His oratorical skills won him rapid support by local Republican politicians, and he was nominated for Stark County prosecuting attorney in 1869. He entered the race as a decided underdog, but campaigned vigorously for the job and won, bucking the normal Democratic tide in county elections. After a two-year term in that post, the Democratic opposition marshalled its forces and managed to deny Mr. McKinley re-election by a margin of forty-five votes.

While still in the prosecuting attorney's office, William McKinley married Ida Saxton, daughter of James Saxton, a Canton banker, on January 25, 1871. Ida's grandfather, John, was founder of the town newspaper, *The Canton Repository*. It was a marriage marred by tragedy, for the McKinleys' daughter, Katie, died at the age of three and a half, and their second daughter, Ida, did not quite live to be five months old. Ida McKinley became a lifelong invalid, but her husband never wavered in his devotion to her. The degree of his attentiveness to his ailing wife won him the sympathy and respect of the electorate throughout his political career.

After their wedding, the McKinleys lived in the St. Cloud Hotel in Canton. This hotel no longer exists. Shortly thereafter, Mr. McKinley's father presented the newlyweds with a home of their own on the corner of Eighth Street and Market Avenue North in Canton. This was their home for the next seven years, until Mr. McKinley, running for Congress in 1876 with his old commanding officer, Rutherford B. Hayes, at the top of the ticket, was elected. The McKinleys sold the house and lodged at Ebbitt House in Washington, D.C., beginning in 1877. When Congress was not in session, the McKinleys stayed with Mrs. McKinley's parents at Saxton House, where the McKinleys had held their wedding reception. Later, William McKinley established a law office at the Saxton House. The law office remained in the home for over twenty years. In the course of his political career, Mr. McKinley used the Saxton House as a retreat from the hassles of public life. Seated at the roll top desk in his third floor law office, William McKinley drafted speeches and legislation and planned campaigns for public office. The office was also a place where Mr. McKinley and his aides discussed policy and politics.

William McKinley served in Congress for 14 years, where he championed the cause of protective tariffs. He did much of his work on tariff legislation in his law office at the Saxton House. He sponsored the McKinley Tariff Act of 1890, which raised tariffs to new highs, and consequently sent retail prices soaring. This legislation was probably the single most important factor leading to the political undoing of Representative McKinley and other House Republicans, who were voted out of office in what proved to be a disastrous election for Congressional Republicans in 1890.

William McKinley's political fortunes rebounded when, in 1891, he was nominated for governor of Ohio. He campaigned even more vigorously for this office than he had for prosecuting attorney, making several speeches each day and appearing in almost all of Ohio's 88 counties. In the end, he won narrowly, and after his first two-year term, was re-elected by a comfortable margin. While in Columbus, he resided at the Chittenden Hotel and, after it burned, lived in the Neill House across from the State Capitol. Governor McKinley fell on financial hard times in the wake of the Panic of 1893. He lost $20,000.00 and was left with $100,000.00 in debts. However, his wealthy friends set up a fund to retire his debts and to pay him back the $20,000.00 he had lost. Gov. McKinley's devotion to his wife became legendary during this period. At precisely 3:00 p.m. each day, he interrupted whatever he was doing and waved his handkerchief at the window to his wife, who was in a hotel suite across the street. Every morning after leaving the hotel, he paused outside, removed his hat, and bowed to his wife's window before proceeding to his office.

In 1892, Governor McKinley had received significant support from Republican National Convention delegates. In 1896, Gov. McKinley's industrialist friends, led by Cleveland millionaire Mark Hanna, were determined to secure the Republican presidential nomination for the governor. These friends financed a seventeen-state tour for Governor McKinley, who made almost 400 speeches in eight weeks. By the time the Republican Convention met in St. Louis in June 1896, Gov. McKinley's support was strong enough to secure his first ballot nomination. The convention also nominated Garret A. Hobart of New Jersey for vice president.

After the Democrats nominated William Jennings Bryan, a passionate advocate of free silver coinage, the central campaign issue became clear. McKinley abandoned his old position in favor of silver coinage and campaigned for retention of the gold standard and a "sound money" policy.

This position endeared him to President Cleveland and other "gold" Democrats. Mark Hanna and other McKinley supporters amassed a campaign war chest of over $3 million, the largest campaign fund in American history up to that time, and won converts who were frightened by the possible economic consequences of a Bryan victory. In November, McKinley received 7,102,246 votes to 6,492,559 popular votes for Mr. Bryan and was elected president with 271 electoral votes, while Mr. Bryan received 176 electoral votes.

In 1896, Mr. McKinley leased his old Market Avenue home and celebrated his silver wedding anniversary there. He used the house for his presidential campaign, making his "front porch" speeches there. Later, in 1899, he repurchased the house for $14,500.00, planning to retire there. He made $3,000.00 in improvements to the house, including an octagonal gazebo. During this period, he also owned a farm in Columbiana County on what is now U.S. 30 near the Stark-Columbiana County line. Many years later, these farm buildings were used as a Western Frontier Museum owned by Robert Lozier. The McKinley farm remains privately owned today.

As for the McKinley home on Market Avenue, it was used as a hospital from 1908-1910, and later as a nursing home. The home was moved in 1930. Eventually it was dismantled, piece by piece, and the pieces were stored, with the idea of rebuilding the house. However, the parts became so badly weathered and vandalized that reconstruction became impossible. Mercy Hospital stood on the McKinley home site for a time. Today, the hospital is known as Timken-Mercy Medical Center and is in an entirely new location.

Once in the White House, President McKinley did his friend Mark Hanna the political favor of naming Senator John Sherman of Ohio his secretary of state. This created a vacancy in the Senate which was filled by Mr. Hanna. Predictably, these political machinations drew sharp criticism.

As president, McKinley proved skillful in dealing with Congress, which passed the higher tariffs he requested. Economic recovery followed. President McKinley also presided over the Spanish-American War, which lasted for four months in 1898. Irrespective of whether the rationale for the war was sound, the United States was militarily successful in defeating Spanish forces in Cuba, Puerto Rico and the Philippines. In July 1898, President McKinley also signed a Congressional resolution approving the annexation of Hawaii. He promoted his "sound money" policies and secured passage of the Gold Standard Act in 1900. He also sent U.S. Marines to China to join with troops from seven other countries in putting down the Boxer Rebellion, which was fomented by a secret revolutionary society. This effort was also militarily successful.

President McKinley was unanimously renominated at the 1900 Republican convention, and he took Governor Theodore Roosevelt of New York as his running mate. (Vice President Garrett Hobart died in 1899.) The Democrats again chose Mr. Bryan as their candidate, and named Adlai E. Stevenson, who had been vice president in the second Cleveland administration, as Mr. Bryan's running mate. While the Democrats scrambled for new issues to add to their free silver and tariff concerns, President McKinley, confident of victory, spent most of the campaign at home in Canton. The president's confidence proved justified; he was re-elected by a wide margin.

President McKinley's second term began quietly. In late April 1901, he left Washington for what was to be a six-week transcontinental tour. However, his wife became ill, and although she recovered, he decided to spend the rest of the summer in Canton. He left from there to deliver a promised speech at the Pan-American Exposition in Buffalo on September 5. On the following day, President McKinley was at the Exposition's Temple of Music shaking hands with a long line of people waiting to greet him, when a man approached whose hand was wrapped with a handkerchief. He fired two shots at President McKinley with a pistol concealed under the handkerchief. As he was helped to a chair, he expressed two concerns: that his wife not be told, and that his assassin not be harmed. President McKinley, who was taken to a private home in Buffalo, died there on the morning of September 14, 1901, eight days after the fatal shots were fired. The assassin, Leon F. Czolgogz, was a neurotic anarchist who said that he wanted to kill a "ruler." He was convicted of murder and later executed by means of the electric chair.

The nation observed five days of mourning. After ceremonies in Buffalo and Washington, President McKinley's body was taken back to Canton, where thousands of people filed past his casket. The McKinley National Memorial was built in Canton, and it is here that President McKinley, his wife and two children were interred in 1907. The structure cost $500,000.00 to build, and the money was raised by more than a million school children from around the world.

Mrs. McKinley, who continued to live at the house on North Market Street, died on May 26, 1907, a few short months before the McKinley National Memorial was dedicated.

Today, the Saxton House is owned by the National Park Service, which leases the building to the Stark County Foundation, a local civic and cultural organization which uses a portion of the building for office space. As befits the ancestral home of a first lady, a first ladies' library is being planned for the building. The precise age of the house is unknown, however, speculation is that the house could have been built around or before the marriage of Ida McKinley's parents in 1846. It is a three-story structure, whose six chimneys were rebuilt. It features a large wraparound porch; a black walnut, spiral staircase leading from the reception hall to the third-floor ballroom; and original mahogany doors, baseboards and moldings. It has twelve open fireplaces and its basement features attractive stone and brickwork, heavy timber lintels, and archways. Today, this beautiful building stands as the only surviving private residence linked to the slain president, whose administration ushered America into the twentieth century and a new era of American involvement in world affairs as a global power.

THEODORE ROOSEVELT

Theodore Roosevelt Birthplace
National Historic Site (reconstructed)
28 East 20th Street
New York, New York 10003
(212) 260-1616

Administered by the National Park Service.

Directions: By subway: Take the IRT to 23rd Street or BMT to 14th Street.

Open: Wednesday through Sunday, except holidays.

Admission: Fee charged.

Features: A thirty-minute tour of the house museum, which includes two rooms of Theodore Roosevelt exhibits and a series of period rooms. Rest rooms. Not handicapped accessible.

Special Events: The site hosts a concert series; contact site for details.

In 1854, a wealthy businessman named Theodore Roosevelt, Sr. and his bride, Martha Bulloch of Georgia, moved into a brownstone house at 28 East 20th Street purchased by his father, Cornelius Roosevelt, as a wedding gift. Built in 1848, the house, a three-story structure, was entered by a Dutch "stoop" over an "English" kitchen basement. (In 1865, a fourth floor was added.) Cornelius Roosevelt had also purchased and presented to his other son, Robert, the house next door at 26 East 20th Street as a wedding gift to him and his bride. About four years later, on October 27, 1858, at the home of Theodore and Martha ("Mittie") Roosevelt, their second child, a son, Theodore Roosevelt, Jr., was born.

Young "Teedie," as he was called, began his life in a manner utterly different from the image he cultivated later in life. He was a pale, thin and frail child who was given to asthmatic coughing fits. In an effort to clear his son's lungs, Theodore Roosevelt, Sr. would sometimes exhale cigar smoke into his son's nose and mouth (in an era where people were unaware of the potential dangers of this practice). Theodore, Sr. also tried picking Teedie up and running down the hallway, taking him on midnight carriage rides, and making him drink strong coffee. Aside from his poor health, young Teedie had all of the advantages that a young boy in a prosperous family could have; at the age of ten he took a one-year trip to Europe with his family, had private tutors and received whatever books or presents he wished. He had an older sister, Anna (called "Bamie"); a younger brother, Elliott; and a younger sister, Corinne. His Aunt Anna Bulloch also lived in the house before her marriage, and acted as tutor and governess for her nieces and nephews. Grandmother Bulloch also came to live with the family until her death in 1864. Teedie grew up with plenty of playmates, including not only his brother and sisters but also his cousins, who lived next door. To allow the children to play outdoors without leaving the house, Theodore, Sr. had the bedroom behind the nursery converted into an open air porch.

As a young boy, Teedie was an avid reader. He began a lifelong practice of keeping a journal. Teedie also developed a strong interest in natural history and in other living creatures, including birds, insects and animal life. In his autobiography, he tells of the time that he passed a market and spotted a dead seal on a slab of wood. He managed to acquire the seal's skull, the first item in the collection that he and two of his cousins called the "Roosevelt Museum of Natural History." Years later, in 1869, while Roosevelt was still collecting specimens, Theodore Roosevelt, Sr. became a founder of the American Museum of Natural History, and its charter was signed in the Roosevelt house. In 1871, young Theodore Roosevelt donated some of his specimens, including a bat, a turtle, a red squirrel skull, twelve mice and four bird eggs to the museum. At the age of thirteen, Teedie took taxidermy lessons from a man who lived nearby.

It was also around this time in his life that Teedie took a stagecoach to Maine and was teased mercilessly by four other boys. Teedie was so puny that he could not fight his tormentors. Worried about his son's frailty, Theodore Roosevelt, Sr. encouraged Teedie to exercise and build up his body. Teedie acted on his father's advice quickly, at first going to a local gymnasium to lift weights, work out on the parallel bars and punch a punching bag. Later, Teedie's father installed a gymnasium on the third floor porch of the house for Teedie's use. Never again did Theodore Roosevelt live in a house that did not have fitness equipment.

At thirteen, Teedie discovered something else about himself. His father gave him a gun, but he was unable to hit the bull's-eye. His parents soon learned that their son was nearsighted and needed glasses. With the glasses, he was able to shoot better and to add other specimens to his collection. His family traveled to Europe and to Egypt that year, and Teedie and his father spent hours shooting birds along the Nile River. At night, Teedie stuffed and mounted the birds he captured.

After leaving Egypt, the family stayed in Dresden, Germany, where Teedie, his brother, and younger sister stayed with a family and learned German. Mrs. Roosevelt and Bamie traveled, while Theodore Roosevelt, Sr. returned to America to conduct business and to prepare a new home for his family.

The Roosevelts left their first home due to the changing character of the neighborhood. The once quiet and fashionable neighborhood, which was close to the Academy of Music, the Fifth Avenue Hotel and the Union League Club, gave way to increasing commercialism, in the form of Lord & Taylor, which was half a block away on Broadway, followed shortly thereafter by Tiffany's, Arthur Constable, and other large stores. These carriage trade establishments drew crowds and traffic, to the extent that the Roosevelts were no longer comfortable there. When the family returned to New York, they moved to a larger home on 6 West Fifty-Seventh Street, near the new Central Park. The Roosevelts thought that the proximity to the park would help alleviate Teedie's health problems. The family also spent summers at "Tranquility," a summer house in Oyster Bay, Long Island, located about two miles southwest of the site that later became Sagamore Hill.

Young Theodore attended Harvard College, where he pursued his studies, including many natural science courses, vigorously. He pursued lightweight boxing at Harvard without much success because of his nearsightedness. However, he was an excellent student and was elected to Phi Beta Kappa on his scholastic achievements. After graduating from Harvard in 1880, he took a hunting trip in Iowa and Minnesota with his brother, Elliott, and then returned to Boston to marry his college sweetheart, Alice Hathaway Lee, the nineteen-year old daughter of a prominent Boston family. In the winter of 1880-81, Theodore Roosevelt attended Columbia Law School, but soon learned that legal studies bored him. He decided to take his new wife on a trip to Europe, and was able to do so because he had come into his inheritance due to the death of Theodore Roosevelt, Sr. three years earlier. While in Europe, he collected material for his first book and climbed the Matterhorn in Switzerland.

Returning to New York in the autumn of 1881, Mr. Roosevelt almost immediately plunged into the political fray. He joined a local Republican club that met over a saloon. A faction of the club convinced him to seek the nomination for New York State Assembly. Theodore Roosevelt became the Republican nominee on October 28, 1881, and twelve days later, was elected. He made a name for himself as a fearless independent legislator, calling for an investigation of corrupt railroad magnate Jay Gould and a state supreme court justice. He bucked the Democratic tide by winning re-election in 1883, the year that Grover Cleveland, running for governor, led a Democratic ticket that swept many of Mr. Roosevelt's fellow Republican legislators out of office. In his second term in Albany, Theodore Roosevelt made an unsuccessful bid for speaker of the New York State Assembly (the Republicans were in the minority in the State Assembly that year). He also opposed two pieces of labor legislation: a bill to reduce the working day of streetcar employees to twelve hours, and another bill to increase the salary of New York City firemen to $1,200.00 a year.

On February 14, 1884, Theodore Roosevelt's wife, Alice, died of Bright's Disease following the birth of their child. Mr. Roosevelt's mother died of typhoid fever eleven hours earlier that same day. Theodore Roosevelt, grief-stricken at his double loss, tried to console himself by working harder than ever. He finished his term as a legislator, went to the Republican National Convention, and campaigned for its presidential nominee, James G. Blaine, despite having opposed his nomination. After the Republicans lost the election, Mr. Roosevelt, determined to make a new life for himself, tried his hand at cattle ranching at the Maltese Cross Ranch in Medora, a town in the Dakota Territory.

Although the Roosevelt family left their house at 28 East 20th Street in 1873 to travel, and did not return to live there, the ownership of the house remained with the Roosevelt family until 1896. In that year it was sold and was taken over for commercial purposes and given a bow-shaped cast iron shop front. Twenty years later, in 1916, a developer purchased the house and demolished it to make way for a small commercial building.

In 1919, Theodore Roosevelt died, and the Women's Roosevelt Memorial Association was formed. The Association decided that the reconstruction and furnishing of President Roosevelt's birthplace would be a fitting memorial to him. They set about raising funds, and in time, acquired both the birthplace site and the Robert Roosevelt home next door. In 1920, the Association cleared the birthplace site and razed the Robert Roosevelt house to make room for a reference library, museum galleries and offices. The project designer, Mrs. Theodate Pope Riddle, was an eccentric with the dubious distinction of having been on board the *Lusitania* during its sinking and surviving. Her design of the birth-

place reconstruction was based in part on the appearance and measurements of the Robert Roosevelt home (which was identical to the birthplace) before its destruction. Unable to find photographs or written descriptions of the house, Mrs. Riddle turned to Mr. Roosevelt's sisters, Bamie (Mrs. Sheffield Cowles, Sr.) and Corinne (Mrs. Douglas Robinson), as well as the president's second wife, Edith (who was a frequent visitor to the house as a child) for their recollections and advice. Their memory of the house, down to wallpaper patterns and furniture placement, was detailed, and the interior was restored accordingly. Mrs. Riddle and the Association managed to assemble about 40 percent of the home's original furnishings.

The other furnishings either belonged to other branches of the family or were donated. The result was a carefully designed, close approximation of the original house as it stood in 1865, the year renowned interior decorator and cabinetmaker Leon Marcotte refurbished the house. The reconstructed birthplace was opened to the public on October 27, 1923, the sixty-fifth anniversary of Theodore Roosevelt's birth.

Over the ensuing years, however, the careful restoration of the house was marred by improper substitutes for wallpaper, drapes and upholstery, furniture shifts, nicks and scratches in furnishings, lack of maintenance, and damage caused by numerous receptions and special events held in the house over the course of the next three decades.

In 1963, the site was acquired by the National Park Service, along with the Roosevelt home at Sagamore Hill, but it was not until 1976 that the birthplace replica and its contents were subjected to a systematic survey, and restoration got underway. Using photographs of the 1923 restoration; carpet samples tucked away in a small closet for fifty years; and the services of the Birge Paper Company of Buffalo, which had made the wallpaper used in the 1923 restoration, the restoration effort was effective. The Park Service engaged a small New York City firm to silk screen the wallpaper for the parlor (Birge, which could no longer print paper by hand, could not reproduce the twenty-three color block-printed paper it had made in 1923). The Park Service's Historical Center analyzed paint samples to determine correct colors and was responsible for repairing or replacing broken or missing hardware. The furnishings were cleaned, polished and reupholstered. The overall result is a house with period rooms which resemble as closely as possible those in the original house in Theodore Roosevelt's early days.

Today, visitors begin their tour in the museum rooms. Here visitors see a partnership desk used by Theodore Roosevelt while serving as Assistant Secretary of the Navy in 1898. This room also contains a saddle given to Theodore Roosevelt while he was president. Here also are Mr. Roosevelt's Rough Riders uniform and an original Teddy Bear. This Teddy Bear once belonged to Morris Michton, the son of the designer of the toy. The idea of the Teddy Bear was developed after President Theodore Roosevelt took a hunting trip to Mississippi in 1902. On that trip, President Roosevelt and his group spent some time searching for wild animals. Finally, the hunting party came across and surrounded a helpless old bear, which a guide cornered and roped. One of Mr. Roosevelt's guides urged him to shoot the bear so that he could win a hunting trophy. However, President Roosevelt refused to shoot the bear, and news of his act of mercy spread throughout the country. This story inspired the famous cartoonist Clifford Berryman to draw a cartoon depicting the incident. Published in the Washington Post on November 16, 1902, the cartoon was entitled "Drawing the Line in Mississippi." After the cartoon came to the attention of a store owner in Brooklyn, New York, he decided to design and to sell a toy which, with the president's permission, he called "Teddy's Bear." Eventually, the figure became known as the Teddy Bear, and was used by Mr. Berryman in many of his cartoons. Of the Teddy Bear, the publisher George Haven Putnam said: "Was there ever a greater compliment paid to the personality of a great political leader than in this association of his name with the pet cherished by children?"

Visitors next see the reconstructed period rooms. First is the library, or back parlor, which served as the family living room. The obelisks on the mantel above the coal-burning fireplace were brought back from Egypt by the Roosevelts in 1871. The Argand lamp on the center table here is supplied from an overhead fixture. (Fixtures were fitted for gas in the Roosevelts' time, but the present fixtures are electric.) Here also is a Wilton carpet, made in France for the 1976 restoration effort.

Next is the dining room, which was above the kitchen in the Roosevelts' time. Food and drink were brought upstairs by a dumbwaiter. The Roosevelt children complained that the horsehair upholstery of the dining room chairs scratched their legs and the walnut chairs seen here today were an 1853 wedding present to Charles and Gertrude Carow, the parents of Theodore Roosevelt's second wife, Edith. The walnut table belonged to Cornelius Roosevelt, Theodore Roosevelt's grandfather. The ceilings in this room, and elsewhere in the house, were molded in 1923. The chimney pieces, fireplace grates and rosettes were salvaged from mid-nineteenth century houses which were in the process of being razed.

Next, visitors see the most elegant room in the house, the parlor, described by Theodore Roosevelt himself as "a room of much splendor." In this room is a 149-year-old Chickering piano, a period piece not original to the 1848 house. One of

the Roosevelt sisters recalled that because there were no globes on the crystal chandelier in the parlor, the gas jets flickered like candle flames. A replica of that chandelier is seen here today. Here also is a marble-topped mahogany table and mahogany settee which belonged to Cornelius Roosevelt (the other identical settee in this room is a reproduction). There is a rosewood Gothic revival side chair, as well as engravings above the settees and garniture on the mantel, all of which were used in the original house. The overall style of the parlor is Rococo revival.

The master bedroom is furnished with satinwood-veneer furniture with rosewood trim. This furniture is original to the 1848 house. Family tradition has it that the furniture was fashioned by Leon Marcotte, the designer who refurbished the formerly "drab rooms" of the original house in 1865. The blue brocade draperies in the room are intended to replace those which were installed in the birthplace replica in 1923, but discarded in the 1940s due to wear and fading without saving so much as a scrap. Above the mantel is a portrait of Theodore Roosevelt's mother, Martha ("Mittie"), painted by Jenette (or Jeanette) S.H. Loop in 1874.

The last room on the tour is the nursery. It is almost entirely furnished with family pieces. By family tradition, the walnut sleigh bed here is the work of Bernard Bosch. (There was no running water upstairs in the original house, and so a chamber pot was placed at the foot of the bed in this room and in the other bedrooms.) An engraving of Sir Thomas Lawrence's painting, "Emily and Laura Ann Calmady," hangs above the bed. Here also is a tiny rush-seated chair used by Theodore Roosevelt as a baby. Another tiny chair here is a doll's chair. Also in the nursery is a period crib with a canopy. The Roosevelt children could reach the gymnasium through the windows of the original nursery.

In the original house, the third floor had more bedrooms, and the fourth floor, added in 1865, had servants' quarters. There were more servants' rooms, as well as a kitchen and storage areas, in the basement. The house had a number of servants, who tended to cooking and cleaning.

This reconstruction of the Theodore Roosevelt birthplace recaptures the elegance of a bygone era. Its original and period furnishings convey to its visitors a sense of the life of a prosperous nineteenth century family and the early years of the first new president of the twentieth century.

Maltese Cross Cabin
Theodore Roosevelt National Park
Medora, North Dakota 58645
(701) 623-4466

Administered by the National Park Service.

Directions: The site is about 135 miles west of Bismarck, North Dakota. Take I-94 to the exit for Theodore Roosevelt National Park (South Unit). Follow signs to the Medora Visitor Center. The restored cabin is located behind the center.

Open:	The cabin is open for 20-minute scheduled guided tours daily, mid-June to mid-September. Open the rest of the year for self-guided tours.
Admission:	A park entrance fee is charged May through September. There are no entrance fees charged from October through April.
Features:	The South Unit of the Park, in which the cabin is located, features a variety of scenic locations and trails, including Scoria Point, Ridgeline Nature Trail, Coal Vein Trail, Buck Hill, Boicourt Overlook, Wind Canyon, Jones Creek Trail, Peaceful Valley, and a petrified forest. Scenic Loop Drive provides motor vehicle access to most of these locations. Interpretive signs are posted along the road to explain some of the park's historical and natural phenomena. Those visitors who approach the South Unit from the east should first stop at Painted Canyon Visitor Center, which is open during the summer months and offers a magnificent view of the badlands from a scenic overlook. Picnic facilities and rest rooms are available here. The Medora Visitor Center displays personal items belonging to Theodore Roosevelt, ranching artifacts, and natural history displays. A scale model of Theodore Roosevelt's Elkhorn Ranch cabin is on display here, and a 13-minute introductory film is shown on a continuing basis. The center also has a book store, and rest rooms. Picnic facilities are nearby and it is handicapped accessible. The North Unit of the Park, accessible by taking I-94 east from Bismarck to Belfield, and then proceeding north on U.S. 85, also has a Visitor Center (which may be closed some winter weekdays). It also features a number of hiking trails. Camping is available at both park units.
Special Events:	The Park hosts a Founders Day celebration in August. On that day, entrance to the Park is free. Cookies and lemonade are served. Special interpretive programs (e.g., a discussion of the history of the National Park Service) are offered.

Having endured the double tragedy of the loss of his wife and his mother on the same day, February 14, 1884, Theodore Roosevelt was determined to find a way to overcome his grief. He had already visited the Dakota Territory on a hunting trip in September 1883 and became interested in the cattle ranching business. Before leaving the badlands to return to New York, he, Sylvane Ferris (whose brother, Joe, had guided him through the Dakota badlands) and William Merrifield became partners in the Maltese Cross Ranch, which was located on the Little Missouri River and was originally owned by Messrs. Hawley and Wadsworth and was operated by Sylvane Ferris and William Merrifield. He initially invested $14,000.00 of his inheritance in the venture. After the tragic deaths, Mr. Roosevelt shuttled between New York and the badlands, finishing his term as a New York state assemblyman and campaigning for James G. Blaine for president in the east, and tending cattle, hunting buffalo and wild animals, and wearing cowboy clothes in the badlands. Upon completing his term in Albany and fulfilling his political obligations, Mt. Roosevelt headed back to the Dakota Territory. In addition to ranching, he was very much looking forward to the prospect of big game hunting, but, upon arrival, was dismayed to discover that disease and hide hunting had virtually wiped out the buffalo herds. On return visits to this area in later years, he witnessed the same phenomenon occurring with other big game species.

Small mammals and songbirds were also vanishing, their natural grassland habitats having been destroyed by overgrazing. These phenomena were abhorrent to Mr. Roosevelt, a natural history enthusiast from childhood. It is quite likely that what Theodore Roosevelt observed here motivated him to establish the United States Forest Service, five national parks, 55 wildlife refuges and many acres of National Forests as president, making him one of America's foremost conservationists.

Wishing to have his own cattle operation, Theodore Roosevelt bought another cattle ranch in 1884 on the Little Missouri River about 34 miles north of Medora, which he called the Elkhorn Ranch, and, using cottonwood logs, built a far larger cabin for this ranch than the one located at the Maltese Cross Ranch. He also continued as a Maltese Cross partner. Two of Mr. Roosevelt's friends from Maine, Wilmot Dow and Bill Sewall, helped him run the Elkhorn Ranch. Mr. Roosevelt spent as much as 14 to 16 hours a day in the saddle tending to his cattle herds. While living in the badlands, he once helped law officers capture a band of outlaws. Years later, Mr. Roosevelt said of this time, "I would never have been president if it had not been for my experiences in North Dakota."

As powerful an influence as Theodore Roosevelt's time in the badlands was on his life, his time as a Dakota Territory rancher was short lived. He returned to New York in

1884, 1885 and 1886 and eventually resumed his political career there. In the winter of 1886-1887, most of his cattle were destroyed by severe snow storms.

After 1886, Theodore Roosevelt visited North Dakota (which became a state in 1889) from time to time, but could not stay for very long on any of his trips there. He did, however, maintain his interest in the ranches until 1898, the year he led the Rough Riders in Cuba. That year, he sold his interests in both sites to Sylvane Ferris.

Today, the cabin at the Elkhorn Ranch no longer stands. However, the Elkhorn Ranch site is today under the jurisdiction of the Theodore Roosevelt National Park. It is possible to visit the site, and it is suggested that interested visitors inquire at one of the park visitor centers or with a park ranger before going there. A scale model of the cabin is on display at the Medora Visitor Center.

The Maltese Cross cabin, which was Theodore Roosevelt's home in the Dakota Territory badlands in 1884, was moved from its original location in 1904, the year Mr. Roosevelt ran for election as president in his own right (having been elected vice president in 1900 and having attained the presidency upon the assassination of William McKinley in 1901). It was exhibited in various cities and on the grounds of the state capitol in Bismarck, North Dakota. It was completely restored and placed in its present location, just north of the Medora Visitor Center at Theodore Roosevelt National Park, by the National Park Service in 1959. (The cabin was originally located seven miles south of its present site.) Each of its hand-hewn, ponderosa pine logs was soaked as part of the restoration process.

The cabin is a three-room structure with mortar chinking and a high-pitched shingled roof. Directly below the high pitched roof were the upstairs bunks where the ranch hands slept. Visitors touring the restored cabin enter from the side, and first see the kitchen, which has a "Miami" lignite coal-burning range. Theodore Roosevelt made "cowboy" coffee on a range similar to this one, using an eggshell as a filter. Atop the range is a Dutch oven for making biscuits.

Next, visitors see the main room of the cabin. This is where Theodore Roosevelt and the ranch hands would socialize and take their meals. A dining table is placed near a whitewashed wall of the cabin. The table is set for dinner with ironstone china, which is turned upside down to avert dust. This room also contains a scale used to weigh small game, a Seth Thomas clock and Mr. Roosevelt's writing desk from the Elkhorn Ranch cabin. Some books of the period are also here, as well as a late nineteenth-century mercury-burning lamp, a cabinet which is original to the Maltese Cross Ranch, and a rocking chair reportedly from Joe Ferris' store.

The third and final room is Theodore Roosevelt's bedroom. Here visitors see his trunk, and period pieces such as a pair of slippers and a wooden bed with a hide and patterned cloth bedspread. While small, this cabin is relatively elegant and reflects the wealth and urbanity of its principal occupant. To be sure, Theodore Roosevelt had become a rugged and energetic adult, but the cabin's furnishings clearly indicate that his background was not that of a rancher or cowboy.

By visiting the cabin and taking the time to explore and to enjoy the park, visitors can acquire some sense of what life was like for Theodore Roosevelt. Clearly, he exhibited characteristic pluck and refined his sensitivity and awareness of the importance of preserving our natural areas for generations to come.

Sagamore Hill National Historic Site
20 Sagamore Hill Road
Oyster Bay, New York 11771
(516) 922-4447

Administered by the National Park Service.

Directions: From New York, take the Long Island Railroad from Pennsylvania Station (Seventh Avenue and 33rd Street) to Oyster Bay. Taxis meet all trains. If travelling by car, take the Long Island Expressway to exit 41 (NY 106 north).

This road leads directly to Oyster Bay. Upon arriving in Oyster Bay, turn right at the sixth traffic light (East Main Street) and follow the signs to Sagamore Hill (about two miles).

Open: Daily, except major holidays.

Admission: Fee charged.

Features: House and grounds, garden, pet cem-
                  etery, gift shop, canteen (summer only),
                  beverage and snack machines, Old Or-
                  chard Museum (formerly home of Gen-
                  eral Theodore Roosevelt, Jr., contain-
                  ing exhibits relating to Theodore
                  Roosevelt's political carreer, family life
                  at Sagamore Hill, and to the lives of his
                  six children, films presented here regu-
                  larly), rest rooms. First floor of house,
                  rest rooms and grounds are handi-
                  capped accessible. No photography is
                  permitted inside the house.

Special Events: The Old Orchard Museum is decorated
                  in Victorian style during the Christmas
                  season. A local band concert and
                  speeches take place on the grounds on
                  the Fourth of July.

Even before the death of his first wife, Alice Hathaway Lee, Theodore Roosevelt was planning a new home for his family at Cove Neck, Oyster Bay, Long Island, where he had spent happy and long summer vacations in his late boyhood spotting birds and shooting small game. At the time, the extended Roosevelt family had two homes in New York: 6 West 57th Street, which was owned by Theodore Roosevelt's mother Martha ("Mittie") Bulloch Roosevelt, and their home at 55 West 45th Street, a small pleasant brownstone. In 1883 he bought 155 acres of land from the Thomas Youngs for $10,000.00 cash and a $20,000.00 20-year mortgage. He kept 95 acres of that land and sold the remainder to relatives. He planned to build a substantial home on that land and to name it "Leeholm," after his beloved wife. He selected New York architects Lamb and Rich to design the home in the Queen Anne style. As envisioned by Theodore Roosevelt, this house would be a fitting home for a family of stature—a house of dignity, comfort and hospitality. It would also have permanence, with 20-inch thick foundations and joists, rafters and roof-boards in proportion. No hurricane or gale would ever destroy this house. As its owner wished, it would have 10 open fireplaces, providing enjoyment and heat to supplement that provided by two hot air furnaces in the cellar.

In March 1884, Theodore Roosevelt was ready to sign a contract for the construction of the 22-room house (the North Room was added to the house in 1905). Tragically, however, on St. Valentine's Day, 1884, his mother died, and within two days of giving birth to her only child, his wife, Alice, also died on the same day. At first, his dream of a home on Cove Neck appeared shattered. But Theodore Roosevelt now had a daughter (whom he named Alice, after her mother), and he realized that she would need a home. Therefore, on March 1, 1884, he signed a contract with carpenters John A. Wood and Son of Lawrence, Long Island, for construction of the home at a cost of $16,975.

The new home was eventually renamed Sagamore Hill for the American Indian Sagamore Mohannis, who had lived on the land two centuries before and who, in Theodore Roosevelt's words, "as Chief of his little tribe, signed away his rights to the land." In 1885, the new home was completed. A grieving Mr. Roosevelt, however, had gone to the Badlands in the Dakota Territory to live the "strenuous life" of a cattle rancher. Theodore Roosevelt sold the family homes on West 57th Street and West 45th Street in New York. His sister Anna ("Bamie") came to the new house and took care of little Alice. After snow storms destroyed most of Mr. Roosevelt's cattle in 1886, he returned to the East.

In October 1886, Theodore Roosevelt attended the Republican County Convention in New York. To his surprise, party bosses approached him and asked him to accept the Republican nomination for mayor of New York. He reluctantly did so, and a lively three-way contest ensued. The results were disastrous for Mr. Roosevelt, who finished third. After the election, Theodore Roosevelt carried out his long-standing plan to travel to London, and there, on December 2, was married to Edith Kermit Carow, his childhood friend, with whom he had corresponded and who had remained close to Mr. Roosevelt's sister Bamie over the years. After the couple traveled through Europe, they returned to Sagamore Hill in April 1887 to make it their permanent home.

For the next two years, Theodore Roosevelt engaged in literary work, welcoming politicians, writers, statesmen, big game hunters and other visitors to Sagamore Hill. This life was much too sedate for a man as active as Mr. Roosevelt, and so, when President Harrison appointed him as a member of the United States Civil Service Commission in 1889, he welcomed the offer. For six years he battled for the cause of civil service reform under both President Harrison's Republican administration and the Democratic administration of President Grover Cleveland. While in this post, Mr. Roosevelt lived at 1720 Jefferson Place in Washington, D.C. Today, Jefferson Place is a street of row houses occupied by professional offices.

In 1895, Theodore Roosevelt left Washington to become president of the New York City Police Board. By 1897, William McKinley had been elected president of the United States, and Roosevelt returned to Washington to take a job he had long sought: Assistant Secretary of the Navy. While at the Navy Department, he moved with his family to 1810 N Street NW, a nineteenth-century development in midtown Washington.

In 1896, the Spanish-American War broke out, and Assistant Secretary Roosevelt left the Navy Department to become lieutenant colonel of the Rough Riders, battling the Spanish in Cuba. He returned home a military hero. He also found that there was a groundswell of support for his nomination to run for governor of New York. After some flirtation with the idea of running as an Independent, Theodore Roosevelt accepted the Republican nomination and ran against the Democratic incumbent, Frank S. Black. On November 8, 1898, Roosevelt, then 40 years old, was elected governor by a margin of 17,794 votes. The following year, Governor Roosevelt and his family moved to the Executive Mansion on Eagle Street in Albany.

Theodore Roosevelt became the Republican nominee for vice president in 1900, and was elected to that office later that year. Vice President Roosevelt returned to Washington with his family and lived at 1215 Nineteenth Street until the fateful day of September 14, 1901, when, following President McKinley's assassination, Theodore Roosevelt, who went to Buffalo to be with the dying president, became the 26th president of the United States.

By 1901, when the Roosevelt family moved into the White House, the Roosevelts had six children (including Alice). Theodore, Jr., Kermit, and Ethel Roosevelt were born at Sagamore Hill, while Archibald and Quentin Roosevelt were born in Washington. During the Roosevelts' time here, the White House was renovated and enlarged, with separate living quarters, new bathrooms, new steel beams, plumbing, heating, and electrical improvements. The first White House press room was established. During the renovation, the Roosevelts stayed at 737 Jackson Place, a four-story stucco row house which later became the Women's City Club. The name "White House" became the official name of 1600 Pennsylvania Avenue under Theodore Roosevelt, who first used the name on his stationery.

During his presidency, Theodore Roosevelt's Sagamore Hill became the Summer White House, and President Roosevelt's children, along with their 16 cousins, would play there in a rough manner. Some of their activities were so daring that the President often accompanied them to prevent casualties. For example, the children sometimes played in an old eighteenth century hay barn (which was the only structure standing on the property when Theodore Roosevelt bought it) and jumped as much as 10 or 15 feet from one floor to another as a test of nerve. The children ran obstacle races there too, with Roosevelt acting as a timekeeper. While at Sagamore Hill, the president himself enjoyed horseback riding, tennis, hiking, wrestling, and boxing. He also chopped firewood and pitched hay.

Sagamore Hill was the scene of many domestic and foreign policy conferences, which took place in the library, on the piazza, or, after its construction in 1905, in the North Room. A significant example was President Roosevelt's role in negotiating with diplomats of the mutually hostile Russian and Japanese Empires in 1905. The diplomats of both empires met aboard the presidential yacht, the *Mayflower*, in Oyster Bay. Through skilled diplomacy, warmth and humor, the president got the diplomats to chat with one another amicably. Returning to Sagamore Hill, the president began the process of negotiating terms which culminated in the Treaty of Portsmouth.

In 1904, President Roosevelt became the first man to succeed to the presidency on the death of his predecessor and go on to election in his own right. He handily defeated Alton W. Parker that year, but, in the course of the campaign, made a pledge which he lived to regret. He promised not to seek another term as president in 1908. Thus, he made it possible for his chosen successor, William Howard Taft, to become president.

Theodore Roosevelt left office in 1909, traveling to Africa to hunt big game, and then to Europe to visit heads of state and to deliver speeches. On that trip, he received the Nobel Peace Prize for his successful resolution of the Russo-Japanese conflict. He returned home to popular accolades.

Theodore Roosevelt shared with many Republicans deep disappointment in what he regarded as the conservative, "stand pat" policies of his successor. So deep was the schism in the Republican Party that in 1912 many Republicans bolted their party and formed a new party, the Progressive or "Bull Moose" Party. Theodore Roosevelt was persuaded to run as the Bull Moose candidate that year. President Taft was renominated by a severely weakened Republican Party, and a newcomer to national politics, Governor Woodrow Wilson of New Jersey, became the Democratic candidate.

In the course of the ensuing campaign, a madman shot Theodore Roosevelt as he was on his way to a rally in Milwaukee. He had on his person a speech draft and a metal spectacle case, which saved his life by diverting the bullet from his right lung. Refusing to have the wound dressed, he went on to the rally and spoke for an hour and a half. Two weeks later, he received a 45-minute ovation after delivering a speech to a crowd of 16,000 at Madison Square Garden in New York.

In the end, Governor Wilson was the beneficiary of the Republican split, and was elected president. Theodore Roosevelt ran a strong third party campaign, and far outstripped President Taft's showing in the Electoral College. But it was simply not enough to beat Woodrow Wilson.

When World War I broke out in Europe, Theodore Roosevelt, believing that America would eventually have to enter the war, urged preparedness. A reluctant President Wilson resisted the idea of American involvement, but, in 1917, came to share Theodore Roosevelt's view and entered the war. Gradually, many of the policies and ideas formulated at Sagamore Hill were reluctantly adopted by Woodrow Wilson.

The war effort drew Theodore Roosevelt's four sons into battle. Two of them, Theodore, Jr. and Archie, were badly wounded. His youngest, Quentin, was killed in the air over German lines in July 1918. The following months were a sad time for the proud but grieving father. He himself had wanted to participate in combat, but his plea was rejected by President Wilson. Now, as he awaited the return of his other three sons to Sagamore Hill, the life was draining out of Theodore Roosevelt. In early January 1919, Theodore Roosevelt was at home in bed. He had been ill, but was convalescing. At midnight on January 6, 1919, he went to sleep in the Gate Room at Sagamore Hill, and at four o'clock that morning, he was dead.

Theodore Roosevelt was barely 60 years old at the time of his death. Had he lived he would almost surely have been the Republican candidate for president in 1920. As it was, his life was relatively short, but few Americans have had as profound an influence on the course of the nation's history. Many of his successors, both Republican and Democratic, have attempted to emulate him, but Theodore Roosevelt, who was the very embodiment of American "rugged individualism," was such a unique personality that it is difficult to imagine that America will ever see his like again.

After Theodore Roosevelt's death, Edith Roosevelt continued to live at Sagamore Hill. In 1937, Mrs. Roosevelt's oldest son, Theodore Roosevelt, Jr., had his own home built a short distance from the Sagamore Hill house. He called his home "Old Orchard." In 1940, Theodore, Jr. served in World War II and died in Europe as a brigadier general shortly after the Normandy invasion in July 1944. Shortly after Mrs. Edith Roosevelt's death in September 1948, the Theodore Roosevelt Association purchased Sagamore Hill, its contents, and 83 acres of surrounding land. It was opened to the public at a formal ceremony conducted by President Eisenhower in June 1953. President Hoover and Roosevelt family members attended. For the next ten years, the Association managed the property, and some rooms were opened to the public. In 1963, the Association presented Sagamore Hill, Old Orchard, the Theodore Roosevelt birthplace reconstruction and a $500,000.00 endowment to the American people as a gift. The National Park Service now administers these sites. Much of Sagamore Hill is now open to the public. Old Orchard was opened to the public as the Old Orchard Museum in 1966.

Today, visitors to Sagamore Hill can see the piazza, which at one time afforded a wonderful view of the Long Island Sound. It was here that Theodore Roosevelt was notified of his nomination for governor of New York in 1898, for vice president in 1900, and for president in 1904. When the North Room was added to the house in 1905, the piazza's old west steps were removed, and the piazza was extended at the southwest corner to create a speaker's platform from which Mr. Roosevelt could address crowds assembled on the lawn below. The piazza was also extended from the west entrance to the south

side of the exterior wall of the North Room alcove, and a new west stairway was added. Above the broad door at the western entrance of the house is carved the family motto: "Qui Plantavit Curabit," or "He who has planted will preserve."

Over the mantel in the oak-paneled entrance hall are the head of an African Cape buffalo and a set of gongs, which are souvenirs of Roosevelt's 1909 African safari. The blue and white Spanish ginger jars on the mantel were used by the Roosevelt children to store tennis balls (a matching bowl in the drawing room was used as the dogs' water dish). The fireplace has andirons made from cannon balls and shells. Near the dining room door is a large Cloisonne urn originally used at the home on 6 West 57th Street in New York. A picture on the south wall of the alcove was painted by a Native American on a buffalo hide. Under the painting is a large chest given to the president by his hunting companion, John M. Parker, after his Mississippi bear hunt in 1902. (It was the imagination of Clifford Berryman, who drew cartoons about that hunt, that led to the creation of the "Teddy Bear.") The other side of the alcove has a carved chair presented to Theodore Roosevelt while he was governor of New York. A horseshoe on the wall was worn by "Dan Patch" when he established a world's record for harness racing.

Next, visitors see the library, which was used by Theodore Roosevelt as an office and study, and was also a family room at times. It was here that some of the Russo-Japanese negotiations took place. On the left bookcase is a bronze "Paleolithic Man" given to the president by sculptor Frederic Remington. To the right is "The Cougar" by I. Phimister Procter, given to the president by his "Tennis Cabinet" when he left the White House. Behind "The Cougar" is a portrait of the president's father, Theodore Roosevelt, Sr. It was placed to look down at Theodore Roosevelt as he sat at his desk. A set of silver plaques on the wall here were purchased by Theodore Roosevelt while traveling in Germany. Pope Leo XIII presented Mr. Roosevelt with the mosaic on the left side of the mantel. There is a great clock to its right, which rings on the quarter hour and was called the "Ting-Tang clock" by the children. Next to it is a silver flagon given to Theodore Roosevelt by King Haaken VII of Norway during Roosevelt's 1910 European trip. Also here is a miniature pepper coal scuttle given by an anonymous coal miner to President Roosevelt, who settled the coal strike of 1902. An oil portrait of Oliver Cromwell and a warrant signed by him hang on the right wall. The desk has a rhinoceros foot inkstand, a silver-plated candlestick that held the candle that sealed the Treaty of Portsmouth in 1905, and a silver tankard given to Theodore Roosevelt in 1905 by his Harvard College classmates.

Next visitors see the drawing room. This room was used primarily by Mrs. Roosevelt as its decor and color scheme suggest. Mrs. Roosevelt used this room to receive visitors, and to manage the household accounts and servants. This room also displays a photograph of Quentin Roosevelt. Two Carow family heirlooms: a leather covered table by the front window and a rosewood etagere in the southwest corner, are also here. There is a polar bear rug on the floor which was given to Mrs. Roosevelt by Admiral Robert E. Perry after he returned from the North Pole. A rosewood desk in this room belonged to Mrs. Robert Kermit, Mrs. Roosevelt's aunt. An oil painting by A.J. Drysdale depicting a Louisiana bayou scene hangs on the wall above the screen and to the right of the piazza door. Here also is a series of old Carow family pieces, including a porcelain service bowl, vases and lamp, which are mounted in bronze on the bookcase and lampstand. The footstool in this room was originally at the home of Cornelius van Schaack Roosevelt, Theodore Roosevelt's grandfather, on East 14th Street.

The next room, the North Room, draws visitors' eyes shortly after they enter the house. This large room, some 30 feet wide and 40 feet deep, was added to the house in 1905. Theodore Roosevelt had been elected to a second term as president the previous year, and realized that he needed a more spacious and formal room in which to receive distinguished visitors and delegations. He commissioned his friend, C. Grant LaFarge, son of artist John LaFarge, to design such a room. The room, which adjoins the northern end of the entrance hall, is constructed entirely of American and Philippine wood and is totally reddish-brown in hue. Its mantelpiece is camogan wood from the Philippines, and its ceiling is made from American swamp cypress and hazel. Its four walls are adorned with black walnut columns set in pairs; between each pair are narrow panels with the initials TR and EKR carved into them. The room is filled with hunting trophies, books, paintings and furnishings. Among the objects in this room are two large elephant tusks, which extend from the barrier, and were a gift from Emperor Menelik of Abyssinia. There are also smaller elephant tusks, to the left and right of the entrance, which were taken from an elephant shot by Theodore Roosevelt in 1909. A large silver loving cup to the left of the entrance was given to Mrs. Roosevelt by the crew of the U.S.S. Louisiana in remembrance of the Roosevelts' 1906 journey to Panama aboard that battleship. This was the first occasion on which a president had gone outside the territorial limits of the United States while in office. The chest on which the loving cup stands was sent by Theodore Roosevelt to Mrs. Roosevelt from Africa in 1909. To the left and right of the entrance are Samurai swords in glass cases. The swords were given to President Roosevelt by Count Kamura, the Japanese peace envoy, at the conclusion of the Treaty of Portsmouth. Six years later, Admiral Togo visited the Roosevelts, and presented Mr. Roosevelt with the miniature suit of Japanese armor that now stands on the large round table in the center of the room. This table, made from a single section of Philippine hatra wood, also holds a cribbage board fashioned on

a walrus tusk, a copy of *Die Niebelunge* given by Emperor Wilhelm II of Germany, and a volume of Frederic Remington's western drawings. There are also two large bookcases set against the west wall. These were given to President Roosevelt by Charles McKim, who directed the remodeling of the White House in 1902. The bookcases were used in the second floor White House Library. On one bookcase is a sculpture by Frederick MacMonnies entitled "Rough Rider." Other sculptures in the room include: a study for "Stone Age in America" by John J. Boyle, "The Puritan" by Augustus Saint-Goudes, "Crossed Hour at San Juan" by James Kelly (which sits on the piano by the east wall), "Kit Carson" by MacMonnies, "Bronco Buster" by Remington (on the mantel), and a bronze rhinoceros by James L. Clark (used by Mrs. Roosevelt to hang her summer hat). A camagon desk in the alcove is made of the same section of wood as the mantelpiece. On the desk is a wooden box containing pictures of Theodore Roosevelt and the German emperor taken in 1910, on the back of which are some rather unflattering captions penciled by the Kaiser. The German chancellor, upon learning of the Emperor's indiscretion, attempted to recover the photos, but Theodore Roosevelt would not give them up. He kept them but showed them only to personal friends. The bisque figurines on the alcove bookcase were given to Mrs. Roosevelt by members of the Rochambeau Commission who visited Washington in 1902 to dedicate a statue of the French Revolutionary Era general. The figurines were used at the White House as table decorations. To the left of the alcove is a Tudor oak armchair made from part of a vessel of explorer Sir Martin Frobisher and given to him by Queen Elizabeth I. It is inscribed "M. Frobisher, 1580." Also here is a chess table used at the president's birthplace home, and P. Marcius Simons' painting "Victory" hangs here as well.

An American eagle with outspread wings encircled with a laurel wreath, carved in wood by sculptor Gutzeon Borglum, is between the tall windows on the north wall. Below the eagle is a copy of a Philip A. de Laszlo portrait of Theodore Roosevelt made for Mr. Roosevelt's British friend Arthur Lee, who was later Viscount Lee of Forcham and First Lord of the Admiralty. Over the piano is another painting, "Porcelain Towers" by P. Marcius Simons.

Above the portrait of Theodore Roosevelt is a flag known as the "Headquarters Flag" in President Roosevelt's administration. It is a copy of the presidential color prescribed by the War Department in 1898. The other flags in the room are copies of the colors and regimental flag of the first U.S. Volunteer Cavalry (the Rough Riders), which were given to Theodore Roosevelt by the secretary of war when the regiment disbanded in September 1898. The large Chippendale chair near the fireplace, a copy of the one used by George Washington at the Constitutional Convention, was presented to President Roosevelt by the First City troops of Philadelphia in 1905. Theodore Roosevelt's sister, Mrs. W. Sheffield Cowles, gave him the fire bench and settee. A leather arm chair used by Theodore Roosevelt in the White House cabinet room is to the right of the fireplace, as is an ormolu cabinet from Theodore Roosevelt's birthplace home. On the cabinet is an ornately engraved silver bowl set on a teakwood stand, which was a gift to Mrs. Roosevelt from the Dowager Empress of China. Also here is an oriental rug, a gift to Mrs. Roosevelt from Sultan Abdul Hamid II of Turkey. The lion and lioness are trophies from Mr. Roosevelt's African safari. The bison were shot by Theodore Roosevelt in Pretty Butte, Dakota Territory, in 1883, and the elk were shot by him in Two-Ocean Pass, Wyoming, in 1891. From the antlers of the elk nearest the entrance hang the sword and hat Mr. Roosevelt wore when leading the Rough Riders in Cuba. The room is filled with a wide variety of books as the Roosevelts read voraciously and also enjoyed reading aloud to one another. Theodore Roosevelt, himself, wrote about 50 books in his lifetime, and could read a book a day.

The dining room has Italian furnishings purchased by the Roosevelts on their wedding trip to Florence. Here the family carried on spirited and occasionally heated conversations on the day's events. The mood was more subdued if company was present, but Theodore Roosevelt was always entertaining, if occasionally indiscreet. Among the items in this room is a settee which came to Sagamore Hill from the house on West 57th Street. On the server below is a silver coffee and tea service that belonged to Theodore Roosevelt's mother. Under the moose head is a silk needlework screen given to Mrs. Roosevelt by the Empress of Japan. On the mantel are Minton plates, which were Carow family pieces and were used at the White House. On the sideboard to the right is a silver bowl presented to President Roosevelt by members of his "Tennis Cabinet." The silver platter on the cabinet between the two entryways was presented to Theodore Roosevelt by Spanish friends in 1914 on the occasion of the wedding of his son, Kermit, to the daughter of the American ambassador to Spain.

There is a doorway through the rear wall of the dining room leading to the pantry. This room was often locked to prevent the children from raiding the sugar and other staples stored here. Here also is an icebox, which was used to keep butter, eggs, and produce from the household's working farm fresh; it was stocked with ice from a nearby pond which was kept in an ice house outside. The first family telephone is also here and was installed after Theodore Roosevelt became President to replace the old method by which messages got to Sagamore Hill—by bicycle from Oyster Bay. Mrs. Roosevelt had an aversion to telephones, and would have removed this telephone after her husband left office, if the children had not persuaded her otherwise. The next room is the kitchen, where the children often had their midday snack.

Up the backstairs is the Red Bathroom, which was, from 1885 to about 1905, the only bathroom in the house. It served primarily as the children's bathroom because the adults and guests took their baths in circular tin tubs which were brought to their rooms and filled with water. The size

and shape of the great porcelain bath tub in this room reminded Alice Roosevelt, Theodore Roosevelt's eldest daughter, of a "sarcophagus." The tub had a wastepipe which, according to Theodore Roosevelt, Jr., "made the most astonishing series of gurgles. We were told by our Irish nurse that these were the outcries of the 'faucet lady' and we watched with care to see if we could catch a glimpse of her head in the pipe."

To the left of the bathroom is the part of the house used by the children. The Southeast Bedroom was used by Alice Roosevelt until her marriage to Congressman (later Speaker) Nicholas Longworth in 1906. She remained in Washington after Theodore Roosevelt left office and for many years was an immensely popular Washington hostess with both charm and an irreverent, and sometimes biting, wit. Several pictures of Alice Roosevelt hang in this room, and a photograph of her mother, Alice Hathaway Lee, hangs over the desk. After Alice Roosevelt's marriage, at least two of the boys, Kermit and Quentin, used this room. Kermit served in World Wars I and II, and died while on active duty in Alaska in 1943. To the left is a door to a little room called "Quentin's Hideaway." The children used it to escape from unwelcome visitors. It had a window opening onto a sloping roof from which a water pipe led to the ground. The children could slide down the roof and pipe and hide in the cornfields below. The northwest bedroom, the room to the other side, was used by all of the boys at various times. Its last occupant, Archie, became a Wall Street bond broker and served in both World Wars.

At the opposite or western end of the second floor is the nursery. There is a Thomas Nast cartoon of Santa Claus filling stockings with names of the Roosevelt children. It was drawn as a Christmas greeting to the new family in the White House. "Clara Doll," which sits in the rocking chair to the right of a tiny table, originally belonged to Edith Roosevelt's mother, Gertrude Tyler Carow.

Next to the nursery is the Gate Room. According to Ethel Roosevelt, it was so named because it had a little gate across the door. It was used by the children after they grew too old for the nursery, "but still had to be contained." Later, Ethel Roosevelt used this room until she married Dr. Richard Derby in 1913. Still later, the room was used as a winter sick room because of its southern exposure. The room contains prayer back chairs from the private chapel of Mrs. James Gracie's house nearby. Mrs. Gracie was Theodore Roosevelt's Aunt Annie, his mother's sister.

To the right of the Gate Room is the Mother's Room. This was the master bedroom, where the family gathered on Christmas mornings. The children's stockings hung at its fireplace. This room's furniture, which is of the "modern gothic" or "reform furniture" style, is attributed to architect Frank Furness and noted Philadelphia cabinetmaker Daniel Pabst. Purchased by Theodore Roosevelt, Sr. in the 1870s, it uses conventionalized floral ornamentation, often in repeating patterns, has architectonic proportions and uses both light and dark woods, in this case, bird's-eye maple veneered over walnut. On the mantel are family photographs, including one of Theodore Roosevelt as a child. Mrs. Edith Roosevelt's favorite photograph of her husband is on the lampstand.

The President's Dressing Room, which adjoins the master bedroom, has A.B. Frost paintings which were used to illustrate Mr. Roosevelt's book *Hunting Trips of a Ranchman*. A miniature of Mrs. Roosevelt sits on the dressing table to the left. The bathroom adjoining this room was added in 1905. So many Roosevelts lived at Cove Neck at the time that Mrs. Roosevelt had the towels monogrammed "R of S" to avoid confusion at the laundry.

The hallway features many family portraits. Here hangs a dark portrait of Quentin Roosevelt by Walter Russell; a portrait of Mrs. Roosevelt's sister, Emily Tyler Carow; a portrait of the colonel of the Rough Riders (Theodore Roosevelt) by Fedor Encke; and a portrait of Mrs. Edith Roosevelt by Philip A. De Laszlo.

The boys' portraits flank the entrances to the single and double guest rooms. In the single room is an enameled Russian object, which was a gift of Czar Nicholas II of Russia. On the wall are illustrations by H. Sandham and R. Gifford Swain used in *Hunting Trips of a Ranchman*. The double room features a walnut bed and stand inherited by Theodore Roosevelt from his parents. Both rooms have stained glass windows, which are characteristic of a Queen Anne house. Eleanor Roosevelt, daughter of Theodore Roosevelt's brother Elliott and later Mrs. Franklin D. Roosevelt, used the single room on occasion.

The South Bedroom, at the head of the stairs, was at one time the nurse's bedroom and was occupied by Mrs. Roosevelt's nurse, Mame Ledwith, who was an old Carow family retainer. At another time, this room was a guest room, and in the latter part of Mrs. Roosevelt's life, it was her winter bedroom. The bed, bureau and washstand in this room are made of Italian walnut. Mrs. Roosevelt's favorite chair, a Shaker rocking chair, is here, and also her silver glove box and black lace shawl. There is a sunflower design on the fireplace, another Queen Anne style touch.

Upstairs on the third floor is the cook's room, which was occupied by Annie O' Rourke for many years. Next door is the sewing room, where Molly Smith, the family seamstress, would mend old clothes and cut new ones using the Wilcox and Gibbs sewing machine in this room. The family stored their luggage in the trunk room, down the hall to the left.

To the right of the schoolroom (which was used for tutoring the Roosevelt children and is not open to the public) is Theodore Roosevelt, Jr.'s room. Originally used by Miss Young, the tutor, the room was used by Theodore Roosevelt, Jr. after his father became president. After Theodore, Jr.'s marriage to Eleanor Alexander in 1910, it became Archie's room. Theodore Roosevelt, Jr. went on to become a New York state assemblyman and assistant secretary of the Navy. He also served in both World Wars and as Governor of the Philippines. In Theodore, Jr.'s room is an oak and pine shaving stand, which was factory-made.

An H. G. Williamson painting of Theodore Roosevelt in a confrontation with Speaker of the House Joe Cannon hangs in the third floor hallway. Across the hall are the maids' rooms, which were used by Rosy McKenna and Mary Sweeny. Mary stayed with the family for almost forty years, retiring after Mrs. Roosevelt's death in 1948. Down the hallway to the right is the linen closet, where the family stored linens and household supplies.

The gun room at the west end of the hall was so named because Theodore Roosevelt's collection of shotguns and rifles are kept here in a cabinet by the south windows. With the exception of the North Room, this room was Mr. Roosevelt's favorite because of its wide views of the woods and water. It was also a retreat from visitors and newsmen at times when their presence made the library an unsuitable place to work. He did much of his writing here, and, upon returning from Cuba in 1898, used the room as an office, dictating correspondence and the text of his book, *The Rough Riders*. When they were small, the children loved playing in this room, especially in the crawl space between the rafters and the floor. They also enjoyed the paraphernalia here, such as ramrods, old pistols and cartridge boxes. This room also has a suit of Philippine armor on the east wall, and a cattlehorn chair, typical of ranching areas in the West in the late nineteenth century. Also here are some Navaho rugs, and a pair of chaps used by Theodore Roosevelt in his ranching days are under a Remington pastel of a member of the Creek tribe hanging on the south wall.

This splendid house captures the multi-faceted nature of the 26th President, and tells as much about the life of an active, spirited, and prominent American family. A truly unique home which is maintained very much as it was in Theodore Roosevelt's day, and still contains most of its original furniture, Sagamore Hill is indeed a fascinating place to visit.

WILLIAM HOWARD TAFT

**William Howard Taft National Historic
Site (Birthplace)
2038 Auburn Avenue
Cincinnati, Ohio 45219
(513) 684-3262**

Administered by the National Park Service.

Directions: From downtown Cincinnati, take Ft.
Washington Way east to I-71 north.
Exit at Reading Road, bear right to
Dorchester Street, and turn left at the
stoplight. Proceed west up Dorchester
Street to Auburn Avenue. Site is on sec-
ond block on right side of the road.
Turn right at Southern Avenue park-
ing lot after passing the site.

Open: Daily (except Thanksgiving Day, Christmas Day and New Year's Day).

Admission: Free.

Features: House museum with three restored
rooms and exhibits concerning William
Howard Taft's public career and the
Taft family. Restrooms, handicapped
accessible (elevator is installed in house
museum). There is a thirty-minute
guided tour. Visitors should plan to
spend at least one hour at the site.

Special Events: **In September the site hosts Constitution Day, in which school children sign a replica of the Constitution.**

The weekend before New Year's Day, the site hosts a Taft family open house, at which refreshments are served.

William Howard Taft was born into the family of a prominent attorney, Alphonso Taft, on September 15, 1857. A native of Townshend, Vermont, Alphonso Taft graduated from Yale College (Yale University) in 1833, and, after graduation, taught at Ellington High School in Connecticut. In 1837, Alphonso Taft returned to Yale for his law degree, and graduated from Yale Law School in 1838. He then decided to visit several cities in search of a place to settle and eventually chose Cincinnati. He corresponded with Fanny Phelps, who was still living in Townshend, and married her on August 29, 1841. The couple had five children, but only two of them, Charles and Peter, lived to be adults.

In 1851, Alphonso Taft purchased a home for $10,000.00 on 1.82 acres of property in Mt. Auburn, a fashionable residential section of Cincinnati. The advent of public transportation in the 1870s changed the character of the neighborhood from wealthy to less affluent. Mr. Taft greatly improved his 1840s Federal brick home, adding a rear wing to the house later that year. The following year, Fanny Taft died of a respiratory ailment but Alphonso Taft did not remain a widower for very long. In 1853, he married Louise Torrey of Millbury, Massachusetts, who became William Howard Taft's mother. "Willie" was the second of Louise Taft's five children. (Her first died in infancy.)

In his childhood and youth, "Willie" was an excellent student. At the age of nine, he had a close brush with death when a horse ran away with a carriage in which he was riding. Young Willie and his four brothers liked to swim, skate, and spar with other boys. He developed a love for baseball; he was a strong batter but a slow runner. When he was of age, he attended Woodward High School, where his size and physique earned him a reputation as a formidable wrestler and fighter. He graduated second in his high school class, and enrolled at Yale in 1874. During this period, Alphonso Taft served in President Ulysses S. Grant's cabinet as secretary of war and later, as attorney general. In 1877, the Taft birthplace home caught fire, but Alphonso Taft was insured, and used some of the insurance money to buy a bay window for the house, perform extensive renovation of its interior rooms and raise its roof.

In 1878, William Howard Taft graduated from Yale, ranking second in a class of 91. He returned to Cincinnati, where he worked part-time for a newspaper and attended Cincinnati Law School (now Alphonso Taft Law School) and, two years later, received his degree and was admitted to the Ohio Bar. He was appointed an assistant prosecuting attorney in Hamilton County in 1881, and the following

year, was appointed by President Arthur to become collector of internal revenue for the First Ohio District. In that post, one of his major responsibilities was collecting taxes from distilleries in Kentucky. In 1882, Mr. Taft's father, Alphonso Taft, was appointed ambassador to Austria-Hungary. In 1883, William Howard Taft resigned as tax collector, visited his parents in Vienna, and then joined his father's law firm, living briefly in his birthplace home. Mr. Taft's father was appointed to another diplomatic post, minister to the Russian czar, in 1884.

On June 19, 1886, William Howard Taft married Helen "Nellie" Herron, daughter of a law partner of former President Rutherford Hayes, after a long courtship. They had three children. The eldest, Robert Alphonso Taft, became a U.S. senator from Ohio and General Dwight Eisenhower's principal opponent for the 1952 Republican nomination. Next was a daughter, Helen, who excelled in educational pursuits, and their youngest child, Charles Phelps Taft II, later became mayor of Cincinnati. The William Howard Tafts established a home of their own at 1763 E. McMillan Street in Cincinnati. Mrs. Nellie Taft's father gave them the lot and Mr. Taft drew on $2,500.00 of savings and financing from his own father to meet the $6,000.00 cost of this three-story home, located not far from Mr. Taft's birthplace. They called their new home "The Quarry." In the 1890s the Tafts rented, and eventually sold this home, and today, the home is a private residence.

In 1887, William Howard Taft was appointed judge of the superior court, and was elected to a five year term the following year. In 1890 President Benjamin Harrison appointed Judge Taft to the post of U.S. solicitor general, which is the third ranking position in the Justice Department. The solicitor general represents the United States government in cases heard by the U.S. Supreme Court. While in this post, Solicitor General Taft and his family rented a home at 5 Dupont Circle in Washington. The building has since been replaced. In 1890, Mr. Taft received another appointment, this time as chief judge of the United States Court of Appeals for the Sixth Circuit, which resided in Cincinnati. Because the house on McMillan Street was rented, the Tafts stayed at the Burnet House, and later rented a house from a friend, Mary Hanna, at Third and Lawrence Streets. The Tafts also established a summer house at Murray Bay, Pointe au Pic, outside Quebec. This home was a rambling, shingled cottage overlooking the St. Lawrence River and was destroyed by fire in the 1950s.

In 1900, President William McKinley appointed Judge Taft as president of the U.S. Philippine Commission. The Tafts went to the Philippines staying at Calle Real in Malate, a suburb of Manila, and later at Malacanan Palace, a Spanish style structure with a sloping roof. Mr. Taft claimed that Calle Real was more homelike and healthful than the palace. His mission was to help the Filipinos establish a civil government but he concluded that they were not educated well enough to the idea of democracy to administer their own government, and consequently accepted President McKinley's appointment as civil governor of the Philippines in 1901. In 1902, Governor Taft was seriously ill with an internal abscess and had three operations over the course of the next several months. While on a visit to Washington for Senate hearings on the Philippines, he became better acquainted with Theodore Roosevelt, who was president by that time. He then went to Europe, stopping in Rome as a special envoy to Pope Leo XIII. His mission was to request of the Pope that the Roman Catholic Church give up hundreds of thousands of acres of farm land that it owned in the islands. President Roosevelt had offered to appoint Mr. Taft to the Supreme Court, but, as much as he wanted the job, Mr. Taft felt that he had to decline because of the work remaining to be done in the Philippines. His wife and brothers also urged him not to accept, fearing that it would ruin any chance Mr. Taft had to become President.

In 1904, William Howard Taft accepted President Roosevelt's appointment to become secretary of war. He maintained strong influence over U.S. activity in the Philippines, whose administration was within War Department jurisdiction. The Taft family lived in a four-story row house at 1603 K Street in Washington for the next five years. Secretary Taft traveled extensively, journeying to Panama to supervise work on the Panama Canal, and going to Japan to encourage American mediation of the Russo-Japanese conflict. He also went to Cuba to quell a threatened revolution in 1906. The following year, he went on a 24,000-mile trip around the world, stopping in Japan to dispel fear of a war with that country. By this time, it was clear that Theodore Roosevelt was grooming Secretary Taft to be his successor as president.

The following year, 1908, William Howard Taft won the Republican nomination by acclamation on the first ballot. The Democrats nominated William Jennings Bryan, who made his third and final run for the presidency that year. Mr. Taft was elected president that November.

In his inaugural address, President Taft urged the reduction of tariffs, calling for a special session of Congress on March 15th for that purpose. He also urged amendments to the Constitution to regulate trusts and interstate commerce. In June 1909, he asked for a Constitutional amendment authorizing an income tax. This amendment was ultimately passed and ratified in the Wilson administration.

In August, President Taft was dealt a severe political blow when the Republican-controlled Congress passed the Payne-Aldrich Tariff Act, which kept tariff rates high. President Taft disliked this legislation, but did not veto it. As the result of his capitulation on this issue, the public blamed President Taft for high prices more than they blamed Congress. This may have been the beginning of progressive Republican disenchantment with President Taft. Despite its political problems, the Taft administration did have many positive accomplishments, including the establishment of postal savings and parcel post services, the admission of Arizona and New Mexico to the Union, and the Federal prosecution of about twice as many antitrust suits.

At the White House, the Tafts were making changes. They doubled the size of the executive office wing, or west pavilion, built under President Roosevelt, thus creating the Oval Office. Mrs. Taft conceived the idea of planting blossoming cherry trees, which were a gift of the mayor of Tokyo. They also added oriental tapestries and teakwood furniture to the White House decor. The Tafts represented the American transition from the nineteenth to the twentieth century by being the last White House family to keep a cow on the premises, and the first to use automobiles; the White House stable was replaced by a garage. Because it was considered inappropriate for a sitting president to vacation outside the United States (Theodore Roosevelt had been the first president to go outside U.S. territorial limits while in office), the Tafts summered at Beverly, Massachusetts while President Taft was in office.

In 1912, the Republican Party was hopelessly divided over President Taft and his policies. Believing that President Taft had fallen under the influence of powerful corporate interests, progressive Republicans, unable to secure the 1912 Republican presidential nomination for their champion, Theodore Roosevelt, bolted the party and formed the Progressive (or the "Bull Moose") party with Theodore Roosevelt as its candidate. The Democrats nominated Governor Woodrow Wilson of New Jersey as their candidate. President Taft felt bewildered, and later bitter, over the actions of his former sponsor, who had single-handedly engineered Mr. Taft's nomination for president in 1908. With the nomination of a badly weakened Republican Party in hand, President Taft made numerous campaign speeches, but knew that he could not win in a three-way race. He wrote: "If I cannot win I hope Wilson will." In the end, it was Woodrow Wilson who won, and President Taft suffered the most crushing defeat of an incumbent president in history, for Theodore Roosevelt ran second in the 1912 election, with President Taft a distant third.

William Howard Taft left the White House in 1913 and returned to his alma mater, Yale, as a law professor. He was extremely popular with the students during his eight years there. He and his family started out living at "Hillcrest," 367 Prospect Street in New Haven, Connecticut, a turreted, "Pseudo-Romanesque" mansion. In 1918 and 1919, Mr. Taft briefly stayed in Washington at 2029 Connecticut Avenue, while serving as co-chairman of the National War Labor Board. By 1919, the Tafts had moved to 70 Grove Street in New Haven, which has since been destroyed. In 1920, Mr. Taft bought a new home in New Haven at 113 Whitney Avenue for $24,000.00. In early 1921, he lived at 60 Yale Avenue.

In the 1920 campaign, William Howard Taft supported his fellow Ohioan, Senator Warren G. Harding, for president. Senator Harding had delivered Mr. Taft's nominating speech at the 1912 Republican Convention. Sen. Harding's campaign victory was extremely pleasing to Mr. Taft, in part because it meant that his friend might make his long-held ambition to be appointed to the Supreme Court a reality. The opportunity arose shortly after President Harding's inauguration, when Chief Justice Edward B. White died. President Harding swiftly nominated Mr. Taft to the post, thus making William Howard Taft's late years the happiest of his life.

In 1921, Chief Justice Taft, who had sold the house on Whitney Avenue in New Haven for $25,000.00, bought a new house at 2215 Wyoming Avenue N.W. in Washington from Congressman Alvin Fuller at a price of $75,000.00. This house is a white brick, Georgian Revival style structure built in 1904. Its third floor library was accessible by elevator. Today, the house is part of the United Arab Republic's (Egypt's) Embassy complex.

As Chief Justice, William Howard Taft's genial nature brought a spirit of personal harmony to the High Court, notwithstanding its divisions on many issues. Perhaps because of his conciliatory nature, Chief Justice Taft never wrote any dissenting opinions in his nine years on the High Court, stating, "I would not think of opposing the view of my brethren if there is a majority against my own." He also lobbied for a separate building for the Supreme Court, which met in the Capitol in his day. In the 1930s the new Supreme Court building was finished, although Chief Justice Taft did not live to see it completed.

Due to heart trouble, William Howard Taft resigned as chief justice in February 1930. On March 8, 1930, he died and was later buried in Arlington National Cemetery. It was a sad ending to the life of the only person to serve as both president and chief justice of the United States.

William Howard Taft's birthplace home remained in the family until 1899. In 1961, the Taft Memorial Association, under the leadership of the president's son Charles Phelps Taft II, acquired the house and grounds. In 1969, the Association donated the property to the American people. The property was designated as a National Historic Site on December 2, 1969.

Today, the William Howard Taft birthplace house has an Italianate appearance. It has a cornice, a small piazza, and a "widow's watch" used by the Tafts, who were amateur astronomers. It has four restored rooms reflecting Taft family life during the years 1857 to 1877 (Mr. Taft's first twenty years of life). The restoration features period fixtures, and venetian blinds and shades. One of the restored rooms is a formal parlor, which was once a double parlor. The doors of this room are wood grained. On its walls hang portraits of four adult members of the Taft family painted by William Walcott, who stayed here in 1858. One mantel in this room (which has two fireplaces) is original; the other was duplicated later. The room has puddle draperies and Rococo revival style furniture, and a three-volume folio, *Indian Tribes of North America*, is on display here. The restored library features a desk made in the 1840s or 1850s which was used by Alphonso Taft. The mantel in the library is original, however, the mantel in another restored room, the nursery, where William Howard Taft may have been born, is not.

The balance of the house is now used as a museum of William Howard Taft's life and family history. Among the exhibits found here are a law office desk marked "A. Taft & Sons," a leather chair with "T" embossed on its back, which was used by William Howard Taft in the Philippines, the Bible used at Mr. Taft's inauguration as president and at his installation as chief justice, and state dinner pieces used by the Tafts at the White House.

Visitors to this house will view a marvelous restoration of the home of a prominent American family and the history of the only man to head both the executive and judicial branches of American government—William Howard Taft.

WOODROW WILSON

Woodrow Wilson Birthplace
24 North Coalter Street (Woodrow Wilson Parkway)
P.O. Box 24
Staunton, Virginia 24401
(540) 885-0897

Administered by the Woodrow Wilson Birthplace Foundation.

Directions: From I-81, take Exit 58/225 to Woodrow Wilson Parkway. Follow signs.

Open: Daily (except Thanksgiving Day, Christmas Day and New Year's Day).

Admission: Fee charged.

Features: Historic house (restored to pre-Civil War appearance); museum featureing seven galleries covering the life and times of Woodrow Wilson, including Wilson's 1919 Pierce-Arrow White House Limousine (purchased by President Wilson from the government when he left office in 1921, used by him until his death in 1924, gift of Mrs. Edith Wilson), gardens, rest rooms, gift shop. First and basement floors of birthplace and museum are handicapped accessible. Tour lasts about 30 minutes and includes touchable artifacts. The museum is self-guided. Educational programs are available for school children.

Special Events: The site hosts an open house in late December in celebration of Wilson's birthday, as well as special tours by guides during Virginia Garden Week (held the last Saturday in April).

Woodrow Wilson, the 28th president of the United States, was born in 1856 in the lovely Shenandoah Valley town of Staunton, Virginia, to very religious parents of Scots-Irish Presbyterian extraction. Woodrow Wilson was born after his father, Rev. Dr. Joseph Ruggles Wilson, had been called to Staunton to serve as a minister for the local Presbyterian congregation. The brick Greek Revival home where they lived from 1855-1857 was never owned by the Wilson family, but was a manse owned by the church. The Wilsons were the second ministerial family to live in the house.

Upon arriving at President Wilson's birthplace home, visitors begin the tour at the Woodrow Wilson Museum, which opened in November 1990. The museum includes seven galleries which trace the life and times of Woodrow Wilson: Family; Princeton; New Jersey; Presidency; War; Peace; and the Garage, which features President Wilson's 1919 Pierce-Arrow limousine. The Museum is self-guided and serves as an introduction to the guided tour of the Manse.

Visitors begin their tour of the birthplace home by entering the hall and turning right into the parlor. The hardwood floor in the parlor, as in every room throughout the house except the kitchen, is original. The parlor was used as the center of entertaining and for many wedding and church receptions while the Wilsons lived there. The Wilson family was very musically inclined, as evidenced by Mrs. Wilson's French-made guitar with its mother-of-pearl inlay, which is on display here, and a melodeon donated by Edith Bolling Wilson, the president's widow. Also featured in this room is a rococo style rocking chair used by Rev. Wilson. In the center of the room is a table with a lamp on it. This table was a Victorian item meant to show off a family's best lamp and to provide a room with the most possible light. Whale oil was used in the lamp originally, but the lamp has since been converted to electricity. The Wilson family Bible can also be seen on the table.

Adjoining the parlor is the formal dining room, in which visitors see French porcelain place settings (which were used by a Staunton family). A silver tea service from 1858, given to the Wilsons as a Christmas gift from Rev. Wilson's congregation in Augusta, Georgia, is also displayed here.

Across the hall is the pastor's study, where Rev. Wilson prepared his sermons. Visitors see his walking cane, a gift from his Wilmington, North Carolina congregation. On the wall is a map of the United States dated 1846, the year the house was built.

In the downstairs bedroom, adjoining the parlor, is an Egyptian Revival bed which belonged to the Wilsons. Also on view is a complete 19th century chamber set used for bathing and a hair receptacle used to save hair for the making of wigs and for embroidery. This is the room in which Thomas Woodrow Wilson was born.

On the second floor is the nursery, in which the Wilson crib is displayed. Woodrow Wilson's sisters, Annie and Marion, shared this room and slept in the same bed. Usually, in the Wilsons' day, children did not have their own bedrooms due to the larger size of the average family. The trundle bed which represents Tommy's bed is of the period and was owned by a Charlottesville, Virginia family. This room also includes a small rocking chair used by all of the Wilson children. Toys and play dresses from the 1800s are also displayed. Across the hall, in the front section of the second floor, is a guest bedchamber.

The Wilson family had three servants. Evidence from census records and oral history suggests that the servants were slaves. However, it is possible that they were hired by the Wilsons.

Reviewing some of the artifacts in the Woodrow Wilson birthplace home, visitors get an idea as to how middle-income families lived in the South prior to the Civil War. Woodrow Wilson came from a strict Presbyterian family, but there was much love here in this home during his childhood. His father's ministerial duties took him south and Woodrow Wilson spent the remainder of his youth in Augusta, Georgia and Columbia, South Carolina. Years later, in 1912, Woodrow Wilson returned to Staunton upon his election as president of the United States. Although living in New Jersey at that time, he always considered himself a Southerner, and acknowledged his heritage by returning to the place where he was born upon his attainment of the highest office in the land.

Woodrow Wilson Boyhood Home
419 Seventh Street
Augusta, Georgia 30901
(706) 724-0436

Administered by Historic Augusta, Inc.

Directions:	The site is located in downtown Augusta at Telfair and Seventh Streets.	**Admission:**	No set admission fee.
		Features:	House and grounds. Not handicapped accessible.
Open:	By appointment only.	**Special Events:**	None.

When the Wilson family left Staunton in 1858, they moved to Augusta, Georgia, where they remained until 1870. They first lived in a Presbyterian Manse located on the north side of the 600 block of Greene Street in Augusta. That site was razed many years ago. "Tommy" Wilson, who grew up to become President Woodrow Wilson, later moved to a manse located at 419 Seventh Street, near the First Presbyterian Church, with his parents, Rev. Dr. Joseph Ruggles Wilson and Janet ("Jessie") Woodrow Wilson, and two sisters. (He had a brother who was born later). The manse, a three-story, ten-room dark red brick house with white trim, was built in 1859 and is of a restrained Greek Revival style. A Colonial revival porch was added around 1900. The manse was purchased by the Church in 1860 and is located diagonally across the street from the Church at the northwest corner of Seventh and Telfair Streets. This site also includes a carriage house. Next door to Woodrow Wilson's boyhood home is the boyhood home of Joseph R. Lamar, an Associate Justice of the United States Supreme Court appointed by President William Howard Taft, who also spent time in Augusta. Justice Lamar grew up in Augusta and was a childhood friend of Woodrow Wilson.

While living here, "Tommy" Wilson experienced the tragedy of the Civil War first hand. His father, Rev. Wilson, was active in the Confederate cause and his church became a war hospital during this period. (It was also at Augusta's First Presbyterian Church that the convention was held forming the Presbyterian Church in the Confederate States in 1861.) Thus, as a young boy, Woodrow Wilson saw much destruction to human life, scarcity of food, and the training and marching of soldiers. It is said that his experience as a child helped to form his lifelong aversion to war, and was a key factor in his efforts to keep America out of World War I during his first term in office. "Tommy" Wilson and his family remained in Augusta through the beginning of the reconstruction period after the Civil War.

Because of the era in which he grew up and the challenges he faced, Woodrow Wilson was prepared to guide the nation through the crisis of World War I with more determination than he might have otherwise had upon attaining the Presidency. It was with that kind of fierce determination that he unsuccessfully fought for United States involvement in the League of Nations, which he hoped would help to avert future wars. He did not realize that dream, but years later, the same essential concept became a reality when the United Nations was formed.

The Wilsons moved to Columbia, South Carolina, in 1870. The manse remained church property until 1930, when it was sold into private hands. It was entered into the National Register of Historic Places on February 28, 1979,

134

and has been carefully maintained. Woodrow Wilson's boyhood home in Augusta was recently sold in 1991 to Historic Augusta, Inc., which plans to restore the house and to open it to the public. Currently, tours of the house are provided by Historic Augusta, Inc. by advance reservation. The significance of this beautiful home and his life in Augusta in the formation of the character of Woodrow Wilson cannot be overstated.

Woodrow Wilson Boyhood Home
1705 Hampton Street
Columbia, South Carolina 29201
(803) 252-1770

Administered by the Historic Columbia Foundation

Directions:	The site is located in downtown Columbia on Hampton Street between Henderson and Barnwell Streets.
Open:	Tuesday through Sunday. Closed Monday.
Admission:	Fee charged.
Features:	Tour of house and grounds. First floor is handicapped accessible. Gift shop and rest rooms nearby.
Special Events:	The site has candlelight tours conducted by guides in period costume in the first week of December.

Woodrow Wilson spent 12 years of childhood in Augusta, Georgia. In 1870, fourteen-year-old "Tommy" Wilson came with his family to Columbia, where he spent his teenage years. The Wilsons first lived with Mrs. Wilson's brother for two years at the Pryor home, located near the Columbia Theological Seminary (where his father was teaching) at Pickens and Blanding Streets, while their own Columbia home was being built at 1705 Hampton Street. The home on Hampton Street is different from the others in which the Wilsons lived in that it is the only house that Rev. and Mrs. Wilson ever owned. It was built expressly for the Wilsons and completed in 1872. Wilson's mother, Jessie, was very happy with the Columbia home, so much so that it was considered "her" home. Here, Woodrow Wilson saw many people struggling to survive in the aftermath of the war. It took many years to complete the rebuilding necessary to make Columbia a beautiful southern town once again, and he later wrote of his reconstruction experience and how it affected his decisions as president.

The home is a Tuscan Villa style structure of the Victoria era; however, because there are not as many gingerbread carvings on this home as on other Victorian homes, it is considered a modest example of Victorian architecture. It is a natural gray color with large bay windows and has cement front steps now, but its original front steps were wooden. Coal was used to heat the house when the Wilsons lived there, and gas light was used for illumination and were only lit for one hour each night. The Wilsons' home was one of the first homes in Columbia which was fitted for gas jets. The house is air conditioned today because maintaining a constant temperature aids in the preservation of antique furniture. Many of the furnishings in the house are period pieces donated by the citizens of Columbia. The property on which the house is situated is enclosed with a white picket fence, and it has fruit gardens in the backyard. The gazebo seen in the front lawn was made in the late 1800s.

The interior of the home underwent restoration in 1992 and today, visitors are able to tour rooms on the first and second floors of the home, which are restored to look very much as they did when the Wilsons lived here.

During the Victorian era, people were very interested in nature and the idea of bringing nature into one's home became popular. This was the era in which indoor plants became fashionable. Many pieces of furniture have flowers carved on them as another way to bring nature into the home. An example of this is a hat rack in the entrance hall of the home. Floral patterns were painted on china, and it is assumed that Woodrow Wilson's mother dried flowers and made arrangements with them.

The living room was painted white in keeping with the plain style of the period. A mark of Victorian decor is the large amount of furniture and clutter in the front room. Gold leaf cornices fit over the top of the curtains. An "S" shaped chair (tete-a-tete) for two, so shaped so that both people can face each other is called a courting bench. Other period touches include the peacock feathers seen on a table here and doilies placed on chairs, which were considered fashionable in the Wilsons' time. (Ironically, peacock feathers were later considered unlucky.) The fireplace and mantel are made with slate which is painted to look like marble.

Visitors can also see an 1870 pump organ in the parlor. Behind the parlor are double doors to the study used by Woodrow Wilson's father. In the study there is another slate fireplace which is painted to look like black marble. Woodrow Wilson's father, Rev. Joseph Ruggles Wilson, was a minister at the First Presbyterian Church in Columbia from 1870 to 1874, and he also taught at the Columbia Theological Seminary while living here. He was consid-

ered a very kind man and tutored many of his seminary students in his study. Students would enter the study by steps leading up to the bay window of this room.

In the dining room, there is a screen in front of the fireplace to protect the heads and faces of those sitting near the fireplace. There is a bay window here, where Mrs. Wilson gazed at the birds and her rose gardens. She planted the roses and magnolias in the garden herself. There is also a sideboard owned by Mrs. Wilson and an oak clawed foot dining room table.

The hallway and winding stairway with archways are original to the home, and there are many family pictures seen throughout the house, including some of Woodrow Wilson's three daughters. Woodrow Wilson's parents' bedroom features such personal items as brushes and hairpins. Calling cards are arranged on the dresser.

This home gives visitors a sense of the days shortly after the Civil War, when the South was rebuilding its heritage and culture. Its white picket fence and gazebo, gracious touches typical of southern middle-class homes of this period, indicate what life was like for young "Tommy" Wilson, who went on to a varied career as a writer, lawyer, political scientist, educator, orator, president of Princeton, governor of New Jersey, and finally, president of the United States. Today, this charming home is a fine tribute to a man of simple, yet gracious origins who rose to become a great world leader. Only one who had observed so much human struggle and determination in his early years could have developed the character necessary to accomplish the great objectives President Wilson achieved.

Woodrow Wilson House
2340 S Street, N.W.
Washington, D.C. 20008
(202) 387-4062

Administered by the National Trust for Historic Preservation.

Directions:	**From Dupont Circle in Washington, D.C., travel northwest on Massachusetts Avenue for seven blocks to S Street. Turn right to 2340 S Street.**
Open:	**Tuesday through Sunday. Closed Thanksgiving Day, Christmas Day and New Year's Day.**
Admission:	**Fee charged. Free to National Trust for Historic Preservation members.**
Features:	**Guided tour of house museum (about 40 minutes); conference room, where a 25-minute film presentation on Wilson's**

last days is shown, exhibits are displayed, and visitor orientation takes place; gift shop; rest room on first floor. House is handicapped accessible (via elevator). Educational materials are available for teachers, and a copy of the film shown in the conference room may be borrowed for educational purposes.

Special Events: In September, the site runs the Kalorama Embassy and House Tour. The tour includes approximately ten homes in the area, including the Woodrow Wilson House.

The site is decorated for the Christmas season as it would have been when the Wilsons lived here.

The site is available for rental during the hours it is closed to the public. Meetings, receptions, and corporate functions can be held here.

In 1873, sixteen-year-old Woodrow Wilson, or "Tommy," as he was then known, left Columbia, South Carolina to attend Davidson College in Charlotte, North Carolina. He did so to continue his studies in preparation for the ministry. While at Davidson, he stayed in the north wing of Chambers Hall, Room 13, however, his poor health forced him to withdraw from Davidson the following year. Later that year, the Wilson family moved to Third Street in Wilmington, North Carolina, where Woodrow Wilson's father, Rev. Dr. Joseph Ruggles Wilson, had a new congregation.

In 1875, Woodrow Wilson's health had improved enough to permit him to travel to Princeton, New Jersey, to attend what was then known as the College of New Jersey. Upon merging with Princeton Theological Seminary later that same year, the College changed its name to Princeton University. While a student at Princeton, Woodrow Wilson returned to Wilmington only for vacations. He made a significant decision during his Princeton days—that he would not follow his parents' wishes and become a minister. Rather, Woodrow Wilson wished to become a statesman.

Woodrow Wilson decided that the first step toward his new goal was to study the law. Accordingly, upon graduating from Princeton in 1879, he enrolled in the University of Virginia Law School in Charlottesville. There he stayed in Room 158, House F, Dawson's Row. He vacationed with his family at Fort Lewis, Green Valley in Bath County, Virginia.

When he returned to school, he stayed at 31 West Range. In 1881, he again fell ill, and was forced to leave Charlottesville. He returned to Wilmington to live with his family and, while recuperating, completed his legal studies and received his law degree in 1882.

Upon receiving his degree, Woodrow Wilson moved to Atlanta, Georgia to establish a law practice in partnership with a friend. He first stayed at a boardinghouse at 344 Peachtree Street, and then relocated to Mrs. James S. Turpin's house, whose location is unknown today. After about a year, Mr. Wilson became discouraged with the number of lawyers competing in Atlanta, many of whom had stronger political connections and local ties than he did, and thus decided to return to school and prepare to teach.

In 1883, Woodrow Wilson entered graduate school at Johns Hopkins University in Baltimore, Maryland. While there, he first lived at 146 North Charles Street, and later moved to 8 McCulloch Street, which was described as "a neighborhood of dignified old brick houses." While at Johns Hopkins, he also courted Ellen Louise Axson, a Presbyterian minister's daughter. They shared many things in common through the similarity of their backgrounds. On June 24, 1885, Woodrow Wilson and Ellen Axson were married.

Just before his marriage, Woodrow Wilson had accepted an offer to become an associate professor of history at a new women's undergraduate institution, Bryn Mawr College, in Pennsylvania. Living on a salary of $1,500.00 a

year, the Wilsons resided in the upstairs apartment in the middle structure in a row of three wooden houses. Their house was appropriately known as the "Betweenery." While teaching at Bryn Mawr, Professor Wilson persuaded the Johns Hopkins faculty to award him his Ph.D. without taking oral examinations, and so in 1886, he received his Ph.D. in economics and political science. His book, *Congressional Government*, was accepted as his doctoral dissertation.

In 1888, Woodrow Wilson accepted another professorship, this time as a Professor of History and Politics at Wesleyan University in Middletown, Connecticut. There the Wilsons lived in an old colonial house on High Street until 1890 when Woodrow Wilson received an appointment as Professor of Jurisprudence and History at his alma mater, Princeton. By this time, the Wilsons had three daughters, who, with their parents, moved to a rented, Federal-style house on Library Place (the first house in the vicinity to have an indoor toilet). The house still stands today and is privately owned.

In 1896, Woodrow Wilson was honored by being invited to be the principal speaker at Princeton's 150th anniversary celebration. It was also in that year that Professor Wilson had a house of his own design built for his family next door to the house on Library Place, off Cleveland Lane. In 1902, the President of Princeton University resigned in a dispute with the trustees, and Professor Wilson, at the age of forty-five, was unanimously chosen by the trustees, including former President Grover Cleveland, to be the new president of Princeton. That year, the Wilsons moved into "Prospect," the university president's residence on the Princeton campus. It is a Florentine-style structure with ironwork of clusters of grapes. Today, it is the Princeton Faculty Club.

In 1907, while president of Princeton, Woodrow Wilson led a fight to abolish the university's private eating clubs in favor of dining halls. The alumni defeated Woodrow Wilson's plan, but the attendant publicity earned him the reputation of a fighter for democracy. In 1910, Woodrow Wilson made a nationally publicized speech in Pittsburgh in which he denounced private universities for neglecting "opportunities to serve the people," castigated Protestant churches for "serving the classes and not the masses," and predicted a revolution with "fields of blood" if the United States did not find "the leadership of men who know her needs." The speech did not sit well with Princeton's conservative alumni, and led to speculation that Woodrow Wilson would leave Princeton for public office given the right opportunity.

The opportunity came after spring graduation exercises, when several powerful figures in the national Democratic Party approached Woodrow Wilson with the idea of his becoming a candidate for president of the United States. These men told him that as a first step toward that goal, he should seek the governorship of New Jersey. They assured him that the Democratic nomination for governor was his for the asking. After receiving assurances that the state party machine would not interfere with his gubernatorial administration, Woodrow Wilson accepted the offer. The New Jersey Democratic state convention nominated Wilson on the first ballot in September, 1910. At the request of the Princeton trustees, Woodrow Wilson resigned his post at Princeton in October. In November, he won the election by 50,000 votes.

As governor, Woodrow Wilson lived with his family in a suite at the Inn on Nassau Street, in Princeton. He skillfully guided one piece of reform legislation after another through the New Jersey legislature during his two-year term. He spent his summers at Sea Girt, New Jersey in "Shadow Lawn," a building that had been erected by the State of New Jersey for the Chicago World's Fair and later moved to Sea Girt. It was loaned to Governor Wilson by Captain J. B. Greenhart. The structure burned in 1927.

Woodrow Wilson was nominated by the 1912 Democratic Convention for president on the 46th ballot. After winning the election, he served out his term as governor, then moved to temporary quarters on Cleveland Lane, behind Grover Cleveland's house and gardens in Princeton. It is fitting that Woodrow Wilson, the first Democrat to occupy the White House since Grover Cleveland, should have so many ties to his Democratic predecessor. In March 1913, President Wilson moved with his wife and three daughters to the White House, where some additional bedrooms were installed in the attic during his administration. While in office, President Wilson eliminated the protective tariff, signed the landmark Federal Reserve Act, and led the battle for U.S. participation in the League of Nations, which, although unsuccessful, inspired a later generation to form the United Nations. He also endorsed the constitutional amendment that gave women the right to vote.

After the death of his first wife, Ellen, in August 1914, President Wilson married again. His second wife, the former Edith Bolling Galt, was a widow who was also a member of a prominent Virginia family which boasted Pocahontas as an ancestor. He married her on December 18, 1915, nine months after their first meeting. As subsequent events showed, she was a woman of tremendous strength and resourcefulness.

In 1919, President Wilson was locked in a struggle with Republican senators over ratification of the Treaty of Versailles, which he saw as a vital step toward realizing his dream of a League of Nations to promote lasting world peace. He took his case to the people by embarking on an 8,000-mile speaking tour of the Midwest and the Pacific Coast. On September 25, 1919, after speaking in Pueblo, Colorado, President Wilson collapsed from exhaustion while on a train, and was taken back to Washington. On October 2, he suffered a stroke, which rendered his left arm useless and caused the left side of his face to sag.

President Wilson spent the next several weeks recuperating. His recovery period was a very reclusive time for him and no one saw the president without first speaking to Mrs. Wilson. Many visitors spoke only to Mrs. Wilson, who would convey their messages to the president, thus isolating him from intrusion to the extent possible for the nation's chief executive.

The 1920 election was of tremendous significance to President Wilson, even though he, himself, could not be a candidate, because he regarded it as a referendum on his position that the United States should join the League of Nations. James M. Cox, the 1920 Democratic nominee, favored U.S. membership in the League. (Mr. Cox's Vice Presidential running mate in 1920 was Assistant Secretary of the Navy Franklin D. Roosevelt.) President Wilson's worst fears were realized when Mr. Cox was soundly defeated by Republican Senator Warren G. Harding of Ohio. However, in December 1920, President Wilson and his League of Nations initiative were honored when he was awarded the Nobel Peace Prize.

In 1920, while still president, Woodrow Wilson decided that he would make the nation's capital his home for his post-presidential years (and remains the only former president to have done so). As a surprise for his wife, he purchased a house located in the Embassy Row section of Washington. The house, a five-story, red brick Georgian Revival town house designed in 1915 by Waddy B. Wood for the Henry Parker Fairbanks family, has a facade which features an arch with Doric pillars of gray stone and black iron grillwork over its entrance, and three neo-Palladian windows on its second floor. Ten of Woodrow Wilson's friends contributed $10,000.00 toward the purchase of the home, and later, Bernard Baruch contributed another $10,000.00 toward its enlargement. President Wilson used this gift to add a billiard room, book stacks for his 8,000-volume library, and a two-car garage to the house; he also added an elevator. In presenting the house to his wife, President Wilson followed an old Scottish custom; he gave her a small piece of sod from the garden and a key to the front door. When the Wilsons first arrived at their new home upon leaving the White House in March 1921, they found that the house was filled with fresh flowers, a delight for Mrs. Wilson, who loved flowers.

Edith Wilson, who had watched over her husband so carefully after his 1919 stroke left him semi-paralyzed, continued to look after him after he left office. She read to him in their second floor library, where they watched silent films on a graphoscope, and took motor trips in their 1919 Pierce-Arrow limousine through Rock Creek Park and into the Virginia countryside. While living here, the Wilsons entertained infrequently due to President Wilson's failing health, but on those occasions on which they did invite guests, a superb table was set. President Wilson rarely ate in the dining room without wearing a dinner jacket, and never allowed guests to discuss business at the dinner table.

After living in this house for almost four years, Woodrow Wilson died here on February 3, 1924. Edith Wilson continued to live here until her death in 1961. The house was then devised to the National Trust for Historic Preservation, which administers it today as a house museum.

Today, visitors begin their tour of the house in a small room on the first floor which President Wilson facetiously referred to as the "dugout," perhaps because among the items on display here is a baseball signed by King George V, who opened a game by throwing this ball out while attending a game played outside of London. President Wilson reviewed his mail in this room. Also on display here are: a desk used by Edith Wilson in the White House; the president's Hammond Multiplex typewriter with both Greek and English characters; a picture of the president's first wife, Ellen Axson Wilson; and pictures of the president's birthplace home in Staunton, Virginia and boyhood home in Columbia, South Carolina.

Moving to the front hallway, which is painted a light yellow, as are all of the hallways in the house, visitors see a statue of a discus thrower, which was a gift to Mrs. Wilson from her first father-in-law (President Wilson was Mrs. Wilson's second husband). Another statue in the hallway is a copy of a figure at the head of Hadrian's tomb in Rome. On a table is a photograph of Woodrow and Edith Wilson, and two landscape paintings in oval frames adorn the walls.

Ascending the stairs to the second floor, visitors notice a neo-Palladian indoor window with an arched top, which allowed light from the windows behind it to fill this part of the house during the day. The molding on the walls is a "diamond in bars" pattern. The clock on the stairway landing, a replica of a clock which was in the White House during the Wilson Presidency, was a gift from Edith Wilson to her husband. On the wall leading up the stairs is a portrait of an Armenian girl titled "L'Esperance." Portraits of Edith Wilson's mother, father, and others believed to be members of Mrs. Wilson's family also hang on the stairway walls.

The first room visitors see on the second floor is the drawing room, whose windows, adorned with dark red damask draperies, look out onto S Street. This room is formal and was rarely used by the Wilsons. A baccarat crystal chandelier (installed after President Wilson's death) is suspended from the ceiling. On the wall opposite the windows hangs the painting "American Landscape" by Eliot Clark. Also in this room is a cupboard with porcelain plates presented to the Wilsons in 1919 by the King and Queen of Belgium. These plates contain scenes of places destroyed in the First World War. A Steinway piano used by President Wilson's daughter, Margaret, is also here. Margaret, who was a concert singer, made a recording of the "Star Spangled Banner" and donated the proceeds of the recording to the Red Cross. On the piano is the sheet music to the song "Oh You Beautiful Doll," which the president, a romantic, was overheard humming as he and Edith Wilson left for their honeymoon. Above the fireplace mantel is a portrait of Edith Wilson. On the opposite wall is an 15' by 18' tapestry, which was originally placed on the floor but later moved to the wall (it is partially rolled up at the bottom because the wall is not quite large enough for it to be completely unfurled).

Visitors move through the second floor hallway, which displays a Victrola, a Statue of Athena, and the "Theodore Roosevelt" pier mirror. The next room they see is the library, a large room with leather-like canvas fabric on its walls. This was the room used most frequently by the president in his retirement. Above the fireplace mantel in this room is a Stanislav Rembski portrait of the president, which was painted in the 1940s. Visitors also see a radio microphone used by the president, which sits on a revolving bookcase he used. A tall, black leather cabinet chair in this room was used by President Wilson in the White House, and a smaller black leather and wood chair also found here was once used in Congress. Also in this room is a display chest filled with "treasures," including freedom chests presented to President Wilson by the people of London, Manchester and Carlisle, in England. A medal presented by the Polonia Restituta (Order of the White Eagle in Poland) is here, as well as the pen used by President Wilson to sign the declaration of war with Germany. Also in the library is a statue of Irish patriot Robert Emmet, portraits of Edith Wilson's ancestors, pictures of the King and Queen of the Belgians, and a samurai sword said to be a gift of the Raw Silk Association.

Next, visitors move on to the solarium, toward the back of the house. This is where the Wilsons often took their breakfast. This room has curved casement windows looking out to the garden. In the hot summer months, these windows could be opened for cross-ventilation. The solarium is cheerfully decorated with various species of indoor plants.

Passing through the solarium, visitors next come to the formal dining room. Its windows are decorated with pale green draperies and lace curtains. It has a Brazilian rosewood dining table and chairs with needlepoint cushions. Against the wall is the Wilsons' marbletop sideboard with mirror. Also here is a loving cup given to Mrs. Wilson by a delegation from Virginia to mark the occasion of her engagement to the president. A dumbwaiter in the butler's pantry was used to bring food and drink to the Wilsons and their guests.

Ascending the stairs to the third floor, visitors see a cedar linen closet made in Portland, Oregon. In the hallway is a petty point depiction of the president. Also on this floor is a portrait of Ellen Wilson, Woodrow Wilson's first wife, and her three daughters. The master bedroom, used by Edith Wilson, is quite cheerful, and the floral patterns of the drapes, upholstery and inlaid carpet reflect her love of flowers. (The house has four bedrooms and five bathrooms in all.) Near the window is Mrs. Wilson's sewing machine. The room also features a statue, drawing and oil portrait of Mrs. Wilson's ancestor, Pocahontas. Visitors can look at her clothes closet, which reveals that Mrs. Wilson was quite tall.

Next, visitors see the president's room, which is still furnished as it was while the president lived here. The bed in which the president died in 1924 is a reproduction of the bed in the Lincoln Room of the White House, which was made for the president according to specifications obtained by Edith Wilson. A desk used by Mr. Wilson during his days at Princeton is also here, as well as his filing cabinet and his shaving table. Above the fireplace mantle facing the bed is a painting entitled "Geraldine J." This painting was purchased by President Wilson from the Cocoran Gallery of Art in Washington. It was painted by artist M. Bradish Titcomb, and its model was the mother of film star Jane Russell. According to his family, President Wilson said that the young woman depicted in the painting reminded him of his first wife, Ellen. Above the door to the bathroom

hangs an original Red Cross poster of a nurse by Harrison Fisher. To the side of the door hangs the Key to the City of Philadelphia, which was presented to the president. Above the key is a horseshoe found by the former president on one of his motor trips with Mrs. Wilson. A remnant of the house's call button system is also in evidence here. A large cedar closet adjoining this room still displays some of the president's clothing, including a beaver coat and a kangaroo coat with a wombat collar. President Wilson's nurse used a room just to the side of the his. Here visitors see a "sensation machine," which generated electrical shocks and was thought to be therapeutic for victims of paralysis, such as that suffered by Wilson after his stroke. Also adjoining President Wilson's room is a sleeping porch, which was useful for comfort at night in the pre-air conditioning era.

On the fourth floor of the house, which is not open to the public, was the laundry room, where clothes were washed and then folded over the bars of a gas dryer. Also on this floor were four servants' rooms, a bathroom and a servants' lounge.

Visitors then go down the backstairs to continue their tour. These stairs look as they did during the Wilsons' time. They are metal and have rubber treads to muffle sound. A neo-Palladian window permitted light into the stairwell during the day. They lead to the butler's pantry, which has its walls covered with fabric as another apparent effort to muffle sound. It also has a zinc metal sink and a warming oven of the period. A dumbwaiter is also here. Near the pantry is a large walk-in safe, which was probably used to store silver, jewelry and important documents.

The tour concludes in the kitchen, which features a large pantry with flow blue dishes, a period ice box, a large cast iron stove which was fueled by a combination of coal and gas, a wooden circular table, two large porcelain sinks (one of which was used to wash pots and pans, the other of which was used to wash and drain fruits and vegetables, a large pantry, a meat slicer, a coffee grinder and a 1930s General Electric refrigerator with a globe housing its motor on top. Large opaque windows allowed light into the kitchen. To further evoke the early 1920s, boxes and cans of products used in the 1920s are on the shelves here.

By touring this house, visitors can learn much about the time period in which President Wilson spent his retirement. It also illustrates a great deal about the public career and private life of one of America's most influential politicians and statesmen who helped establish the status of the United States as a world power and also advanced the cause of peace on the heels of a devastating war.

WARREN GAMALIEL HARDING

Warren G. Harding Home
380 Mt. Vernon Avenue
Marion, Ohio 43302
(614) 387-9630

Administered by the Ohio Historical Society.

Directions: From Columbus, take Route 23 north to Marion. Take the interchange for Route 95 west. Route 95 becomes Mt. Vernon Avenue. The site is a three-story green frame house with white trim, and an historical marker is on the front lawn. Turn into the driveway just west of the house and park behind it.

Open: Memorial Day through Labor Day, Wednesday through Sunday.

Admission: Fee charged.

Features: Home, grounds and gardens, picnic table. Building at rear of home, which served as a press office in the 1920 Presidential campaign, is now a museum and gift shop, which includes rest rooms. The house is not handicapped accessible.

The Harding Memorial, where the President and Mrs. Harding are interred, is also in Marion.

Special Events: The site celebrates President Harding's birthday on the weekend closest to November 2. It also holds a Christmas open house one weekend in December.

The twenty-ninth president of the United States, Warren Gamaliel Harding, was born in a small salt box clapboard cottage on what is now Route 97 in the small, north central Ohio town of Blooming Grove, on November 2, 1865. The cottage was torn down in 1896, but the site now has an historical marker and a small stone marker resting on the southwest corner of the actual location of the cottage. Warren Harding was the first of eight children born to George Tryon and Phoebe Dickerson Harding. George and Phoebe Harding were Baptists, and Warren Harding was raised in that denomination although his mother, Phoebe Harding, converted to the Seventh Day Adventist Church while the Hardings lived in Caledonia, Ohio. In 1867, George Harding finished building his son's second home on the site of his ancestor's cabin; the cottage was too small for the growing family once the Hardings' second child was born. Warren Harding's second home, which still stands, is a white two-story frame house with a covered front porch and a rear lean-to addition located 0.6 miles west of Route 288 on Route 97.

Young Warren Harding's family originally lived on a farm, and so the boy spent his early years doing day to day farm chores and attending his small school in Blooming Grove. In 1873, when Warren Harding reached the age of eight, his father completed a course in homeopathic medicine in Cleveland, and he would sometimes accompany his father on horse and buggy calls. That same year, the Harding family moved a short distance southwest to Caledonia, Ohio, where they lived in a home on the northwest corner of South and Main Streets and south of the Public Square. The house was a small yellow-brown frame house with gingerbread trimmings. Today, it is a modernized, white frame residence and is privately owned. An historical marker can be seen from Main Street. Warren Harding's father became part-owner of a local newspaper, the Caledonia *Argus*, and young Warren Harding soon learned to set type, run the press, and clean ink from press rollers here. Warren Harding also played a coronet in the Caledonia band.

When Warren Harding turned fourteen, he went to Ohio Central College in Iberia, which is about midway between Blooming Grove and Caledonia. There he learned to play the alto horn and edited the school yearbook. In 1880, his family moved to a forty-acre farm two miles east of town. Today, the farmhouse is a white frame house with a large stone stoop and is privately owned.

In 1882, Warren Harding graduated from Ohio Central College at age seventeen. His family first moved to a house near the intersection of State and Center Streets behind the Fite Building, in Marion, Ohio, where the Marion *Daily Star* was once published. It was to this home that Warren Harding rode a mule after graduating from college. Neither the home nor the Fite Building still stand. Later, the family again moved to what is described as a turreted white box at what is now 500 East Center Street in Marion. Warren Harding began his life after college as a country school teacher, earning $30.00 a month. He later tried his hand at studying law and selling insurance, and, for recreation, played in a band in Marion and also participated in a local baseball team.

Warren Harding found his stride in the newspaper business, in which he started out as a $1.00 a week reporter for the Marion *Democratic Mirror*. By this time, however, he was already an ardent supporter of the Republican Party and its presidential candidate, James G. Blaine. The Democratic owner of the *Mirror* dismissed Mr. Harding after a few short weeks when he learned of his new reporter's political views. Undaunted, Mr. Harding teamed up with two friends, John Sickel and Jack Warwick to buy the bankrupt Marion *Daily Star* for $300.00. The revived paper began to publish anew on November 26, 1884. Eventually, Mr. Harding's partners bowed out of the venture, but Warren Harding persisted. The *Star* became firmly established and, after several moves, found a permanent home on 195 E. Center Street in Marion. By the end of the 1890s, the paper was clearly a financial success. (Mr. Harding remained the owner of the *Star* until 1923, when he finally sold it.)

On July 8, 1891, at the age of twenty-five, Warren Harding married Florence Kling DeWolfe, the daughter of the richest man in Marion. The new Mrs. Harding had been deserted by her first husband and left with a small child to care for herself, as her father provided her with no support. The Hardings were married in a home they had built for themselves at 380 Mt. Vernon Avenue in Marion, and they resided there for the rest of the time they spent in Marion.

In 1892, Warren Harding began his political career by running unsuccessfully for county auditor. He continued as editor and publisher of the *Star* with Mrs. Harding running the business end of the publication. In 1899, Warren Harding, a strong and handsome orator, won the Republican nomination for Ohio state senator, and was elected to that post. He proved to be a personally popular legislator and was skilled at effecting compromises between the competing factions of the state party, led by Joseph Benson Foraker of Cincinnati and Mark Hanna of Cleveland. The Republicans, grateful to State Senator Harding for his services to the party, suspended their rule against renominating incumbent state senators to allow Mr. Harding to seek re-election, which he won handily. While the legislature was in session in Columbus, State Senator Harding stayed in a parlor-bedroom suite in the Great Southern Hotel, which was a labyrinth of buildings across from the State House known as "the little capitol."

In 1903, Warren Harding was nominated and elected to the post of lt. governor of Ohio. During the campaign for lt. governor, the front porch of the Harding home collapsed. Consequently, Warren Harding built a new front porch with a rotunda extension, ornate railing and Ionic columns. The new front porch made an excellent speaker's platform in 1920, when U.S. Senator Harding conducted his "front porch" campaign for the presidency. At the end of his term as lt. governor, Mr. Harding did not seek public office, but returned to Marion to work at the *Star*. His political career resumed when he ran unsuccessfully for governor of Ohio in 1909. His campaign was managed by Harry M. Daugherty, a small town lawyer who later became Mr. Harding's chief political advisor and attorney general of the United States in the Harding administration. The gubernatorial effort was lost by a badly factionalized Republican Party. However, three years later, Warren Harding had the honor of delivering the nominating speech for President William Howard Taft at the Republican Convention. Mr. Harding was deeply disappointed at President Taft's loss in the election that November, but later, when Warren Harding himself became president, he made President Taft's lifelong dream a reality by appointing him Chief Justice of the United States.

Despite the 1909 defeat, and Warren Harding's initial misgivings, Mr. Daugherty and Mrs. Harding persuaded him to run for United States Senator from Ohio in 1914. Mr. Harding secured the Republican nomination by winning Ohio's first direct primary, then went on to soundly defeat his Democratic opponent in November. As a Senator, Warren Harding was a party loyalist who never openly criticized his colleagues of either party. From July 1917 to the end of his Senate term, he lived at 2314 Wyoming Avenue in Washington, a neo-Georgian style duplex with a terrace and a side entrance, which he purchased for $50,000.00. Today, that home is privately owned.

In 1919, Mr. Daugherty tried to persuade Senator Harding to run for president and in December of that year, the Senator finally agreed to do so. His name was entered in primaries in Ohio, Indiana and Montana. He carried Ohio but lost badly in the other two states. However, Mr. Daugherty, apparently sensing that the Republican convention in Chicago would deadlock, urged his candidate to continue. In the end, the convention did deadlock between General Leonard Wood and Governor Frank Lowden of Illinois. A series of meetings took place, the most famous being the "smoke-filled room" meeting of uncommitted Republican senators at the Blackstone Hotel in Chicago, about which much has been written, although it was certainly neither the first, nor the last, occurrence of the brokering of a deadlocked Presidential nominating convention. In looking back on that meeting, Senator Wadsworth of New York, a friend of Warren Harding's in the Senate, said of those at the meeting, "They were like a lot of chickens with their heads cut off." After reviewing the possibilities, the meeting participants agreed that Senator Harding should be the nominee. On the following day, General Wood and Governor Lowden were in first and second place, respectively, for eight ballots, but on the ninth ballot, Sen. Harding, whose strength had increased with each ballot, moved into the lead. On the tenth ballot, Warren Harding became the Republican nominee for president. The next day, the delegates selected Governor Calvin Coolidge of Massachusetts, who had earned a national reputation for toughness because of his firm stand in the Boston police strike the previous year, as Sen. Harding's vice presidential running mate. Warren Harding's opponent, former Governor James M. Cox of Ohio, running on a ticket with Assistant Secretary of the Navy Franklin D. Roosevelt, tried to make his support of President Wilson's proposal for American affiliation with the League of Nations the issue. But a war-weary electorate was swayed by Sen. Harding's plea for a "return to normalcy," the theme of a campaign which took Sen. Harding on five railroad trips into a total of twenty-four states. During the campaign, Senator Harding delivered over one hundred "whistle stop" speeches as well as thirty-five campaign addresses in various cities. He also delivered speeches on the front porch of his house on Mt. Vernon Avenue in Marion. The lawn and street in front of the house were packed with journalists and citizens who travelled to Marion to hear the Republican candidate. In the end, the voters, which included women for the first time in American history, elected Warren Harding as the twenty-ninth president of the United States by a wide margin.

After the election, Warren Harding arranged to rent the house on Mt. Vernon Avenue to Millard Hunt. He then moved to the White House, where, as president, he was responsible for improving fiscal management of the government budget, reduced expenditures and wartime taxation, and advocated United States membership in the World Court, a dream which was eventually realized. He also returned the nation's railways to private control. Significantly, on November 12, 1921, representatives of the United States, Great Britain, France, Italy and Japan met at President Harding's invitation to draw up limitations of naval armaments treaties. It was the first international peace meeting of its kind, and drew worldwide acclaim. He also fought with the steel industry to shorten the twelve-hour working day, to which steel companies agreed after the president's death. The president also courageously vetoed a huge soldier's bonus bill, saying that the bill did not provide for the additional revenues to pay the bonus. In 1922, he signed into law the Fordney-McCumber Tariff Act, which raised protective tariffs to new highs.

The Harding Presidency ended tragically. In 1922, President Harding became aware of a scandal concerning the Veteran's Bureau, which had sold war surplus materials far below value to favored purchasers without competitive bidding. The Bureau had also bought new materials well above their cost. He allowed the head of the Bureau, Charles R. Forbes, who had been an intimate of President Harding's, to leave for Europe in January 1923. This was followed by the suicide of Charles R. Cramer, counsel to the Bureau, who had bought from Warren Harding the home he lived in while a senator. To make matters worse, the Republicans had fared badly in the 1922 Congressional elections, and that result has been attributed to the ongoing economic recession following World War I. Worried that the results were essentially a vote of no confidence in his administration, President Harding resolved to travel on what he called a "voyage of understanding," in which he would take his case to the people and try to strengthen his popularity. He left for the trip on June 20, 1923, and was met in Kansas City by Mrs. Albert Fall, wife of the former Secretary of the Interior, who had resigned several months earlier. The speculation is that Mrs. Fall told the president at this meeting about her husband's role in opening up to private oil companies two huge oil fields reserved by the government for naval use, one located in Elk Hills in California and the other located at Teapot Dome in Wyoming, in exchange for bribes. Mr. Fall was convicted of bribery in 1929, but there has never been a trace of evidence linking President Harding with either the "Teapot Dome" scandal or the Veteran's Bureau scandal. However, these revelations, and others, apparently affected the president, who muttered comments about friends who had betrayed him by the time he reached Alaska.

On July 27th, the president was stricken in Seattle with what his doctor, Surgeon General Charles E. Sawyer, at first diagnosed as indigestion. Later, it was suspected that the president had a heart attack. By the time the president arrived in San Francisco on July 29, he seemed to be recovering. Then he was stricken with pneumonia, and was attended by a team of distinguished physicians but also appeared to be recovering from this attack. Finally, on August 2nd, the president died in bed while being read to by Mrs. Harding. The doctors speculated that his death was caused by a blood clot which had been carried to the brain, but were unable to perform an autopsy to prove their hypothesis because Mrs. Harding would not allow it. A funeral train carried the president's body across a mourning nation to his home in Marion, where it was buried in a temporary tomb at Marion Cemetery. Mrs. Harding returned to Marion staying at the home of Dr. Sawyer due to her kidney ailment. Mrs. Harding died in Marion the following year, and upon her death, the Harding house on Mt. Vernon Avenue was deeded to the Harding Memorial Association.

In 1926, the bodies of President and Mrs. Harding were taken to be interred in the newly constructed Harding Memorial in Marion, not far from their Mt. Vernon Avenue home. The Memorial, which cost $786,000.00 to complete, is currently undergoing a four-year renovation at a cost of over $1,200,000.00 in state and federal funds. At the dedication ceremony for the Memorial in 1931, President Herbert Hoover, who had served in President Harding's cabinet, said, "Warren Harding had a dim realization that he had been betrayed by a few of the men whom he had believed were his devoted friends. That was the tragedy of Warren Harding."

Years later, in the winter of 1964-65, the Harding Memorial Association undertook the task of restoring the house to its appearance at the turn of the century. The Association arranged to have the home's original gas lights reinstalled; the decoration, especially wallpaper, duplicated, and the original furnishings returned to their positions in the home. The building which had served as the press office in the 1920 campaign became the Harding Museum and Administrative Office.

Today, a tour of the house, which is a two-story frame house with an attic, begins on its Colonial Revival porch. As stated above, this porch was built after the old porch collapsed in 1903. The porch has a rotunda at one end, which served as a speaker's platform during Mr. Harding's campaign for lt. governor, as well as during the 1920 "front porch" campaign. Green wicker furniture decorates this large porch.

Once inside the house, visitors enter the parlor to see that it has walnut woodworking, an oak parquet floor, and a gas lighted fireplace adorned with tiles from a Cincinnati pottery. Also in the parlor is Mrs. Harding's Gebhardt piano, which was made in Marion, caned furniture and one of three stained glass windows imported from Germany. Mirrors above the mantel reflected light. On the stairs leading from the hallway is a clock, made circa 1891 and given to the Hardings by a Marion jeweler as a wedding present.

In the dining room, which is in the rear of the house on the first floor, is a stained glass window above a mirrored sideboard. A cabinet built into the wall contains a set of White House blue and white china, wedgewood china and Dresden china. Also here is a free standing wicker basket, a large model of the Mayflower made in Massachusetts and a miniature statue of Simon Bolivar. (The life-sized original is in New York's Central Park).

Also on the first floor of the house is a kitchen with wainscotted walls. The kitchen contains an old waffle iron, a large ice box, a six-burner gas stove made by A B Stove Co. of Battle Creek, an old toaster, a phlanged spoon, a deep fryer and coffee mill. A Sears & Roebuck bicycle is also here. The floor in the kitchen is linoleum. Adjacent is a pantry, which has cabinets with bevel-edged doors to keep mice out.

The library, also on the first floor, displays the desk and chair used by Warren Harding at the State Senate. This room also has a stained glass window. A portrait of Mr. Harding's parents hangs here. Visitors see a set of stackable bookshelves, and another of the three fireplaces in the house, all of which use the same flue. Also on display here is a box used to store wood, coal and a portable gas heater.

The wash room on the first floor has wainscotted walls. It has a ceramic design in the sink, which has a third spout for cistern water (although the house was on the Marion city water system beginning in 1891).

On a wall in the hallway on the second floor is a painting of a sacrificial lamb. It was found by a soldier in World War I who sent it to Mr. Harding, who in turn had it framed.

Also upstairs is the master bedroom, whose twin beds are made from bird's eye blond maple wood. The master bedroom has a bow window. The guest room features bordered posted wallpaper, a rocker, a large mirrored chiffarobe, and a cigar humidor from Havana. Also here is an impressive quilt made by a Ladies Republican Club which reads "G.O.P. Layton, Utah 1920," and the names of the women who stitched it radiate from an American flag.

Also on the second floor is the room used by Mrs. Harding's son Marshall Eugene DeWolfe, who died at the age of 35. In this room is a University of Michigan pennant, a guitar, and an elephant model. The second floor also includes a maid's room, another bathroom and a closet. The maid's room displays Mrs. Harding's dress and her shoes. Also here is a cricket cage, made in keeping with the Chinese belief that crickets bring good luck.

The site is maintained in excellent condition, and its grounds are attractively kept.

CALVIN COOLIDGE

The Plymouth Notch Historic District
(President Calvin Coolidge Birthplace)
Plymouth Notch, Vermont 05056
(802) 672-3773

Administered by the Vermont Division for Historic Preservation.

Directions: The site is six miles south of U.S. 4 on Vt. Route 100A.

Open: Daily, late May through mid-October.

Admission: Fee Charged.

Features: Self-guided tour of ten buildings, Aldrich House (originally President Coolidge's stepmother's house, open year-round with exhibits), two walking trails, Visitor Center museum, restaurant, gift shop, cheese factory, post office, rest rooms. Handicapped accessible.

Special Events: The site holds a July 4th Coolidge birthday parade and barbecue. Also on that day there is a ceremony at which a wreath, flown up from the White House, is placed on President Coolidge's grave.

It was in the small, hilltop community of Plymouth Notch, Vermont that Calvin Coolidge, 30th president of the United States, was born on July 4, 1872. His birthplace was a modest, one and a half story framed structure attached to the town's general store, which his father John Coolidge owned. To the left of the entrance door is the room in which President Coolidge was born. This small room still includes the bed in which he was born and, like the rest of the cottage, contains original Coolidge family furnishings.

The president's father was a man of great versatility who, because of his neighbors' respect, was referred to as Colonel John Coolidge. Indeed, he was a colonel on the staff of Governor Stickney of Vermont, but he held many other public offices, including state legislator, state senator, road commissioner, postmaster, and notary public.

John Coolidge married the president's mother, the former Victoria Josephine Moor, who was also a Plymouth Notch native. They were married in her family home, now called the Wilder House, which still stands as part of the Plymouth Notch Historic District.

The first story of the Coolidge birthplace includes a main center room, a small bedroom to the left, a kitchen to the right, and a pantry. A passageway leads to the rear of the general store that the president's father ran. Among notable furnishings in the house are: a doll belonging to the president's sister, Abbie, found resting on the Coolidge bed, a large desk used by the president's father, a baby's highchair, and a "nanny bench" designed so that the baby could be placed on one end and the mother at the other. Two small bedrooms, closed to the public, are on the second floor. The cottage was Calvin Coolidge's home until 1876, when the family moved across the road to a larger, yet still modest, homestead that was to become the home of the president's father for the rest of his life.

The white-framed, two-story Coolidge homestead was purchased by the president's father for $375. It includes a front living area, a tool shed, and a barn, all reached without having to go outside (a blessing in cold, Vermont winters!). Today, the house has been restored to its appearance as of August 3, 1923, the date Calvin Coolidge took the oath of office as the 30th president of the United States. Visitors to the house may take a self-guided tour by walking through a corridor leading from the barn to the front of the house.

The barn contains the buggy made by the president's father, which he used for business trips. The horses were stabled on the main floor of the barn, and hay was stored in the loft. Corn was hung in sacks from the rafters of the barn and used as seed for the following year's crops. A saddle used by Calvin Coolidge on his grandfather's horse, Captain, is also on display.

An entrance leads to the next wing, consisting of the tool room, the back buttery, and the shed bedroom. The tool room contains tools found at the time the property was donated to the state of Vermont in 1956. Some of these tools are housed in an old post office box, brought to the house by Carrie Brown, who became the second wife of the president's father in 1891, six years after the death of his first wife. The room was later used for storage by Miss Aurora Pierce, the housekeeper for the president's father. Miss Pierce lived in the house for over thirty years after the president's father died. Among the items she collected over the years were about twenty bushel baskets of birch bark.

The back buttery contains a dry sink and a series of shelves where milk pans rested until the cream was ready to be skimmed. The shed bedroom includes a quilt made by Calvin Coolidge when he was ten, as well as a miniature chest of drawers which he also made. The room was subsequently used as a bedroom by Vice President Coolidge's chauffeur.

Next along the corridor is the woodshed. This was used to store the wood for the stoves in the kitchen, parlor, and sitting room. It was Calvin Coolidge's daily chore as a boy to split the kindling wood for the morning fire. Also in the room is the box used by the president's father to smoke his hams outdoors. Beside the woodshed is the privy, which was the only sanitary facility on the premises until 1932.

The next room is the laundry, where all of the family washing and ironing was done. Clothes were boiled on the kitchen stove using the copper wash boiler. Each item was hand scrubbed on a washboard, put through a wringer, and then rinsed in another tub. The clothes were then placed outside to dry and finally ironed with irons heated on the kitchen stove.

Adjacent to the laundry are the pantry and kitchen. The pantry was used for storing dishes and for the preparation of baked food. The kitchen houses a large wood-burning stove, an iron sink, and the family eating table. It was near the kitchen door where shy, young Calvin Coolidge would stand to compose himself prior to meeting the visitors his parents would bring to the house.

One can see out onto the porch, now part of the corridor. Also in sight is the sitting room, or "oath of office room," where in the early morning of August 3, 1923, John Coolidge, in his capacity as a notary public, administered the presidential oath of office to his son (an event unique in American history). Next to the sitting room door is the secretary used by the president's father, which still contains many of his papers. Many family pictures adorn this room, including one of Calvin Coolidge's sister, Abigail Coolidge, and his sons Calvin Coolidge, Jr. (who died at 16) and John Coolidge. This small, simply furnished room also contains several items of knitwear, including a pair of mittens made by the president's mother and two hand-woven shawls.

Stepping back out onto the back porch, one can see the large, gray farmhouse across the meadow, built by the president's great-grandfather circa 1815. Near the farmhouse is also the two and a half story addition, originally attached to the homestead in 1931, which was used as modern living quarters by the president. It was moved to its current location in 1956 when the Homestead was donated to the state of Vermont. Its removal restored the Coolidge Homestead to its 1923 appearance.

Facing the front is a bedroom used in 1923 by Calvin Coolidge's father. Today, the room contains furnishings used by the president and Mrs. Coolidge. Featured in the room is a hand-decorated set of country furniture and a quilt made by Abigail. The room also contains photographs of the president's father and his grandfather. On the commode is a chamber set consisting of matched crockery. Pairs of President Coolidge's small (size 7 and a half) shoes are also on display.

The final room accessible from the back porch is the parlor, or "Best Room." Unlike most Vermont homes where parlors were seldom used, except for formal occasions such as funerals and weddings, church services were often held in this parlor when it was too cold to have them in the Union Church across the street. (John Coolidge, the president's father, was deacon of the Church.) The black walnut furniture with horsehair upholstery in this room was purchased by the president's father in Boston. He also bought the piano to the side of the room in Boston for his second wife, Carrie. Also contained in this room is the only photograph of young Calvin Coolidge and his sister, Abigail Coolidge, together, taken during a Sunday school picnic in 1887. The hassock near the horsehair sofa contains a secret compartment for holding valuables.

While Plymouth Notch was Calvin Coolidge's true home, his long career brought him to many other residences. From 1885 to 1890, when he attended Black River Academy in Ludlow, Vermont, and spent one term at St. Johnsbury Academy, he boarded at various homes. He also stayed in various private residences while attending Amherst College from 1891 to 1895. During the period from 1895 to 1905, Calvin Coolidge studied law and was admitted to practice in Northampton, Massachusetts. He boarded at Round Hill, in the home of Mr. Robert N. Weir, the steward of the school where his future wife, Grace, taught, and dined at Rahat's Inn. Shortly after his marriage in 1905, he moved into the Norwood Hotel, then to a small furnished house for a few months. Later in 1905, he rented a home for $28.00 a month at 21 Massasoit Street in Northampton, which was his official residence until 1930. When he became governor of Massachusetts, his rent was raised to $40.00 a month. The house, which was furnished in an austere fashion, is a simply designed duplex with a front porch and three bedrooms. The front porch was Mr. Coolidge's favorite sitting place. Ever frugal, the Coolidges bought linens and silverware from a local hotel after it closed, and did not hesitate to display the hotel insignia on each item. Governmental duties had Mr. Coolidge commuting to Boston, where he stayed in a room at the Adams Hotel. After he became lieutenant governor he rented two rooms for his wife and himself. The house on Massasoit Street was maintained as one of the Coolidges' residences while Mr. Coolidge was vice president and president, and he returned to the house upon leaving office. In 1930, the Coolidges moved to "The Beeches," which they bought for $45,000.00 from Smith College President Dr. Henry Noble MacCracken in an effort to achieve more privacy. This house, which was President Coolidge's

home until his death on January 5, 1933, is a shingle-sided house with twelve rooms and includes a tennis court and swimming pool. The rear sleeping porches on the house overlook the meadows and the Connecticut River. Today, both of Mr. Coolidge's Northampton homes are privately owned.

As vice president from 1921 to 1923, Mr. Coolidge stayed in a small suite at the Willard Hotel, on 14th Street and Pennsylvania Avenue, N.W. in Washington, D.C. This Beaux Arts style hotel closed in 1968, but was recently reopened under new management. After Mr. Coolidge became president, a new roof and third floor were added to the White House to allow for more privacy and housekeeping areas. As first lady, Grace Coolidge requested that Congress pass a resolution accepting "rare old pieces" as gifts to the White House. She also crocheted a bedspread for the Lincoln Bed.

During the White House renovation, the Coolidges stayed at 15 Dupont Circle, N.W. in Washington. This residence, a four-story mansion with thirty rooms and ten baths, was designed by Stanford White in 1902 and was known as the Patterson House. Its second floor has a large hall, a ballroom, a library and a dining room with a butler's pantry. Many fine parties including one honoring aviator Charles Lindbergh, were held here. Today, the mansion is the Washington Club, and is one of the few mansions remaining on Dupont Circle. In contrast to these posh surroundings, the Coolidges spent their summers in a cottage in the Black Hills of South Dakota. It was while staying here at the cottage that President Coolidge made his famous statement, "I do not choose to run for President in 1928."

Today, the Calvin Coolidge Birthplace, general store, and Homestead are part of a historical district owned and operated by the state of Vermont, Division for Historic Preservation. Among the other features of this village is the Plymouth Cheese Corp. reopened by the president's son John Coolidge in 1960. On July 4, 1972 (the 100th anniversary of Calvin Coolidge's birth), a visitors center was formally opened by the state of Vermont in his memory. It includes a museum store, a sitting room containing portraits of the president and his family, displays of presidential gifts from around the world, and another room featuring a photograph exhibit with text taken from Calvin Coolidge's autobiography.

Two additional buildings were recently added to the historic tour here: Coolidge Hall, which was used by the president as his 1924 Summer White House office, and a circa 1927 tourist cabin (which, according to local tradition, was used by the president's chauffeur and secret service.)

Set in the magnificent Green Mountains of Vermont, so dearly loved by President Coolidge, this historic village is a fitting monument to the 30th president. President Coolidge is buried in the town cemetery here, along with six generations of his family. One cannot fail to be moved by the simple beauty of this land, and though his spoken words were few, Calvin Coolidge spoke with great feeling about the days he spent here and how they influenced his life.

HERBERT HOOVER

Herbert Hoover National Historic Site (Birthplace)
P.O. Box 607
West Branch, Iowa 52358
(319) 643-2541

Administered by the National Park Service.

Directions: The site is one-half mile north of I-80, exit 254, about eight miles east of Iowa City.

Open: Daily (except New Year's Day, Thanksgiving Day and Christmas Day).

Admission: Fee charged.

Features: Birthplace cottage, grave site, Herbert Hoover Presidential Library-Museum, blacksmith shop, schoolhouse, Friends meeting house, other period houses, visitor center, book store, gift shop, picnic shelters, rest rooms. 75 acres of restored native tall grass prairie. Handicapped accessible.

Special Events: Herbert Hoover birthday celebration ("Hooverfest") the first weekend in August. Free admission for all on Sunday of that weekend. "A Christmas Past," first weekend in December. Other special events throughout the year.

In 1874, West Branch, Iowa, was a small settlement on the west branch of the Wapsinonoc Creek, populated mostly by people who had recently migrated from Ohio. Among the inhabitants of this tiny settlement were a young blacksmith and his wife. The blacksmith, Jesse Clark Hoover, and his wife, the former Hulda Randall Minthorn, had a child by the name of Theodore in January 1871. On August 10, 1874, a second son was born to this young couple, and this boy, who was born into such humble circumstances in the small Quaker community, was destined to serve much of the 90 years of his life in the service of others. The boy's name was Herbert Clark Hoover.

The house where Herbert Hoover was born is a small board-and-batten structure standing on the corner of Downey and Penn Streets, measuring fourteen by twenty feet. The lot on which the small cottage stood was purchased at a cost of $90.00 on March 12, 1870. After the birth of their third child, Mary, in 1876, the cottage proved to be quite cramped, but the Hoovers remained in the cottage until 1879. Herbert Hoover's father and grandfather, Eli, built this cottage in 1871, making some of the furnishings of this cottage with their own hands. For example, in the small bedroom located in the left-front portion of the cottage, visitors find a small wooden cradle used by the Hoovers during this period. As the children grew older, they slept in a trundle bed stored under the parents' bed in the small bedroom. Each of the Hoover children, including Herbert Hoover's younger sister, Mary Hoover, used the high chair. The parents' bed was a rope bed with a feather tick. The wooden couch in the living room contains a mattress also stuffed with a feather tick.

During the winter months, the Hoovers kept the stove inside the living room and did their cooking there, which also provided heat for the small cottage during the winter. During summer months, the cooking stove was moved into a small room located behind the living room. This summer kitchen was accessible from the back porch. Today, this room is used to display various kitchen tools of the period of Herbert Hoover's childhood, including a sauerkraut maker and a sausage stuffer.

Behind the cottage the Hoovers kept a small flock of chickens, which provided fresh eggs for the household. Another food source was the vegetable garden located in the back yard. Out of season, the vegetables were stored in a root cellar, accessible through a trap door in the floor of the porch.

These early years must have created a strong impression of the value of hard work and honesty in young Herbert Hoover's mind. He had, after all, spent his early years growing up in a Quaker family, and in a cottage built by his father and grandfather. Because of the scarcity of wood on the prairie, the wood used to build the structure was probably rafted down the Mississippi River from Minnesota. Herbert Hoover remained in this tiny cottage for only five years, at which point the family moved to a larger, two-story, four room home a block south and across Downey Street from the birthplace cottage. (The larger home is no longer in existence today; it was sold for $500.00 in April 1886 and razed in the fall of 1923.) However, Mr. Hoover never forgot his birthplace, as evidenced by the fact that he is buried on a knoll overlooking the tiny cottage where he began his life.

On December 13, 1880, Jesse Hoover died at the age of 34, but Hulda Hoover was determined to keep her family together. Herbert Hoover traveled to stay with relatives from time to time during the next few years. In the summer of 1881, "Bertie" Hoover traveled with his mother and his brother, Tad, to stay with Mrs. Hoover's brother, Pennington Minthorn, in his sod house in Sioux County in northwest Iowa. Bertie Hoover also traveled by train to spend eight or nine months with Mrs. Hoover's sister, Agnes, and her husband, Laban J. Miles, in Pawhush, Indian Territory (today Oklahoma), where Mr. Miles worked as a government agent to the Osage and Kaw nations. Years later, Herbert Hoover recalled that his Aunt Agnes was kind and that he had a boy and a girl cousin who lived at the Miles home. The three of them attended schools with native American children.

Bertie Hoover returned to West Branch, where tragedy struck on February 24, 1884, when his mother, Hulda Hoover, died from typhoid fever and pneumonia at the age of 35. Lawrie Tatum, a pioneer farmer and a Quaker, was appointed guardian for Tad and Bertie Hoover. Several relatives offered to care for the orphaned Hoover children.

Today, the village that Herbert Hoover knew as a young child has been preserved and restored, thanks to the efforts of the National Park Service. Visitors can take a self-guided tour of a replica of Jesse Hoover's blacksmith shop, as well as the restored one-room schoolhouse and the Friends Meeting House where the Hoover family worshipped. The birthplace cottage is the original cottage in which Herbert Hoover was born, and it is indeed fortunate that it has been preserved in a condition which, as nearly as feasible, replicates its appearance in the year 1874.

The small cottage was sold in May 1879 by Jesse Hoover, who at the same time sold his blacksmith shop and all of the adjoining property for a sum of $1,000.00. The birthplace cottage was eventually acquired in 1889 by R. P. Scellers, a drayman. Mr. Scellers, after purchasing the birthplace cottage, bought another house, moved it onto the lot and turned the cottage 90 degrees so that it faced south, after which he joined the buildings. Hence, for a time, the birthplace of Herbert Hoover was used as a kitchen for the larger house to which it was attached.

Mrs. Scellers acquired the cottage after the death of her husband, charged ten cents admission for each tourist who wished to see the cottage, and sold souvenirs. She carried on this small business, which earned her an average of $600.00 per year, until her death in 1934. After her death, her heirs decided that they would sell the cottage. The following year, through the offices of a friend, the property was sold for the sum of $4,500.00 to the president's son, Allen Hoover.

Once the property had been reacquired by the Hoover family, Mrs. Herbert (Lou) Hoover supervised its restoration to its 1874 appearance. By this time, Herbert Hoover had served as president of the United States. After Mrs. Hoover had restored the cottage, a group called the Herbert Hoover Birthplace Society was formed in 1939 for the express purpose of managing and maintaining the cottage as a shrine to the 31st president. Today, it is part of the Herbert Hoover National Historic Site. The Herbert Hoover Presidential Library-Museum, which is operated by the National Archives and Records Administration, is located a short distance from the birthplace.

Every year during "Hooverfest" weekend, a memorial ceremony takes place at President Hoover's grave site with some of his descendants attending. They gather in honor of a man who accomplished much in his 90 years of life, including successful careers in engineering and business, during which he amassed a large fortune, but which never deterred him from devoting himself unselfishly to public service. He was a man who knew both praise and scorn, but whose tenacity would not allow him to retire from the arena of public life. He was a world statesman whose success in life was based on the lessons of honesty and hard work he learned from the place he was born and where he was laid to rest.

The Hoover-Minthorn House
115 South River Street
Newberg, Oregon 97132
(503) 538-6629

Administered by the National Society of the Colonial Dames of America in the state of Oregon.

Directions:	The site is located at the intersection of River and Second Streets in Newberg.
Open:	Wednesday to Sunday in March through November. Closed in January. Open weekends only in December and February. Closed Thanksgiving Day and the day after, Christmas Eve and Day, New Year's Eve and Day.
Admission:	Fee charged.
Features:	Tour of home, picnic at park across the street. No rest rooms. Site sells one book, *The Homes of the Hoovers*. Teachers can borrow a video presentation of

the home (for a $35.00 deposit which is returned upon return of the tape). Tour lasts about 30 minutes. Not handicapped acessible. A brochure in Japanese is available.

Special Events:	Free old fashioned ice cream social the last weekend in July. The yard is available for rent for a small parties. On August 10th the site celebrates Herbert Hoover's birthday.
	On the first weekend in December, the site hosts a Victorian Christmas with living history and live music of the early 1800s.

In 1883, Herbert Hoover was orphaned, his father having died in 1880 and his mother having passed away in 1883. He went to live with his aunt and uncle, Millie and Allen Hoover, on their farm about one mile north of the depot in West Branch, Iowa. In 1885, at the age of eleven, he moved west to live with another aunt and uncle, Laura Minthorn and Dr. Henry John Minthorn, in Newberg, Oregon, at their invitation. The Minthorns had recently lost a son, and they thought that having another boy in the house might ease their grief. He spent four of his formative years in Newberg, which was a dry, Quaker town at the time.

The Minthorn House, where Herbert Hoover came to live, was built in 1881 by Jesse Edwards, a Quaker from Indiana (who also bounded and plated the present site of the city of Newberg) and was the first residence built and still standing in Newberg. Dr. Henry John Minthorn, who bought the house from Mr. Edwards in the fall of 1885, was the first medical doctor in the community, as well as the first superintendent of Friends Pacific Academy, which later changed its name to George Fox College. Young Herbert Hoover came to live with his Uncle John and Aunt Laura a month after Dr. Minthorn bought the house. There "Bertie" became reacquainted with his aunt and uncle and his two younger female cousins, Tennessee (nicknamed "Tennie") and Gertrude. The Minthorns' youngest daughter, Mary, was born in the house two years later.

While living in Newberg, Herbert Hoover attended Friends Pacific Academy, a Quaker school attended by dignitaries and foreign students. From Newberg, he moved with his aunt and uncle to Salem, Oregon, in 1889. They first lived temporarily in a barn and then at a home on Hazel and Highland Avenues in Salem. He interrupted his education to become an office boy at the Oregon Land Company, and attended night classes to prepare for further education at Stanford University in Palo Alto, California. He first lived in Encina Hall on the Stanford campus and spent some of his second year at Romero Hall. It is said that at one point he lived at "the Camp," a barracks-like series of rooms built for the campus workers, where rent was cheaper and he could pay less than the $15.00 a month he paid at Encina Hall. He eventually returned to Romero Hall and spent his final two years at Encina Hall. During his student years, from 1891 to 1895, he spent his summers doing geological work in Arkansas, Nevada and California. He supported himself through college by doing typing, running a laundry service, and handling a paper route.

After graduating from Stanford in 1895 (Stanford's first graduating class) with an A.B. in engineering, Herbert Hoover worked as a miner in Nevada, and then as an aide in a mining firm in San Francisco, California. From 1897 to 1899, he managed a gold mining operation in Australia, living in a bungalow in Kalgoorie, western Australia and then at Mt.

Lenora, 150 miles north of Kalgoorie. On February 10, 1899, he married his college sweetheart, Lou Henry, in Monterey, California. The newlyweds then departed for Shanghai, and then for Tientsin, China, where Mr. Hoover became chief engineer of China's bureau of mines. Mr. Hoover traveled throughout China while Mrs. Hoover stayed at the Astor House Hotel in Tientsin and with friends. Later, the Hoovers rented a two-story, blue brick house on Racecourse Road. In 1901, Mr. Hoover became general manager of the Chinese Engineering and Mining Company.

In 1901, Herbert Hoover became a partner in a British engineering firm, and traveled throughout the world in that capacity. The Hoovers first lived in the "White House" at Ashley Drive, Walton-on-Thames, a few miles southwest of London. Later they rented an apartment at 39 Hyde Park Gate in the Kensington section of London, where their sons, Herbert Hoover, Jr. and Allen Hoover were born. In 1902, desiring a "home base" in the United States, Mr. Hoover built a small cottage in Monterey.

On December 20, 1907, the Hoovers moved to "The Red House," on Hornton Street West in the Kensington section of London. The Red House was a rambling two-story structure built in the 1830s. It had steam heating, large bathrooms and an oak-paneled library with leaded glass bookcases. Its dining room had walnut panels and a dais reachable by two or three steps which could be used as a stage.

The grounds were surrounded by a high brick wall and had a garden, an old mulberry tree and a fish pond with a fountain. The Red House lease terminated in 1917, and the Hoovers returned to the United States. In 1907, Mr. Hoover also arranged for the construction of a six-room cottage at 623 Mirada Avenue on the Stanford University Campus. Later, this became the site of the Lou Henry Hoover Home.

From 1908 to 1914, Herbert Hoover headed his own engineering firm and supervised projects in many countries. In 1914, he became Chairman of the Commission for Relief in Belgium. From 1917 to 1919, he was the United States Food Administrator. In those capacities, he stayed at many places in different countries. His last stop before returning to the United States in 1919 to live in the Hoovers' new home on the Stanford University campus was Paris.

As for the Minthorn House in Newberg, the Minthorns left the house in 1889, selling it to the Nicholson family, who in turn sold it to Henry and Mary Mills in 1904. In 1909, the Mills gave the house to the Pacific College (George Fox College), an institution they strongly supported. A Mr. Crozier was the next owner, followed by the Downeys. Then Pacific College became the owner for the second time in 1945. Sometime prior to 1945, the house was remodeled, and in 1947, the house was purchased by the Herbert Hoover Foundation, and a restoration process began with the participation of volunteers and interested citizens. The restoration effort produced a result which was very faithful to the original design of the house.

When Herbert Hoover visited the house for its dedication on August 10, 1955 (his eighty-first birthday), he remarked that the rooms were very much as he remembered them. On that occasion, President Hoover reminisced about the days, seventy years earlier, when he lived in the house, and his memories were indeed fond. He recalled the pear tree growing on the property, and the delicious pears it yielded, which were used to make pear butter. His Aunt Laura showed him how to stir the pear butter, and told him that he must keep stirring without stopping. She also told him that as long as he did so, he could eat all the pears he wished. "Bertie" Hoover, who had never eaten a pear before arriving in Oregon, loved the pears so much that he ate too many of them and became so sick that he had to be put in bed to recover. After that, "Bertie" did not eat another pear for a long time.

The Herbert Hoover Foundation administered the house until 1981, when the house was turned over to the National Society of the Colonial Dames of America in the state of Oregon.

Today, only six to eight visitors at one time can tour Herbert Hoover's boyhood home in Newberg, the Hoover-Minthorn House. Visitors are taken on a guided tour, which includes the parlor, living room, kitchen, back porch, and three bedrooms that are upstairs. The house contains some original pieces used by the Minthorns, but all furnishings on display today are of the Minthorn era and evoke the flavor of that period. The siding of the home is also original, but only a few of its windows and window panes are original.

The yard surrounding the home accents the loveliness of the setting in which Herbert Hoover grew up. When visitors tour the house in the spring, they find its corner lot adorned with blooming flowers. Lilacs also grow on the property on which the house is situated. A well house, an outhouse, and a boardwalk were also located there, and are replicated today at their original locations. Today, the house sits on a busy street corner across from a lovely park appropriately named Hoover Park. In Herbert Hoover's day, the house looked down into a canyon and Hess Creek, a setting of quiet pastoral beauty where cows grazed. The house gives visitors a feeling for what life was like for a Quaker family just before the turn of the century.

The first room visitors see is the parlor, where the Minthorns spent much of their leisure time. In one corner of the parlor is a carefully crafted secretary, which contains Dr. Minthorn's medical books. Also in this room are a pump organ, unusual rocking chairs, and a Victorian era sofa. A portrait of Dr. Minthorn hangs on a wall here. Bertie Hoover enjoyed the family gatherings and singing to the music of the pump organ in the parlor. The stereoscope placed in this room was a source of amusement for family members, who could use it to view scenes of faraway places. A Bible, with a beautifully carved wooden cover, is also on display here.

In the dining room is a table dating back to 1845 which is one of the rarest in Oregon. It was the property of Joel Palmer, an Indian agent in Dayton, a city a few miles from Newberg. The dishes are royal ironstone china manufactured by Alfred Meekin of England, and represent a style very popular in the 1880s and 1890s. It is rare to see as complete a set of such dishes as those on display here. A silver napkin ring inscribed "Tennie" with a cock crowing, as well as a silver cup and saucer given to Dr. Minthorn by his students, are also here. A pie closet, or pie safe in this room, originated at about the same time as the house, although it is not an original furnishing. The holes in the pie safe allow air to circulate without letting insects get to the contents inside. On the wall hangs a charming letter written by a lovestruck Bertie Hoover to a girl he knew while living here.

The kitchen displays black iron utensils, a period stove and oven. On a kitchen table sit certain period pieces, including a tin lunch pail with its own early day "thermos." On the wall hangs a candle dipper and a corn-shaped muffin tin. A large cabinet referred to as the "kitchen queen" was used as a work area, as well as for storage, and is thought to be an original piece owned by the Minthorns. The utensils on display here include: an apple corer, a sausage stuffer and other well-used items.

Going through the pantry and up the stairs, visitors come to an upstairs bedroom. At the top of the stairs is the room shared by the three Minthorn daughters. Here is a hand-knitted bedspread, one of many fine examples of needlecraft on display in the house, including embroidery, lace and a hair weave made from human hair. Given the number of chores to be completed before turning to needlework (probably by late evening working by candlelight), the quality of the weaving on display here is remarkable. The small youth bed in the daughters' room is a Minthorn original. Here also are a tiny pair of shoes from Herbert Hoover's birthplace, and a tiny dress which, in the late nineteenth century, could have been worn by a small girl or a boy.

Down the hall a few steps is Herbert Hoover's room. The hall is adorned with patterned wallpaper which, according to the youngest Minthorn daughter, Mary Minthorn Stinch, is an exact copy of what was used when she was a child there. In "Bertie" Hoover's room is his bed, with a spread and mattress very similar to those he used. The mattress was regularly stuffed with fresh straw. Here also is a collection of recreational items which display Herbert Hoover's love for the outdoors. A trunk here belonged to Mrs. William Lord, whose husband was the ninth governor of Oregon. It was donated to the house by her daughter Elizabeth. Elizabeth Lord and Edith Schreiber were the landscape architects responsible for the restoration of the yard and garden area surrounding the house. The carpets throughout the house are period pieces representative of the carpets originally in the house.

The master bedroom, where Mary Minthorn was born, displays two leather cases used by Dr. Minthorn to carry medicine vials for patients in need of medicines. A sewing machine patented in 1872 is also here, as well as a large commode set and a leather razor strap used for both shaving and the discipline of unruly children. A beautiful, handwoven paisley shawl is also on view here. A pot belly stove located here may be the original stove used by the Minthorns. Herbert Hoover recalled at the dedication of the house that one of his chores was to split the wood for the stove. Also on display on the property is Dr. Minthorn's buggy whip and a lantern used to light his way while traveling to make house calls.

Herbert Hoover spent a short but significant period of his life here under the care of his beloved Aunt Laura and Uncle John before embarking on a path to a varied career as engineer, academic, world leader and statesman. It is a pleasant experience to view these surroundings and obtain first-hand information concerning the early years of a man who eventually became the thirty-first president of the United States.

Lou Henry Hoover House
c/o Stanford University
623 Mirada Avenue
Stanford, California 94305
(415) 723-3419

Administered by Stanford University.

Directions: The site is on the Stanford University campus between Mayfield and Santa Inez Streets.

Open: By appointment only.

Features: Home on one-acre property on the campus of Stanford University.

Special Events: None.

In 1919, after Herbert and Lou Hoover returned to America from Paris, where Herbert Hoover headed the U.S. Food Administration, the Hoovers took up residence at Stanford University in a temporary home. They had rented seven different houses in Palo Alto and Stanford between 1914 and 1920, which they used when not traveling abroad on relief missions.

The Hoovers, however, were planning a permanent home. In 1917 or 1918, they commissioned a San Francisco architect, Louis Mulgardt, to design their home. Shortly after engaging Mr. Mulgardt, the Hoovers had an unpleasant surprise—Mr. Mulgardt had made his contract with the Hoovers public, and the national news services publicized the plans. Given the nation's economic situation, the Hoovers felt that

the news was ill-timed. Moreover, they felt that Mr. Mulgardt's plans for the house were too pretentious. They decided to dismiss Mr. Mulgardt, paying him for his services up to that date.

This unfortunate episode delayed the Hoovers' plans for their new home. Their intentions to build were revived by September 27, 1919, when Herbert Hoover, upon his return to California, made public his plans for a home "containing seven rooms and a basement, a kitchen and a garage." By this time, Mr. Hoover was being considered as a possible presidential candidate, and one politician, who was clearly not enamored of Mr. Hoover, was quoted as saying, "Herbert Hoover lives in a palatial residence on his estate at Stanford University." Mr. Hoover maintained

that the "estate" was only seven rooms on one acre. While there are seven rooms on the first two floors, Mr. Hoover neglected to mention the servants' rooms or the guest rooms on the other floors of the home, which was built at a cost of $137,000.00. Still, the house, while elegant, is not "palatial" in appearance. Rather, Mrs. Hoover wanted the house to blend with others in the community.

To avoid overwhelming other houses in the area, the Hoovers selected a vacant hillside lot on San Juan Hill, overlooking the Stanford campus, as the site for their new home. It was on that hill that the Hoovers used to sit and enjoy the view, and perhaps courted. The Hoovers leased the land from the university, and selected new architects: Arthur B. Clark, head of Stanford's Art Department, and his son, Birge. As Arthur Clark was quite busy, the lion's share of the planning effort fell to Birge Clark.

The design and planning of the house was of the utmost importance to Lou Hoover. Herbert Hoover, continually involved in public matters in Washington and Europe, showed little interest in the details of the project, although his wife tried to involve him. Lou Hoover, as reflected in her correspondence with Birge Clark, was not only interested in the project, but she involved herself in the design of the house down to the smallest details. For example, in a letter dated February 14, 1920, Mrs. Hoover wrote, "From

the one door handle on the small piece of wood I should think the color scheme very good, although I fancy it would be better still if the metal were considerably darker." Or this telegram from Mrs. Hoover to Birge Clark, dated June 28, 1928, which reads, "Decided basement room imperative with cement floor some one get hunch for cheap appropriate fireplace how about indian plaster stop." As Birge Clark later wrote: "Though Mr. Hoover paid no attention, Mrs. Hoover paid a great deal of attention, far more than the average client ever would."

The result is an eclectic, tasteful style, and while Birge Clark was the architect, the home is every inch a reflection of the taste and influence of Lou Henry Hoover. As for the overall architectural style of the house, an article in the February 1929 issue of *Western Homes and Gardens* perhaps states it best: "At first glance the exterior of this residence suggests the Pueblo influence, but a closer study of the various elevations reveals the true motif, the Algerian, with every roof an outdoor living room, accessible by a staircase... [T]he house...is a mass of piled up blocks with terraces, outer staircases and fireplaces everywhere inviting freedom and comfort. A dignified unpretentiousness prevails." As for the Hoovers themselves, they intended to have a house which was liveable and fun, as well as fire resistant. With these considerations in mind, the house was designed with low walls, wide terraces and many windows. Mrs. Hoover also intended that the house be architecturally reminiscent of Hopi pueblos.

In June 1920, the Hoovers moved into the new house, which remained their principal home until Mrs. Hoover's death in 1944. While living in the house, the Hoovers, particularly Mrs. Hoover, enjoyed the special amenities of their home. For example, Mrs. Hoover's study is accessible both by the main stairway and by a "secret," winding stairway leading from her dressing room. In front of the desk in that study were three little windows from which Mrs. Hoover could look at the entrance to the house and, if she saw someone coming, she could come down to greet that person or remain "out of the house" at her election.

The house has fireplaces in every principal room, and one on the terrace for toasting marshmallows. The house had a swimming pool, which was used by the Hoovers for many swimming parties.

The Hoovers' sons, Herbert, Jr. and Allen, also lived in the house, and once used its basement to build a car, powered by a motorcycle engine. The car had to be removed from the basement by a window. Mrs. Hoover enjoyed driving the small car around the Stanford campus.

Beginning in 1921, the Hoovers spent most of their time in Washington, and during that time Herbert Jr. lived in the house while a student at Stanford. As secretary of commerce in the Harding and Coolidge administrations, Herbert Hoover lived at 2300 S Street, N.W., in Washington, D.C.

This home, occupied by the Hoovers from 1921 to 1928, was originally the home of Major Thomas M. Gales, whose realty firm developed the Kalorama Heights section of Washington in 1901 and 1902. That house has been described as "a nineteenth century house trying to become Georgian."

While president, Herbert Hoover used a log cabin on the Rapidan River in Virginia as a presidential retreat. Today, the cabin is a part of Shenandoah National Park and is open to the public each year on Herbert Hoover's birthday.

During the Hoovers' long absences, someone always stayed in their Stanford house to look after it. After leaving the presidency in 1933, President Hoover lived in the house for another two years. He then lived at a suite at the Waldorf-Astoria Hotel in New York City, where he remained until his death on October 20, 1964. He spent his post-presidential years as an active participant in civic affairs and as a world statesman, and was appointed to head various government commissions, notably a commission on government reorganization, by President Truman. He served in these appointive capacities from 1946 to 1949.

After Mrs. Hoover's death in 1944, Herbert Hoover presented the house on San Juan Hill as a gift to Stanford University. President Hoover stayed in the house for periods lasting several weeks in the 1940s and 1950s, but the Lou Henry Hoover House, as it is now known, became the official residence of Stanford University's presidents, and remains so today. The home was designated a National Historic Landmark on April 29, 1985.

FRANKLIN DELANO ROOSEVELT

Home of Franklin D. Roosevelt
National Historic Site
Route 9
Hyde Park, NY 12538
(914) 229-9115

Administered by the National Park Service.

Directions:	Site is just north of Poughkeepsie on Route 9. Entrance is on left side of the road.	**Features:**	Home, museum, library, gardens, grave sites of Franklin and Eleanor Roosevelt, restrooms, and two gift shops. Handicapped accessible.
Open:	Wednesday through Sunday (except Thanksgiving Day, Christmas Day, and New Years Day).	**Special Events:**	A grave site ceremony is held every year on January 30th, Memorial Day, and October 11th.
Admission:	Fee charged.		

The magnificent grounds of the Franklin D. Roosevelt Home command a fine view of the Hudson River Valley, stretching southward toward Poughkeepsie. This panorama was one of the virtues of this site that continued to draw the thirty-second president back to his home throughout his life. It was here that Franklin Delano Roosevelt was born on January 30, 1882, and it was here that he was finally laid to rest. His attempt to spend as much time as possible at his family home, Springwood, reflects his great love of that home. Because of his frequent stays at this home during his presidency, a series of historic events took place here.

Although commonly referred to by the name of the town in which it is located, Hyde Park, the home is actually known as "Springwood." Built about 1800, the two-story structure was bought by the president's father, James, in 1867. Franklin Roosevelt and his mother, Sara Delano Roosevelt, later hired architect Francis W. Hoppin to modernize the structure and add wings to the north and south. The stone and stucco alterations were completed by 1916 and the house remains unchanged to this day.

To be sure, Franklin Roosevelt occupied other homes in his lifetime. From 1896 to 1904, he spent much of his time on the campuses of Groton School in Massachusetts, then Harvard University, and then Columbia Law School in New York City. From 1908 to 1929, he shared with his mother, Sara, a neo-Georgian double row house with drawing room and dining room doors which, when opened, provided free access between the two dwellings. This home, at 47-49 East 65th Street in New York, was purchased by students at Hunter College in 1941, and serves as a memorial to Sara Delano Roosevelt. From 1911 to 1913, Franklin Roosevelt was a New York State Senator and lived in Albany. In 1913, he became Assistant Secretary of the Navy, and he and his wife, Eleanor, lived at 2131 R Street in Washington, which has seventeen rooms and six and a half baths. He left that home in 1920, the year he ran unsuccessfully for vice president. Today, that home is the Malinese Embassy. He also spent much time at his cottage on Campobello Island, lived at the New York State Executive Mansion while governor and, while president, at the "Little White House" in Warm Springs, Georgia, where he died in April 1945. Of course, he also occupied the White House from 1933 to 1945, and established the presidential retreat he called "Shangri-La" (later renamed "Camp David" by President Eisenhower) at the Recreational Demonstration Area in the Catoctin Mountains in Maryland in 1942. At the White House during the Roosevelt administration, the west and east wings were rebuilt, an underground cabinet room was redesigned, a swimming pool was constructed by public subscription, office space for the first lady was provided, and the first electric dishwasher and first bomb shelter were added. President Roosevelt himself designed the American Eagle Pedestals for the Grand Piano in the East Room. At "Shangri-La," two hours away from Washington, an existing cabin was enlarged to include a living/dining room, screened-in porch, bedroom wings, and a kitchen wing with an exterior of hardwood and local stone. A communications building, a guest lodge and a gatehouse were added to the site, making it suitable for a president, his aides and guests. Because the temperature at the retreat is generally cooler than in Washington, it is an appealing place for a working president and his aides during the warm summer months.

The largest of Springwood's 35 rooms is the library. Here, above the two fireplaces, are portraits of two of the president's ancestors: Isaac Roosevelt, who was active in the Revolutionary War, and James Roosevelt, a former New York state assemblyman who became the first Roosevelt to settle in Dutchess County in 1819.

The Dresden Room contains a Dresden chandelier and mantel bought in Germany by James Roosevelt in 1866, and upstairs is the bedroom where Franklin Roosevelt was born in 1882.

The first floor study (called the "Summer White House") was the site of a historic signing with British Prime Minister Winston Churchill, on June 20, 1942. It launched the Manhattan Project, under which the atomic bomb was developed. It was also from this study that Franklin D. Roosevelt broadcasted his last campaign speech on November 6, 1944.

Upon his death on April 12, 1945 in Warm Springs, Georgia, President Roosevelt's body was transported by train to his Hyde Park home and was laid to rest on the grounds three days later. His wife Eleanor and the children surrendered their rights and interests in the house and 33-acre estate, transferring title to the U.S. Department of the Interior on November 21, 1945. On November 10, 1962, Eleanor was laid to rest beside her husband in the Rose Garden, which is surrounded by a 150 year-old hemlock hedge.

Today, the home and grounds are administered by the National Park Service. A tragic fire struck the property on January 22, 1982, eight days before the centennial of Franklin D. Roosevelt's birth, but alert National Park Service staff managed to rescue many of the precious artifacts contained in the home. A thorough restoration of damaged portions of the house has preserved it as a shrine to the memory of the man who held our nation's highest office longer than any other.

**Roosevelt Campobello
International Park
Campobello Island, New Brunswick,
Canada EOG 3HO
(506) 752-2922**

**Administered by the Roosevelt Campobello International
Park Commission.**

Directions: From U.S. 1 North of Ellsworth, Maine:
Take Route 189 to Lubec and cross the
Franklin D. Roosevelt Memorial Bridge
to Campobello Island.

Open: For twenty weeks beginning on the Saturday preceding Memorial Day from
9:00 a.m. to 5:00 p.m. E.D.T. seven days
a week.

Admission: Free.

Features: Reception Centre, parking, Roosevelt
Cottage, James-Sara Roosevelt Cottage
site, Prince Cottage, Hubbard Cottage,
Wells-Shober Cottage, natural areas
(2,800 acres of R.C.I.P. land) for picnics, but not for camping. Restrooms
in Reception Centre. Handicapped accessible.

Special Events: Weddings are sometimes held on the
park grounds, but not in the cottages.

For the natural beauty of its waters and woodlands, no site can surpass that of the tiny Canadian island just off the eastern coast of Maine known as Campobello. The magnificent scenery afforded to visitors who stand on its high cliffs looking out toward the coast of Maine, facing the Bay of Fundy, has drawn people to this spot ever since its first settlers arrived on the island in 1770. A little over 100 years after its first settlement, a group of wealthy Americans saw the island's potential as a summer resort and developed a cluster of magnificent summer homes, calling them cottages. Among the wealthy individuals drawn to Campobello was a country gentleman and businessman named James Roosevelt. He purchased a four-acre estate and a partially-completed house overlooking Friar Bay in 1883. The Roosevelts spent their first summer on Campobello in 1883, when James came to the island accompanied by his wife, Sara Delano Roosevelt, and their one-year-old son, Franklin Delano Roosevelt.

From 1883 to 1921, Franklin Delano Roosevelt spent most of his summers on this tranquil island. He became familiar with the sites of bicycles and horse-drawn buggies, the principal modes of transportation on the island. Despite the wealth of the summer residents, their homes were not furnished with electricity as it was not available on the island until 1948. Instead, their homes were lighted by oil lamps, kerosene, and candles, and on colder summer nights, the fireplaces and the coal and wood-burning stoves of the kitchen became the principal sources of heat. Summer residents generally traveled to Campobello via a railroad train to Eastport, Maine, and because no bridges to Campobello existed, the rest of the trip was by boat.

It was here on Campobello Island that Franklin Roosevelt's lifelong love of the sea developed. He spent time at the fishing wharfs watching the fishermen ply their trade and was taught to sail by a local sea captain. Young Franklin Roosevelt spent many happy hours sailing in the Bay of Fundy.

In the summer of 1904, Franklin Roosevelt, an attorney at this point, brought his fiancee, Eleanor Roosevelt, to Campobello to become better acquainted with her future mother-in-law. The beauty and tranquility of the island did little to soothe the tensions between Sara and her future daughter-in-law, who boldly, yet politely, once remarked to Sara, "I do wish you'd learn to love me a little."

This tension did not prevent Eleanor Roosevelt's marriage to her cousin Franklin Roosevelt the following year and Sara Roosevelt, resigned to the marriage, presented the young couple with a large, Dutch-colonial cottage situated just to the south of her own. (Eleanor and Franklin Roosevelt did not own the cottage outright until many years later.) The home had been purchased by Sara Roosevelt in 1897 at the price of $5,000.00 from the Kuhns, a Boston family. Here, Eleanor and Franklin Roosevelt spent many happy summers with their young and growing family, including their daughter, Anna

Roosevelt; and their sons, James, Elliot, John, and Franklin Roosevelt, Jr., who was born in the cottage.

Franklin Roosevelt spent his time here relaxing, away from the pressures of political and legal life. He taught his own children how to sail here, just as he had been taught as a child. During the years the Roosevelts spent hiking, sailing, and picnicking with their children, Franklin Roosevelt rose from New York state senator to Democratic candidate for vice president in 1920.

Having been defeated in his vice presidential bid, Franklin Roosevelt went to work as the vice president of the Fidelity & Deposit Company of Maryland in their New York office. He looked forward to an active, yet restful, summer at Campobello in August 1921, and was planning to build a new boat for his children, having ordered some of its parts in advance. Shortly after his arrival there, he and his family plunged into their usual whirlwind of activity.

On August 10, Franklin Roosevelt took his family sailing on the *Vireo*. The rest of that day included assisting in fighting a forest fire, running across the island, and a swim through the chilly waters of the Bay of Fundy. Mr. Roosevelt returned home too tired to do anything but read the newspaper. He then developed a chill which, the following morning, became a fever. His illness, at first, appeared to be a cold, but then further symptoms developed. His left leg weakened and, after a time, refused to move. Shortly thereafter, the right leg became similarly afflicted. A Lubec doctor, Dr. Bennet, was contacted. He diagnosed the illness as a bad cold. The next morning, Dr. Bennet returned. He and Eleanor Roosevelt agreed that a second opinion was warranted. Louis Howe, a Roosevelt confidante and friend, contacted Dr. William Keen, an eminent eighty-four year old Philadelphia surgeon, in Bar Harbor, Maine. Dr. Keen thought that Franklin Roosevelt's symptoms were caused by a blood clot from a sudden congestion which had settled in the lower spinal cord, temporarily removing the power to move. Louis Howe wrote letters to Franklin Roosevelt's uncle, Fred Delano, in New York, describing the symptoms in detail and asking him to relay the symptoms to specialists. Specialists contacted in Boston suspected that the illness was infantile paralysis.

Dr. Samuel Levine of the Harvard Infantile Paralysis Commission diagnosed the illness as polio. In September 1921, Dr. Robert Lovett, the foremost specialist on infantile paralysis, came to Campobello. Ultimately, it was decided that Franklin Roosevelt would undertake a program of treatment in New York City. He was carried on an improvised stretcher by some fisherman friends to a boat that would take him to the train at Eastport. His words of encouragement to two of his sons, holding back tears as they watched their father being carried off to the boat, were: "Don't worry, kids! I'll see you soon!"

After 1921, Franklin D. Roosevelt returned to Campobello only three more times, and by the time of the first of these visits (June 1933) he had already been elected president of the United States. At this point, President

Roosevelt had altered his traditional vacation plans to include frequent visits to Warm Springs, Georgia, where he received therapeutic treatment for his polio. Eleanor Roosevelt and the five children had continued to visit Campobello, and continued to do so even after President Roosevelt's death. In 1933, however, a mixture of sentimentality and the need for relaxation after enduring the pressure of his first 100 days in office induced him to plan a sailing trip to Campobello. President Roosevelt arrived there on June 30th, having sailed the schooner "Amberjack II" from Marion, Massachusetts. Like his other two visits (in 1936 and 1939), his stay was only overnight, and he was greeted by a large crowd. After 1939, the demands of office never permitted President Roosevelt to visit his "beloved island" again.

Seven years after Franklin Roosevelt's death in 1945, the Campobello cottage and its surrounding acreage was sold to the late Dr. Armand Hammer, who was chairman of Occidental Petroleum Corporation. The Hammer family used the cottage as a summer residence, but became interested in the idea of converting the property into a shrine dedicated to the memory of Franklin Delano Roosevelt. In 1962, President John F. Kennedy's administration, at the urging of Senator Edmund S. Muskie of Maine, negotiated with the Canadian government concerning the concept of converting the property into an international park. The Roosevelt Campobello International Park was established under an agreement signed on January 22, 1964, by President Lyndon B. Johnson of the United States and Prime Minister Lester B. Pearson of Canada. The park was officially opened on August 20, 1964, with a ribbon-cutting ceremony attended by Mrs. Lyndon B. Johnson and Mrs. Lester B. Pearson. On August 26, 1966, Prime Minister Pearson and President Johnson jointly laid the cornerstone of the new Visitor Centre. Her Majesty Queen Elizabeth, the Queen Mother, declared the Visitor Centre open on July 13, 1967.

Today, the Roosevelt Cottage, a modified, Dutch-colonial frame structure, stained terri red with tavern green shutters and a green roof with gray dormers, dominates a park whose pathways are lined with flowers and whose surrounding acreage may be explored via nature trails. The completed cottage contains 34 rooms, including 18 bedrooms and seven bathrooms. The house has seven fireplaces, and while it was not originally wired for electricity, it does have indoor plumbing dependent on an outside water tower, a windmill powered pump, and a gravity-fed system that drew water from the third floor to the bathrooms and kitchens.

Visitors take a self-guided tour through the home, ably staffed by both American and Canadian park personnel, ready to answer any questions, they notice several recurring features. Many of the doors are of the Dutch style (meaning that the top half of the door may remain open while the bottom half is closed). The original blue and white oriental rugs used by the Roosevelts may be seen in several of the first and second floor rooms. A couple of the

furnishings are knotty pine, manufactured at the Val-Kill factory near Hyde Park, instituted by Eleanor Roosevelt and two partners as a means to provide jobs to unemployed craftsmen. The pleasant summer feeling visitors detect in this house is accentuated by the lovely wicker furniture. On display throughout the house are captioned photographs illustrating highlights of the Roosevelts' lives.

Among the noteworthy rooms is the first one seen on the self-guided tour. Contained in the children's wing, this room was originally used as a nursery, but later became a schoolroom. Today, it is used as a Roosevelt museum, containing many Franklin Roosevelt artifacts and mementos. Notable items in the collection include: a stretcher chair made especially for Franklin Roosevelt during his visits as President, a set of Mongolian prints given to Eleanor Roosevelt by Madame Chiang Kai-Chek of China, a pair of dueling pistols purchased by Franklin Roosevelt as collectors' items when he and Eleanor Roosevelt were in Paris on their honeymoon in 1905, his sculling oars from Harvard, and a small pony chair used by Franklin Roosevelt at Hyde Park when he was young. A leather chair used by President Roosevelt at the White House is also on exhibit here.

From the museum room, there is a short hallway. Flanking the hallway are rooms used by Eleanor and Franklin Roosevelt's son, James Roosevelt, and by Franklin Roosevelt after he was stricken with polio. The Franklin Roosevelt room was used briefly by him after he was stricken with paralysis in order to avoid the problem of transporting him upstairs to his former room on the second floor. In addition to the usual bedroom furnishings, a battered fedora, his trademark, rests on a small chair.

At the other end of the hallway is a writing room. As in many of the other rooms, the wallpaper is reproduced from patterns originally used in the cottage. This room, which contains a breakfront, was used by Eleanor and Franklin Roosevelt for writing their correspondence, or as a study.

A tour of the cottage continues through the front entrance hallway, which features many Roosevelt photographs, and turns left towards the living room, which is filled with wicker furniture. A tabletop radio plays President Roosevelt's famous fireside chats. A large window on the rear wall affords a majestic view of Friar's Bay, and one can also see the beach to the rear and the remains of the pier where the Roosevelts docked their boat. At the rear of the living room visitors emerge onto the first floor porch and see Franklin D. Roosevelt's old Indian birch bark canoe resting there. An enclosed portion of the same porch contains a pair of the family's bicycles, a set of driftwood chairs, and an old-style hammock.

In front of the enclosed portion of the porch, and to the side of the living room, is a dining room. Several small throw rugs depicting sea scenes, made by women on the island, cover the floor. Large megaphones used by the Roosevelts to call their children to the house for dinner and talk to the captain aboard the yacht are also here in the living room and dining room.

Adjacent to the dining room is the butler's pantry. It includes wooden cabinets, a marble countertop, and a large built-in icebox. Also on display in the pantry is a wicker picnic basket with compartments belonging to the family.

The kitchen, located to the side of the pantry, displays both a wood and coal burning oven and a kerosene stove. Visitors also notice a large, copper hot-water tank and a cake box. The large wooden table in the center was used for preparing the family meals.

At the end of the servants' wing is a small washroom, filled with the washing appliances of the period. Included are two types of clothes wringers, a clothes tree for drying, a rug beater, and a potbellied stove to heat the irons. The irons were placed around the outside on the stove. The first floor of the servants' wing contains a second pantry, rest room, and storage closets, all closed to the public.

The main section and children's and servants' wings each contain a set of stairs leading to the second and third floors. The third floor, closed to the public, contains a water tank used for plumbing, and storage space. Most of the rooms of the second floor are bedrooms, including several guest rooms and servants' quarters. Also on the second floor is the master bedroom (where Franklin, Jr. was born and where his father noticed his first symptoms of polio). Adjacent is the room Eleanor Roosevelt used during her later visits to Campobello.

Arched hallways on either side of the main section of the second floor lead to the servants' and children's wings. The Roosevelts would bring with them four to six servants during their summer stays. The other wing includes the room used by Anna Roosevelt, filled with lightly stained furniture and a wicker chair. Next door is a sewing room, also including wicker chairs, as well as a Davis sewing machine table, and tables used for hand-sewing.

Beyond the sewing room are the rooms used by the Roosevelts' younger sons. Elliot Roosevelt's room is to the side of the hallway and has a door leading to the second floor porch. Its bedspread has a nautical pattern similar to that in the room which was used by Franklin Roosevelt, Jr. and John Roosevelt (whose room also includes a large, hanging mobile representing "the Jennie," a World War I airplane, a small school writing desk, and lamps with more nautical design).

A visit to Campobello is not complete without exploring its magnificent grounds. A pathway leading from the cottage passes the Roosevelts' icehouse, and continues on a downward slope towards a rocky beach where the family used to sail and swim. Adjacent to the property is the site of the original cottage occupied by Franklin Roosevelt's parents in 1883, now torn down due to disrepair. There is a plaque on this site showing the James-Sara Roosevelt Cottage. The Hubbard Cottage, sometimes open to the public, is adjacent to the site of the James-Sara Roosevelt Cottage and is another example of the summer homes used by wealthy American families of the late nineteenth century.

Visitors should not leave Campobello Island without taking the opportunity to explore its Natural Area, which has been acquired by the Park Commission to prevent encroachment by commercial developers. It is the natural beauty of Campobello that drew the Roosevelts and others of their time to the island. In the Roosevelts' day, there was a system of surrey and carriage paths leading to natural points of interest on the island. Adhering as closely as possible to the direction and land contours of those paths, the drives have been relocated and are now passable for cars.

After a tour of the International Park and a drive around the island, one can easily understand why Franklin D. Roosevelt referred to Campobello as his "beloved island." It has not lost its attractiveness or charm in the generations since he last visited it. The island is a treat for the botanist, the architect, the swimmer, and the hiker—a fitting monument to the friendship between two great nations.

Little White House and Museum
Warm Springs, Georgia 31830
(706) 655-5870

Administered by the Georgia Department of Natural Resources.

Directions:	From Atlanta: Take Interstate 85 to Newman exit. Follow State Route Alt. 27 South to Warm Springs, turning right at marked intersection (near general store and railroad car display). Entrance to site will be on the right hand side of the road.
Open:	Daily (except Thanksgiving Day and Christmas Day).
Admission:	Fee charged.
Features:	"Little White House," guest house, servants' quarters/garage, museum, walkway of stones and flags of the states, fountain, gift shop, snack bar, picnic grounds and rest rooms. "Little White House" is not handicapped accessible.
Special Events:	On April 12, the anniversary of Franklin D. Roosevelt's death, the site holds a special commemorative ceremony. Every September 16th is "Fala Day."

The Little White House stands today as a monument to the indomitable courage of a man stricken with a debilitating, lifetime disease. In 1921, the year after Franklin Delano Roosevelt had suffered his only electoral defeat as the Democratic candidate for vice president of the United States, he was stricken with infantile paralysis while vacationing at his beloved Campobello Island. His legs were paralyzed and his political aspirations threatened. Thanks to the devotion of his wife, Eleanor Roosevelt, and his trusted aide and companion, Louis Howe, Franklin Roosevelt recovered his will and determination, and set out in an effort to find a cure for his paralysis and pain.

The search for a cure was both frustrating and discouraging. Medical treatments and physical therapy were of little help, either to Franklin Roosevelt's physique or his sagging spirits. In 1924, however, he learned of a young engineer, Louis W. Joseph, who had been stricken with polio and had made dramatic improvements in his condition thanks to the naturally buoyant, warm waters of a small village in western Georgia known as Warm Springs. Mr. Roosevelt resolved to travel to Warm Springs immediately.

Shortly after Mr. Roosevelt arrived at Warm Springs and bathed in its waters, there was a noticeable improvement in both his limbs and his disposition. In time, his health improved and he was strengthened by the relaxing, tingling sensation created by the warm pool of water. He swam in the waters daily, until it was no longer necessary for him to do so. When his strength had improved sufficiently, he returned to New York, but occasionally travelled to Georgia to receive treatments at Warm Springs, residing in various summer cottages over the course of his visits.

The eight years following Franklin Roosevelt's first visit to Warm Springs were years during which his political career blossomed. When Al Smith, the 1928 Democratic candidate for president, needed a candidate to succeed him as Governor of New York, he turned to Franklin D. Roosevelt. Mr. Roosevelt bucked the Hoover Republican tide and became a narrow upset winner in the New York gubernatorial contest. He was re-elected to a second two-year term in 1930, and was regarded as a strong contender for the 1932 Democratic nomination based upon his record as governor and his exuberant personality. He went on to become the Democratic candidate and winner of the 1932 presidential race against Republican incumbent Herbert Hoover, whose political fortunes had taken a turn for the worse as a result of the Great Depression.

It was in 1932 that Governor Roosevelt constructed a small wooden cottage overlooking a ravine in the Warm Springs area. The building was completed in the spring of 1932 at a total cost of $8,738.14. In May of that year, Gov. Roosevelt first occupied his new cottage, and was delighted with it. This first of many visits was capped by a house warming party for the local residents and others who, like Franklin Roosevelt himself, sought the healing effects of the waters of Warm Springs to aid their own handicapped limbs.

After his election as president, Franklin D. Roosevelt, who never was a man to keep his own company or shun the public, continued to join other patients at the Warm Springs Foundation in bathing in the therapeutic waters. He seemed to feel a special affinity with all who had come to seek treatment, but especially enjoyed being with the children who came there.

Franklin D. Roosevelt mixed his presidential duties with private enjoyment during his stays at the cottage, which came to be known as the "Little White House" during his years in office. He enjoyed driving his specially-equipped automobiles, including a 1938 Ford convertible, on display in the garage today. The special hand instruments used to depress the clutch, apply the brake, and accelerate the car were designed with the assistance of the president himself.

The cottage is a one-story structure, with the exception of a basement housing the boiler and storage area. It is a very simple structure: a frame cottage with a four-column portico and pine wood interior walls. One of the dominant features of the cottage is its abundance of ship models and nautical fixtures, reflecting Franklin Roosevelt's great love for the sea. The entrance to the cottage has a ship's lantern over the portal and a brass door knocker in the shape of an anchor.

Visitors enter the pine-walled interior of the cottage from a side ramp, passing an ice box. The first room is on the right front portion of the cottage. Here visitors see a note written by Daisy Bonner, Franklin Roosevelt's cook, which says: "Daisy Bonner cooked the first meal and the last one in this cottage for the President Roosevelt." The note was written on April 12, 1945, the day Franklin Roosevelt died here. Also in this room is Mr. Roosevelt's old fashioned hand cranked ice cream freezer.

Passing through a small room which doubled as a butler's pantry and china closet, the visitor comes to the entry way of the house. Here one finds the wheelchair used by the president and the dog chain used for President Roosevelt's scottie, Fala. Ship models are located above the doors of the room.

Behind the entry is the cottage's combination living room and dining room. This room has French doors and the floor-length windows that fill the room with light on sunny days. On one side of the room is the living area, centered around a fieldstone fireplace, surrounded by bookshelves. The floor is covered by a hooked rug symbolizing the New Deal. Three telephones which were used by the president are on the bookshelves to the side of his favorite chair, in which he was sitting when fatally stricken on April 12, 1945. The chair is brown leather, and was used while the president was posing for a portrait to be painted by Madame Elizabeth Shoumatoff. It was while he was sitting for the portrait that he complained of a headache and was taken to his sick bed. Shortly thereafter, President Roosevelt died, having suffered a cerebral hemorrhage.

Passing through the double French doors, visitors next see a magnificent sun deck, which traverses the length of the cottage (54 feet) and is shaped like the fantail of a ship. Its rustic furnishings were a gift of the president's mother, Sara Delano Roosevelt, and it offers a wonderful view of a ravine and mountainside.

Next is the president's bedroom. Here visitors see a hooked rug with his named embroidered on one side, a chest of drawers, a sea chest, a "Storm-O-Guide" on the wall, a bed table with a lamp, and an arm chair custom made for him. The bed is three-quarter size and has a tufted coverlet and a folded blanket at its foot. Also in this room is a flat top desk and a matching chair given to the president by CWA workers in Fitchburg, Massachusetts.

On the other side of a connecting bath is Eleanor Roosevelt's room, which has twin beds. It also has a framed cartoon by Lewis Gregg depicting "Marse Franklin" on a "possum" hunt. The cartoon was presented to Franklin Roosevelt by friends in nearby White Sulphur Springs in 1930. On the other side of the living-dining room, and accessible from the sun deck, is the secretary's bedroom, used by any one of a number of private secretaries who accompanied Mr. Roosevelt during his stays here.

In front of the cottage are two buildings: the garage and servants' quarters to the north, and the guest house to the south. The garage features President Roosevelt's specially equipped 1938 Ford convertible. The guest house is decorated in the same nautical style as the cottage and most of its furniture was fashioned at Val-Kill Shops in Hyde Park, New York. Val-Kill was established by Mrs. Roosevelt as a means of providing jobs for the unemployed.

The grounds were secured by a bump gate, which was raised when activated by pressure from an automobile bumper. When Franklin Roosevelt became president, sentry houses and eight green sentry boxes were added to the grounds, manned by a detachment of 65 Marine guards, 24 hours a day.

Since President Roosevelt's death, other features have been added to the grounds. Significant among these additions is a Memorial Fountain, a gift of Mr. and Mrs. Lawrence W. (Chip) Robert, Jr. of Atlanta. Mr. Robert, an assistant treasury secretary during Franklin Roosevelt's first term as president, later became treasurer of the Democratic National Committee. The fountain was built and dedicated in 1959. The fountain is now the "hub" of the grounds, from which three paths emanate: one leading to the entrance building (which has a gift shop and snack bar), and another leading to the cottage. The third is a pathway of state flags and stones leading to a museum, which contains a variety of Franklin D. Roosevelt gifts, mementos and curios. A 12-minute movie on Franklin Roosevelt at Warm Springs is shown at the museum.

It should also be noted that two subsequent Democratic presidential candidates paid visits to this site. On October 10, 1960, Senator John F. Kennedy spoke in front of the cottage here, and on Labor Day, 1976, Georgia governor Jimmy Carter officially opened his campaign as the Democratic nominee for president here. Both campaigns were successful.

For its simple beauty, and the story this small cottage tells of the private life of a world-renowned leader, the Little White House is a unique place to visit.

HARRY S TRUMAN

Harry S Truman Birthplace
State Historic Site
Truman and Eleventh Streets
Lamar, Missouri 64759
(417) 682-2279

Administered by the Missouri Department of Natural Resources, Division of State Parks.

Directions: From U.S. 71: At Lamar, proceed east on U.S. 160 two miles, turning left at Truman Street. Site is one block north of U.S. 160, at the northwest corner of the intersection.

Open: Daily (except New Year's Day, Easter Sunday, Thanksgiving Day and Christmas Day).

Admission: Free.

Features: Guided tour of house lasting at least fifteen minutes, reception office (sells postcards and books), UAW memorial, tree planted by President Truman's father, flower and vegetable gardens. One rest room. Not handicapped accessible.

Special Events: President Truman's birthday is celebrated on the first weekend in May with entertainment and arts and crafts. A Victorian Christmas celebration takes place in December.

Harry S Truman was born May 8, 1884 in the quaint town of Lamar, Missouri. President Truman's father, John Anderson Truman, a mule trader, purchased the home in which Harry Truman was born in 1882 at a cost of $685.00. Despite the fact that it had no electricity, running water or bathroom, it was an elegant home in its day. Lamar, as many other cities in the area, was still undergoing reconstruction from the Civil War. The streets were paved with gravel and the main square of town had 5 local bars (or saloons, as they were called). The population of the town was 700 with 5 people practicing medicine.

The home was built between 1880 and 1881 and has 6 rooms. It stood at the corner of 11th Street and Kentucky Street. Today Kentucky Street has been renamed Truman Street. Harry Truman's father planted an Austrian pine tree in the yard the day Harry Truman was born and nailed a mule shoe over the front door to celebrate his son's birth. The tree is still alive today, and is over 100 years old.

This little early Victorian white frame house was the home of the Trumans from 1882 to March 1885. The home was built in 1880 or 1881 by a Mr. Blethrode. Railroad service was available for the town, as was telephone service installed for a 24 mile area, which cost the town $1,500.00. There was a barn across the street from the house which John Truman used in his business as a livestock dealer and farmer. Harry Truman's mother, the former Martha Ellen Young, was born in Kansas City and married John Truman in 1881, and then came to Lamar in a covered wagon.

1840-1890 period furniture, wallpaper and carpet can be seen throughout the home. Although not original to the Truman family, this furniture can help one appreciate the humble life style that the Truman family shared. The house has four bedrooms, two of which are upstairs and two downstairs. The bedroom to the southwest side of the parlor is the room in which Harry Truman was born. This room contains a 3/4" counter pin style walnut bed and a 1840 handmade cradle.

Harry Truman's grandparents names were Solomon and Shippe. He was given the middle initial "S" after both of his grandparents. He always used the initial "S" and to this day no one knows which name it represented.

The parlor, the room through which one enters the house, has a wood burning stove dated 1870. On the wall is a picture which is based on John Greenleaf Whittier's "Barefoot in the Park."

The kitchen has a table in the center, which is surrounded by chairs. The kitchen cook stove cost $6.00 at the time and it was marketed by Sears, Roebuck and Co. A bedroom behind the kitchen houses a ginger bed, platform rocker, and a wishbone race track trim dresser.

The yard on this property was raked or swept at that time because no grass was planted, but there were a few flowering plants in the yard. The yard was surrounded by a wire fence and probably had a few cows wandering in it.

The Trumans left this house in 1885 and moved to a farm in Harrisonville, in the area where Harry Truman's parents had been raised. The location of the farm house is unknown. Later in 1885, the Trumans moved again to a farm southeast of Belton, Missouri, which today is owned by Mr. C. K. Frank. In 1887, the Trumans moved once again, this time to Grandview, 60 miles north of Lamar. It took them a month to get to their new residence by horse and buggy and they couldn't take many belongings because Harry Truman's mother decided to take her piano with her. Harry Truman took piano lessons and loved to play even into adulthood.

Incidentally, Harry Truman's mother did not bid a final farewell to Lamar in 1885. She was forced to return in 1934 to get a new birth certificate for her son because he needed it to run for office.

Today, the Harry S Truman birthplace is listed in the National Register of Historic Places, and the state of Missouri took title to the house in 1957. After visiting the site of President Truman's birth in Lamar, one can see how the simple life style depicted here profoundly influenced his life.

The Truman Farm Home
12301 Blue Ridge Boulevard
Grandview, Missouri 64030
(816) 254-2720

Administered by the National Park Service.

Directions:	**From Kansas City, take I-70 east to I-435 south to U.S. 71 south. Take Blue Ridge exit to Blue Ridge Extension. Farm Home is on left.**
Open:	**Summer months only. Call for hours.**

Admission:	**Free.**
Features:	**Farm Home, old post office used as a garage by Mr. Truman, old chicken house, and various stone section markers.**
Special Events:	**None.**

After leaving Lamar, Missouri in 1885, Harry S Truman and his family lived in various towns within the state of Missouri, including Harrisonville and Belton. From 1887 to 1890, the Trumans lived at the farmhouse in Grandview owned by Harry Truman's paternal grandparents. In 1890, the Trumans moved to the city of Independence, and until 1896, lived in a two-story white frame house at 619 South Crysler Street which they acquired for $4,000.00. Harry Truman's poor eyesight meant that he had to wear thick-lensed glasses, and could not engage in rough-and-tumble play, so he spent much of his time reading the Bible, biographies and history. In 1896, when Harry Truman was twelve, his family moved to 909 West Waldo in Independence, a frame, two-story, gabled-front home with large verandas. In 1902, the Trumans moved once again, this time to 902 North Liberty Street. The Truman boyhood homes in Independence are still standing as private residences, but have been substantially remodeled since Mr. Truman's day. In 1900, Harry Truman got his first taste of politics when he worked as a page at the 1900 Democratic Convention in Kansas City. He was impressed at hearing the presidential nominee, William Jennings Bryan, speak. While living in Independence as a youth, Harry S Truman met Elizabeth ("Bess") Wallace at a Sunday school gathering. Their friendship, however, was interrupted when Harry Truman's family moved to Kansas City, Missouri.

The Truman family lived two years at 2108 Park Avenue in Kansas City, one year at 2650 East Twenty-Ninth Street, a two and a half story frame house with a front porch, and two years at 1314 Troost Avenue. While in Kansas City, Harry Truman took various jobs, including a $7.00-a-week job in the mailroom of the Kansas City Star, a job as a bank clerk, and a job as a bookkeeper. While a bank clerk, he roomed in a boarding house with a fellow clerk, Arthur Eisenhower, who had a brother named Dwight.

In 1906, Harry Truman's father asked him to return to Grandview to help run his grandmother's farm, which had fallen into the hands of Harry Truman's parents. It was in the farm's box-like, frame house, located on a 600 acre farm, that Harry Truman lived from 1906-1917 (ages twenty-two to thirty-three), assisting his father in the many chores necessary to farm life, such as raising corn, hogs and cattle. This period of his life as a dirt farmer came to an abrupt halt upon the entry of the United States into the European conflict in World War I. Answering the call of his country, Harry Truman enlisted in the service and became a field artillery captain in France. He stayed in the service until 1919.

The two-story frame farmhouse in Grandview was built in 1894, and has been authentically restored. It is a white-framed house with green trim, featuring a porch with four columns. The first floor contains a central hallway enclosed by a parlor to the left as the visitor faces the front of the house, and a living room to the right. These rooms are decorated in patterned wallpaper and the parlor features an instrument very dear to the heart of Harry Truman's mother: a piano. This piano, which was donated by an area resident, may very well be similar to the instrument hauled by the Trumans on a covered wagon during a one month journey from Lamar, Missouri to the northwestern portion of the state by the Truman family in 1885.

The house appears to be late Victorian in its style, and includes an ell extending toward the back of the property. The ell contains a dining area and a small back room, probably used as a kitchen.

Beside the ell is a porch containing a swing suspended from the ceiling. The swing was used to enjoy the breezes of warm summer evenings or, perhaps, for courting. Behind the house were the garden, fruit trees and the out-house. Behind the garden was the main barn where the farm animals were kept and a grainery to the east. North of the house was the chicken house, and farther north was the hay barn.

When Harry S Truman returned from his service in World War I, he did not return to Grandview Farm, which became known as Truman Corner. At the age of thirty-five, he determined that upon completion of his military service he would return to Independence, where he had spent so many years of his childhood, to wed his childhood sweetheart, Bess Wallace, and did so on June 28, 1919. The Grandview house and property still exist however, as a reminder of Harry S Truman's devotion to his family and his willingness to devote himself to the basic values in which he believed.

The site was acquired by the National Park Service on May 8, 1994. Tentative plans are to restore the site to its 1906-1917 appearance.

Harry S Truman National Historic Site
223 N. Main Street
Independence, Missouri 64050-2804
(816) 254-7199

Administered by the National Park Service.

Directions:	From Kansas City, take I-70 West to Noland Road, in Independence. Take Noland Road north and turn left on Truman Road to Ticket/Information Center, where tour begins.
Open:	Daily (except New Year's Day, Thanksgiving Day, Christmas Day, and Mondays from Labor Day to Memorial Day).
Admission:	Fee charged.

Features:	Harry S Truman Home, Harry S Truman Library, Jackson County Courthouse (where 30 minute slide program entitled "Man from Independence" is shown), Missouri Pacific Railroad Station, First Presbyterian Church, Trinity Episcopal Church, Harry S Truman National Historic Landmark District. Ticket/Information Center has twelve minute slide show with narration, showing the inside of the Harry S Truman Home. Rest rooms.

Special Events: As announced.

After returning from service to his country during World War I, Harry S Truman settled in the home that became his principal residence for the rest of his life. The house at 219 North Delaware Street is striking because of its simple Victorian charm. Its most unique feature, however, is that although it was the principal residence of a president of the United States until the end of his life, it remained situated in what is still a residential neighborhood.

The house shows few signs of the trappings of office so often found in the homes of other modern American presidents. The only security precautions taken during the Truman presidency were the installation in 1949 of an iron fence surrounding the property and a security checkpoint placed in front of the house. In addition, a row of large bushes obstructed the view of passersby, insuring the privacy of the president, who frequently enjoyed reading the newspapers on the porch. The porch was also used by Mrs. Bess Truman when she played card games with her friends.

The original section of the house, which later became the kitchen, was built in 1850. In 1867, George Porterfield Gates, the grandfather of Mrs. Bess Truman, expanded the house in a Victorian style, adding the portions used by the Trumans as a library and dining room. The main addition to the house was made in 1887 by Gates, who commissioned

builder John W. Adams to add an extension at a cost of $8,000.00. This extension, facing out onto North Delaware Avenue, includes the current entrance hall and living room.

The resulting house was a two and half story late-Gothic Revival home, with a wrap-around porch and a gabled roof. With the exception of such modernizations as central heating, electricity and telephones, the house remained virtually unchanged since the newly married Trumans moved into a second floor bedroom in 1919.

Harry Truman shared this house not only with his wife, but also with his mother-in-law, Madge Gates Wallace, for 33 years. When dinners were taken in the dining room, it was Mrs. Wallace who always sat at the head of the table, while Mr. Truman was consigned to the foot of the table. Despite Harry Truman's numerous attainments outside of this house, it was Mrs. Wallace who was the undisputed leader in matters concerning the home until her death in 1952. Harry Truman's election to the presidency changed the house and property in only one major respect aside from the addition of minimal security precautions: a flag pole was donated to the property by the citizens of Independence to be placed on the front lawn. Characteristically, however, the Trumans were satisfied with the house as it had remained through so many years of their lives and saw no reason to make major alterations in its structure.

Good friends of the Trumans always entered this house by walking around the side to the rear entrance. They would then pass through a kitchen which appears to have changed little since the 1930s, with its green-painted wainscoting and repatterned wallpaper intact. As in many other American kitchens, the linoleum floors show signs of wear and tear, but were never replaced or repaired by the Trumans. From the kitchen, friends would then pass through a small pantry into the dining room and, turning right, would perhaps approach the library, in which Mr. Truman's books and a comfortable chair can be found. Or perhaps the visitor might turn left and walk into the music room, still containing a baby piano received by daughter Margaret as a Christmas gift when she was eight years old. Margaret, who had made clear her desire for a train set, darted under the piano upon seeing it and engaged in a frantic search for the train set. When she realized that there was no train set to be found, she sat under the piano and wept—unable to conceal her disappointment.

During the Truman presidency, a great wall of separation between the activities of welcomed friends who stopped by the Truman home and those of the many dignitaries who came to Independence to visit with the president was evident. These dignitaries were escorted up the front walk and through the front door, and into the living room, located to the right of the entrance hall. Once seated on the comfortable chairs, they would discuss matters of state in this very homespun atmosphere. They seldom saw any other part of the house.

The hallway of the house features a portrait of Margaret Truman Daniel, depicting her in the dress she wore for one of her singing recitals. The dark wainscoting in the hallway appears to be wood but is actually made of a linoleum-based substance. Closer inspection of the gold-leaf border on the wainscoting reveals it to be made only of plaster of Paris. The house is filled with many such money-saving trompe d'oeils. The woodworking interior of the house appears to be rich, dark wood such as oak or chestnut, but is actually stained white pine. Looking at the house from the outside and facing the front, visitors see two long, slender stained-glass windows. These windows are in fact composed of transparent glass backed by colored cellophane.

Behind the home is a backyard containing a beautiful garden and a two-car garage. Relatives of Mrs. Bess Truman had built homes of their own on either side of the house many years earlier.

Harry Truman lived in this house full-time until 1935. In 1919, he and an army friend opened a men's clothing store in Independence, which they closed in 1922. In 1922, he was elected Jackson County judge, a nonjudicial post which was concerned largely with road and bridge building and maintenance. During this period, he took courses at Kansas City Law School, but did not obtain a law degree. In 1924, his daughter, Mary Margaret (Mrs. Margaret Truman Daniel) was born. That same year, Harry Truman was defeated for re-election, largely because of Ku Klux Klan opposition based on a mistaken belief that Mr. Truman was part Jewish because one of his grandfathers was named Solomon Young. In 1926, Harry Truman was elected presiding judge of Jackson County, a post which controlled hundreds of patronage jobs and ten of millions of dollars in public works projects.

Despite the support Mr. Truman received from the Tom Pendergast political machine in winning these posts, and despite the patronage and public works money that found its way to Mr. Pendergast's company, there was no suspicion of dishonesty on Mr. Truman's part.

In 1934, Mr. Pendergast was searching for a candidate for the U.S. senate, and came up with Harry Truman who went on to win a three-way primary and the senate seat in November. Senator Truman and his family went to Washington, where they rented various apartments. In 1935, they lived at 3016 Tilden Gardens; in 1936, the Sedgwick Gardens at 3726 Connecticut Avenue, NW; in 1937, the Carroll Arms, 301 First Street, NE; in 1938, the Warwick Apartments at 3051 Idaho Avenue, NW; in 1939, the Tilden Gardens; 1940, 3930 Connecticut Avenue, and from 1941 to 1945, 4701 Connecticut Avenue, NW. The Trumans lived in Independence during senate recesses.

In 1944, President Roosevelt requested Senator Truman as his vice presidential running mate, and the Democratic ticket went on to defeat Governor Thomas E. Dewey of New York, the Republican presidential candidate, in November. On January 20, 1945, Harry Truman was sworn in as vice president. On April 12, the vice president was summoned to the White House by Mrs. Roosevelt, who told him, "Harry, the president is dead." Shortly thereafter, Chief Justice Harlan Stone swore in Harry Truman as the thirty-third president of the United States.

Under President Truman, World War II ended after he made the difficult decision to drop the atomic bomb on Hiroshima and Nagasaki; the Marshall Plan to provide aid to war-torn Europe was conceived and implemented; and, as part of his "Fair Deal" program, a full-employment bill was passed. President Truman won a term in his own right in 1948 by his upset victory over Governor Dewey, who was making a second presidential bid.

In 1947, President Truman ordered that a second floor balcony be added to the south portico of the White House to shade the windows of the Blue Room. Consequently, a leg of Margaret Truman's piano forced the floor to give way, and a subsequent inspection revealed that the original wooden beams on the second floor had rotted, and that the building structure was in danger of imminent collapse. The Trumans then moved across the street to the Blair-Lee House, at 1651-1653 Pennsylvania Avenue. Blair House was built in 1824 by Dr. Joseph Louel, the first U.S. Army Surgeon General. In 1836, Francis Preston Blair lived here, and had the Lee House built next door for his daughter. The two buildings are today combined as one. The House is a four-story yellow stucco building with a white stone lintel over the windows and paneled green shutters. An Ionic portico covers the fanlighted entrance door. On November 1, 1950, while President Truman was living here, two fanatical Puerto Rican nationalists attempted to assassinate the president by shooting their way into the house. One of the would-be assassins and a Secret Service agent was killed in an exchange of fire. President Truman was not harmed. Today, Blair-Lee House is used by the State Department for visiting dignitaries, and State Department clearance is required to visit the house.

Meanwhile, the White House renovation was proceeding. It was gutted, with only its outer walls retained, a new basement and sub-basements were dug for added office space, and reinforcing concrete and steel was added to the interior. The interior was redone to look as much like the original as possible. After the three-year renovation project was completed, President Truman conducted the first tour of the renovated White House himself.

After retirement from his high office, Harry and Bess Truman made good their promise to return to their home town as private citizens of Independence. Mr. Truman enjoyed walking through his neighborhood and visiting with people of the community.

President Truman spent his post-presidential years writing his memoirs, lecturing, and playing an occasional role in politics. He lived to the age of eighty-eight, and died on

December 26, 1972, at the Research Hospital and Medical Center in Kansas City, of a respiratory infection and other complications. Mrs. Truman continued to live in the house on Delaware Street until her death.

The house in Independence stands as a reminder of the story of a remarkable couple who, to the extent possible, remained unaffected by the public notoriety and world acclaim they received. Harry Truman's elevation to the presidency did not affect his view of himself as a servant of the people while in office, and as a member of the general public while out of office. Perhaps his special charm was in his perception of himself as no greater than any other American citizen and his joy in living out the rest of his life as a citizen of the city he loved best.

The Little White House Museum
111 Front Street—Box #6443
Key West, Florida 33041
(302) 294-9911

Administered by the Little White House Company. The home is listed on the National Register of Historic Places and is designated a Literary Landmark because of President Truman's numerous writings.

Directions:	**Drive from Miami south on U.S. 1 (approximately three hours) until you reach Whitehead Street. Turn right, then turn left at Caroline Street. The museum is on Caroline Street through the Presidential Gates. At that point there will be signs directing you to the home. Alternatively, small planes take passengers from Miami to Key West (the trip takes approximately a half hour).**
Open:	**Daily.**
Admission:	**Fee charged.**

Features:	**House Museum, guided 30 minute tour (tour begins every 10 to 15 minutes), video, grounds, lawn chairs, bookstore and gift shop food and gift shop.**
Special Events:	**Dinner parties and receptions are held on the poker porch. The lawn outside the house is available for rent for large receptions.**
	On December 31, 1996, the site hosted former president Jimmy Carter and his family at New Year's Eve dinner.

In the period of over seven years that Harry S Truman was president (1945-1953), there were many changes in the nation and the world which had lasting significance. World War II came to an end, Eastern Europe closed behind the Iron Curtain, the NATO alliance was formed and the United Nations came into being. Harry Truman did not command widespread respect during his term in office, but over the past 30 years, historians have come to recognize his accomplishments. It is believed that most students of the American presidency would rank Truman among the top five to hold the office.

Harry Truman was a warm, outgoing and unpretentious man. He loved to play poker, but was also an accomplished pianist. Contrary to popular belief, his favorite pieces were the classics, not the Missouri Waltz. The president's vacation home in Key West embodies much of the spirit of the nation's thirty-third chief executive, and will bring back many memories for those old enough to recall the Truman Era.

Harry Truman first visited Key West in 1946 at the advice of his doctor, Brigadier General Wallace, who ordered him to take a vacation. He stayed there seven days and was immediately attracted to the tranquility, quaintness and the warm tropical climate of the island. The former commandant's residence (base commander's Home) at the Key West submarine naval station became the president's vacation home. He stayed there eleven different times for a total of 175 days. His wife and daughter, Bess and Margaret Truman, accompanied him on four of his stays. His wife thought of the house as a place for boys to get together and play cards, sip bourbon and fraternize. All of the president's vacations were working vacations; his visitors included key people in

his administration such as General Marshall, Dean Atcheson, Clark Clifford, and many world leaders, who made the journey to Key West to confer with the president.

The house was renovated and refurbished by the Navy for $35,000.00 following the president's election in 1948. (Mr. Truman had been elected vice president four years earlier, and assumed the presidency upon the death of President Franklin Roosevelt in 1945, but was not elected in his own right until 1948.) The refurbishing was directed by Haygood Lasseter, a Miami interior designer. The house and furnishings have the light airy touch of a summer vacation home and there are two pieces of furniture that are especially evocative of Harry Truman. A unique poker table was designed and built by the Navy and can be seen on the enclosed poker porch; the piano was used by the president on his presidential yacht, the U.S.S. *Williamsburg*, which was berthed at the Navy base while he was in Key West.

The home at Key West was built in 1890. The Little White House is on 2.27 acres of property which was purchased by the Navy in 1854 for $10,400.00. In 1896, a New York contractor built two frame dwellings for $7,489.00. Then, in the twentieth century, the two frames were convened into one home for the base commander and served as a temporary home for various senior Navy

officials until 1945. Thomas Edison also stayed there for a short period of six months during World War I to finish the development of a depth charge. After President Truman left office in 1953, the house reverted to its former use by the Navy as the base commander's home. In 1974, during the waning months of the Nixon administration, the Navy base was closed and supervision of the property was turned over to the General Services Administration. The house remained empty and neglected from 1974 to 1986 and suffered from considerable vandalism during this period. While abandoned, vagrants slept in the house and various fixtures of the house were later found to be missing or destroyed.

In 1986, the General Services Administration auctioned the land and buildings at the Naval base to a real estate developer, Pritam Singh of Massachusetts, for $17 million. He transferred the title back to the State of Florida and then leased it from the state. The restoration of the former "Little White House" began in 1989. The restoration team used state archives, historical and other records to guide them in their efforts to make the home look as it did during the Truman administration. On January 22, 1991, Singh sold his interest and improvements of the Little White House to the Little White House Company, a Florida corporation that completed the restoration process. A major effort was undertaken to finish restoring the house to its appearance in its glory days in the late 1940s and early 1950s. This process was completed in April 1991, and, since that time, the house has been opened to the public every day.

Visitors touring the house today first view a ten-minute video on the life of Harry Truman. The video is shown upstairs in the area that was used as staff bedrooms in the Truman administration. Visitors then proceed to Mrs. Bess Truman's bedroom to begin their tour. What they see is a home filled with rattan furnishings decorated with carefully reproduced flowered upholstery, which gives the house a casual, light and tropical look. The furnishings are positioned as they were during Truman's last stay here. Visitors also see the ceiling fans which were positioned throughout the house to keep it cool for President Truman, his staff and guests. In the bedroom used by Mrs. Truman and her daughter, Margaret Truman, during their visits here, one can see their pink hats and gloves. Behind their beds are mystery novels, which were greatly enjoyed by the Trumans. (Today, Margaret Truman Daniel is the author of numerous mystery books and a biography of her father.) When his wife and daughter were not there with him, President Truman used the desk in this room to write to the First Lady, and some of the letters he wrote to her can be seen here. Also in this room are the president's Stetson hat and cane, and the Trumans' travel trunks. Next, visitors view the president's bedroom, which is painted blue in an effort to make the room more conducive to rest. The second floor rooms are painted in light colors, and the bathroom on this floor is green tiled and has a tub, but no shower.

Downstairs, visitors have the opportunity to view the president's poker porch, where he enjoyed playing cards for relaxation. The room has a bar, and one can imagine the president having a ready supply of bourbon there for himself and his poker-playing companions. The ash trays on the table are made of shell casings.

The dining room features a Sheridan mahogany dining room table, which seats twelve. Visiting officials and members of the president's staff would dine here together with the president himself. On the table are admiralty candle holders. The dining room also has a corner cabinet for silverware and china.

Also on the first floor is the living room, where history was made. Here, President Truman ordered the firing of General MacArthur and planned the North American Treaty Organization (NATO) with a visiting Winston Churchill. On the more personal side, President Truman listened to his daughter Margaret's singing recital on the radio here, and watched newly released newsreels in this room. He also used the living room for daily, two-hour meetings with his staff. In keeping with the light, restful decor of the house, the furnishings in the living room are made of wood and have flowered upholstery. This room also contains the piano that President Truman played on the U.S.S. *Williamsburg*. The piano is the only significant piece of furniture in the house that was not originally located in the house when Truman used it. All of the other furnishings have been restored to their exact appearance during the times when President Truman stayed in the house.

A look at the living room caps the tour of this home, which is made all the more enjoyable by the reminiscences of many of the tour guides. Although Truman did not return to this house after he left office, he made many return visits to Key West, and his last visit was in 1969. Visitors to Key West, a lovely enclave of stores, restaurants and galleries, will readily experience the sunny climate and restful surroundings that lured President Truman here for so many visits.

Harry Truman was called "the last human being" because he was "no nonsense"—he said and did what he believed. His Key West "Little White House" reflects his simple but very satisfying lifestyle as president and beyond.

DWIGHT DAVID EISENHOWER

**Eisenhower Birthplace State
Historic Site
208 East Day
Denison, Texas 75020
(903) 465-8908**

Administered by the Texas Parks and Wildlife Department.

Directions: Take U.S. 75/Highway 75 to exit 120 East (Morton Street). Turn right on Tone Avenue and proceed to Main Street, and turn left onto Main Street to Crockett Avenue. Proceed on Crockett Avenue and follow signs to the site.

Open: Daily (except Thanksgiving Day and Christmas Day).

Admission: Fee charged.

Features: House, visitor center, gift shop, statue of Eisenhower, picnic facilities, rest rooms. Handicapped accessible.

Special Events: The site hosts a President's Day celebration in February, an Earth Day fair in April, and a historic homes tour in December.

David Dwight Eisenhower, as he was originally named, was born in a small northern Texas town called Denison. His name was later changed to Dwight David Eisenhower because his mother, Ida Elizabeth Stover Eisenhower, was not happy with "David" as her son's first name and did not want him to be called "Dave." He was nicknamed "Ike" throughout most of his life. Many people mistakenly think that Abilene, Kansas was Dwight Eisenhower's birthplace. Apparently, even Ike himself was mistaken at one time as to where he was born, for when he applied to West Point, he listed his birthplace as Tyler, Texas. In fact, he was born in a modest two-story white house on the corner of Lamar and Day Streets in Denison, across from the train tracks on which his father worked. He was the third of seven sons (one of whom died young) born to David and Elizabeth Eisenhower and the only one born in Texas; all of General Eisenhower's brothers were born in Kansas. The Eisenhower family remained close throughout their lives; in fact, Milton Eisenhower, the Eisenhower's youngest son, became an aide and advisor to his brother, Dwight Eisenhower, when the latter became president.

Dwight Eisenhower's parents came to Denison because his father's store and business in Kansas didn't work out. While living in Denison, David Eisenhower worked for the railroad on an engine known as a "Katy" (derived from the Missouri/Kansas/Texas, or "MKT" Railroad) and took a correspondence course at night in mechanical engineering. The Eisenhowers lived in Denison for three years and returned to Kansas when David Eisenhower was able to get work there as an engineer in a creamery.

The birthplace home, a frame house with three gables, was built circa 1880 and is situated on a six and one-half-acre site. It was rented by his parents when Dwight Eisenhower was born on October 14, 1890. The family lived there between November 1888 and the spring of 1891. The furniture now in the house didn't belong to the Eisenhowers, but dates from the period they lived in the house. There are no original floors or wallpaper in the house, but similar paper with authentic patterns and floor boards similar to the original are now on display.

Visitors enter the front door and see a hallway with a bedroom to the right and a front parlor to the left. There is a replica of an old windup telephone which plays a recording of President Eisenhower's voice made in 1958. In the parlor is a picture of General Eisenhower's parents. His father and grandson, both named David, bear a strong resemblance. In the bedroom behind the parlor is a picture of Dr. Bailey, the doctor who delivered the future general and president. In the parlor there are pictures of Dwight Eisenhower at the age of two and one-half years and of his parents at their wedding, which took place in 1885 in Hope, Kansas.

General Eisenhower's 1950 painting of a native American, which is on display here, demonstrates that he was a talented painter. Also seen here is a 1952 campaign pic-

ture of General Eisenhower's family and a picture of his three grandchildren. Dwight Eisenhower had two sons, John, surviving, and his other son, Doud Dwight, who died in infancy and today is buried with his parents in Kansas.

There are two attic bedrooms, one of which was rented out to a boarder for extra money, and the other was used by the two boys. The Eisenhower family took all of their meals together in the dining room. The house was designed with seven doors to the outside to provide for cross-ventilation. In the room in which Ike was born is a quilt made by Mrs. Ida Elizabeth Eisenhower, which is the only authentic possession of the Eisenhowers in the house today.

One can see an early model of the "Morris Rocker Recliner" in the parlor, and there is a wood/coal stove in the kitchen, which was built in 1890 by Majestic of St. Louis. Wood and coal were plentiful in this area and both proved useful as a source of warmth. The home had no electricity and no running water when the Eisenhowers lived there. There was a well outside by the large oak tree used by the family to get water for the house.

In the kitchen are many items that indigenous to the time period depicted. Some examples are: a clothes stomper, which is a forerunner to today's washing agitator; a butter churn; a wooden lemon squeezer; a German sausage link stuffer; a turkey feather duster; a metal popcorn popper; and an old Borden's milk bottle for delivery.

The Eisenhower family belonged to the River Brethren denomination, which advocates a strict religious life style. They adhered to its tenets while living here. A family Bible seen in the home symbolizes the strong religious beliefs which influenced the moral values Ike carried with him his entire life.

The Eisenhowers didn't have a yard as we know it today. At this time in Texas people didn't maintain grass yards, but they did have a gravel yard which they raked. Mrs. Eisenhower planted a few flowers around the yard.

Years after the Eisenhowers left Denison, Ms. Jennie Jackson, the principal of Lamar Elementary School, remembered rocking a baby named David (Dwight) Eisenhower. When, as a general, Dwight Eisenhower became famous during World War II, Ms. Jackson set out to promote interest in preserving the home of the great general. This house is unusual among restored presidential homes in that, because of General Eisenhower's popularity as a war hero, it was restored before he even became president.

Ms. Jennie Jackson organized a group of citizens interested in preserving the home. The group purchased the home and deeded it to the city of Denison. On October 14, 1953, the Eisenhower Birthplace Foundation Inc. was chartered and then took on the task of restoring the house. One of the first steps taken in the preservation was the conversion of the surrounding block to a park to prevent encroachment. Mr. Fred Conn continued to lead the research and restoration of the house after Ms. Jackson's health failed, and in 1958, the property was deeded to the Texas State Parks Board, which is now the Texas Parks and Wildlife Department.

Viewing this home makes one feel very nostalgic for the so-called "good old days." The tour takes no more than ten people into the home at one time and lasts approximately fifteen minutes. While waiting, however, visitors are welcome to sit on the porch. Visitors can buy post cards at the house itself, as well as "I Like Ike" buttons, mugs, and tee shirts.

Eisenhower Center
200 S.E. Fourth Street
Abilene, Kansas 67410
(785) 263-4751

Administered by the National Archives and Records Administration.

Directions:	From I-70, take the Abilene exit and travel two miles south on Kansas Highway 15 (also called Buckeye Avenue).
Open:	Daily (except Thanksgiving Day, Christmas Day and New Year's Day).
Admission:	Fee charged.
Features:	Eisenhower boyhood home, Dwight D. Eisenhower Library, Eisenhower Museum, Visitors' Center and Place of Meditation. The Visitors' Center shows a movie about General Eisenhower's life and work and contains a gift shop and public rest rooms. The Place of Meditation is the burial site of General and Mrs. Eisenhower and their son, Doud Dwight. Handicapped facilities consist of chair lifts at the Home, Museum, and Library. Level entrances are provided at the Visitors' Center and the Place of Meditation. Research facilities are open free of charge Mondays to Fridays, except holidays, from 9:00 a.m. to 4:45 p.m. to those who make advance, written application to the director.
Special Events:	Contact site for special events.

In 1891, before Dwight Eisenhower was even two years old, the Eisenhower family moved back to Kansas from Denison, Texas. The Eisenhowers settled in Abilene, where they lived in a small rented house on S. E. Second Street through 1898. Dwight Eisenhower's father took a job in the Belle Spring Creamery Co. as a head mechanic. As soon as Dwight Eisenhower and each of his five brothers (a sixth brother died in infancy) was old enough, each boy worked in the family garden where vegetables were grown for the dinner table, and, when somewhat older, began other work, usually at odd jobs. In Dwight Eisenhower's case, he worked in the creamery after school and during school vacations to aid his struggling family.

In November 1898, when Dwight Eisenhower reached the age of eight, his family purchased for $1,000 a larger, Victorian house at 201 S.E. Fourth Street at the corner of Chestnut Street. Built in 1887, the home is simple in design and typifies nineteenth-century Kansas family homes. The property also had a large barn. Here, young Dwight Eisenhower grew into adolescence. He was brought up in a house where prayer and Bible reading were a daily ritual. Dwight Eisenhower and three of his brothers shared an upstairs bedroom, which had 2 full-sized beds. The oldest boy, Arthur Eisenhower, had his own small bedroom upstairs.

As a youth, Dwight Eisenhower developed severe blood poisoning in his leg from a scratch and his doctor advised amputation. He was spared a needless loss when he and his older brothers resisted the doctor's advice, and the leg healed. As a student, young Dwight Eisenhower developed a fondness for history, and especially enjoyed reading about military heroes of the past. He graduated from Abilene High School in 1909, and his class prophecy was that he would become a history professor at Yale. But his parents could not afford to send both Dwight Eisenhower and his brother, Edgar, who graduated from high school at the same time, to college, and so from 1909 to 1911, while Edgar Eisenhower

went to college, Dwight Eisenhower worked full-time at the creamery. After a year, Dwight Eisenhower applied for admission to the U.S. Naval Academy at Annapolis. He learned that he was too old to enter Annapolis, and so he applied to West Point, where he received an appointment. Dwight Eisenhower's parents, who were opposed to violence on religious grounds, were troubled by their son's decision to attend a military academy. When young Dwight Eisenhower left for West Point through the back porch of the house, his mother remained in the kitchen and cried for two and a half hours, but neither she nor her husband impeded their son, who left to begin a new life.

Dwight Eisenhower, or "Ike," as he was nicknamed, began his military career as a West Point cadet in 1911. He graduated from West Point in 1915, having distinguished himself in football until a knee injury in the 1912 season ended his football career. As a second lieutenant, Dwight Eisenhower was first assigned to Fort Sam Houston in San Antonio, Texas, where he met Mamie Geneva Doud, the nineteen-year-old daughter of a well-to-do Denver businessman. On July 1, 1916, he married her, and was promoted to first lieutenant that same day. They had two sons, Doud Dwight, who died in infancy, and John Sheldon Doud, who, like his father, became a career officer in the U.S. Army.

From San Antonio, Dwight Eisenhower went on to numerous assignments, including: Leon Springs, Texas; Fort Oglethorpe, Georgia; Fort Leavenworth, Kansas; and Camp Meade, Maryland. In the spring of 1918, he was assigned to command the Tank Training Center at Camp Colt near Gettysburg, Pennsylvania. (He later built a home and retired in Gettysburg.) He then went to Camp Dix, New Jersey, and then spent two years at Camp Gaillard in the Panama Canal Zone. He went to Fort Logan in Denver, Colorado in 1925, and then, in 1926, was sent to the Army General Staff School at Ft. Leavenworth, where he graduated first in his class of 275 officers. As a result, Captain Eisenhower was picked to attend the Army War College in Washington, D.C.

In 1926, Dwight Eisenhower was assigned to Paris, where he stayed in a Rue d'Anterrel apartment. In 1929, he returned to Washington, where, as a major, he served on the staff of the assistant secretary of war. In 1932, he was appointed an aide to General Douglas MacArthur, who was then chief of staff of the army. In 1935, he accompanied General MacArthur to the Philippines, where MacArthur was assigned to help the Filipinos build an army, and Major Eisenhower was his assistant. While in the Philippines, Dwight Eisenhower was promoted to lieutenant colonel. He returned to the United States in 1939, where he was assigned to Fort Ord in California, then to Fort Lewis in Washington, and then to Fort Sam Houston, where he was promoted to colonel and became chief of staff of the Third Army. His role in big maneuvers held in Louisiana by the Second and Third Armies led to his promotion to brigadier general.

Five days after the Japanese attack on Pearl Harbor, General Eisenhower was ordered by Army Chief of Staff George C. Marshall to report to the War Department in Washington, D. C. In April 1942, Dwight Eisenhower was appointed assistant chief of staff in charge of the Operations Division of the War Department general staff, in which capacity he and his staff developed the strategy of opening a "second front" by invading German-occupied France. In June 1942, General Eisenhower reported that the plans were ready for execution and General Marshall swiftly appointed him commanding general of the European Theater of Operations. He was later appointed Supreme Commander of the Allied Forces by President Roosevelt in December 1943. While in Europe, one of General Eisenhower's headquarters was in the Dendreton on Park Lane, in London. Meanwhile, Mrs. Eisenhower lived in the Wardman Park Hotel, which is now part of the Sheraton Washington Hotel at Connecticut Avenue and Woodley Road in Washington, D.C. General Eisenhower also stayed at an apartment at Scotland's Culzean Castle (where he held a life tenancy) and an eighteenth century chateau near Versailles, in France.

After World War II, General Eisenhower was hailed as a military hero, and in December 1945, President Truman appointed him Army Chief of Staff. He served in that post until May 1945, and lived in Quarter One, which was built in 1899 and has been the home of Army Chiefs of Staff since 1908. It was located on Officer's Row in Arlington Heights, Virginia.

In May 1948, General Eisenhower retired from active duty and served as president of Columbia University. He lived in the university president's twenty-one room mansion at 55 Morningside Drive in New York City. In 1950, he purchased a farm in Gettysburg, Pennsylvania, where he later built the only house he and Mrs. Eisenhower ever owned.

In 1950, President Truman returned General Eisenhower to active duty and appointed him supreme commander of NATO. General Eisenhower lived in Paris during this period and his career was about to take a new turn. As a popular military hero, he was an obvious potential presidential candidate in 1952, and both the Democrats and Republicans made overtures to him. After Governor Thomas E. Dewey of New York, the 1944 and 1948 Republican presidential candidate and a leader of the liberal wing of the G.O.P., publicly supported General Eisenhower, Dwight Eisenhower, who had never expressed a party preference, declared that he was a Republican, and, in mid-1952, was nominated by the delegates at the Republican National Convention on the first ballot. As his running mate, the delegates nominated Senator Richard M. Nixon of California. The Democrats nominated Governor Adlai E. Stevenson of Illinois on the third ballot, and named Senator John I.

Sparkman of Alabama as his running mate. General Eisenhower, who already had an enormous advantage in popularity and name recognition, capped his campaign with his promise, "I shall go to Korea," referring to a planned journey to that country to end the military conflict there. He made good on that pledge in December 1952, before his inauguration as president, and an agreement ending the Korean conflict was signed on July 27, 1953.

In his two terms as president, Dwight Eisenhower's achievements include the building of the Interstate Highway System; his 1957 directive instructing the National Guard to enforce the law of the land by making it possible for black students in Little Rock, Arkansas to attend school; and his initiation of the American space exploration program with the launching of the Explorer I satellite in January, 1958. Alaska and Hawaii were admitted to the Union in his second term, which he won by soundly defeating Adlai Stevenson a second time in 1956.

While the Eisenhowers lived in the White House, they added a kitchen to its third floor, where President Eisenhower sometimes relaxed by practicing his cooking hobby. He often visited the Maryland presidential retreat which had been named "Shangri-La" by President Franklin D. Roosevelt, but was renamed "Camp David" by President Eisenhower in honor of his grandson. The main lodge at Camp David was renamed "Aspen." The Eisenhowers also added a flag stone terrace, and a picnic and outdoor cooking facility at the lodge, as well as a golf green on the grounds.

After leaving office, General Eisenhower retired to his Gettysburg farm and spent winters in California. He died of congestive heart failure at Walter Reed General Hospital in Washington, D.C., on March 28, 1969. Today, he is buried at the Place of Meditation at the Eisenhower Center in Abilene, beside his wife, Mamie Doud Eisenhower, and their first born son, Doud Dwight, who died in infancy.

General Eisenhower's parents continued to live in the home on S.E. Fourth Street in Abilene until his father's death in March 1942, and his mother's in September 1946. Following her death, her sons gave the house to the Eisenhower Foundation, which preserved it in its original location along with family furniture and mementos, and restored it in 1947. On Veteran's Day, 1954, a museum near the site was dedicated and, in 1962, the Dwight D. Eisenhower Library was dedicated. In November 1966, the Eisenhower Foundation conveyed the boyhood home and museum to the United States. Today, these buildings, together with the Place of Meditation and the Visitors' Center, form the Eisenhower Center. A statue of General Eisenhower is located in a spot on the grounds between the library and the museum.

Today, visitors may tour the Dwight Eisenhower boyhood home. The wallpaper in the house was reproduced from the original patterns in each room. Entering through a screen door visitors see the front parlor, where the family Bible can be seen. Hanging on the wall is General Eisenhower's parents' marriage license. His parents were married at Lane University, where they both studied. In the back parlor, which was accessible from the front parlor by way of sliding wooden doors, is an 1883 upright piano, an old model radio, quilted pillows with family members' names on them and an inlaid bench inscribed "AHS" (Abilene High School). The back parlor also features an 1885 Seth Thomas eight-day clock, which was a wedding present to Dwight Eisenhower's parents (along with a Gilbert eight-day clock located in the dining room). The furniture in the back parlor is adorned with cloth and doilies.

The cooking area in back of the house features a coal and gas burning stove. Visitors are told that the kitchen used to have a cistern from which water was drawn. The bathroom was at one time a bedroom used by Dwight Eisenhower's grandfather, who lived in the house for a time.

The simplicity of this charming home reflects the simple, puritanical values in which the Eisenhowers believed. Clearly this was the foundation from which Dwight Eisenhower built his long and successful military and political career.

Eisenhower National Historic Site
97 Taneytown Road
Gettysburg, Pennsylvania 17325
(717) 334-9114

Administered by the National Park Service.

Directions:	To the Eisenhower Tour Center: The Eisenhower Tour Center is one-half mile south of the center of Gettysburg on State Route 134. Tour begins at the Eisenhower Tour Center. (Note: Visitors are not permitted to travel directly to the site. A shuttle bus takes you to the site.)
Open:	Daily, April through October; Wednesday through Sunday, November through March (closed Thanksgiving Day, Christmas Day, and New Year's Day and four weeks each winter).
Admission:	Fee charged.
Features:	Eisenhower Tour Center, which holds an 11-minute orientation program, sells tickets to the site, has rest rooms and is handicapped accessible. The site itself includes the farm house, barn, guest house, and a reception center which sells books, gifts and cards, and has rest rooms. First floor of the farm house, and the rest of the tour, is handicapped accessible.
Special Events:	An Eisenhower Christmas is held annually from the second weekend in December through New Year's Day.

In early 1950, General Dwight D. Eisenhower, with his World War II military command behind him, was the president of Columbia University and looking forward to retirement. He and his wife, Mamie, had shared a life which necessitated constant relocation from place to place, and they had never, even during his tenure at Columbia, owned a home of their own. Their desire for a quiet life out of the public eye led them to search for a place to establish such a home.

The Eisenhowers' good friends, George and Mary Allen, encouraged them to purchase a 189-acre farm owned by Allen Redding in Gettysburg, Pennsylvania. In 1950, after looking at several farms in the area, the Eisenhowers decided to buy the Redding farm.

The Eisenhowers were no strangers to Gettysburg. General Eisenhower visited the area for the first time as a West

Point cadet, and during that first sojourn, his lifelong fascination with the famous 1863 Battle of Gettysburg began. From March to December, 1918, he commanded the Army's tank corps at Camp Colt in Gettysburg, and grew fond of the area. His fond memories of the area were a great incentive in the decision to retire in Gettysburg. However, their retirement plans were delayed by two subsequent and unforeseen events: General Eisenhower's appointment as commander of the NATO forces in Europe, and his 1952 election to the office of president of the United States.

The Eisenhowers planned to use the Allen Redding farmhouse, once remodeled, as their retirement home. When the architects began the remodeling of the home, however, they made an incredible discovery. The brick walls of the farmhouse were a veneer for a 200-year-old log cabin supported by timbers which were quickly dete-

riorating. Acting on Mrs. Eisenhower's instructions, construction workers tried to save as much of the original farmhouse as possible. They salvaged a two-story brick section of the old house and the fireplace and bake oven from a summer kitchen which stood nearby. By 1955, a new house was constructed around the remains of the Redding farmhouse under the guidance of the chief architect, Milton Osborne. The new house, a modified Georgian farmhouse, includes eight bedrooms, eight bathrooms, a living room, a formal dining room, an attic studio, and a porch.

As president, Dwight Eisenhower hosted distinguished visitors at his Gettysburg farm, including Prime Minister Nehru of India and former Prime Minister Winston Churchill of Great Britain. After General Eisenhower left office in 1961, guests at the Gettysburg farm were mostly family and a small circle of friends. Visiting dignitaries and friends alike were usually given a tour of the farm, and possibly the Gettysburg battlefield. General Eisenhower was very fond of the Angus cattle he raised on his farm, and, for virtually all guests, a visit to the cattle barn was obligatory. Even Nikita Khrushchev, Premier of the Soviet Union, visited the Angus cattle barn. After the tour of the farm, visitors would return with General Eisenhower to the farmhouse, where they would be greeted by Mrs. Eisenhower. Mrs. Eisenhower normally insisted that her guests sign the guest book, which is currently on display in the entrance hall of the house. Her rule even applied to her grandchildren, who were to sign the book every time they entered the house.

Today, visitors to the site arrive by shuttle bus from the Eisenhower Tour Center. As the bus enters the main driveway of the farm, visitors see the Norway spruce trees which line the driveway, a birthday gift to the president from the state Republican committees in 1955. Passing the large barn (built in 1887) and the two-room guest house, visitors come into the entrance hall of the main house, which is custom wallpapered. The paper depicts the seals of the 48 states that comprised the United States at the time of the construction of the home, plus the seal of the territory of Hawaii and the Great Seal of the United States.

Entering the living room to the left, visitors see a room filled with numerous furnishings and gifts received by the Eisenhowers during their years in public life. The room, which contains portraits of General Eisenhower, Mrs. Eisenhower, and Mrs. Elivera Doud, Mrs. Eisenhower's mother, was seldom used by the Eisenhowers, but served as a space to exhibit the furnishings, gifts, and curios they collected for many years. Until the house was built, Mrs. Eisenhower, who had a fondness for collecting "knickknacks," had to place many of her furnishings and curios into storage. Today, many of these objects and furnishings are on display in the entrance hall and living room. Among these items are: a circular couch obtained by Mrs. Eisenhower and her sister, a painting of the city of Prague, Czechoslovakia, given to the Eisenhowers by Prague's mayor, and items of lead crystal and Steuben glass.

Turning to the right, visitors enter the Eisenhowers' porch, their favorite room in the house. While at the farm, General and Mrs. Eisenhower spent most of their time in this room. It is a glass enclosed, white walled room, furnished in a comfortable, informal manner. The dominant colors in the room are white and green. Here, the Eisenhowers entertained guests, took most of their meals, and pursued various interests. Mrs. Eisenhower was fond of watching television soap operas on the porch, and asked for absolute silence during "As The World Turns." The General's favorite programs included westerns such as "Gunsmoke" and "Bonanza." He also pursued his painting hobby and read history and western books on the porch.

Stepping back into the entrance hall and turning left, visitors next see the dining room. The dining room suite, purchased in 1927, traveled with the Eisenhowers during their moves from place to place. A tea service, an early gift to Mrs. Eisenhower from General Eisenhower, is also on display in the room. The chandelier in the dining room was a gift from a Texas oil millionaire.

Going upstairs, visitors turn right and enter a sitting room, in which hangs one of General Eisenhower's oil paintings. The books on the shelves include the westerns, biographies, and history books that the General enjoyed reading. The draperies in this room depict nine of the Eisenhowers' residences. Ahead is the "General's Room," where he relaxed or napped, and his portrait of two of his grandchildren hangs on a wall in this room. Adjacent to this room is his bathroom.

Down the hall to the right is the master bedroom, which reflects Mrs. Eisenhower's tastes. In brief, her preferences were for "pink, pearls, and photographs." Her pink tiled bathroom is next to this room, which contains some of her jewelry and other small items. In addition, many family photographs are on a dresser here, and a portrait of the Eisenhowers' grandchildren is prominently hung across from the bed. After her husband's death, Mrs. Eisenhower used this room as an office for household and personal business.

A long, narrow hallway leads past the maid's room, where Mrs. Eisenhower's personal maid used the Eisenhowers' earliest furniture, and leads toward the guest wing of the house. Two guest rooms, separated by a dressing room and a bathroom, are located here, and were used by such distinguished guests as Prime Minister Nehru of India.

When visitors come to a second set of steps, located beside the guest wing, they enter the portion of the house which was once part of the Redding farmhouse. The stairs lead to the first floor kitchen. Occasionally, General Eisenhower used this room for cooking, a hobby he enjoyed; however, the kitchen was used most frequently by the cook.

Across from the kitchen entrance is the entrance to the den. The exterior of the den is faced with stone, while the interior is wainscoted with wood salvaged from the old house. The den also contains an old fireplace and oven used in the summer kitchen which serviced the Redding farm house. General Eisenhower often played cards with friends or read in the den.

The hallway adjacent to the den, which leads to a side entrance to the house, served as the general's farm office. At the time of his heart attack in 1955, it served as a "temporary White House" while he recuperated at Gettysburg. A desk in this room was reproduced from a desk used by George Washington, and is made with pine boards recovered from the White House's 1948-1950 renovation.

Behind the house is a garden, a brick barbecue, a large flagpole and a putting green. The farm on which the house is located used the 189 acres owned by the Eisenhowers, and 285 acres owned by a friend, to grow corn and wheat, to produce hay, and to first raise dairy cows, and later, Angus cattle. Flying on the flagpole, besides the American flag, is a red flag which depicts in white the five star emblem of the rank of General of the Army, to which Dwight Eisenhower was reinstated after leaving the presidency.

When touring the Eisenhower Farm, visitors see the private lifestyle of a modern chief executive during his term of office, and during retirement. For the Eisenhowers, retirement was a dream that was delayed, but not denied, by Dwight Eisenhower's eight years in the Oval Office. For General Eisenhower, the special pleasure here was the farm, and for Mrs. Eisenhower, the joy was in the house itself.

JOHN FITZGERALD KENNEDY

John Fitzgerald Kennedy National Historic Site
83 Beals Street
Brookline, Massachusetts 02146
(617) 566-7937

Administered by the National Park Service.

Directions: From Plymouth, Quincy and other points south of Boston, take I-93 to the Massachusetts Turnpike (I-90) west. Exit the turnpike at the Allston Cambridge toll booths (Exit 20). Follow the Allston-Brighton off ramp. This merges into Cambridge Street. Follow Cambridge Street approximately three-quarters of a mile to Harvard Avenue. Turn left onto Harvard Avenue. Follow Harvard Avenue across two sets of trolley tracks. The sixth street on the left is Beals Street (approximately three-quarters of a mile along Harvard Avenue). Drive down Beals Street to #83, a green house with a flag pole. The site is three-quarters of the way down the street, on the right.

Open:	May through October, Wednesday to Sunday.
Admission:	Fee charged.
Features:	A Park Service ranger conducts a guided tour of the house. The basement of the house serves as a reception area

with exhibits, a video presentation and sales center. The house is not currently handicapped accessible.

| Special Events: | Free one hour guided walks in the neighborhood John F. Kennedy knew as a child are available during the spring, summer and fall. Contact the site for specific dates. |

The descendant of two distinguished families of Irish-American Bostonians, John Fitzgerald Kennedy was born on May 29, 1917 at 83 Beals Street in Brookline, a suburb of Boston. The house in which the 35th President was born, a three-story frame house built in 1909, was purchased by his father, Joseph Patrick Kennedy, in 1914 in anticipation of his marriage to Rose Fitzgerald, daughter of John F. ("Honey Fitz") Fitzgerald, who served two non-consecutive terms as mayor of Boston and also served in the U.S. House of Representatives. Joseph P. Kennedy was the son of a well-to-do East Boston family. He graduated from Harvard University in 1912 and went into the business of investments, especially stocks, real estate and banking. At age 25, one year before his marriage, he became president of the Columbia Trust Company, thus becoming the youngest bank president in America at that time. In 1917, the year of John F. Kennedy's birth, he moved into the managerial field by becoming assistant general manager of the Fore River Shipyards.

The Kennedys had four children while living on Beals Street: Joseph, Jr. (born at Hull, Massachusetts) in 1915, John in 1917, Rosemary in 1918 and Kathleen in 1920. The young family dined together each evening, prayed together at nearby St. Aidan's Catholic Church, and entertained occasionally. While Joseph Kennedy was at work, Rose set about the business of running the household and raising an active group of children.

In 1921, the growing family moved to a larger home at the corner of Abbottsford and Naples Roads in Brookline. This three-story shingled frame house has a large wrap-around porch with columns and dentils, and two brick chimneys. Three more children, Eunice, Patricia and Robert, were born here. (Jean and Edward were born later in Boston.) While living here, Joseph Kennedy took the steps which led to the considerable family fortune. John and his older brother, Joseph, Jr., first attended The Edward Devotion School, a public school, and then the Lower Noble and Greenough School (which later became the Dexter School), a private, nonsectarian school, while living here. Today, the Kennedys' second Brookline house is privately owned.

In 1927, when young John Kennedy was ten years old, the family moved to Riverdale, a well-to-do section of the Bronx, in New York City. Later, they moved to a palatial home in Bronxville, which is just outside of New York City in Westchester County. That home was later demolished.

The Kennedys also had a residence in Manhattan and a rented villa on the Riviera. After completing sixth grade in the Bronxville public schools, thirteen-year-old Jack Kennedy went on to attend Canterbury School in New Milford, Connecticut, then Choate School in Wallingford, Connecticut. The Kennedys spent their winters in Palm Beach, Florida and summered at Hyannisport, on Cape Cod, Massachusetts. There they swam, sailed and played on the beach.

In the summer of 1935, after graduating from Choate, Jack Kennedy went to England, where he studied under Professor Harold Laski at the London School of Economics. Jack Kennedy, who had been sickly as a child, developed jaundice while on this sojourn, and was compelled to drop out of school. After returning to the United States, he matriculated at Princeton University, but a recurrence of jaundice after two months forced him to leave that institution as well.

When he recovered his health, Jack Kennedy enrolled at Harvard, his father's alma mater, and while there lived at Winthrop House. There he wrote his acclaimed senior thesis, which was published as a book, *Why England Slept*, in 1940. After graduating from Harvard with honors, he accompanied his father, who had been appointed American ambassador to the Court of St. James (Ambassador to Great Britain), to London, where he lived at 14 Princess Gate. After Joseph Kennedy was forced to resign as ambassador for having made certain anti-British statements, Jack Kennedy enrolled in the graduate business school at Stanford University in the winter of 1940-41. However, with the Second World War approaching, Kennedy sought to enlist in the army, but was turned down because of a back injury he had received while playing football. After a course of strenuous exercises, he passed a Navy physical and became a seaman in September 1941.

For his first year of service, even after the attack on Pearl Harbor, Jack Kennedy 's assignments were routine desk jobs. He served in Washington, D.C., and later in Charleston, South Carolina, where he roomed at 48 Murray Road and later rented on Sullivan's Island. He persuaded his father to use his influence to get him sea duty, and he was then assigned to officers' training in Chicago and PT training in Melville, Rhode Island. He then received a commission as a lieutenant (j.g.) and, in March 1943, was given command of his own torpedo boat, the PT-109, in the South Pacific. That boat was sunk by a Japanese destroyer on August 2, 1943, killing two crew members, but Lt. Kennedy and ten of his crew members survived by clinging to the wreckage and making their way through the cold Pacific waters for fifteen hours until they finally reached a tiny island. Lt. Kennedy kept up his men's courage, and they swam from island to island for four days until they found some natives who carried a message carved on a coconut to the nearest navy base. After their rescue, Lt. Kennedy discovered that he and his crew had been given up for dead prior to the successful delivery of the message, and their families had been so notified.

Jack Kennedy returned to the United States, where he was admitted to a Navy hospital near Boston to be treated for malaria and a recurrence of his old back injury. While there, he learned that his older brother, Joe, Jr., had been killed while flying a bomber in Europe. In 1945, Jack Kennedy received an early discharge from the Navy due to his physical condition, and left for San Francisco to cover the United Nations organizational meeting as a reporter for the Hearst newspapers. After reporting on the British elections for the Hearst chain, he ended his brief career in journalism and decided to enter the political realm.

Long before, Joseph Kennedy, Sr. had resolved that his oldest son, Joe, Jr., would become president of the United States. With his oldest son lost forever, Joseph Kennedy now pinned his ambitions on Jack, who had been a sickly, somewhat shy youth, but was now a war hero due to the PT-109 incident. Father and son went to the family winter residence at 1095 Ocean Drive, Palm Beach, to map out young Jack Kennedy's political future. The house is a white stucco structure with a red-tiled roof and six bedrooms, where Jack Kennedy had spent vacation time as a child. That house is now privately owned.

Jack Kennedy returned to Boston in 1946, and set his sites on Boston's Eleventh Congressional District, where a vacancy had occurred. He knew that the seat was his if he could win the Democratic primary, which was tantamount to election in this heavily Democratic, blue collar district. He established residence by occupying a Beacon Hill apartment at 122 Boudoin Street, Boston. In a much celebrated campaign, in which most of his family members participated, Jack Kennedy was an active, energetic candidate who managed to touch a chord among the working class primary electorate, notwithstanding his affluent background. Campaigning under the slogan, "The New Generation Offers a Leader," Jack Kennedy won the primary, beating out nine other candidates for the nomination. He went on to an easy victory over his Republican opponent in November.

In Washington, Representative Kennedy, not quite thirty years old, rented a three-story row house with a patio garden at 1528 31st Street in Georgetown for $300.00 a month. He served in the House of Representatives for three terms. In 1952, he ran a statewide campaign in Massachusetts against incumbent Republican U.S. Senator Henry Cabot Lodge. With his twenty-seven-year-old brother, Bobby, as his campaign manager, Rep. Kennedy beat Senator Lodge by 70,000

votes, even though General Eisenhower was at the top of the Republican ticket and the Republicans won the governorship of Massachusetts that year. The following year, as if looking for a more luxurious residence in keeping with his new office, Senator Kennedy retained Hickory Hill, a fifteen-room house on seven acres in Virginia that once served as Civil War headquarters for Union General George McClellan. He later passed Hickory Hill on to his brother Bobby, whose widow, Ethel Skakel Kennedy, still lives there. On September 12th that same year, Senator Kennedy married Jacqueline Lee Bouvier, whom he had met two years earlier while she was attending George Washington University. At the time of their marriage, Jacqueline Bouvier was an inquiring photographer for the Washington *Times-Herald*. Their wedding took place in Newport, Rhode Island, and the reception was held at her mother's home in Newport, Hammersmith Farm, which is open to the public today.

In 1954, Senator Kennedy underwent surgery to correct his old back injury, and while recovering wrote the bestseller *Profiles in Courage*, a series of stories of political courage in American history. That book won the Pulitzer Prize for biography after its publication in 1956. 1956 was also the year that Senator Kennedy attempted, over his father's strong objections, to secure the Democratic nomination for vice president on a ticket headed by former Illinois governor Adlai E. Stevenson. In a rare political move, Stevenson threw the choice of his running mate open to the delegates at the Democratic convention. After three ballots (Senator Kennedy was the top vote-getter on the second ballot), the nomination went to Senator Estes Kefauver of Tennessee, who had been a Democratic primary opponent of Stevenson's earlier that year. Senator Kennedy campaigned vigorously for the Democratic ticket in the ensuing general election campaign, but the ticket was nonetheless defeated by an Eisenhower landslide in November, although the Democrats remained in firm control of Congress. However, the ever-vigilant Kennedys learned much from the failed Democratic effort, and were determined not to repeat the mistakes made in 1956 in the next presidential election, in which Senator Kennedy and his brother, Robert, had all but decided that the senator would be a candidate.

It was around this period that Senator Kennedy established a summer residence at Irving and Marchant Avenues, in Hyannisport. It was close to the summer home that Joseph Kennedy, Sr. owned since 1928. John F. Kennedy's home is a two-story white-shingled home built in the early 1900s which was expanded until it had eleven rooms, five baths, and a brick paved patio. The homes of Joseph, Sr., John, and Robert Kennedy comprise the Kennedy compound. These residences are still owned by the Kennedy family today. During the Kennedy administration, security was extremely tight at the Kennedy compound whenever the president was in residence there, and curious motorists were turned away by the Secret Service.

In 1957, Senator and Mrs. John F. Kennedy purchased a residence at 3307 N Street N.W. in Washington for

$78,000.00. It had a double drawing room and a rear garden. The home was renovated for $20,000.00 and then sold for $105,000.00. Senator Kennedy also maintained a suite on the thirty-fifth floor of the Hotel Carlyle, on Madison Avenue in New York.

The following year, 1960, was the presidential election year that Senator Kennedy, his father, and brother Robert had long planned for. Through a combination of masterful strategy, political acumen, and energetic campaigning, Senator Kennedy successfully negotiated the potential obstacles in the path to the Democratic nomination, first by winning the Wisconsin primary, which established his national appeal, and then by defeating Senator Hubert H. Humphrey in the West Virginia primary, thus dispelling the impression that a Roman Catholic candidate could not appeal to an overwhelmingly Protestant electorate. Primary victories such as these convinced the Democratic bosses that Senator Kennedy was a strong vote-getter, leading to a first ballot nomination for Senator Kennedy at the 1960 Democratic Convention in Los Angeles. Much to his brother Robert's chagrin, John F. Kennedy chose Senate Majority Leader Lyndon Baines Johnson of Texas as his running mate. Ironically, Johnson had been one of Senator Kennedy's rivals for the presidential nomination. The choice was politically motivated; John F. Kennedy felt that he could not beat the Republicans without carrying Texas. Moreover, the choice of Senator Johnson would help to unify the party in November. As expected, the Republicans nominated Vice President Richard M. Nixon as their choice to succeed President Eisenhower. In an apparent political swipe at Senator Kennedy, Henry Cabot Lodge of Massachusetts was chosen as Mr. Nixon's running mate.

A highlight of the fall presidential campaign was the unprecedented Kennedy-Nixon debates, the first televised presidential debates in American history. The conventional wisdom on these debates is that while Vice President Nixon answered questions impressively and showed a command of the issues, Senator Kennedy, who fared quite well as an orator, was the more "telegenic" of the two candidates, and appeared to be more assured and attractive in appearance than his Republican rival. In the end, the election was extremely close, with Senator Kennedy ahead by a razor-thin margin in the popular vote, but considerably ahead in the electoral vote. He carried the crucial states of Illinois and Texas to win the presidency, although, to this day, stories persist of voting fraud in those two states. Resisting pleas to contest the election results, Vice President Nixon graciously conceded the election to John F. Kennedy, who was inaugurated as the 35th president on January 20, 1961.

As president, John F. Kennedy's notable successes included the Nuclear Test Ban Treaty, and his handling of the Cuban Missile Crisis, in which his brother Robert played a key role in getting the Soviet Union to remove nuclear missiles from Cuba that were aimed at American targets in October 1962. Almost certainly his greatest failure, which haunted him long afterward, was the failed Bay of Pigs in-

vasion of Cuba, an initiative conceived during the Eisenhower administration by American intelligence operatives which was designed to overthrow Cuba's Communist leader, Fidel Castro.

Under President Kennedy, the fifth White House renovation took place. The Fine Arts Commission was formed for the purpose of gathering historical pieces for display and use. The goal of the restoration was to reflect the history of the presidents and their families. While in office, the Kennedys rented "Wexford," at Glen Ora, Fauquier County, Virginia. Built in 1810, Wexford is a modified French provincial style home on land which includes tall groves of trees, stables, a greenhouse, a smokehouse, a springhouse, tennis courts, and an unfiltered pool. Today, Wexford is privately owned.

No one will ever know what further achievements President Kennedy might have accomplished, for on November 22, 1963, he was assassinated while riding in a motorcade on a political swing through Dallas, Texas. His body was laid to rest at Arlington National Cemetery. Vice President Lyndon B. Johnson succeeded John F. Kennedy as president.

Just before President Kennedy's parents left his birthplace home in 1921, they sold the house to the wife of Edward E. Moore, a close friend and business associate (after whom the Kennedys' youngest child, Edward Moore Kennedy, was named). In 1961, the town of Brookline placed a commemorative plaque on the house, and in May 1965, it was designated a National Historic Landmark. After having been occupied by a series of owners, the Kennedy family repurchased the house in 1966. Mrs. Rose Kennedy supervised the restoration of the house to its 1917 appearance. In 1967, Congress authorized the inclusion of the house in the National Park System as a National Historic Site.

Today, visitors begin their tour in the hallway, which had a coat closet and a small table for the telephone. They then see the living room, which is filled with furnishings and objects belonging to the Kennedys while they lived here. A red chair against the northwest wall was Mr. Kennedy's usual chair, and Mrs. Kennedy normally sat in an armchair on the other side of a mahogany gateleg table. The piano, which Mrs. Kennedy often played while the family sang, was a wedding present from her uncles, James and Edward Fitzgerald. It has a brocade cover which is also original, as are a pair of mantel vases and an oriental rug. All of these furnishings are in their original positions. The living room also has a gas-log fireplace, but Mrs. Kennedy seldom allowed it to be used because of the danger to the children, who would play in the living room in the evening before bed.

Next, visitors return to the hall, ascend the stairs and turn to the right at the top to view the master bedroom, where John Fitzgerald Kennedy was born. Its twin beds (including the bed where John F. Kennedy was born), dresser, mirror and night table are all original to the house. On the day of President Kennedy's birth, May 29, 1917, Mrs. Kennedy used the bed closer to the window (which faces out onto

Beals Street) to provide as much light as possible for the attending physician. In this room are other objects which belonged to the family, including: silver toilet articles sitting on the dresser, a chest of drawers and a silver vase on the vanity. There are a number of family pictures here, including: Mr. Joseph Kennedy's parents, Mr. and Mrs. Joseph Kennedy themselves, and several of Joseph Kennedy, Jr. The pictures beside the dresser are of the first four children: Joseph, Jr., John, Rosemary and Kathleen, when each was six months old. The bathroom adjacent to the master bedroom was the only bathroom in the house, and was used by all members of the family.

Across the hall is the nursery, which was used for that purpose beginning with Joseph, Jr.'s birth in 1915. After John's birth, the two boys shared the room. After Rosemary was born in 1918, the boys were relocated down the hall, and the room remained a nursery. There are several objects of interest in this room, including a bassinet used by Rose Kennedy for all of her newborn children, and later, probably for visiting grandchildren. It originally had a canopy. The christening dress (a reproduction of the original, which is now at the John F. Kennedy Library in nearby Dorchester), bonnet, outer coat and cape were worn by all of the Kennedy children as infants, as well as by President Kennedy's son, John F. Kennedy, Jr. This christening outfit was handmade by the Franciscan Missionaries of Mary in East Boston. On a chair is a children's book, *King Arthur's Knights*, which was a favorite of the president as a child.

The next room visitors see is the guest room. After Rosemary's birth in 1918, this room became a children's room, but at the time of John F. Kennedy's birth, the room was used by visiting family or school friends. The dresser and bed footboard seen in this room were originally used here; the headboard is a reproduction. The room also features a silver vase and bud vase, which were wedding gifts, and an original silver toilet set. The toilet set includes a hand mirror, brush, powderbox, loose-hair jar, container for smelling salts, shoehorn, nail file and polisher, button hook and pin box.

The last room visitors see on the second floor is a tiny study. This is the room Mrs. Kennedy used to keep a card file on the growth and health of each of her children. She also wrote letters here, read, and did such household chores as mending and button-sewing. In this room are an original mahogany desk and a Martha Washington sewing cabinet. A framed Mother's Day poem from the Kennedy children to their mother hangs on the wall above the desk. Other framed items on the wall in this room include: a wedding day photograph of the Kennedys, their wedding announcement, and Joseph Kennedy, Sr.'s birth announcement. In the hall, visitors can see a photograph of Mrs. Rose Kennedy and her sisters with Sir Thomas Lipton, taken on his yacht.

The stairs to the third floor are closed to the public. Once the third floor included the cook's and nursemaid's rooms; today it is used for the site's administrative offices. Visitors return to the first floor to view the dining room. The dining room table was too large for the small Kennedy children to manage, so they sat at the small table nearby, once they were old enough to dine on their own. Mrs. Kennedy kept a watchful eye on her children at the small table when meals were served. The Kennedys normally spent holidays with the children's grandparents, but used the dining room for several birthday parties for the children. This room has more furniture originally used by the Kennedys than any other room in the house. With the exception of the china cabinet and children's table, the furnishings in this room are original. The forks, spoons, napkin rings and porringers on the small table are those used by Joseph, Jr. and John Kennedy, and are marked with their initials. The room also has original family china and silver. Also displayed here are: a handpainted punchbowl; Limoges porcelain (Mrs. Kennedy's bridal service) which was decorated by Margaret Kennedy Burke, Mrs. Kennedy's sister-in-law; and silver flatware from Mrs. Kennedy's original table service. There is a ruby cut-glass decanter and wine glasses which were made in Prague and had belonged to Mrs. Kennedy's mother. Six tea cups and saucers given to Mrs. Kennedy before her marriage by Sir Thomas Lipton, who formerly used them on his yacht, Erin, are in the china cabinet.

Behind the dining room is the kitchen, where the cook and the nursemaid prepared meals, baked bread, and washed dishes. For the seventeen years when an infant was part of the Kennedy family, bottles were sterilized on the stove while formulas were prepared in this kitchen and in the kitchens of later Kennedy family homes. The cook and the nursemaid took their meals here.

As visitors tour this house, they get a sense of what life was like for an active, growing American family around the time of the First World War. It is fortunate that Mrs. Rose Kennedy took such an active part in restoring a place where American history was made, and where one can learn of the formative years of a man who grew up to become a renowned and, tragically, martyred world leader.

LYNDON BAINES JOHNSON

Lyndon B. Johnson State Historical Park
Stonewall, Texas 78671
(830) 644-2252

Administered by the Texas Parks and Wildlife Department.

Lyndon B. Johnson National Historical Park
(Stonewall Unit)
Stonewall, Texas
(830) 844-2241 ext 3

Administered by the National Park Service.

(Johnson City Unit)
Johnson City, Texas
(830) 868-7128

Administered by the National Park Service.

Directions:

To National Historical Park, Johnson City Unit:
From Austin: Take Interstate 35 and use exit for U.S. 290 West. Take U.S. 290 West for 50 miles to Johnson City. Turn left at F Street in Johnson City and drive two blocks. Boyhood home is on the southeast corner of 9th and G Streets. Visitor Center and parking is located on F and 10th Streets.

To State Historical Park and National Historical Park, Stonewall Unit:
From Austin: Take Interstate 35 and use exit for U.S. 290 West. Take U.S. 290 West for 64 miles. Entrance to site will be on the right side of the road. (Note: A tour of this site begins at the State Park Visitors Center, as the birthplace and LBJ Ranch are accessible only via a tour bus operated by the National Park Service. Tour bus tokens are sold at the state park visitor center on a first-come, first-served basis.

Open:

National Historical Park, Stonewall Unit:
Daily (except Christmas Day).
State Historical Park: Daily. (Pool open from Memorial Day to Labor Day only.)

National Historical Park, Johnson City Unit: Daily (except Christmas Day and New Years Day).

Admission:
Fee charged for swimming pool and tour bus to LBJ Ranch. Free for all other units.

Features:

National Park, Stonewall Unit: Reconstructed birthplace home, cemetery, LBJ Ranch and home, junction school, church.

State Park: Visitor Center, Sauer-Beckmann "Living History" Farm and swimming pool.

National Park, Johnson City Unit: Boyhood home, Visitor Center, Johnson settlement, exhibit center.

Special Events:
In the fall a Crafts Day is held at the Johnson Settlement, located in the Johnson City Unit of the National Park. Crafts of the 1800s and early 1900s are demonstrated.

On August 25, the National Park celebrates National Park Day.

On President Johnson's birthday, August 27, a wreath-laying ceremony takes place at the Stonewall Unit of the National Park.

From Thanksgiving Day to New Year's Day, both parks participate in the local "Light Spectacular," in which buildings and trees are decorated with white holiday lights. The Lyndon Johnson boyhood home in Johnson City is not decorated with lights because electricity was not used in the house at the time Lyndon Johnson lived there. Instead, a lamplight tour takes place in mid-December.

In December, the Christmas season is celebrated with a tree lighting ceremony on the state park grounds and evening bus tours of the Sauer-Beckmann Farm (on the State Park grounds) and the reconstructed Lyndon Johnson birthplace (in the Stonewall Unit of the National Park). Both the farm and the birthplace are decorated with period Christmas decorations.

Contact sites about specific dates and times, and other special events.

In 1867, shortly after the close of the Civil War, Sam Ealy Johnson, Sr. brought his new bride, Eliza Binton Johnson, to settle in his native land near the Pedernales River. This dry-soiled, rugged land of low-lying hills, which Sam Ealy Johnson, Sr. called home, stretches east from Austin about 80 miles. It reaches Fredericksburg, and encompasses towns such as Llano to the north, and San Marcos to the south, and is known as the Hill Country of Texas, Blanco County.

Sam Ealy Johnson, Sr. had greater dreams than merely sustaining his family; he desired success and comfort for himself and his household. In 1867 he decided to work together with his brother, Jesse Thomas Johnson, as a cattle drover, hoping that their business partnership would prove highly successful. They purchased many herds of cattle on credit and drove them north up the Chisholm Trail to the railheads in Kansas—an extremely hazardous, difficult journey. At first, the business appeared promising. However, in 1872 financial obstacles proved too great, and the partnership had to be dissolved and their assets sold. The Blanco County property they had used as headquarters for their business was sold to James Polk Johnson, a nephew of Sam, Sr.'s, who established the settlement from which the village of Johnson City takes its name.

In 1872, Sam Ealy Johnson, Sr. and his family moved to Hays County, where they engaged in farming until 1889. They then moved on to Gillespie County near Stonewall, Texas, built a house there and continued to farm. They remained there until 1905, and then moved to another house about one-quarter of a mile west.

After Sam E. Johnson, Sr. left his original house and farm in Stonewall, his son, Sam Ealy Johnson, Jr., rented them from his father. Sam Johnson, Jr. had been elected to the Texas State Legislagure in 1904. On October 20, 1907, he married Rebekah Baines, the daughter of a former Texas state legislator. Rebekah Baines Johnson had an education unusual for a woman of her day; she had received a degree at Mary Harden-Baylor College and, like her husband, held a teaching license.

Sam Ealy Johnson, Jr. brought his new bride to live in the rented farmhouse where Lyndon Johnson was born on August 27, 1908. The house was called a "dog-trot" house

because of the open breezeway running between the two enclosed sections of the house. Today, visitors see a reconstruction of the open-air birthplace, which is in far better condition than its 1889 predecessor. The "new" birthplace home was designed to serve as a guest house during the Johnson administration. Nonetheless, the reconstructed birthplace does provide an idea of what life was like for young Lyndon Johnson and his family while they lived there.

Facing the front of the house, the kitchen and dining areas are located in the left section, and the parlor is contained within the right section. The house contains some original furnishings belonging to the Johnson family, including a dining room table and chairs used by Lyndon Johnson's grandparents, and some replicas such as a duplicate of a bedspread made by Lyndon Johnson's Grandmother Baines. The left section of the house also contains a nursery and bedroom, and the latter features the bed in which Lyndon Johnson was born. Additional beds are located in the parlor on the other side of the house. The roof of the house extends over the front porch, and the outer walls of the house have board-and-batten siding and are painted white. The ceiling is beaded and the inner walls are wainscoted.

In 1913, Sam Ealy Johnson, Jr. moved to Johnson City with his family. There he held several occupations, as a teacher, a real estate agent, and an insurance agent. The new home of Sam and Rebekah Johnson and their three children, Lyndon, Rebekah and Josefa, was located on what is now the corner of 9th and G Streets in Johnson City. This house, built in 1886, was considered to be on the edge of town in 1913, and is of a style known as "folk Victorian." It is a "double L" structure, shaped like a plus sign as viewed from above, and sits on a one and three-quarters-acre lot. Sam Ealy Johnson, Jr. paid $3,000.00 for this property, which is located very near the Johnson Settlement where his father had once lived.

Like many of his neighbors, he kept some livestock, including a cow and a few chickens on his land, and grew some vegetables on the premises. He continued to make his way in a variety of pursuits, including acting as the town barber. Rebekah Johnson, who had a degree in journalism, wrote articles for the local paper. She also practiced her natural teaching talents on her own children, attempting to strengthen their powers of observation and their ability at public speaking. At dinner, Sam Johnson, Jr. often listened, along with his family, to radio speeches by politicians and other important figures and then questioned his children about the content of what they had heard. Current events were a frequent topic of conversation at dinner. These conversations and parental lessons were the beginning of the political education of Lyndon Johnson.

A tour of Lyndon Johnson's boyhood home in Johnson City begins on the front porch, where Rebekah Johnson conducted extended elocution lessons for her own children and other children in town. The wooden platform of the porch, elevated above the wooden benches extending from the house, enabled Rebekah Johnson to address her young charges with authority. Years later, in 1937, it became the platform from which Lyndon Johnson announced his candidacy for Congress.

Stepping through the screen door of the house into the east wing, visitors come to Sam Ealy Johnson, Jr.'s study. The study resembles a small hallway with a writing desk. Hanging on the wall here is a photograph of Sam Johnson, Jr., at his desk in the Texas State Legislature, in which he served for six two-year terms.

As the tour continues, visitors are told several other facts about the house. No electricity was used in this house during the period Lyndon Johnson lived here, from 1913 to 1920 and from 1923 to 1927 (the Sam Ealy Johnson, Jr. family returned to the farmhouse in Stonewall, lived there from 1920 to 1923, and then moved back to the house in Johnson City), as the period precedes the advent of rural electrification. Later, Representative Lyndon Johnson played an instrumental role in bringing electricity to the Hill Country. However, when young Lyndon Johnson was growing up, the house used kerosene lamps for illumination. Although the house is currently decorated and furnished in proper period fashion based upon the recollections of Lyndon Johnson and some of his siblings, most of the furnishings are not original. However, the house still has its original floorboards, which were inverted to extend their use.

A side door from Sam Ealy Johnson Jr.'s study leads to the girls' bedroom on the left, where Lyndon's sisters, Rebekah, Josefa and Lucia, slept. To the right, in the north wing of the house, is the parlor, the only room in the house holding many of the original furnishings. A mirror, hanging prominently on the northwest wall of the parlor, was used as a teaching tool in Rebekah Johnson's "classroom" for her children. One by one, the children stood in front of this mirror and practiced speeches. Over the mantel in the parlor is a picture which, at a distance, appears to depict a human skull. Upon closer examination, the picture is actually that of a woman primping before a mirror.

Moving from the dining room, the central room of the house, to the west wing, visitors come to the parents' bedroom, which, because it was used to entertain the tobacco-chewing, smoking or swearing politicians who visited Sam Ealy Johnson, Jr., was also known as the politicians' room. Rebekah Johnson did not feel the parlor was suitable for such political sessions. The bedroom is so small, however, that some of Sam Ealy Johnson, Jr.'s political visitors probably sat on the bed during their gatherings.

Adjacent to the parents' bedroom is the tiny boys' bedroom that Lyndon Johnson shared with his brother, Sam Houston Johnson, until Lyndon departed for Southwest State Teachers' College in 1927. One can imagine that the boys overheard many of the political discussions Sam Ealy Johnson, Jr. had with his colleagues from this room. In this manner, young Lyndon Johnson must have learned about another aspect of politics besides the civic and public issues; he learned how to strategize, and how to make trade-offs and compromises. These are lessons that Lyndon Johnson carried with him throughout his congressional career, and to the presidency.

Coming back through the parents' bedroom and dining room, the next room visitors see is the kitchen. A solid slab of linoleum, unusual for the time and place of Lyndon Johnson's boyhood, rests on the wooden kitchen floor. The cooking took place on a large woodburning stove. Also on display are a baker's table, a butter churn and a variety of antique containers of various kitchen products which recall a bygone area.

Beside the kitchen to the east, is the rear, or southern porch. Visitors notice a bed on the porch which represents the fact that the children often slept on the back porch to take advantage of the cool breezes on hot summer nights. Sam Ealy Johnson, Jr. shaved on this porch, as represented by a shaving table with a mirror, bowl and kitchen pitcher. An ice cream maker used by Rebekah Johnson also sits on the porch, as does a wooden ice box. Ice was delivered to the Johnsons and their neighbors from Austin once each week and was placed in the top compartment of the ice box, keeping the food in the lower compartment cold. A drip was placed below the ice box to catch the drops of melted ice, and emptied four times a day.

Outside the house itself, to the west, is the vegetable garden where Sam Johnson, Jr. and Rebekah Johnson grew vegetables for their own use. An above-ground well with a chute leading toward the house supplied water for the family, and they kept their cow and chickens behind the house. Currently the property has a grass lawn and a paved road but in Lyndon Johnson's boyhood the grounds had only clumps of grass in the yard and was reached by dirt roads.

In 1922, during the time when his parents and siblings were living on the Stonewall farm for the second time, Lyndon Johnson boarded with his grandparents in Johnson City so that he could enroll in the local high school. Two years later, while young Lyndon Johnson and his family were again living together in their Johnson City home, he and some friends decided to make their way to California as an adventure. He spent much of 1924 traveling along the California coast doing odd jobs, but returned home after nearly a year and took a job doing manual labor with a road gang. Yielding to his parents, who urged that he continue his education, he enrolled at Southwest State Teachers' College in San Marcos, Texas in 1927 at the age of eighteen. While a student there, he enrolled at Pittle House, where Willard Deason was his roommate. He spent one year away from college teaching Mexican children in a tiny school in Cotulla, Texas, and while there boarded with Miss Sarah Tinsley in a house with stilts. He returned to college and continued to work his way through school by taking such jobs as a janitor and an office helper for the college president. In 1930, he graduated from college.

After graduation, Lyndon Johnson moved to Houston, where he spent a year teaching debate and public speaking at Sam Houston High School. In 1932, he began his political and governmental career in earnest when he accepted the invitation of U.S. Representative Richard Kleberg to come to Washington as his secretary at a salary of $3,000.00 a year. Lyndon Johnson found lodging at the Dodge Hotel on Capitol Plaza for $20.00 a month, and, working as a Congressional aide from 1932 to 1935, learned the workings of Capitol Hill in the waning days of the Hoover administration and in the exciting initial days of the Roosevelt administration. In 1934, while on a trip to Texas, Mr. Johnson met Claudia Alta Taylor, who was called Lady Bird by her family and friends. After a whirlwind courtship lasting only two months, the two were married on November 17, 1934. Later, Mr. and Mrs. Johnson had two daughters: Luci and Lynda. Mrs. Johnson's family was well-to-do and, by a series of shrewd investments using money she had inherited from her mother, beginning with a small radio station in Austin, Mrs. Johnson, with her husband's assistance, eventually turned the Johnsons' assets into a multi-million dollar empire.

Back in Washington, Lyndon Johnson, with his new wife, rented an apartment for $42.50 a month on Connecticut Avenue and City Columbia Road in northwest Washington. In 1935, President Franklin Roosevelt established the National Youth Administration (NYA), an agency whose mission was to help unemployed young people earn money and go to school. Lyndon Johnson applied for a post with the new agency and received President Roosevelt's appointment as NYA administrator for Texas. At the age of twenty-six, Lyndon Johnson was the youngest of the NYA administrators. The Johnsons returned to Texas and rented their lodgings in Austin from friends. Mr. Johnson lost no time in organizing programs that resulted in tens of thousands of jobs for youth.

1937 was a significant year in Lyndon Johnson's life. Due to the death of the U.S. Representative from the district which included the Hill Country where Mr. Johnson grew up, a special election was called. Lyndon Johnson became one of ten candidates for the Congressional seat, presenting himself to the electorate as an ardent supporter of President Roosevelt and his policies. President Roosevelt's initiatives in rural electrification and other areas made him very popular in the Congressional district, and, by stressing his support of the Roosevelt administration and tireless personal campaigning, Lyndon Johnson won the special election. In his early years in the House of Representatives, Lyndon Johnson focused upon providing electrical services for farms in his district and pushed for public housing in urban areas.

When Senator Morris Sheppard of Texas died in April 1941, Representative Johnson determined that he should enter the race to succeed him. He ran a vigorous statewide campaign that year, but lost to the popular Texas Governor W. Lee "Pappy" O'Daniel. Rep. Johnson returned to his duties in the house, but, not long thereafter, the Japanese bombed Pearl Harbor. Rep. Johnson immediately asked for active duty as a member of the Naval Reserve (in which he

had the rank of lieutenant commander), and became the first member of Congress to go on active duty in World War II. While on a fact-finding mission in the South Pacific for President Roosevelt in May 1942, Lyndon Johnson flew in a bomber which was attacked by Japanese fighter planes. Later, he was on board another plane that crash-landed in Australia, and as a result of these incidents, General Douglas MacArthur presented Lyndon Johnson with the Silver Star for gallantry under enemy fire. Lyndon Johnson's tour of duty ended in July 1942 when President Roosevelt ordered him and all other members of Congress to return to Washington and to resume their legislative duties.

In 1948, Representative Johnson made another attempt to win a seat in the U.S. Senate. He was one of eleven candidates in the Democratic primary and, when the votes were counted on primary day, Rep. Johnson came in second to former Texas Governor Coke Stevenson. Under Texas election law, a runoff primary election between the top two vote getters was held. The results of that election are the subject of controversy to this day; the official results showed Rep. Johnson winning the contest by a margin of only eighty-seven votes out of 988,295 cast! Gov. Stevenson unsuccessfully challenged the results, and later supported Rep. Johnson's Republican opponent in the fall election, but Rep. Johnson won the Senate seat by a two-to-one margin in November 1948.

In 1949, Lyndon Johnson's first year as a senator, he purchased a Norman-style mansion located in the Spring Valley section of Washington, from Washington society hostess Perle Mesta, which he sold in 1963 when he became president. Today, the mansion is privately owned. He also began a rapid political rise and in 1951, his fellow Democratic senators elected Senator Johnson party whip, or assistant leader, of the senate Democrats. That same year, Senator Johnson purchased a ranch including about 2,000 acres of land from his widowed aunt in Stonewall. The size of the ranch was later expanded by subsequent purchases and came to be known as the LBJ Ranch, and, during President Johnson's administration, as the Texas White House. The ranch house itself has been expanded greatly since the purchase of the property, and today, the National Park Service owns 550 acres of the property, which was donated by the Johnson family. (The property includes the site of Lyndon Johnson's birthplace, where the reconstructed birthplace is situated today.) Because the LBJ Ranch house is a private residence of Lyndon Johnson's wife, Lady Bird Johnson (who has a life tenancy), the house is not open to the public, although the National Park Service tour buses pass by the house and allow visitors to view the exterior of the home from a distance. The house, which is mostly white on the outside, was originally built with eighteen-inch thick limestone as a precaution against attacks by members of local tribes. The house currently contains eight bedrooms and nine bathrooms, a great expansion from its original 1894 appearance. An office wing was added by the Johnsons for the president's use, outside of which is a porch with a series of rockers on which the president and a legion of distinguished guests would sit and confer on many vital matters. The wing on the opposite side of the house contains a dressing room and the president's bedroom; outside the bedroom door is a swimming pool. Concrete stepping stones to the house bear the signatures and greetings of some famous visitors to the LBJ Ranch.

Currently, the National Park Service manages the LBJ Ranch as a working ranch on which registered Hereford cattle, descendants of the original LBJ herd, are kept looking as they did when President Johnson was alive. The ranch also contains numerous specimens of trees and cacti, in accordance with the president's wishes to allow wildlife to live on unimproved land within the ranch.

Visitors also notice many reminders of the Johnson presidency in a tour of the ranch. A secret service checkpoint is located at the gate of the ranch, and a large hangar, used for press conferences, is located near a landing strip upon which a small plane would land bringing the president or his guests to the ranch. Near the hangar is the president's car collection, including a white convertible he used to take guests on tours of the ranch.

After 1951, Lyndon Johnson's political rise continued, largely due to his unswerving loyalty to the Democratic party during the 1952 presidential campaign, when Governor Adlai Stevenson was the underdog Democratic candidate opposing Republican General Dwight D. Eisenhower. In January 1953 Senator Lyndon Johnson was elected senate minority leader (the Democrats were a minority in the Senate for the first two years of the Eisenhower administration), becoming the youngest man ever to be elected to senate leader of either party at the age of forty-four. As minority leader, and even as majority leader beginning in 1955 when the Democrats regained control of the Senate, the hallmark of Lyndon Johnson's role was that of cooperation and, where possible, compromise with the Republican Eisenhower administration. He proved to be a master of the art of compromise and of the legislative process, and these skills were key to the passage of important civil rights bills in 1957 and 1960.

1960 was the year that a presidential election was held to determine who would succeed Dwight D. Eisenhower, who was constitutionally ineligible to run for a third term. Senate Majority Leader Lyndon Johnson hoped to be the Democratic candidate for president that year, but he did not compete in the presidential primaries, and did not announce his candidacy until shortly before the Democratic National Convention met in Los Angeles. Senator John F. Kennedy, who had actively competed in and won key primaries and caucuses, had more than enough support to capture the Democratic nomination on the first ballot. But Senator Johnson did have significant delegate support (he received 409 votes to Senator John F. Kennedy's 806 votes on the first ballot at the Democratic Convention); he was obviously a leading figure in the Democratic party, and he came from Texas, a state which Senator Kennedy, a shrewd political analyst, knew he had to carry in order to be elected in November.

Phil Graham, then publisher of the Washington *Post* and a close friend of Senator Kennedy, is credited with being the first to suggest to Kennedy that he ask Johnson to be his running mate. Notwithstanding the bitter opposition of his brother Robert to the choice, Senator Kennedy did offer the vice presidential nomination to Johnson, and he accepted. The Kennedy-Johnson ticket went on to victory in November, and when President Kennedy was assassinated on November 22, 1963, Lyndon Johnson succeeded his slain predecessor as president.

At first, President Johnson tried to provide continuity in leadership by retaining members of the Kennedy cabinet and by carrying on the Kennedy administration's policies. But after Johnson won a term as president in his own right by running on a ticket with Minnesota Senator Hubert H. Humphrey for vice president, which overwhelmed the Republican ticket of Arizona Senator Barry Goldwater and New York Representative William Miller, he felt that he had a mandate to carry out his own policies. These policies amounted to bold initiatives on the domestic front and political disaster in foreign policy. The domestic initiatives were labeled the "Great Society" programs, including the Office of Economic Opportunity, the Mobilization for Youth, and the Model Cities Program. These programs and others were intended to be the weapons in a "War on Poverty," intended to alleviate the plight of poor people in America by providing housing, employment and services. The political benefits of that "War" were counterbalanced by the Vietnam Conflict. After the 1964 election, the Johnson administration escalated ground and air support for the American-supported regime in South Vietnam in an effort to achieve a military victory over the Communist-dominated North Vietnamese. Despite these efforts, military victory was not achieved, and as graphic film of the conflict was broadcast on nationally televised news, public opposition to President Johnson's Vietnam policy increased, and the political benefits of Johnson's domestic initiatives were virtually eradicated as Vietnam became a national obsession. The degree of opposition became palpable in early 1968, when Democratic Senator Eugene McCarthy of Minnesota, running for the 1968 Democratic presidential nomination as an opponent of the Johnson Vietnam policy, came surprisingly close to defeating Johnson in the New Hampshire primary. Later, another opponent of President Johnson's Vietnam policy, Senator Robert F. Kennedy of New York (brother of President Kennedy) entered the race. In a memorable address to a national television audience on March 31, 1968, President Johnson announced a partial bombing halt in North Vietnam, but then, in the last few minutes of his speech, made the surprise announcement that he would not be a candidate for renomination or re-election as president in 1968. President Johnson's protege, Vice President Humphrey, became the Democratic candidate that year, and the Johnson administration pinned its hopes for an end to American involvement in Vietnam on a combination of a continuing military effort and peace negotiations with the North Vietnamese regime in Paris. The Paris peace talks yielded no solid progress that year, and on October 31, 1968, President Johnson announced a bombing halt in Vietnam in the apparent hope that the change in strategy would benefit Vice President Humphrey in the closing days of the 1968 presidential campaign. It did not. Rather, former vice president Nixon was elected president in a close contest. However, the successful manned space flight of the Apollo VIII mission to the moon, which took place during Christmas week in 1968, provided a more upbeat close to the Johnson administration by demonstrating the success of the American space program, which President Johnson enthusiastically supported.

After Johnson left office in January 1969, he retired to a quiet life on the LBJ Ranch and wrote his autobiography, *The Vantage Point: Perspectives on the Presidency, 1963-1969,* which was published in 1971. While at the LBJ Ranch on January 22, 1973, President Lyndon Johnson died of a heart attack at the age of sixty-four. He is buried in a family cemetery not far from the LBJ Ranch house, and today visitors may visit his modest grave site as part of the bus tour of the LBJ Ranch (the Stonewall Unit of the Lyndon B. Johnson National Historical Park).

Together, the reconstructed birthplace, Johnson City boyhood home, LBJ Ranch and facilities of the Lyndon B. Johnson State and National Historical Parks tell the story of a boy who came from humble origins to become a prosperous world leader, only to return time and again to the land of his origin and, finally, to be laid to rest by the banks of the Pedernales. The influence of strong parents, the beauty and lure of his native soil, and the persistence and tenacity of the people of the Texas Hill Country, all combined to mold the character of a man who achieved the highest office in our land. There is no better way to learn his story than to visit the places where it began and ended.

RICHARD MILHOUS NIXON

The Richard Nixon Library & Birthplace
18001 Yorba Linda Boulevard
Yorba Linda, CA 92686
(714) 993-3393

Administered by The Richard Nixon Library & Birthplace.

Directions: From Los Angeles, go south on I-5 to Highway 91. Exit east on Highway 91 and proceed to Highway 57. Exit north on Highway 57 and proceed to Yorba Linda Boulevard. Exit east on Yorba Linda Boulevard to the site.

Open: Daily (except Thanksgiving and Christmas Day).

Admission: Fee charged.

Features: Restored birthplace home with audio presentation by President Nixon, library, museum, grave site, gardens, movie theater showing a 28-minute film entitled "Never Give Up: Richard Nixon in the Arena," 75-seat amphitheater, reflecting pool, First Lady's Garden, gift shop/bookstore. Handicapped accessible.

Special Events: President Nixon's birthday is celebrated at the site each January 9th. During December, a special White House Christmas Program is presented to the public.

Richard Milhous Nixon was, to quote his memoirs, "born in a house that [his] father built." The house, a small one and one-half story, five-room frame house, was constructed by Richard Nixon's father, Frank Nixon, who had a lemon and orange grove on the property. He purchased the twelve-acre property in Yorba Linda in 1911, and built the house in 1912 using materials which cost $800.00. Richard Nixon was born in his parents' bedroom on the first floor to the left of the front entrance to that house.

Frank Nixon and his wife, Hannah, to whom Richard Nixon referred as "a saint," were Quakers. They instilled a respect for peace and the value of an education in their five sons, and Richard Nixon took these lessons seriously. He studied hard and learned to play six instruments: the piano, violin, organ, clarinet, saxophone and accordion.

In 1922, the Nixon family left Yorba Linda to run a combination gasoline station and grocery store on East Whittier Boulevard between Whittier and LaHabra. Their residence was located above the station/store. Later, they moved to a single family home at 15844 East Whittier Boulevard, and ran The Nixon Market, which was located next door. The boys worked at the store when they were not in school. In 1924, Richard Nixon went to Lindsay, California to live with his aunt and to study piano and violin. He also spent two summers in Prescott, Arizona, while Hannah Nixon attended Richard Nixon's older brother, Harold Nixon, who had tuberculosis and later died of the disease at the age of twenty-two. Richard Nixon also had three younger brothers: F. Donald Nixon, who died several years ago; Arthur Nixon, who died of tuberculosis and encephalitis at the age of seven and a half; and Edward Nixon.

Richard Nixon distinguished himself as a high school student, and later as a student at Whittier College, which he attended from 1930 to 1934. He also acted in plays, played the organ at the Quaker meeting house, and played the piano at parties. He was an excellent debater, winning prizes for public speaking. At Whittier College, he was elected president of the student body, and graduated second in his class. From there, he went on to Duke University Law School in Durham, North Carolina. While there he first lived in a room he rented for $5.00 a month, and later shared a house in Duke Forest, which has been described as a "shack" and was called Whippoorwill Manor, with three law school classmates. He graduated third in his law school class in 1937.

Richard Nixon returned to California, passed the bar examination and joined a Whittier law firm. He became involved with an amateur theater group, through which he met a red-haired high school typing teacher named Thelma Catherine ("Pat") Ryan. After a two-year courtship, the couple married on June 21, 1940, and had their reception at Frank Nixon's house at 6799 Worsham Drive in Whittier. In 1941, the Nixons took up residence in an apartment at 12336 East Beverly Boulevard. They did not remain there long, however, for after the Japanese attack on Pearl Harbor on December 7, 1941, Mr. Nixon decided to participate in the war effort. He took a job as a lawyer at the Office of Price Administration for $61.00 a week, living in an apartment in Virginia, but later decided that he should be more directly involved in the fighting. He applied for and received a commission as a lieutenant (j.g.) in the Navy in September 1942. Naval assignments took the Nixons to Ottumwa, Iowa; San Francisco; Washington; Philadelphia; New York and Baltimore. In 1943, Mrs. Nixon remained in San Francisco while her husband went to the South Pacific for fifteen months. He returned for shore duty and, by the end of the war, had advanced to the rank of lieutenant commander.

In November 1945, a banker friend told Lt. Commander Nixon that a Republican committee back home in California was looking for a candidate to oppose veteran Congressman Jerry Voorhis. After his discharge from the Navy, Richard Nixon answered the committee's advertisement and became the Republican candidate. He took on Representative Voorhis in a series of debates in which he attacked his opponent as an ultra-liberal New Dealer. Thus, Mr. Nixon transformed himself from a political unknown into a force to be reckoned with. In the end, Richard Nixon won the election in what proved to be a landslide year for Republicans, 1946, in which the Republican-controlled Eightieth Congress (later called the "Do Nothing Congress" by President Truman in his campaign speeches) was elected. During the 1946 campaign, it is believed that the Nixons lived in an apartment at 13217 East Walnut Street in Whittier. Once elected, Representative Nixon bought a house at 14033 Honeysuckle Lane in South Whittier, and stayed in a hotel in Washington until they found more permanent lodging there. While in Congress, Representative Nixon worked for passage of the Taft-Hartley labor bill (over President Truman's veto), debating the measure in McKeesport, Pennsylvania with another freshman congressman, John F. Kennedy.

Representative Nixon traveled to Europe as a member of the Herter Committee, whose mission was to determine the need for the Marshall Plan to provide economic aid to war-torn Europe. As did other members of the committee, Nixon returned home convinced that foreign aid was needed to prevent the spread of communism. From that time onward, Richard Nixon became a fervent advocate of foreign aid, a view which did not bring him favor in the eyes of some conservative members of his own party. Most significantly, Nixon gained national notoriety by his dogged pursuit of the case against Alger Hiss, a former State Department official who Nixon was certain was a Communist spy. Hiss was convicted of perjury by a federal jury in 1950, vindicating Nixon's efforts.

Having earned a national reputation as a Communist hunter, Representative Nixon entered the race for United States senator from California, and overwhelmingly defeated his Democratic opponent, Rep. Helen Gahagan Douglas. At the age of thirty-seven, Richard Nixon became the youngest Republican U.S. senator. As a senator of the minority party with no seniority, his senatorial assignments were not significant, but he continued to grow in political popularity, and was a speaker at Republican gatherings throughout the country in 1951. He also went on a trip to Europe, where he met with General Dwight David Eisenhower. Senator Nixon agreed to join the Eisenhower campaign for president.

General Eisenhower went on to receive the Republican nomination for president at the Republican National Convention in Chicago in 1952. He asked Senator Nixon to be his running mate. The popular general and Communist-hunting senator proved to be a strong ticket in November. However, Senator Nixon's candidacy ran into trouble in September 1952, when the New York *Post* ran a story stating that he had an $18,000.00 "secret fund" collected by a "millionaires' club," which he used for personal expenses. After the story was released, General Eisenhower received numerous demands to drop Nixon from the ticket. Five days after the story ran, Senator Nixon appeared on nationwide television with his wife. He told sixty million viewers that the fund was used solely for the political campaign, and not for personal expenses, and he described his assets. At the end of his speech, he told a story about a man from Texas who sent a small dog to the Nixon children (Tricia and Julie) that they named Checkers, and that he would not take that gift away from them just because he was a candidate and a public office holder. He also said that he did not believe he should quit "because I am not a quitter." The response to the speech was overwhelmingly in favor of retaining Senator Nixon on the ticket. In November, the Eisenhower-Nixon ticket won handily.

As vice president, Nixon was given more responsibility than any previous holder of that office. He presided over 19 cabinet meetings and 26 National Security Council meetings during his eight years as vice president. And he made numerous goodwill trips abroad. On one such trip to Venezuela in 1958, angry Communist-led mobs jeered and spat at the vice president, and even tried to overturn his car and kill him. He remained cool under fire despite those violent incidents, and earned a national reputation for courage. Politically, the Eisenhower-Nixon ticket was even more successful in 1956 than it had been in 1952, winning the election over Democrat Adlai E. Stevenson of Illinois in both of those years. In 1957, the first year of Mr. Nixon's second term as vice president, the Nixons moved to a lovely field-stone house at 4308 Forest Lane, N.W. in the Wesley Heights section of Washington.

In early 1960, Vice President Nixon was the favorite to become the Republican presidential candidate; he had the backing of President Eisenhower, who, as the first president subject to the constitutional amendment limiting the number of years that an incumbent president can hold office, could not seek another full term. Vice President Nixon's principal Republican rival was Governor Nelson Rockefeller of New York, who had demonstrated political prowess by winning office in 1958, a landslide year for Democrats nationally. Vice President Nixon traveled to New York to meet with Rockefeller and to address his demands for a more liberal

GOP platform. After they agreed on the wording of the platform, Vice President Nixon's path to the nomination was clear. Presidential candidate Nixon chose UN Ambassador Henry Cabot Lodge of Massachusetts (the home state of his Democratic opponent, Senator John F. Kennedy) as his running mate.

The 1960 presidential campaign is most memorable for its series of unprecedented live television debates, to which Vice President Nixon reluctantly agreed. The conventional wisdom is that while Vice President Nixon scored points on articulating the substantive issues of the campaign, Senator Kennedy's poise, appearance, and demeanor in front of the camera made a favorable impression on the voters. In the end, Senator Kennedy won by a narrow margin in the popular vote. Some of Vice President Nixon's supporters, who became aware of vote fraud allegations concerning the key states of Illinois and Texas, urged their candidate to contest the election, but Nixon graciously declined and conceded the election.

Out of office for the first time in fourteen years, Richard Nixon returned home to California. He was the first member of the family to arrive in the Los Angeles area in February 1961. He lived in an apartment at the Gaylord Apartments on Wilshire Boulevard for a few months, while Mrs. Nixon remained in Washington with their daughters to allow them to finish the school year in June 1961. The rest of the family then joined Mr. Nixon in the Los Angeles area where they leased a house in Brentwood while using $48,000.00 in equity accumulated during their Washington years to build a new home, completed in the spring of 1962, at 410 Martin Lane in Beverly Hills. Mr. Nixon joined the Los Angeles law firm of Adams, Duque & Hazeltine and worked on his book, *Six Crises*, which was published in 1962. However, Mr. Nixon's political advisers and supporters were eager to have him re-enter the political arena. Some of his backers urged him to run for governor of California in 1962 against incumbent Democratic Governor Edmund G. ("Pat") Brown. Despite Mr. Nixon's personal view that this was the wrong office for him, he was encouraged by favorable polls and agreed to make the race. The effort was marred by three factors: a Republican primary contest forced by a Republican state assemblyman who was perceived as more conservative than Mr. Nixon, and who took 37% of the primary vote; the October 1962 Cuban Missile Crisis, which distracted voter attention from the gubernatorial campaign; and the ability of Mr. Nixon's Democratic opponent, Gov. Pat Brown, to articulate his detailed knowledge of the workings of state government. Although he knew as early as October that the missile crisis meant that the race was lost, Mr. Nixon became angry on the morning after the election, telling the press that "you won't have Nixon to kick around anymore, because, gentlemen, this is my last press conference." That morning, even Richard Nixon himself thought that his political career was over.

Thus began what Mr. Nixon himself called his "wilderness years." He decided that he and his family would move to New York City, and they did so in 1963, living in a ten-room cooperative apartment on Fifth Avenue. He became a partner in the law firm of Nixon, Mudge, Rose, Guthrie, Alexander & Mitchell. He did not seek the Republican presidential nomination in 1964, thus leaving the Republican contest a battle between the principal spokesman for the conservative wing of the party, Senator Barry Goldwater of Arizona, and the principal spokesman for its liberal wing, Governor Rockefeller. After Goldwater was nominated, Mr. Nixon hit the campaign trail on behalf of the Republican ticket, although it soon became evident that the campaign against President Lyndon Johnson would fail. After Senator Goldwater's crushing defeat, the need to heal and rebuild the GOP was clear, and Mr. Nixon, whose political philosophy was generally perceived to be more moderate than that of either Goldwater or Rockefeller, seemed to be the ideal person to unite and to revive the party. He did so by campaigning actively for local Republican candidates in 1965 and 1966, and built a network of support and goodwill for himself in the process. By 1967, Mr. Nixon was once again a leading contender for the presidency, and polls indicated that he was more popular than President Johnson.

1968 proved to be a year of turmoil and division, and the dominant political issues were Vietnam and civil rights. These issues shattered the Democratic Party in 1968. The first clear sign of the depth of the political schism was the 1968 New Hampshire presidential primary, where Senator Eugene McCarthy, running as an advocate of peace through withdrawal from Vietnam, made a surprisingly strong showing against incumbent President Johnson. Shortly thereafter, Senator Robert F. Kennedy of New York (brother of President Kennedy), who also opposed the Johnson administration's Vietnam policies, entered the race. On March 31, President Johnson made a surprise announcement at the end of a televised speech on Vietnam that he would not be a candidate in 1968, and Vice President Hubert Humphrey later became the candidate backed by President Johnson and his partisans. Then came the assassination of the noted civil rights leader, Rev. Dr. Martin Luther King, Jr., in April, which fueled the atmosphere of social and political tension. On June 5th, Senator Kennedy was assassinated in Los Angeles on the night he won the California primary. Later, while the Democratic convention was meeting in Chicago, violent clashes between demonstrators and police were televised around the world, and inside the convention hall, tensions ran high. Despite the similarity of their views, the Kennedy forces (nominally backing Senator George McGovern of South Dakota in place of the slain Senator Kennedy) and the McCarthy delegation did not unite, and Vice President Humphrey was nominated in an atmosphere that unquestionably damaged his campaign from the start. Senator Edmund S. Muskie of Maine was chosen as his running mate.

Mr. Nixon's path to the 1968 Republican nomination, although arduous, appeared smooth by comparison. He turned back primary challenges from Governor George Rom-

ney of Michigan and Governor Rockefeller. At the Republican convention in Miami Beach, Mr. Nixon was the clear favorite, but Rockefeller and a newcomer to the national political scene, Governor Ronald Reagan of California (who was identified with the conservative wing of the GOP) both had their names placed in nomination. Mr. Nixon won the nomination on the first ballot and named Governor Spiro T. Agnew of Maryland as his running mate.

The fall campaign was further complicated by the entry of Alabama Governor George C. Wallace into the race as a third party candidate. Mr. Nixon, comfortably ahead in the polls, campaigned in a relatively relaxed manner at first. But then in the final weeks of the campaign, Vice President Humphrey's efforts to disassociate himself from the Johnson Vietnam policies seemed to be attracting more voters to his camp. On election night, the early returns showed Mr. Humphrey in the lead, but later it became clear that Mr. Nixon was on his way to a decisive electoral college victory. Ironically, in the popular vote, Nixon led Humphrey by only seven-tenths of a percentage point. Despite this narrow margin, Richard Nixon was elected the thirty-seventh president of the United States, thus achieving an unprecedented political comeback.

As president, Nixon wrestled with the problem of American involvement in Vietnam, sending envoys to peace talks in Paris, gradually withdrawing troops while stepping up air attacks, and attempting to turn over prosecution of the war to the South Vietnamese in a program he called "Vietnamization." He struggled with a sagging economy by instituting wage and price controls. But perhaps his most memorable achievements were in the area of diplomacy. He will always be remembered as the president who "opened the door" for formal diplomatic relations with China, symbolized by his trip to China in February 1972. Encouraged by progress in the Strategic Arms Limitation Talks (SALT), he also forged a new relationship with the Soviet Union by making the first visit by an American president to the Soviet capital in Moscow in May 1972. President Nixon's summit meeting with Soviet leader Leonid I. Brezhnev did much to advance the cause of peace and the spirit of detente between the two superpowers. During his visit, President Nixon delivered a televised address directly to the Soviet people. Mr. Brezhnev flew to the United States for further summit meetings with the president in June 1973, and these meetings succeeded in erasing much of the antagonism of the Cold War era. One year later, President Nixon paid a second visit to Moscow, but this summit meeting with Mr. Brezhnev resulted in little substantive progress. However, both leaders stated that the meeting was a fine expression of the spirit of friendship between the two nations.

At the White House, the Nixons proudly hosted the wedding of their daughter Tricia to Edward Cox in June 1971. While Mr. Nixon was president, the practice began of flying the flag over the White House both day and night (under illumination). He also owned two homes in Key Biscayne, Florida, which he used as a "Winter White House" and as base of operations during the 1972 Republican convention in Miami Beach. He also used Camp David, Maryland as a retreat for both working and relaxation.

The Nixons established a "Western White House" at San Clemente, California. This home, called "La Casa Pacifica" ("The House of Peace"), was built in 1925 and was the estate of Henry Cotton before the Nixons acquired it. It is a twelve-room Spanish-style mansion which sits on five acres of property surrounded by an eight foot wall. The property is located on a bluff and affords a magnificent view of the Pacific Ocean. The Nixons returned to San Clemente when the president left office and lived there until 1980, when they sold the property to a partnership of three businessman. Today, the house is privately owned by Mr. Gavin Hebert.

1972 was a turning point for the Nixon administration. Early that year, the president made his memorable trips to China and the Soviet Union. 1972 was also a presidential election year, and the Democratic Party, which had altered the guidelines of its nomination process in an attempt to select convention delegates who were more representative of its rank-and-file members, nominated Senator George S. McGovern of South Dakota, who was the most liberal of a field of candidates which included both former Vice President Humphrey and Senator Muskie (the 1968 Democratic ticket). Senator McGovern's views were perceived as too liberal for many of the moderate and conservative members of his own party to accept, and, in the fall campaign, the trend of support for President Nixon among both Democrats and independents was evident. In November, the voters returned President Nixon to office by the biggest electoral college landslide in American history up to that time; the Nixon-Agnew ticket carried every state except Massachusetts and the District of Columbia. This was the first election in which 18 to 20 year-old voters, under a constitutional amendment supported by President Nixon, had the right to participate. The Nixon re-election chant, "Four More Years," appeared to have been confirmed.

But it was not to be. Even before the nominating convention, the chain of events culminating in President Nixon's resignation had begun. In June 1972, seven men were arrested for breaking into Democratic national headquarters at the Watergate complex in Washington. It has been speculated that their aim was to obtain information embarrassing to the Democrats in order to ensure Democratic defeat in 1972. However, the reason for the break-in is still debated by historians. Later press accounts alleged that the break-in was authorized by leaders of the Nixon re-election organization, the Committee to Re-Elect the President. As time went on, more and more stories about the Watergate scandal appeared, which accused both campaign and administration officials of a series of illegal activities and a subsequent effort to "cover up" those activities. By mid-1973, President Nixon's second term was well under way, but the Watergate scandal had become a national obsession. Millions of Americans watched on television as the Senate Select Committee on Campaign Activities, chaired by Senator

Sam Ervin of North Carolina, conducted hearings on the Watergate scandal. As the hearings proceeded, Senator Howard Baker of Tennessee, the ranking Republican on the committee, articulated the question on everyone's mind, "What did the president know, and when did he know it?" The key revelation of these hearings was made by Alexander Butterfield, who disclosed that the president had installed a taping system in the Oval Office which had recorded all Oval Office conversations for posterity. From that time onward, the president was pressed to release the tapes, but Nixon, stating that his conversations should remain subject to "executive privilege" because of the potential that revelations of such conversations might jeopardize the separation of powers, refused to turn over some of the tapes sought by the committee. Later, the special prosecutor appointed by Nixon to investigate the Watergate allegations also unsuccessfully sought certain tapes. Because Nixon refused to produce the tapes, the special prosecutor brought legal action against him, seeking a court order compelling him to produce the tapes.

The president's troubles were compounded when Vice President Spiro Agnew resigned his office after pleading no contest to a bribery charge stemming from his activities as governor of Maryland. Acting under the powers conferred upon him by a recent constitutional amendment, President Nixon nominated House Minority Leader Gerald R. Ford of Michigan as his new vice president. The nomination was confirmed by the Senate, and Vice President Ford, once in office, became an effective advocate for the administration and for President Nixon in particular.

But the charges would not go away. In the summer of 1974, the House Judiciary Committee, chaired by Representative Peter Rodino of New Jersey, voted to impeach President Nixon for obstruction of justice and on other grounds. Impeachment is a trial of a holder of a high government office before the United States Senate. If two-thirds of the Senate votes to convict, the official is removed from office. President Nixon knew that unless he could maintain the support of at least one-third of the Senate, he could not remain in office. The pressure mounted even further when the Supreme Court, ruling on an appeal of the special prosecutor's legal action, held that President Nixon had to produce the tapes. When it became evident that he did not have the support he needed, he reluctantly decided to resign his office. On the evening of August 8, 1974, he announced his decision on national television. On the following day, he made an emotional farewell speech to his White House staff, and, at 12:00 p.m. eastern time, he and his family boarded a helicopter on the White House lawn and began the journey to San Clemente. That same day, Vice President Ford was sworn in as president. On Sunday, September 8, 1974, President Ford pardoned former President Nixon for all acts in which he may have engaged related to the Watergate matter.

Characteristically, President Nixon spent his post-presidential years quietly at first, but later gradually re-emerged into the public arena, writing eight books and many articles and making television appearances. In 1980, he sold La Casa Pacifica and returned to New York City, where he purchased a ten-room, four story townhouse at 142 E. 65th Street for $750,000.00. One year later, he sold the townhouse and purchased, for about $1 million, a home in Upper Saddle River, New Jersey. Later, the Nixons moved to a townhouse in the nearby community of Park Ridge. There they spent their remaining days, and in 1994, Mr. Nixon passed away in a New York hospital within months of the death of his beloved wife. The Nixons are buried beside each other at a gravesite located on the grounds of his presidential library.

Today, Richard Nixon's birthplace, a National Historic Landmark, has been restored, and his presidential library, entirely funded by private donations, is also located on the site. The home is surrounded by lovely flowers, and a bench is situated directly in front of the house for resting visitors. The front door leads into the living room, a cozy room with window seats, a fireplace, and simple wooden furnishings. (While living here, Frank Nixon earned extra money by building fireplaces for neighboring houses.) Almost all of the furnishings on display in the house are original; they were placed in storage or dispersed among family members for many years. The Crown piano on which Richard Nixon learned to play is also in this room, along with his violin and clarinet. In the other corner of the room are bookshelves which contain books Richard Nixon read as a child, including *Pilgrim's Progress* and the autobiography of Benjamin Franklin. Among the pictures on the wall is a framed collage of photographs of Richard Nixon and his four brothers as young boys. On the shelves in the rear of the room are small blue "everyday" dishes used by the Nixon family.

Adjoining the living room is the bedroom where Richard Nixon was born. Unlike most of the home's other furnishings, Mr. Nixon's birth bed was not taken out of storage, but was salvaged from a garden, where it was used to hold up snow pea plants. On the bed is a wool blanket marked "Ohio 1837," a family heirloom presented to Frank and Hannah Nixon on their wedding day in 1908. On the wall in this room is a framed fan which was carried by Hannah Nixon on her graduation day. It is said that the photograph and poem dedicated to "Mother," both of which are hanging above the bed, were framed by Richard Nixon.

Also adjoining the living room is Hannah Nixon's sewing room, behind which is a narrow stairwell leading to the small bedroom which the Nixon brothers shared as children. (The stairs and upper floor of the house are not open to the public.) In the rear of the house is the kitchen, which contains an antique coal and oil stove and an ice box, neither of which is original to the house. However, a high chair used by the Nixon children is also here.

From the modest, yet dignified origins suggested by this house, Richard Nixon rose to become one of the most influential figures of modern American history.

GERALD RUDOLPH FORD

Gerald R. Ford Birthsite Park
32nd and Woolworth Streets
Omaha, Nebraska 68105
(402) 444-5955

Administered by the Omaha Department of Parks & Recreation.

Directions: From I-80, take exit for I-480 north. Use exit 1A (Martha Street). At end of off ramp, turn left onto Ed Creighton Avenue. Proceed past Hanscom Park on the right, and turn right at 32nd Avenue. The street dead ends at the site, which is across Woolworth Street.

Open: Daily.

Admission: Free.

Features: Model of home in which President Ford was born, gardens, roster of names and home states of presidents.

Special Events: None.

Gerald R. Ford, 38th president of the United States, was born Leslie L. King, Jr. on July 14, 1913 in a home at 3202 Woolworth Avenue in Omaha, Nebraska. He was the son of Dorothy Gardner King and Leslie King, the manager of his father's wool trading company. The house was a Queen Anne mansion built in 1893 and owned by Mr. King's father, Charles H. King, who was away on an extended trip to the west at the time of Leslie King, Jr.'s birth. The birth, which was on a 101-degree day, was not easy for Mrs. King, who struggled with weakness, ill health and a troubled marriage. On July 30, 1913, Mrs. King left Omaha with her newborn child to live with her aunt in Oak Park, just outside Chicago, Illinois. The birthplace mansion was sold in 1916, and, in 1971, was destroyed by fire.

The Kings were divorced in January 1914. Sometime that year, Mrs. King and her young son moved to 457 Lafayette Street, SE in Grand Rapids, Michigan. Today, that home is privately owned. Mrs. King and her son then moved to 1960 Terrace Avenue, SE (today, the street name is Prospect), a one and a half-story frame house with a full size front porch which is privately owned today. In 1916, the future president's mother met a paint salesman named Gerald Rudolph Ford, whom she soon married. Mr. Ford formally adopted young Leslie, who was renamed Gerald R. Ford, Jr. Beginning in 1917, the Fords rented a two-family house at 716 Madison Avenue, SE. Today, the home no longer stands; a recreation center is now on the site, which is owned by the Kent County government.

About 1921 or 1922, the Fords moved to 620 Rosewood Avenue, SE, in East Grand Rapids, a two-story frame house which is privately owned today. Mr. Ford's paint selling business grew and was quite successful in the long run, but in 1923, business reverses resulted in foreclosure on the house, and the family moved to 649 Union Avenue, SE, in Grand Rapids. Young Gerald Ford, or "Junie," grew from childhood into adolescence in this house, a three-story residence with a large front porch and a bay window. He participated actively in competitive sports and outdoor recreation, and became a Boy Scout, earning enough merit badges to attain the status of eagle scout. He also used the two-car garage in the rear of the property to organize a clandestine social club and to play penny-ante poker. By the time young Gerald was fourteen, he had three half-brothers: Thomas, Richard and James Ford. Because of the belief in those times that it would be harmful to an adopted child to learn of his adoption, the Fords never told young Gerald about his adoption or his natural father. So it came as a complete surprise to sixteen-year-old Gerald Ford when, one day, a stranger approached him at the sandwich shop across from the high school, where young Gerald was working to earn extra money, and said, "Leslie, I'm your father." He later confronted his mother and adoptive father, who told him the whole story. While this incident was a shock, Gerald Ford understood his parents' motive for not having told him of his adoption and went on with his life. He became a star football player in high school, and was a conscientious student.

In 1929 or 1930, the Fords left their home on Union Avenue. The house was later donated by the Veterans Administration, which had acquired it, to the Public Museum of Grand Rapids, an agency of the city. In 1990, it was sold to private citizens. The Fords' new home was on 2163 Lake Drive in East Grand Rapids, and the Ford family remained there until 1933. Gerald Ford, Jr., who enrolled at the University of Michigan in Ann Arbor on an athletic scholarship in 1931, visited his parents here when not in school, and worked at his father's paint and varnish business during the summers. In 1962, this home was demolished.

At the University of Michigan, Gerald Ford, Jr. continued to demonstrate his skill at football. He joined the Delta Kappa Epsilon fraternity there, and lived in their fraternity house. In 1934, his parents moved again, this time to 1011 Santa Cruz Drive, SE, a two-story colonial-style stone house with a side screened-in porch. This was Gerald Ford, Jr.'s home in Michigan until his marriage in 1948.

After Gerald Ford graduated in 1935, he received an offer to become an assistant football line coach and boxing coach at Yale University in New Haven. He spent the summer of 1936 working at Yellowstone National Park and was based at Canyon Station, which was later demolished. In 1938, he applied for admission to Yale Law School, convincing the faculty to give him the opportunity to study there. After successfully completing two law courses, he took on a full-time schedule of courses the following semester, and, while continuing to work as a coach, studied nights and weekends. His determination paid off, and he graduated in 1941 in the upper third of his class.

After graduation, Gerald Ford returned to Grand Rapids, was admitted to the Michigan bar, and set up a law practice with his friend Philip Buchen, who later became his counselor at the White House. But in December, the Japanese attacked Pearl Harbor, and the twenty-eight year old lawyer volunteered for service in the U.S. Navy, which gave him a commission as an ensign. He began his service in 1942 as a physical education instructor in the naval air cadet training program at Chapel Hill, North Carolina. After a year, he applied for sea duty and was first assigned to gunnery training at Norfolk, Virginia, and was then assigned to a new light aircraft carrier, the U.S.S. *Monterey*, which was being readied at Camden, New Jersey. The *Monterey* joined the Pacific fleet, enduring a typhoon in December 1944 in which Gerald Ford narrowly escaped death. He participated in ten battles and rose to the rank of lieutenant commander.

Gerald Ford returned to Grand Rapids on terminal leave in December 1945 and resumed his law practice. His interest broadened into politics, spurred by his adoptive father, Gerald Ford, Sr., who was elected Kent County Republican Chairman. Gerald Ford's first political effort was to form a veterans' committee to push for low-cost housing for returning GIs. Building upon this experience and the network of support he acquired, he set his sights on the Congressional seat held by Representative Bartel J. Jonkman since 1940. To win the seat, Ford had to beat Jonkman, a Repub-

lican, in a primary. With his college fraternity brother Jack Stiles as his campaign manager, candidate Ford charmed the voters with his refreshing candor. He even helped farmers with their chores while asking them for their support. His primary opponent counted on the regular Republican organization to carry the campaign for him and refused to debate Gerald Ford. Mr. Ford triumphed in the primary, taking 62.2% of the vote. Virtually assured of election in the heavily Republican district, Gerald Ford went ahead with his plans to marry Elizabeth Bloomer Warren, a former Martha Graham dancer who had divorced her first husband the previous year. Their marriage took place at the Grace Episcopal Church in Grand Rapids. Their first child, Michael, was born in 1950, followed by John ("Jack") in 1952, Steven in 1956, and Susan in 1957.

As expected, candidate Ford easily won the election in November 1948 with 61% of the vote. The Fords had already moved into Mrs. Ford's ground-floor apartment at 330 Washington Street, S.E., a two-story brick house with a columned porch. In Washington, they rented a one-bedroom apartment at the Carlin Apartments, located at 2500 Q Street, NW, in Georgetown. This was their Washington address from November 1948 to June 1951. In 1950, the Fords moved to a new home in Representative Ford's congressional district, 1624 Sherman Street, SE, in East Grand Rapids. That home is a two-story stucco, two-family house, and served as the Fords' official residence. However, the Fords

spent relatively little time there in the twenty-six years that they owned the house because of Gerald Ford's duties in public office. In 1979, the Fords donated that home to the Gerald R. Ford Commemorative Committee.

In June 1951, the Fords moved their Washington-area home to 1521 Mount Eagle Place, a two-bedroom ground floor garden apartment at Park Fairfax, Alexandria, Virginia. In March 1955, they moved to a brick and clapboard house built for them at a cost of $34,000.00 at 514 Crown View Drive in Alexandria. Here, the Ford children grew up, and when Steven and Susan were born, they used the same wicker bassinet, decorated with ruffles and ribbons, that Gerald Ford had used as a child. The Ford family added a swimming pool to the backyard of this property in later years, and Gerald Ford regularly used it for exercise. This was the family home until Gerald Ford became president in August 1974. In January 1977, the Fords sold the house privately. In 1968, they acquired a condominium at a ski resort in Vail, Colorado, which was sold in 1979. Eventually, however, in 1982, the Ford family moved into a newly constructed winter and summer resort home in Beaver Creek, Colorado.

As a congressman, Gerald Ford worked quietly and earnestly, and was very loyal to Republican Party positions. He attained a seat on the House Appropriations Committee, and in 1963, he was appointed to serve on the Warren Commission, which investigated the assassination of President John F. Kennedy. In 1965, Ford was elected house minority leader by the House Republican membership. He opposed key Johnson administration policies, attacking President Johnson on Vietnam in particular, but was loyal to the policies of President Johnson's successor, President Nixon.

In 1973, Vice President Spiro T. Agnew resigned his office after pleading no contest to bribery charges, and President Nixon, the first president with the opportunity to exercise the power conferred upon him by the Twenty-Fifth Amendment to the U.S. Constitution, sought a nominee for the office of vice president. Seeking a candidate with a reputation for honesty and loyalty who could be easily confirmed by the Congress, President Nixon made his choice: Gerald R. Ford. Because of the possibility that the Watergate scandals could result in the impeachment of President Nixon, the congressional investigations and confirmation hearings for vice president designate Ford were quite probing. In the end, Gerald Ford's nomination was easily confirmed by both houses of Congress.

As vice president, Gerald Ford essentially had two political missions: to stem the tide of eroding public confidence in President Nixon and his administration, and to demonstrate that he would be a capable leader in the event that President Nixon should resign or be otherwise removed from office. Vice President Ford criss-crossed the country, speaking to both live and television audiences, and carrying his two messages to anyone who would listen. Even in the face of the unraveling of the Nixon administration, Vice President Ford's popularity in public opinion polls was rising.

On the evening of August 8, 1974, President Nixon announced his resignation, and, on the following day, Vice President Ford was sworn in as the thirty-eighth president of the United States. Declaring that "our long national nightmare is over," President Ford set about the task of restoring public confidence in the presidency, which had been so badly shaken by the Watergate scandals. He retained the Nixon cabinet at first, but gradually replaced each cabinet official except Secretary of State Henry Kissinger and Treasury Secretary William Simon. On August 20th, President Ford became the second president to invoke the Twenty-Fifth Amendment by nominating former New York Governor Nelson Aldrich Rockefeller as his vice president. After many months, Mr. Rockefeller's nomination was confirmed by Congress.

On Sunday, September 8, 1974, President Ford made the surprise announcement that he intended to pardon his predecessor, former President Nixon. The controversy over the pardon raged for a long time afterward, and was an issue in the 1976 campaign. Later, President Ford announced an amnesty for Vietnam draft resisters and deserters, another controversial pronouncement. His domestic and economic policy efforts were hampered by increasingly strained relations with the Democratic-controlled Congress, which passed many measures vetoed by the president. In foreign policy, Ford became the first sitting president to visit Japan, and met in Vladivostok with Soviet Leader Leonid Brezhnev to lay the groundwork for a strategic arms limitation agreement. Later, these two leaders and many others signed the Helsinki Accords, which guaranteed the boundaries of European nations as established after World War II. President Ford also took decisive military action to free the crewmen of the *Mayaguez*, an American freighter that was captured by Cambodian communists in May 1975. Perhaps the saddest chapter of American foreign policy under President Ford was the fall of South Vietnam to the North Vietnamese communists in 1975. (The North Vietnamese broke the truce fashioned under the Nixon administration in 1973 and overran South Vietnam).

By 1975, President Ford, who was ready to retire from public life before he received the call in 1973 asking him to become vice president, had decided that he wanted to keep his job and wanted to run for a full term in 1976. At that time, it was unclear who the Democratic candidate would be, but the public opinion polls suggested that former governor Ronald Reagan of California, who had become the leading spokesman for the conservative wing of the GOP, would be a formidable candidate for the Republican nomination. President Ford decided to face him head on. In the New Hampshire primary, President Ford won narrowly, suggesting that the race for the GOP nomination would be a fight down to the wire. It was a close race, although the president won every primary until North Carolina, which was a turning point for the Reagan campaign. By the time that the Republican national convention met in Kansas City, Missouri, it was still not entirely clear who would be the GOP nominee. In the end, President Ford was nominated, although narrowly, suggesting that this was not the last appearance of Ronald Reagan on the national political scene. With the nomination he fought so hard to secure safely in hand, President Ford sought a running mate who would be both qualified to serve as president and who would be acceptable to the members of the GOP who had supported Mr. Reagan. Using these criteria, President Ford chose Senator Bob Dole of Kansas, a conservative and a party stalwart.

The Democrats, whose nomination battle was just as fierce as the Republicans, nominated former governor Jimmy Carter of Georgia, whose grassroots campaign transformed him from a long shot candidate to the front-runner of the 1976 campaign. Despite his incumbency, the polls showed that President Ford was starting out as the underdog in the fall campaign, and the president was determined to close the gap. He attempted to do so by challenging Governor Carter to a series of nationally televised debates, reminiscent of the 1960 Kennedy-Nixon campaign. In an unprecedented move, the two major vice presidential candidates, Senator Dole and Senator Walter F. Mondale of Minnesota, also held one nationally televised debate. Despite an aggressive campaign, President Ford was unable to overtake Carter by election time, although Carter managed to take only 51% of the popular vote as opposed to 48% for President Ford. On the following morning, President Ford, hoarse from campaign speaking, turned the microphone over to First Lady Betty Ford, who read to the nation President Ford's moving concession to Governor Carter.

After assisting the Carter team in a smooth transition, the former president and his wife, Betty, moved to Palm Springs, California, where they rented a home while building a new one on the grounds of the Thunderbird Country Club in nearby Rancho Mirage. Mr. Ford has remained active in his post-presidential years, serving on the boards of directors of corporations, participating in policy forums, writing books, making speeches and enjoying sports. He resisted the encouragement of friends who wanted him to seek the GOP nomination in 1980, and was the subject of a stir at the 1980 Republican convention in Detroit, when it was suggested that the former president might agree to become Ronald Reagan's running mate in exchange for an understanding that as vice president, Mr. Ford would effectively share power with Mr. Reagan. The speculation ended when Mr. Reagan announced his recommendation that George Bush be nominated for vice president.

Today, visitors may see the site on which Gerald Ford was born, which is now a lovely park. Unfortunately, the house was destroyed by fire in 1971. The Gerald R. Ford Museum in Grand Rapids, Michigan, and the Gerald R. Ford Library, located on the campus of the University of Michigan in Ann Arbor, are also open to the public. At these sites, visitors may learn the story of a man of integrity who answered a call to serve his country and did much to restore the faith of the American people in their own system of government.

JAMES EARL CARTER

Jimmy Carter National Historic Site
P.O. Box 392
Plains, GA 31780
(912) 824-3413

Administered by the National Park Service.

Directions:	The site is located ten miles west of Americus, Georgia on U.S. 280.	
Open:	Daily (except Christmas and New Year's Day)	
Admission:	Free.	
Features:	The Plains depot (now used as the visitor center), Plains High School, Carter	

Boyhood Home (not open to the public) and the Carter Home on Woodlawn Drive (occupied by the Carters and enclosed as a compound; visitors are not allowed to enter, but may see it from a viewing area). Rest rooms at the visitor center, which is handicapped accessible.

Special Events: The site celebrates Plains Country Day on a Saturday in May.

Jimmy Carter, the first president of the United States from his region of the nation since Zachary Taylor, was also the first president born in a hospital. James Earl Carter, Jr., was born in Wise Hospital on October 1, 1924, in Plains, Georgia. His father, James Earl Carter, Sr., who was called "Mister Earl," was a farmer and a store keeper, and his mother, who was affectionately and reverently referred to as "Miss Lillian," was a registered nurse at the local hospital and an unselfish devotee to social causes. Later, the Carters had three other children: Gloria (born in 1926), Ruth (born in 1929) and Billy (born in 1937). For the first few years of his life, Jimmy Carter lived with his family at a rented house on South Bond Street, next door to the home of the Smith family, whose eldest daughter, Rosalynn, later became Mrs. Jimmy Carter. At the age of four, Jimmy Carter moved with his family to a farm located three miles west of Plains on Preston Road near a railroad flag stop called Archery. Many crops were raised on this farm, including cotton, corn, watermelons, Irish potatoes, sweet potatoes and, of course, peanuts. In the farm house, a modest clapboard cottage which had no indoor plumbing or electricity until after he was thirteen, young Jimmy Carter grew up, tending to farm chores and reading in silence at the dining room table, a family custom. Today, this home, along with Jimmy Carter's present home on Woodlawn Drive, the Plains train depot which was the nerve center of the Carter presidential campaign, and the Plains High School comprise the Jimmy Carter National Historic Site.

From the time he was five, young Jimmy Carter sold boiled peanuts on the streets of Plains. With the money he saved, he bought several bales of cotton. He stored and sold the bales much later when cotton prices increased, thus tripling his income.

As a child, Jimmy Carter had many playmates who were the children of black farm workers who lived nearby. When Jimmy Carter was old enough for school (starting in 1930), he, like many other white children of his region in his day, took a bus to an all-white school, while his black friends went on foot to a one-room schoolhouse. Mr. Carter says that it was not until he reached adulthood that he realized the discriminatory nature of this practice and fought to end it. With his parents' encouragement, and that of his teacher, "Miss" Julia Coleman, he read well beyond his grade level. At the age of twelve, he first read one of his favorite books, Tolstoy's *War and Peace*.

Because his family was too poor to finance a four-year college education, Jimmy Carter determined at an early age that he would apply for admission to the U.S. Naval Academy at Annapolis, where tuition was subsidized by the government. He applied for the appointment, and then graduated from Plains High School at the age of sixteen. While awaiting word as to whether he would receive an appointment, he attended Georgia Southwestern College at Americus, Georgia. In 1942, he was notified that he would be appointed to the Naval Academy the following year. For the 1942-43 academic year, he enrolled at the Georgia Insti-

tute of Technology in Atlanta. While a student there, he lived in a Georgia Tech dormitory and took courses in mathematics recommended by the Navy. Then it was off to Annapolis, where he lived in Bancroft Hall. While there, he participated in cross country track, played intramural football and learned how to fly. He graduated after three years and received a commission as an ensign. One month after his graduation, on July 7, 1946, Jimmy Carter married eighteen-year-old Rosalynn Smith, the best friend of his sister Ruth. The Carters had four children: Jack, Chip, Jeff and Amy Carter.

Ensign Carter's first naval assignment was at Norfolk, Virginia, where the Carters lived in an apartment. There Ensign Carter served as a gunnery and electronics instructor for enlisted men assigned to the battleships *Wyoming* and *Mississippi*. He was then assigned to submarine duty. He prepared for this by attending six months of training at the officers' school in New London, Connecticut. Afterward, he was assigned to the U.S.S. *Pomfret*, in the Pacific. He got to the submarine by way of California, and then to Oahu, Hawaii, where he boarded the vessel. He almost lost his life while on this duty when a storm broke out and a wave swept him off the bridge and carried him along the deck. Fortunately, he was able to grab a cannon barrel and save himself.

After two and a half years of service aboard the *Pomfret*, Jimmy Carter was assigned to become the senior officer for the pre-commissioning assembly of an experimental submarine, the U.S.S. *K-l*. He later became one of the officers aboard that vessel. His naval duties took him to San Diego, California and Groton, Connecticut. When the nuclear-powered submarine program began, Jimmy Carter applied for the program, and in 1952 was assigned to become engineering officer aboard the U.S.S. *Sea Wolf* upon its completion. In the interim, he was assigned to take graduate courses in nuclear physics at Union College in Schenectady, New York. He then began his work in the atomic submarine program under the command of Admiral Hyman Rickover, the man who, by Jimmy Carter's own account, had a profound influence on his life by challenging him to do his best. During this period, the future president's base of operations was at the Atomic Energy Commission in Washington, D.C.

In 1953, Jimmy Carter was granted an emergency leave to go home to Plains to be with his father, who was dying of cancer. After spending some time there, he decided that he wanted to end his naval career and come home. He resigned from the Navy, and he and his family moved in with his mother at first, and then moved to a red brick public housing project two blocks from his mother's house on Church Street. Later, the family moved again, this time to the home of Dr. Thad Wise on Old Preston Road in Archery. Jimmy Carter took over the family farm and built a thriving peanut business. He also became active in civic affairs and, beginning in 1955, served on the Sumter County Board of Education.

In 1961, the Carters built a new, architect-designed home on Woodlawn Drive in Plains. That house remains the home of Jimmy and Rosalynn Carter to this day. The home is a

brick ranch-style house with light green trim, full-length windows in some areas, and a lovely stand of trees surround the house. Today, the house is secured as a presidential compound, and visitors are not allowed on the property.

In 1962, Jimmy Carter decided to seek a seat in the Georgia state senate. His opponent was backed by the local political machine. On Democratic primary day, Mr. Carter saw for himself that a ballot box was being stuffed in one of the cluster of cities in the senatorial district. Later, after the votes were counted, the apparent result was that Mr. Carter had lost the race by a narrow margin, and that the votes from the city where the ballot box stuffing had been observed accounted for his opponent's victory margin. Jimmy Carter decided that he would challenge the results, and, after protracted hearings, was declared the Democratic nominee just three days before the general election. After the returns from the general election were counted, Jimmy Carter was declared the winner.

From 1962 to 1967, the years that Jimmy Carter was a state senator, the Georgia Legislature had three month terms. While the legislature met, State Senator Carter stayed at the Henry Grady Hotel, and later at the Piedmont Hotel, both in Atlanta. As a state Senator, Carter was aghast at the influence of lobbyists and special interest groups in state government. He concluded that the only way to fight the corrup-

tion was to attain higher office. He entered the 1966 race for the Democratic nomination for governor of Georgia, and, after a three month campaign, lost to segregationist restaurant owner Lester Maddox, who became governor. For the next four years, Jimmy Carter continued to campaign for governor, making speeches throughout the state. This long and determined effort culminated in Jimmy Carter's election as governor in 1970.

In 1971, the Carters moved into the Governor's Mansion at 391 West Paces Ferry Road, N.W., in Atlanta. The mansion, which sits on eighteen acres of property, is of the Greek Revival style, three stories high and 25,000 square feet in size. The residence was completed in 1967.

As governor, Jimmy Carter did much to ease racial tensions in the state of Georgia and to reform the system of state government. His state budgetary reforms resulted in budget surpluses and the number of black state employees increased by 40 per cent during his term in office.

By 1972, Governor Carter, ineligible to succeed himself as governor under a Georgia state law in effect at the time, was already beginning to lay the groundwork for a presidential campaign by chairing the Democratic Governors' Campaign Committee, which supported gubernatorial candidates throughout the country. In 1974, he chaired the National Democratic Party Campaign Committee, and participated personally in sixty key races. The 1974 election, which occurred on the heels of President Nixon's resignation, was a landslide for the Democrats.

Thus, Jimmy Carter built a national base for his quest for the presidency. Although his efforts had won him some recognition and contacts within the Democratic party structure, he was still virtually unknown to the public outside of Georgia. In late 1975, public opinion polls still indicated that Senator Hubert Humphrey of Minnesota, the 1968 Democratic presidential candidate and former vice president, had the support of a plurality of Democrats for the 1976 nomination. Jimmy Carter realized that if his campaign for the nomination was to have any chance of success, it would require an early start, a solid grassroots organization, and public financing. He decided that he would enter every primary and every caucus possible. He officially declared his candidacy on December 12, 1974, the first major candidate to do so.

Having prepared for the initial Democratic contest for over a year, Carter scored impressively, first by an overwhelming victory in the Iowa caucuses, then by a plurality in the New Hampshire primary. To be sure, Jimmy Carter did not win every contest he entered; he suffered setbacks in Massachusetts and New York, but his victories in many other states convinced the Democratic party establishment that Jimmy Carter was a force to be reckoned with. The last hope of those Democrats searching for an alternative to Jimmy Carter faded when Senator Hubert Humphrey called a press conference announcing that he would not be a candidate in 1976 and would not spearhead a "stop-Carter" drive. By mid-1976, Jimmy Carter had captured the imagination of the public with his wide grin, his promise never to lie to the American people, and his image as an outsider with a humble background as a peanut farmer. By July 1976, when the Democratic convention met in New York City, Jimmy Carter's nomination was assured. Even his primary season opponents, in allowing their names to be placed in nomination, praised Jimmy Carter for his tenacity and offered their support for the fall campaign. In accepting his first ballot nomination, the Democratic nominee entered the convention hall from the floor, shaking delegates' hands as he approached the speaker's platform, then gave his acceptance speech. In order to assuage the Democratic party establishment, the party's liberal wing, and Washington "insiders," while at the same time picking a candidate eminently qualified to serve as president, should the need arise, Jimmy Carter chose as his running mate Senator Walter F. Mondale of Minnesota, who began his political career as Senator Humphrey's protege.

In a break from Democratic party tradition, Jimmy Carter opened his fall campaign against incumbent President Gerald R. Ford at the "Little White House," which is located in candidate Carter's home state of Georgia. By doing so, he touched both the New Deal traditions of his party and his own regional roots. He participated in a series of televised debates with President Ford.

Overall, the race started out as Jimmy Carter's to lose (the public opinion polls generally showed him to be far ahead of President Ford), but as the campaign progressed, President Ford gained ground in many of the polls, to the point where the race looked close. Indeed the election was quite close, and it was not until the early morning hours of the day after Election Day that it became clear that Carter won. Carter's victory was based on wins in all southern and most northeastern states, plus Texas and Hawaii. In the popular vote, Jimmy Carter received slightly over 50%.

President Carter's inauguration was informal in style. He wore a plain business suit to the ceremony, eschewing the traditional morning coat, and walked up Pennsylvania Avenue with Mrs. Carter and daughter Amy in the inaugural parade. President Carter made an effort to bring the White House closer to the people by enrolling Amy in a public school (he was the first president to send his child to public school since Theodore Roosevelt), participating in a radio "call-in" show, and by inviting grassroots campaign helpers to his state dinners. From time to time, as he had during the campaign, he stayed overnight at the homes of ordinary Americans.

Among President Carter's domestic policy initiatives was a reorganization of the federal government which not only abolished several agencies but also created two cabinet level departments: the Department of Energy and the Department of Education. He also backed measures deregulating the airline, trucking, and railroad industries. He supported income tax cuts, which were enacted, but galloping inflation rendered these tax cuts illusory as taxpayer income was pushed into higher brackets.

In foreign affairs, President Carter saw both his greatest triumph and his greatest tragedy. The triumph came on September 17, 1978, when President Carter, President Anwar el-Sadat of Egypt and Prime Minister Menachim Begin of Israel emerged from seclusion to announce that they had, after lengthy negotiations, reached a peace agreement that came to be known as the Camp David Accords. The tragedy began when, on November 4, 1979, militant supporters of Ayatollah Ruhollah Khomeini rushed the American embassy in Teheran and took embassy personnel and American visitors as hostages. The hostage crisis became a national obsession and dogged Carter for the rest of his administration, as the president struggled to find a way to free the captives. On his last day in office, January 20, 1981, the hostages were finally freed, but in a last taunting gesture, the hostages did not fly out of Teheran until one hour after President Carter's successor, President Ronald Reagan, was inaugurated.

The perceived weakness in the Carter administration drew challenges to President Carter's re-election effort in 1980. On the Democratic side, President Carter faced a challenge from Senator Edward M. ("Ted") Kennedy of Massachusetts, brother of slain President John F. Kennedy and the late Senator Robert F. Kennedy. Any effect that Senator Kennedy's criticisms of the Carter administration may have had on the voters was offset by doubts about Senator

Kennedy's own character, and President Carter scored victories in the early primary and caucus states. But the Carter campaign was negatively affected by a failed attempt at a military rescue of the hostages as well as a perceived lack of commitment to Israel. This combination of factors was probably significant in Kennedy's victory over President Carter in New York. Senator Kennedy also won victories in other big states, including Pennsylvania, California and New Jersey (Kennedy had previously won in his home state of Massachusetts). When the Democratic Convention met in New York City that summer, while it was clear that President Carter would be re-nominated, the Kennedy forces were well represented, and Senator Kennedy never formally endorsed President Carter despite direct public requests from the president to do so. This meant that heading into the fall campaign, President Carter did not have the united party apparatus that he had previously had in his 1976 effort.

The Republicans, sensing an opportunity for victory, held primaries involving several contenders, including: George Bush, a former CIA director and ambassador to China who had served as Republican National Chairman during the Nixon administration; former governor Ronald Reagan of California, who narrowly lost a battle for the 1976 nomination to President Gerald R. Ford; and Representative John B. Anderson of Illinois, a progressive Republican. Mr. Bush's triumph in the Iowa caucuses made him an early favorite for the GOP nomination, but then Ronald Reagan, long regarded as the leading spokesman for the conservative wing of his party, won the primary in conservative New Hampshire, and was regarded as the front runner for the nomination from that time forward. At the Republican National Convention in Detroit, Governor Reagan received the nomination, and, in a gesture to achieve party unity, selected his former rival, George Bush, as his running mate.

President Carter's re-election effort was further hampered by the decision of Representative Anderson, whose candidacy appealed to some members of both major parties, to run as an independent. Rep. Anderson attempted to broaden his bi-partisan base of support for his "National Unity Campaign" by selecting former Governor Patrick J. Lucey of Wisconsin, a liberal Democrat, as his running mate.

In 1980, televised debates among the presidential candidates were delayed by the question of whether Anderson should be included. Finally, in the last week of the campaign, President Carter and Governor Reagan debated head-to-head in a forum in which Reagan apparently scored heavily with the voters with his warm delivery, his rejoinder, "There you go again, Mr. President," after many of President Carter's responses, and his closing question for the voters, "Are you better off now than you were four years ago?"

In November 1980, Reagan handed President Carter a crushing defeat, carrying all but seven states. In conceding defeat, President Carter stated, "I can't say that it doesn't hurt." He devoted the remainder of his administration to negotiating successfully the release of the American hostages in Iran.

After President Reagan's inauguration, President Carter returned with his family to Plains. He and Mrs. Carter have written books; worked to establish the Carter Center, a combined presidential library, museum and policy institute in Atlanta; and spent much time working with Habitat for Humanity, a project which is dedicated to building homes for the underprivileged. The former president himself still personally participates in building some of the new homes. President Carter also speaks out publicly on significant policy issues, and has traveled to many countries to negotiate peaceful solutions of regional conflicts.

For relaxation, the Carters began visiting their friends John and Betty Pope (a Carter cousin) at their home at Walnut Mountain, not far from Plains. The area is wooded and is ideal for fishing. The Carters loved the area, and decided to work together with the Popes to build a log cabin for both couples to enjoy. In 1982, Mrs. Carter selected the site for the cabin, a wooded area owned by the Popes and located on Turniptown Creek. By 1983, the cabin, a small, unpretentious two-story structure, was completed. It has a wood shape roof and hemlock logs with joints filled with styrofoam; metal laths and two coats of cement provide good insulation. It has a small porch, and its rooms are filled with furniture made by President Carter, a skilled wood worker. The furniture includes slat-back chairs made with wood taken from a hickory tree from the backyard of the Carters' home in Plains, and a lazy-Susan table fashioned from pine boards salvaged from the attic of a demolished house which, at one time, belonged to the Murrays, Mrs. Carter's grandparents. Wood from the same house was also used to form the frame of a cushioned armchair and a spindle-backed bench which are placed near the stone fireplace in the living and dining room. The downstairs bedroom has a four-poster bed featuring square, tapering pencil posts; and two wardrobes with bracket feet, a raised-panel door and cornices. These furnishings were all crafted by President Carter in his workshop at his home in Plains.

The cabin's floors, doors and interior walls are also made of hard heart pine salvaged from the former home of Mrs. Carter's grandparents. The living and dining area features a long, high shelf on which President Carter's antique bottle collection is placed. The cabin's bright red front door is a board-and-batten antique from Plains, made of two wide pine boards and one narrow one.

The Carters' friend, John Pope, brought in 130 tons of gravel for the road to the cabin and also instigated the renaming of the nearby waterfall leading to Turniptown Creek. It was decided by the neighbors that it should be called Rosalynn Rapids in honor of Mrs. Carter.

Dividing much of their time between their home on Woodlawn Drive in Plains, and the cabin at Walnut Mountain, the Carters demonstrate that, despite their status as world renowned and influential figures, they have never lost their love for the simple pleasures of life, or their affinity for the beauty of the natural surroundings in their native Georgia.

The Georgia Governor's Mansion
391 West Paces Ferry Road, N.E.
Atlanta, Georgia 30305
(404) 261-1776

Administered by the State of Georgia.

Directions: The site is located in northern Atlanta, on the northern side of West Paces Ferry Road.

Open: Tuesdays, Wednesdays and Thursdays,

Admission: Free.

Special Events: None for touring visitors.

From 1971 to 1975, while Jimmy Carter was governor of Georgia, the Carters lived in the Georgia Governor's Mansion. The Mansion, a Greek Revival style residence designed by Georgia architect A. Thomas Bradbury, was completed in 1968. It contains 24,000 square feet and is located on an 18-acre property. Consistent with the architectural style of the mansion, its furnishings, paintings and porcelain are neoclassical. Most of the furniture was manufactured in the Federal period, and is considered to comprise one of the finest collections of furnishings of that period in the United States.

Visitors to the mansion first see the entry hall, which features a marble floor with a large bronze seal of the state of Georgia inlaid in the floor as they enter. Also on display here are bronze busts of George Washington and Benjamin Franklin, signed by French sculptor Jean Antoine Houdon and dated 1778.

Visitors also see the library, which is paneled in cherry wood and contains a collection of works by such celebrated Georgia authors as Joel Chandler Harris, Flannery O'Connor, Erskine Caldwell and Carson McCullers. The library also includes a collection of county histories and other books about Georgia. On a Pembroke table, near an antique scroll-arm sofa, is an engraved portrait of General James Oglethorpe, the founder of Georgia. On the floor is a Persian Tabriz carpet, made circa 1875.

The state dining room features an accordion-style table which can seat eighteen. The table is attributed to John Seymour of Boston. Also in this room is an Empire sideboard made by Henry Connelly, a Philadelphia cabinetmaker, and a Turkish Sultanabad carpet dating to about 1820.

Visitors also view the state drawing room. On display here are an Aubusson tapestry weave carpet and a large English breakfront. Other furnishings include mahogany Pembroke tables and square-back Grecian scroll-arm sofas. The matching card tables are attributed to Duncan Phyfe, and above them are eagle-topped convex mirrors, dating to the early 1800s. Here also are portraits by John Neagle of Lt. and Mrs. John Marston of Philadelphia.

From the circular hall, a winding staircase ascends to the second floor. An early nineteenth-century Italian giltwood chandelier, which once hung in the Yaarab Shrine Temple, now hangs here. The carpet, which reproduces a Federal design, was made in Georgia. Above the stairs is a portrait by an unknown artist of Hugh McCall, one of Georgia's first historians. A portrait of George Washington, painted by Samuel King after an earlier portrait by Charles Willson Peale, is found on the wall opposite the foot of the stairs. The circular hall also features the rarest piece in the mansion: a nineteenth-century Sevres porcelain vase on which a portrait medallion of Benjamin Franklin can be found.

The family living room, an informal gathering place, is paneled in butternut. An Austrian (French-style) Savonnerie carpet made in 1890 is bordered by two early nineteenth-century square-back, scroll-arm sofas from New York (although the sofas are not a pair). The English mantel is framed by a pair of Chinese eglomise, reverse paintings on glass. Also seen here is an oil portrait of Andrew Jackson by artist Ralph E.W. Earl.

The family dining room, used by the governor's family each day, has an American dining table and chairs. The sideboard in this room, the only piece of furniture on the first floor which is fully documented as having been made in Georgia, dates to about 1810. There are two paintings here: a still-life by Severin Roesin, and a landscape by Thomas Doughty entitled "View of the Berkshires."

Also on the second floor is the guest bedroom, which features an alcove bed made in New York circa 1815 and an English needlepoint carpet dating to about 1805. Over the bed is a wallpaper scenic panel, printed in the mid-nineteenth century from wood blocks made at an earlier time in France. The second floor contains private living quarters for the governor's family, including a den and office space for the governor. Visiting dignitaries stay on this floor in the presidential suite, which includes a spacious guest room, a sitting room and an aide's quarters. There are a total of six guest bedrooms on the second floor. One bedroom contains the bed and furniture used by former President and Mrs. Jimmy Carter while Mr. Carter was governor. The mansion also has a lower level, where the office of the First Lady of Georgia, the security office and a large ballroom which can accommodate formal dinners for 200 are located. On the east and west sides of the mansion are its lovely formal gardens. The gardens on the west side are terraced, and descend to a fountain surrounded by statues representing the four seasons.

This mansion, one of four executive mansions in the United States once occupied by at least one state governor who went on to become president of the United States, is the most modern of the four, and yet retains a traditional flavor and beauty which makes a visit there a worthwhile experience indeed.

RONALD WILSON REAGAN

Ronald Reagan Birthplace
111 Main Street
Tampico, Illinois 61283
(815) 438-2815

Administered by Helen Nicely.

Directions: From Chicago, take I-88 to the Sterling Rock Falls. Pass exit sign for Dixon (boyhood hometown of Ronald Reagan) and proceed west to second Sterling Rock Falls exit. Take Illinois Route 88 south to Route 172 West and then turn south on Route 172, which passes through Tampico.

Open: By appointment only.

Admission: Donations requested.

Features: Second floor birthplace apartment, Reagan Museum on first floor, gift shop. Birthplace apartment not handicapped accessible.

Special Events: None.

In 1906, attracted by the lure of the construction of a new canal near the hamlet of Tampico, Illinois, and the wave of new business it might bring, John Edward ("Jack") and Nelle Wilson Reagan came to Tampico to open a dry goods store. The Reagans had met as store clerks in the town of Fulton, Illinois and were married shortly thereafter. They rented a small apartment on the second floor of a three-story building from the building's owner, The First National Bank of Tampico, through Mr. R. F. Woods, who had a controlling interest in the bank. In 1908, their first son, John Neil ("Moon") Reagan was born.

On February 6, 1911, the Reagans' second son, Ronald Wilson Reagan, was born in their modest apartment. It is said that when Jack Reagan first saw his new baby son, he remarked that the infant looked like a "fat little Dutchman." For many years after that, Ronald Reagan was known by his nickname, "Dutch." (Today, the eatery two doors up from the birthplace is named the Dutch Diner in Mr. Reagan's honor.)

Ronald Reagan moved from place to place in his early childhood while Jack Reagan moved from job to job. In May 1911, the Reagans moved to a house on Glassburn Street in Tampico. That house was just across the park and opposite the depot. In December 1914, the Reagans moved to 832-834 E. 57th Street in Chicago, which was near the University of Chicago. From early 1915 to late 1917, the Reagan family lived on N. Kellogg in Galesburg, Illinois. In 1916, they moved to another house a block away, and it is believed that the address of that house is 1460 N. Kellogg.

In late 1917, the Reagans moved to yet another town, Monmouth, Illinois, and until August 1919, a span of two years, they lived in three different houses in Monmouth.

The Reagans returned to Tampico in August 1919. They lived in an apartment on Main Street above H.C. Pitney's General Store, which Jack Reagan managed. In December 1920, when Ronald Reagan was nine, the family left Tampico for Dixon, Illinois, 27 miles north, where Jack Reagan managed a shoe store that Mr. Pitney had opened there. The Reagans' first home in Dixon was at 816 S. Hennepin Avenue.

Today, Helen Nicely maintains the Ronald Reagan birthplace apartment, and has established a museum on the ground floor. Through donations and purchases, Mrs. Nicely has assembled a collection of period furnishings and mementos from Mr. Reagan's entertainment and political careers. The museum displays the mementos, and the period furnishings are used to decorate the six-room apartment, which includes a living room, library, two bedrooms, a dining room and a wash room/pantry.

Maintaining the birthplace and museum has not been easy for Mrs. Nicely, who has been plagued by vandalism and whose application for a state historical grant to renovate the birthplace and museum was rejected. However, Mrs. Nicely, who deserves commendation for her efforts to preserve a significant historical landmark, is happy to open the site to interested visitors, who should pay a visit to Tampico to see the modest birthplace of the fortieth president of the United States.

Ronald Reagan Boyhood Home
816 South Hennepin Avenue
Dixon, Illinois 61021
(815) 288-3404
(815) 288-5176

Administered by the Ronald Reagan Home Preservation Foundation.

Directions:	**From Chicago, take I-88 west to Dixon. Turn right onto Galena Avenue (Route 26 north). Turn left at 9th Street, and right again into the parking lot for the site.**
Open:	**December, January, and February— Open Saturday and Sunday.**
	March through November—Daily.

Closed Easter Sunday, Thanksgiving Day, Christmas Day and New Year's Day.

Special arrangements for group tours available by advance reservation.

Admission:	**Free.**

Features: Boyhood home, reception center, park featuring 8-foot bronze statue of President Reagan, barn housing a fully restored 1919 Model T automobile, vegetable garden, offstreet parking lot for cars and buses. A ten minute video presentation on Ronald Reagan and his life in Dixon is shown at the reception center. Gift shop, rest rooms, benches in park. No food or refreshment concession. Reception center and rest rooms are handicapped accessible, but the boyhood home is not (a video tour of the home is available for the handicapped). Guided tour of home lasts about 30 minutes.

Special Events: On February 6 (President Reagan's birthday), the site holds a celebration with cake and punch.

On December 6, 1920, Jack and Nelle Reagan moved with their two sons, Neil ("Moon") Reagan, age 11, and Ronald ("Dutch") Reagan, age 9, from Tampico, Illinois, to Dixon, Illinois, where Jack Reagan managed a shoe store in town owned by H. C. Pitney. The Reagan family moved into a two-story Victorian frame house located at 816 South Hennepin Avenue. The house, which stands on a lot originally owned by Father John Dixon, founder of Dixon, was originally built in 1891.

Because money was tight for the Reagan family, Mrs. Nelle Reagan supplemented the family income by utilizing her talents in sewing, mending and clothing alterations. Later, Mrs. Reagan worked at selling apparel at a dress shop. Because of the family's financial struggles, Ronald Reagan learned at an early age to save his money. As a child, he hid his pennies under a loose ceramic tile in the hearth in the front parlor. Despite the family money problems, "Dutch"

Reagan was an active youngster, and later called his Dixon years "the happiest times of my life." He and his brother, "Moon," attended the South Side School, later called the South Central School, from 1920 to 1923. The school building, which still stands, is currently being renovated and will become the home of the Dixon Historical Center. It will feature Reagan exhibits. "Dutch" Reagan also made use of the Dixon Public Library, the First Christian Church, and the Dixon YMCA. Both Reagan brothers had various childhood hobbies. They raised rabbits in the barn behind the house, and collected bird eggs and bird nests. They played football together and with their friends in the side yard.

In 1924, the Reagan family moved to 338 Everett Street in Dixon. This was where the Reagans lived while young "Dutch" Reagan attended high school. He continued to play football and other sports in high school, and his popularity resulted in his election as president of the student council.

213

He also became a very able swimmer, and, after his sophomore year, worked as a lifeguard at Dixon's Lowell Park. Over the course of seven summers as a lifeguard, he is credited with saving seventy-seven lives.

Using the money he saved as a lifeguard, Ronald Reagan was able to enroll at Eureka College, a small Disciples of Christ school near Peoria, Illinois. While a student there, he lived in the T.K.E. (Tau Kappa Epsilon) fraternity house on Burton Avenue in Eureka, Illinois. He played football as a running guard, acted in college plays and was involved in campus politics. When he was home from college, he stayed with his parents, who lived in an apartment at 226 Lincolnway from 1928 to 1931, then moved to N. Galena Avenue in 1931. In 1932, Jack and Nelle Reagan moved to 107 Monroe Avenue, where they lived from 1932 to 1937. This was where Ronald Reagan stayed for one last summer as a lifeguard after graduating from Eureka College in 1932.

Ronald Reagan decided that he wanted to become a radio announcer. In the late summer of 1932, he left Dixon for Chicago, where he stayed a few days for a radio tryout. He went from place to place searching for a station to work at until he reached Davenport, Iowa, where the program director of station WOC gave him a tryout. He worked there from the fall of 1932 until April 1934, when he moved to a larger station, WHO in Des Moines, Iowa, and became a sports announcer. There his play-by-play descriptions of football, baseball and other sports earned him quite a following. While in Des Moines, he lived at 400 Center Street.

In June 1937, Mr. Reagan traveled with the Chicago Cubs on a spring training trip to California. He visited Hollywood, where a friend arranged for him to have a screen test. As a result of the screen test, Warner Brothers offered him a contract, which he accepted. In his first film, *Love Is On the Air*, he played a familiar role—a radio announcer. When he first arrived in Hollywood, he stayed at the Montecito Apartments, located at 6650 Franklin Avenue.

In 1938, Mr. Reagan made his first "A" film, *Brother Rat*, which also featured Jane Wyman, whom he married on January 25, 1940. They had two children, Maureen, born in 1941, and Michael, an adopted son who was born in 1945. The newlyweds shared an apartment in Beverly Hills and, in late 1940, moved to 1128 Cory Avenue, in Hollywood. Before the year was out, they moved again, to 1326 Londonderry View, where they stayed until early 1941. Later that year, they moved to a new house they had built at 9137 Cordell Drive, in Los Angeles. They lived in this house until at least August 1945, and possibly until their divorce in 1948.

Meanwhile, Mr. Reagan was enjoying a successful acting career. Perhaps his most memorable role was that of the dying football player George Gipp in the 1940 film *Knute Rockne— All-American*. (The nickname "the Gipper" has stuck with Mr. Reagan even through his presidential years.) In *King's Row*, a 1941 film in which he played a young man whose legs were amputated, he uttered the memorable line, "Where's the rest of me?" This line became the title of Mr.

Reagan's 1965 autobiography.

At the outbreak of World War II, Mr. Reagan, who had joined the U.S. Army Reserve while still a sportscaster in Iowa, was called up for active duty. He was commissioned a second lieutenant, but his nearsightedness prevented him from being assigned to combat duty. Rather, he was transferred to an army motion picture unit, and helped to make films for the military. From April to June 1942, he was stationed at Ft. Mason in San Francisco. From January to November 1944, he was assigned to New York City to participate in a War Loan Drive. He was promoted to the rank of captain, and refused a promotion to major.

After the war ended, Mr. Reagan returned to his acting career. In 1945, he acquired a ranch property in Northridge, California which was used as a retreat, not a full-time residence. He sold this property in 1951. He became active in the Screen Actors Guild, a labor union for film performers, and served as its president from 1947 to 1952. In that capacity, he attempted to stave off the perceived threat of communist infiltration of the film industry. A liberal Democrat in those years, he supported President Harry S. Truman's 1948 presidential campaign and Representative Helen Gahagan Douglas in her 1950 senatorial campaign against Representative Richard M. Nixon. Years later, in 1959 and 1960, Mr. Reagan again served as president of the Screen Actors Guild and during that term, led a strike that resulted in allowing actors to receive a share of the profits of the sale of their old films to television networks.

It is thought that after he and Jane Wyman were divorced in 1948, Mr. Reagan lived at 939-943-1/2 Hilgard in Los Angeles until early 1949. As of August 1949 until sometime in the early 1950s, Mr. Reagan lived at 333 S. Beverly Glen in the Holmby Hills section of Los Angeles. In 1951, having sold the ranch in Northridge, Mr. Reagan acquired a second ranch property in Malibu, which he owned until 1967, his first year as governor of California.

While still president of the Screen Actors Guild, Ronald Reagan was asked to help a young actress named Nancy Davis. He agreed to meet her at a restaurant, where she talked to him about her problem with receiving communist propaganda in the mail. This encounter blossomed into a romance, and on March 4, 1952, with actor William Holden as best man, Ronald Reagan and Nancy Davis were married. Mr. Reagan, who had been living in an apartment on Camden Drive in Hollywood just before the marriage, moved to the new Mrs. Reagan's residence on Beverly Glen Boulevard, where they stayed until July 1952. They then moved to Amalfi Drive in Pacific Palisades, where they lived until approximately 1957. The Reagans then moved to a new house they had built at 1669 San Onofre Drive in Pacific Palisades, which was their home until Mr. Reagan's inauguration as president in January 1981. The Reagans had two children: Patricia (Patti Davis), born in 1953; and Ronald Prescott, born in 1958. Ronald and Nancy Reagan made one film together, *Hellcats of the Navy*, in 1957, which was the last of eleven films with Nancy Davis (Reagan).

In the 1950s, Mr. Reagan's entertainment career shifted its emphasis from films to television. From 1954 to 1962, he served as host of the General Electric Theater, and sometimes starred in its dramatic presentations. From 1962 to 1965, he was the master of ceremonies for Death Valley Days, a western series in which he sometimes performed. During these years, Mr. Reagan's political views also shifted. Although a nominal Democrat, he supported the presidential campaigns of Dwight D. Eisenhower in 1952 and 1956 and of Richard M. Nixon in 1960. He also served as a corporate public relations spokesman for the General Electric Company, making many personal appearances and delivering after-dinner speeches throughout the country. In his appearances, he espoused conservative principles. In 1962, he changed his voting registration from Democrat to Republican.

On October 27, 1964, Mr. Reagan made a nationally televised speech in support of Senator Barry Goldwater's 1964 GOP Presidential campaign. The speech resulted in hundreds of thousands of dollars in contributions to the Goldwater campaign. The speech was a turning point in Ronald Reagan's life, for while Senator Goldwater went on to defeat in that contest, Ronald Reagan's political star began to rise at that point, and began a series of events resulting in his replacement of Senator Goldwater as the leading spokesman for the conservative wing of the Republican Party. The good-natured, anecdotal fashion in which Mr. Reagan delivered that speech while attacking big government and high taxes convinced well-heeled California conservatives that Ronald Reagan had significant potential as a candidate. Wealthy conservative activists approached Mr. Reagan with the idea of running for governor of California in 1966. At first, Mr. Reagan laughed and brushed such entreaties aside. But by autumn of 1965, Mr. Reagan became convinced that he had a chance to win. He ran in 1966 against Democratic Governor Edmund G. "Pat" Brown, who, having defeated Richard M. Nixon four years before, was seeking a third term. Governor Brown did not take Mr. Reagan's challenge seriously; he did not believe that the voters would choose an actor who was inexperienced in government over an experienced government official. Mr. Reagan turned his inexperience to an advantage, calling himself a "citizen politician" and thereby tapped into voter resentment of professional politicians. In the end, Ronald Reagan was elected governor of California by a margin of nearly one million votes, and had taken a giant step on his road to the White House.

Today, visitors to Ronald Reagan's boyhood home can view the surroundings in which Mr. Reagan spent some significant and happy years. The white frame house in which "Dutch" Reagan lived from 1920 to 1924 is filled with furniture similar to that which was in the house when the Reagans lived here, as confirmed by the recollections of Neil Reagan, who visited here, and President Reagan, who also visited here on his birthday on February 6, 1984. Upstairs are three bedrooms, the first of which was shared by Neil and Ronald Reagan, the second was Mr. and Mrs. Reagan's bedroom, and the third was used by Mrs. Reagan as a sewing room. The boys' room features school pennants and other relics of South Side School, and the sewing room features a rocking chair donated by friends of the Reagans.

Downstairs is the kitchen, which features a top loading icebox, a gas stove and a pantry. Also on the first floor are a parlor, a sitting room and dining room, all of which are furnished with period pieces. Outside the house is a vegetable garden similar to that maintained by the Reagan family alongside the barn. Inside the barn is another item evocative of the period—a restored 1919 Model T. When the Reagans lived here, they also kept their car parked in the barn.

The surrounding property has been augmented by an adjacent park with an 8-foot statue of the fortieth president. This site is a charming and restful spot fashioned in tribute to President Reagan, who built two successful careers, in entertainment and in politics, upon the lessons he learned here.

The California Governor's Mansion
1526 H Street
Sacramento, California 95814
(916) 323-3047

Administered by the California Department of Parks and Recreation.

Directions:	From Business I-80, take 16th Street to H Street. The site is at the corner of 16th and H Streets.
Open:	Daily. (Tours last approximately 45 minutes.)
Admission:	Fee charged.
Features:	Mansion, reception center showing introductory video and selling postcards and souvenir books. Rest rooms in reception center. First floor of the Mansion is handicapped accessible.

Upon becoming governor of California on January 2, 1967, Ronald Reagan moved into the Governor's Mansion together with his wife, Nancy, and son, Ron Reagan. He was the thirteenth governor to occupy the Victorian-style home. However, the Reagans' stay at the mansion was brief, for, as gracious as the house is, its proximity to the corner of 16th and H Streets in Sacramento, and the increasing street traffic, meant that the noise level and degree of privacy of the mansion was no longer what it was in earlier times. In addition, there was concern about fire safety at the mansion.

For those reasons, the Reagans moved to 1341-45th Street, an English Tudor-style home in a residential area which served as their Sacramento home for the balance of Mr. Reagan's two terms as governor. At this writing, none of Mr. Reagan's successors as governor have chosen to live in the mansion, which is now a State Historic Landmark and open to the public for tours.

Governor Reagan managed his state government in corporate board style, calling semi-weekly cabinet meetings at which top state officials would present reports and recommendations to the governor. Some of the participants in these meetings later became federal officials and advisers during the Reagan presidency, notably Edwin Meese III, the gubernatorial cabinet secretary who became a top White House adviser and later attorney general.

The California state legislature was Democratically-controlled throughout Mr. Reagan's years as governor, so compromises had to be made in order to pass his legislative initiatives. Significant state debts forced Governor Reagan to forego his pledge to reduce the cost of government and to call for new taxes, which the legislature enacted. After inflation caused state revenues to far exceed projections, a revenue surplus resulted, and the state government rebated much of the surplus to the taxpayers. Governor Reagan left office with a state treasury with a surplus of over half a billion dollars. He also cut thousands from the state's welfare relief rolls, but, despite promises to reduce the number of state employees, could not hold the line on their number, which grew by more than forty thousand. He served two terms as governor, winning 53% of the vote against Democrat Jesse M. Unruh, who was the Democratic Majority Leader of the California State Assembly, in 1970. Governor Reagan did not seek a third term, and left office at the beginning of 1975.

Almost immediately upon becoming governor, Ronald Reagan was viewed as a contender for the Republican presidential nomination in 1968. After resisting pressure to enter the race (he had pledged in his gubernatorial campaign to serve a full term if elected), Governor Reagan finally announced his availability for the nomination while the 1968 Republican National Convention was in session. It was far too late, and Richard Nixon won the nomination on the first ballot and went on to become president.

In 1974, his last year as governor, Mr. Reagan purchased "Rancho del Cielo" ("Ranch of the Sky") for $527,000.00, at 3333 Refugio Road in Santa Ynez, California. This is a 688 acre ranch located at an elevation of 2,300 ft. in the Santa Ynez mountains, not far from Santa Barbara. The ranch house, a five room adobe heated by fireplaces, is over ninety years old and is still owned today by the Reagans. During his presidency, Mr. Reagan used this California retreat to relax and to exercise by horseback riding or tending to ranch chores such as fence mending and rail splitting.

In 1975, when Governor Reagan left office, Gerald Ford was president. Some GOP conservatives were becoming increasingly disenchanted with President Ford, perceiving him as insufficiently conservative due to his support of amnesty for Vietnam draft resisters and other factors. President Ford was also perceived as politically vulnerable; he was the only president to have become chief executive without having been a candidate for president or vice president. In consultation with his advisors, Mr. Reagan decided that a challenge was appropriate and, on November 20, 1975, announced formally that he was a candidate for the 1976 Republican presidential nomination.

The contest for the nomination was nip and tuck. In the first primary, in New Hampshire, President Ford edged Governor Reagan to win, and went on to more decisive victories in Florida and Illinois. Prospects looked grim for the Reagan challenge, but he then won an upset victory in North Carolina—the first time that an incumbent president had been defeated in a primary. Mr. Reagan went on to victories in Texas, Georgia, Alabama and Indiana, while President Ford won in Michigan and Ohio.

By the time the Republican National Convention began its session in Kansas City, the race for the nomination was so close that a shift of a small number of delegates would have given the nomination to Mr. Reagan. Grasping for a means to sway some delegates, Mr. Reagan decided to announce a vice presidential running mate prior to the vote on the presidential nomination. He chose Senator Richard S. Schweiker of Pennsylvania, a liberal Republican, in the hope that the prospect of an ideologically "balanced ticket" would sway some of the GOP delegates to support him. This tactic failed, and President Ford went on to narrowly win the GOP nomination and to narrowly lose to former Governor Jimmy Carter of Georgia in the fall. Although Ronald Reagan had to sit out of presidential politics for the next four years, he was, nonetheless, regarded as a contender in 1980. During Jimmy Carter's term as president, Ronald Reagan lived comfortably on his income from investments and lectures and did planning and fund-raising for a 1980 presidential candidacy.

Because of the perceived vulnerability of President Carter as a candidate for re-election, nine other Republicans besides Mr. Reagan announced their candidacies, and former President Gerald Ford was still considered a possible contender, although he never entered the race. Nonetheless, a confident Ronald Reagan announced his candidacy on November 13, 1979, borrowing President Franklin Roosevelt's "rendezvous with destiny" phrase.

At the outset, Mr. Reagan's chief rival for the GOP nomination was George Bush, the former director of the Central Intelligence Agency who had held numerous other significant party and government posts. Mr. Bush defeated Mr. Reagan in the first GOP test, the Iowa caucuses, but Mr. Reagan rebounded in the New Hampshire primary and never lost ground after that, taking such a commanding lead that the other Republican candidates withdrew one by one. One of them, Representative John B. Anderson of Illinois, the most liberal of the Republican contenders, ended his quest for the GOP nomination but announced that he would continue to campaign on an independent "National Unity" ticket.

At the Republican National Convention in Detroit, Mr. Reagan's nomination was so certain that the only real question was who would be nominated for vice president. Mr. Reagan held several conferences with former President Gerald Ford about the possibility of offering the vice presidential nomination to him. However, in the course of these discussions, it became clear that the former president would not accept unless he was promised an unprecedented expansion of the powers and influence of the vice presidency, which would have amounted to a "co-presidency." In the end, Ronald Reagan made an unprecedented personal appearance at the nominating convention prior to the vote on the vice presidential nomination, at which he announced that President Ford would be of more value as a campaigner than as a candidate on the national ticket and requested that his erstwhile rival, George Bush, be nominated. The delegates responded with cheers and nominated Mr. Bush on the following night. The Reagan-Bush ticket went on to defeat the Carter-Mondale and Anderson-Lucey tickets in November. The "Reagan Revolution" had begun.

The Reagan administration began with the release of the American hostages who had long been held captive in Iran. Shortly after taking office, President Reagan announced a major program for drastic reduction of government expenditures and an increase in defense spending. He also hoped to balance the federal budget and to cut income taxes by one-third. These Reagan economic initiatives were swiftly dubbed "Reaganomics," and although they did not stave off a national recession in late 1981, the president stood by his belief that his measures would turn the economy around.

Some of President Reagan's other notable contributions include his nomination of the first woman to serve on the United States Supreme Court, Sandra Day O'Connor, in 1981. In foreign affairs, he was faced with a tragedy that occurred in October 1983, when 241 American Marines and 58 French military personnel lost their lives as Arab terrorists bombed the American and French military headquarters in Beirut, Lebanon. Consequently, he sent a joint peace-keeping force with Britain, France, and Italy to Beirut to supervise Israeli efforts to expel the members of the Palestinian Liberation Organization (PLO) terrorist group. President Reagan was also involved in an incident that occurred in January 1981, when he cut off economic aid to Nicaragua, whose government was perceived as communist by the administration, and increased aid to Nicaragua's Central American neighbors and the anticommunist Nicaraguan rebels, the "Contras." Most memorably, when infighting broke out among communist leaders in Grenada, President Reagan ordered the invasion of that Caribbean island on October 25, 1983, with the stated purpose of protecting American students on that island.

In 1984, a lively contest for the Democratic nomination for president culminated in the nomination of former Vice President Walter F. Mondale, despite spirited campaigns by

Senator Gary Hart of Colorado, Rev. Jesse Jackson, and other Democrats. As his running mate, Mr. Mondale made an unprecedented selection by naming a woman, Representative Geraldine A. Ferraro of New York. In his acceptance speech, Mr. Mondale made the candid, but politically damaging, announcement that if elected president, he would have to propose a tax increase to reduce the national deficit. The Reagan-Bush team was unchallenged for renomination, and was the Republican ticket for a second time. President Reagan and former Vice President Mondale engaged in a series of televised debates, and Vice President Bush and his opponent, Rep. Ferraro, engaged in one such debate. These debates had little apparent effect on the thoughts of most of the electorate, and President Reagan won a landslide victory in November, carrying every state except Mr. Mondale's home state of Minnesota and the District of Columbia, a traditional Democratic stronghold.

Terrorism continued to plague international affairs in the second Reagan administration, and President Reagan struck out at one perceived source of terrorism, the government of Libya, by ordering that Libyan assets in the United States be frozen and that diplomatic relations be severed in March 1986. He responded to a dare by Libyan leader Colonel Muhamar Qadhafi that Libya would wage war with the United States if American ships crossed what he called the "line of death" and entered the Gulf of Sidra, where American naval exercises were scheduled as a show of force. Reagan ordered the U.S. Navy to fire on land-based missile sites and damage two Libyan patrol boats after Libyans had fired six missiles at American ships during the exercises. A few days after this incident, on April 5, 1986, a bomb planted in a Berlin discotheque popular with American military personnel exploded, killing one American soldier and injuring 155 other people. Strong evidence linked the bombing to Libya and in response, President Reagan secretly ordered U.S. bombers to bomb the Libyan capital, Tripoli. The bombs landed in an affluent section of Tripoli and hit Colonel Qadhafi's headquarters. Fifteen people, including Qadhafi's fifteen month-old daughter, were killed. One U.S. plane was lost.

In November 1985, President Reagan met with the new leader of the Soviet Union, Mikhael S. Gorbachev, thus beginning a process which eventually led to a treaty which provided for the elimination of medium and short-range nuclear missiles and stringent verification procedures in 1987. The two men met five times during President Reagan's second term, and the last such meeting was held in New York in December 1988 with President-elect George Bush in attendance.

The revelations in November 1986 that the President's National Security Advisor, Admiral John Poindexter, and his deputy, Lt. Colonel Oliver North, had been involved in a plan to sell arms and military spare parts to Iran and divert the proceeds to the Contras in Nicaragua touched off a wave of controversy which raised questions about the Reagan administration. This made Lt. Colonel North, in particular, a controversial figure who became a hero to some and a villain to others. The president appointed an investigating commission and Congress held hearings on the matter that year. Scholars and commentators are still debating what role, if any, President Reagan and then Vice President Bush played in this incident.

At the Republican Convention in 1988, President Reagan endorsed Vice President Bush as the man most capable of carrying on his policies, and signaled the impending close of his administration. He was the first president since Dwight Eisenhower to serve two full terms, and left office with the same enormous popularity he had enjoyed when he first took office. Having used 10960 Wilshire Boulevard in Los Angeles as his California mailing address throughout his presidency, he made plans to have a permanent home in the Los Angeles area upon leaving office. Together with several investors, he acquired such a home, at 668 St. Cloud in the well-to-do Bel-Air section of Los Angeles. While enjoying their life at this home and their Rancho del Cielo retreat, the Reagans remained active as travelers and President Reagan lectured on frequent occasions.

The Governor's Mansion, which was the Reagans' home in early 1967, was built in 1877 for Albert Gallatin, one of the partners of the Central Pacific Railroad. This palatial Mansard styled Victorian mansion was the home of thirteen California governors, from George C. Pardee to Ronald W. Reagan. Governor Pardee, the first governor to reside here, lived in the mansion from 1903 to 1907. This large house has seventy-seven doors (Mr. Gallatin paid $0.20 per door knob.) Governor Earl Warren, who lived here from 1943 to 1953 (and later became Chief Justice of the U.S. Supreme Court) was responsible for extensive renovation of the mansion.

Today, visitors may tour the first and second floors of the mansion. Passing through the entrance, visitors first see the entry hall, whose ceiling was embellished using a cake decorator's tool. The trim around the arches and baseboards is mahogany. Looking through the archway to the front, or formal, parlor, visitors see the original red English linen velvet drapes which adorn the windows, an Italian marble fireplace with metal inserts, and petticoat mirrors. Mirrors are placed above the fireplaces in this and other rooms to reflect light. The furniture in the formal parlor is Victorian, and was brought in by Governor Warren in the 1940s.

The informal parlor is decorated with furniture brought in by Governor Pat Brown in the 1960s. It evokes the feeling of a typical family living room of the 1960s, complete with a television set. Crossing the hallway to the music room, visitors note the reproduction Persian rug on the floor. In the music room is a Steinway piano purchased by Governor Pardee; its other furnishings were purchased by Governor Hiram Johnson. Incidentally, the original use of this room was as a library, reflected by the Shakespeare and Byron moldings on the wall.

Walking down the hallway and passing a gallery of pictures of California's first ladies, visitors come to the formal dining room. The wainscoting on the walls has molded images of food, suggesting the purpose of this room. The Victorian-style furniture here was purchased from Gump's of San Francisco. The table is covered with a lace table cloth, on which rests china and crystal service for six.

Ascending the curved stairway, whose steps are partially covered by a Persian rug, visitors come to the second floor, where there is a pink bedroom, a green bedroom, and a blue bedroom (originally a child's room). There are also two bathrooms, one of which was originally a nursery, and the servants' wing was also on this floor. On display in the pink bedroom are gowns worn by California's first ladies. The tour concludes when visitors descend a set of stairs and view the kitchen.

This ornate mansion, a California registered historical landmark, should be visited by those who treasure fine architecture as well as those who wish to learn more about the history of both the state of California and the United States.

GEORGE HERBERT WALKER BUSH

George Bush Birthplace
173 Adams Street
Milton, Massachusetts 02187

Bush Summer Home/Summer White House
Kennebunkport, Maine
(409) 260-9553

Privately owned. Not open to the public.

George Herbert Walker Bush, the forty-first president of the United States, was born in a Victorian mansion on Adams Street in Milton, Massachusetts on June 12, 1924. Adams Street is so named because the family of Presidents John Adams and John Quincy Adams lived on the same street in the "Old House," which is several miles away in Quincy. President Bush's father, Prescott Sheldon Bush, Sr., was an executive at U.S. Rubber and a graduate of Yale College. President Bush's mother, Dorothy Walker Bush, gave birth to her second son in a makeshift delivery room on the second floor of the mansion, which remains privately owned today.

In 1925, when U.S. Rubber relocated its headquarters to New York City, the Bush family moved to the affluent suburb of Greenwich, Connecticut, into an English Tudor-style home there. Young George Bush lived there until the age of seven, walking a mile to get to school. In 1931, the growing family (President Bush has three

brothers, Prescott, Jonathan and William; and a sister, Nancy Bush Ellis) moved to an eight bedroom house on Grove Lane in Greenwich, where young George was known to have taken his shotgun to an upstairs window and shot rats foraging in the trash.

In 1937, thirteen-year-old George Bush entered Phillips Academy in Andover, Massachusetts, where he was known as "Poppy." While there, he lived in what is now an all-female dormitory. After graduating in 1942 (several months after the attack on Pearl Harbor), George Bush enlisted in the Navy on his eighteenth birthday. He enrolled in flight school and was sent to Chapel Hill, North Carolina for pre-flight training. In early 1943, he became one of the youngest pilots in the Navy, and was assigned to a bomber squadron. After being shot down during a bombing raid on the island of Chichi Jima, he was awarded the Distinguished Flying Cross. He had been hit but managed to find his survival raft and stayed afloat until a U.S. submarine found him. He rejoined his squadron in the Philippines and flew 58 combat missions before being sent home for Christmas of 1944.

On January 6, 1945, George Bush married Barbara Pierce, who he had met at a Christmas dance three years before. They were engaged before he left for the Pacific. The newlyweds went to Trenton, Michigan, renting rooms from Grace Gargone while George Bush trained with the Navy. Before he received another assignment, the Japanese surrendered, and World War II ended in August 1945.

With the war over, George Bush lost no time enrolling in college. He attended Yale, as had his father, where he majored in economics. He also joined Skull and Bones, the Yale secret society. He excelled at soccer and baseball, and even dreamed about an offer to play baseball professionally, but the offer never came. For their first year in New Haven, George and Barbara Bush rented a small railroad flat next to a mortuary. The following year, 1946, with Barbara Bush pregnant with their first child, George, Jr., the couple moved to a house in New Haven, where George Bush refused a doctor's request to carry his pregnant wife up the stairs, joking that she "was as big as anyone on the Yale football team." Later in 1946, they moved next door to the Yale president, who, on one occasion when he was expecting an important visitor, asked George Bush to remove his infant son's diapers from the clothesline.

After graduating from Yale in 1948, George and Barbara Bush, with their young son George, Jr., hopped into their Studebaker and set off for Odessa, Texas, where Mr. Bush took a job as a trainee with a subsidiary of Dresser Industries. They lived in a duplex in Odessa situated on what is now a vacant lot. There, George Bush set about learning about the oil business and how to get involved in the postwar oil boom. After less than a year in Odessa, they relocated to California, where Mr. Bush took a series of jobs with Dresser Industries. In 1949, the Bushes stayed at what is now the Pierpont Inn in Ventura, California, while Mr. Bush was involved in the sale of oil drilling equipment. They also stayed in a number of other hotels along the west coast, and, for a time, lived in what is now a run-down building in Compton, California. By this time, the Bushes had a second child, a daughter, Robin, who died tragically three and a half years later of leukemia. In addition, the Bushes later had four other children: Jeb, Neil, Marvin, and Dorothy.

In 1950, the Bushes returned to Texas. They settled in a house in Midland, Texas in 1951. The house, which is located on "Easter Egg Row" (so-called because of its brightly painted houses) cost $7,500.00, and is privately owned today. During this time, Mr. Bush and his friend, John Overbey, formed an independent oil company, the Bush-Overbey Oil Development Company, Inc. In 1953, the Bushes moved to a second house in Midland, across from "the most stylish neighborhood," according to Mrs. Bush.

In 1954, Mr. Bush's company merged with another small company to form Zapata Petroleum. The following year, a subsidiary, Zapata Off Shore, was formed to manage the parent company's interests in offshore oil drilling, a new technology at the time. That same year, 1955, the Bushes again moved, this time to a ranch-style house with a two-car garage which they had built for themselves. The house bordered on a group of athletic fields.

Zapata Off Shore became a separate entity in August 1959, and Mr. Bush became president of his own oil exploration company. At that point, the Bushes moved to Houston, Texas, and, in 1960, moved to a house in which they lived until 1967. The house was later razed to make room for five new houses. By 1962, George Bush, pursuing new challenges, started to become politically active. (His father, Prescott Bush, Sr., was U.S. Senator from Connecticut from 1952 to 1962.) He became the Harris County Republican Chairman that year, and, during his two years in that post, worked to revitalize the Texas GOP and to increase its membership. In 1964, he challenged incumbent Democratic Senator Ralph Yarborough, and was defeated despite an energetic race. Two years later, in 1966, he ran for U.S. Representative from a new district in Houston, and won. Having been elected, he bought a home in Washington, D.C. which is today a home for Italian diplomats. He also moved his Houston residence to a town house, which, according to Mrs. Bush, was burglarized three times while Congress was in session and the family was away.

In 1969, the Bushes moved to a brick two-story home in Washington. By this time, Richard Nixon was president, and Bush was being urged to consider giving up his House seat to make another race against Senator Yarborough. Bush agreed to make the race but Senator Yarborough was defeated in the Democratic primary by a more conservative newcomer, Mr. Lloyd Bentsen, leaving him to run against a different opponent than he had anticipated. Most of the voters followed their partisan traditions and elected the Democrat, Mr. Bentsen, to the post.

After the election, President Nixon nominated George Bush to be the United States ambassador to the United Nations, and the Bushes moved to the ambassador's official residence in New York. After two valuable years in the area of foreign policy, President Nixon called upon Mr. Bush once again, this time to serve in a party office as chairman of the Republican National Committee. Mr. Bush served in this post when President Nixon resigned and President Ford succeeded him. President Ford wanted to offer Mr. Bush an ambassadorship. The two met, and Bush told the president that he wanted the opportunity to represent the United States in China. Since the United States had not yet formally recognized the People's Republic of China, there could be no ambassador to that country, so Mr. Bush was appointed chief of the U.S. Liaison Office in China. The Bushes lived in Beijing for thirteen months, during which time they studied t'ai chi and invited guests over for entertainment, such as Marx Brothers films and the American moon landing. In 1975, President Ford asked George Bush to return to Washington to become director of the Central Intelligence Agency. While in that post, Mr. Bush had bulletproof screens installed at his Washington home. Those screens were still in place when the house was sold in 1977, as were Yale decals on some toilet-seat covers.

After Jimmy Carter became president in 1977, George Bush, out of government for the first time in ten years, returned to a private home in Houston. There he determined that he might be a viable contender for the Republican presidential nomination in 1980. He knew, however, that Ronald Reagan would also be a formidable contender. He mapped out a strategy that he thought would be effective in the 1980 primary season. At first, the strategy seemed to be working when Mr. Bush won the Iowa caucuses, but Mr. Reagan overcame Mr. Bush's self-proclaimed "Big Mo" (big momentum) in New Hampshire by winning that primary. While Mr. Bush won later primary contests, attacking Mr. Reagan by denouncing his economic proposals as "voodoo economics" while campaigning in Pennsylvania, it became evident in due course that Mr. Reagan would be the presidential nominee. At the Republican National Convention in Detroit, after considering the possibility of placing former President Ford on the ticket, Mr. Reagan personally addressed the convention and recommended to them that they nominate George Bush as his running mate. The delegates ratified Mr. Reagan's choice, and the Reagan-Bush campaign was born. Fall strategy was mapped out at Mr. Bush's home in Houston, and he loyally adopted the Reagan campaign issue positions as his own, notably in the area of economics (the "voodoo economics" phrase dogged him throughout the campaign and beyond). The Republican ticket won handily in November, and George Bush became vice president of the United States on January 20, 1981.

In 1981, Vice President Bush sold his Houston home, and took a Houston hotel suite as his legal residence and voting address. (In 1988, local Democrats teased then Vice President Bush by renting the three-room suite for a party). He and his family moved into the vice president's official residence on the grounds of the Naval Observatory in Washington. This turreted, eleven room house was formerly the home of the base commander at the observatory, and became the vice president's official residence during the Ford administration, when Nelson Rockefeller held the office. While she was still living there, Mrs. Bush quipped that the house rocked when she jogged on her treadmill. When they left the house in 1989, President-elect Bush noted that he and Mrs. Bush had lived in that house longer than they had lived in any other single residence in their more than forty years of marriage.

George Bush's vice presidential years are best characterized by his unswerving loyalty to President Reagan, who delegated responsibilities to him, including participation in cabinet meetings, and an arrangement for him to occupy offices in the White House. For about eight hours in 1985, presidential powers were actually transferred to Bush while President Reagan underwent cancer surgery. Despite taking political heat when questions arose about his past dealings, as CIA director, with Panamanian leader General Manuel Noriega, who had been indicted for drug trafficking (Vice President Bush was given responsibility for illegal drug interdiction, and critics claimed that he should have known sooner about the illegal activities of General Noriega, who at one time

was a paid CIA informant) and for his possible role in the Iran-Contra matter, Bush remained a leading candidate to succeed President Reagan.

Going into the 1988 presidential campaign, there was little doubt that Vice President Bush would be a candidate. The position in which he found himself was not dissimilar to the position in which Ronald Reagan found himself in 1980, when Mr. Reagan's claim for the GOP nomination was challenged by an upstart named George Bush. This time, the role of "upstart" was played by Senator Bob Dole of Kansas, the Senate minority leader who had been President Gerald Ford's running mate in 1976. Senator Dole's political credentials in 1988 were perhaps even stronger than those with which George Bush had entered the 1980 contest; Dole was a veteran Republican politician, and his wife, Elizabeth Dole, served in the Reagan cabinet. As George Bush had done eight years earlier, Dole won the Iowa caucuses. Television evangelist Pat Robertson, another candidate, was second, followed by Vice President Bush, who came in a humiliating third.

To have any hope of remaining viable, Vice President Bush knew that he had to win the New Hampshire primary. He campaigned vigorously against Senator Dole, pounding him both in speeches and on the airwaves. This strategy won the primary for him, and from that point onward, neither Dole nor any other announced Republican candidates seriously challenged Vice President Bush for the nomination. Senator Dole withdrew and supported Vice President Bush after the latter scored a string of impressive primary victories in southern states in March.

The Democrats, thinking that 1988 was an opportune year to regain the White House, also had several contenders for their nomination, notably Massachusetts Governor Michael Dukakis, Reverend Jesse Jackson, and Tennessee Senator (later Vice President) Albert Gore, Jr. Although Senator Gore scored well in some southern primaries, and Reverend Jackson carried Michigan, Governor Dukakis won such key states as Texas, New York, and his home state of Massachusetts. He managed to unite the disparate factions of the Democratic Party sufficiently to capture the nomination. For his running mate, Dukakis looked to George Bush's adopted state of Texas and picked an old Bush opponent, Senator Lloyd Bentsen. Coming out of the Democratic convention, things looked good for the Dukakis-Bentsen ticket; national polls showed them to be about seventeen points ahead of Mr. Bush.

George Bush's choice for a running mate was a controversial surprise. He named Senator J. Danforth ("Dan") Quayle of Indiana, a little known, conservative senator who had deposed former Democratic Senator Birch Bayh in the 1980 Reagan sweep. Despite the doubts of some commentators and political pundits as to Senator Quayle's capacity to serve in the nation's highest office, Mr. Bush insisted that he was equal to the job. Mr. Bush also thought that Senator Quayle's appeal to youth, and to the conservative wing of the party, would be an asset to the ticket. In a subsequent televised debate between the vice presidential candidates,

Senator Bentsen appeared to be focusing on public doubts about Senator Quayle when he faced him and said, "Senator, you're no Jack Kennedy!"

On the last night of the 1988 Republican Convention, Vice President Bush delivered a highly praised and much quoted speech in accepting the nomination. Drafted by speechwriter Peggy Noonan, the speech was peppered with memorable phrases, such as his metaphor for the nation's complexity, "a thousand points of light;" his call for "a kinder, gentler nation;" and his pledge, "The Congress will push me to raise taxes—and I'll say to them, read my lips, no new taxes." (Later, economic pressures forced President Bush to abandon this pledge.)

The 1988 presidential campaign will probably be remembered more for symbols than substance. Except for Senator Bentsen's comment to Senator Quayle in the vice presidential debate, the Bush campaign seemed to be defining the contest and the issues to be addressed. First, Governor Dukakis was accused of condoning the burning of the American flag, and then he was attacked for allowing Boston Harbor to remain a polluted disgrace. Vice President Bush also labeled Dukakis as a card-carrying member of the American Civil Liberties Union, and the man whose furlough program allowed a convict, Willie Horton, to go free and to commit the crime of murder while out on furlough. As a candidate, Governor Dukakis did not effectively rebuff these attacks. He also proved to be self-defeating, notably by climbing into a tank to drive it around a military base, with the intention of making himself appear tough but instead looking foolish, and by giving a intellectual, passionless answer to a question concerning what he would do if his wife were raped, which was asked during a nationally televised debate.

In the end, George Bush was elected president by a comfortable margin, winning about 54% of the popular vote, and carrying about 40 states. His first term was supported by remarkable events abroad, notably the collapse of the Soviet Union, the liberation of the eastern European states and the reunification of Germany, all of which President Bush claimed are part of the emergence of a "new world order." Also notable was "Operation Desert Storm," the military action in which Iraq was invaded and Iraqi troops were driven out of neighboring Kuwait, whose oil resources were an incentive for Iraqi leader Saddam Hussein to invade that country. On the domestic side, the United States was in the grip of a recession in 1991 and 1992, and President Bush, who easily overcame a primary challenge by conservative commentator Pat Buchanan, faced Democratic Governor Bill Clinton of Arkansas and Texas billionaire H. Ross Perot, an Independent, in the 1992 election.

While president, George Bush had frequent occasion to take working vacations in the Bush summer home at Kennebunkport, Maine. This large summer retreat, which sits on a bluff overlooking the coast of Maine, has been a Bush family retreat since the president's grandfather built it in 1901. While the property is private and not open to the public, visitors to Kennebunkport may view the property from a distance by driving along a coastal road.

WILLIAM JEFFERSON CLINTON

The Arkansas Governor's Mansion
1800 Center Street
Little Rock, Arkansas 72206
(501) 376-6884

Administered by the state of Arkansas.

Directions: From I-30, take 2nd Street exit (Little Rock) and turn (left from I-30 north, right from I-30 south) onto 2nd Street. Turn left again at Center Street. The site is located at the end of Center Street at the intersection of Center and West 18th Streets.

Open: Tuesdays and Thursdays by appointment.

Admission: Free.

Features: Mansion, state police guard house, guest house, lawns, and gardens. Tour of first level of mansion only. Tour is handicapped accessible, although rest rooms are not.

Special Events: Please contact the site for information about special events.

William Jefferson "Bill" Clinton, the forty-second president of the United States, was born on August 19, 1946 at Julia Chester Hospital in the small, rural community of Hope, Arkansas. President Clinton's mother, the former Virginia Cassidy, grew up in Hope and married William Jefferson Blythe III, a salesman from Sherman, Texas. Tragically, Mr. Blythe died in an auto accident in May 1946. He was driving to Hope to rejoin Virginia, who was five months pregnant at the time. Four months later, William Jefferson Blythe IV was born.

When Virginia Cassidy left Julia Chester Hospital with her newborn son, she took him to live at the home of her parents, Eldridge and Edith Grisham Cassidy, at 117 South Hervey Street in Hope. The house, a two-story frame structure with a front porch and a dormer on the second floor, was built shortly after World War I by Charles Garrett, who served in France during the war and modeled the house after one he had admired in that country. Mr. Garrett and his wife, Irene, lived in the house for a number of years prior to its ownership by the Cassidys. From 1946 to 1950, young Billy Blythe grew up in the house on South Hervey Street. He was entrusted to the care of his grandparents while his mother received training as a nurse-anesthetist at schools in Shreveport and New Orleans, Louisiana. Today the house on South Hervey Street is fully restored and was opened to the public in 1997 as an Arkansas State Historic Site.

In 1950, the year that Billy Blythe turned four, his mother married Roger Clinton, the owner of a Buick dealership in Hope. The Clintons and young Billy moved to 321 East 13th Street, a modest but charming one-story home with three bedrooms. The house was one of a series of homes built in 1945 by George Peck, who intended for them to be occupied by returning World War II veterans. The Clintons lived there until 1953. Later, the house was owned by Helen Aldridge, who ran a pet grooming business on the property for many years. The home was later renovated by another owner, Donna Williams, who added a large awning to the side of the house, installed new carpeting, but kept the essential character of the house. The house was sold recently to two women, a school teacher and a probation officer, who maintain a sign noting that this charming white home with green trim was the boyhood home of Bill Clinton.

In the summer of 1953, Billy Blythe and his family moved to a rented home outside Hot Springs, Arkansas, where his stepfather joined his brother's car dealership. After a few months, the family moved into a permanent home at 1011 Park Avenue, a two-story Tudor-style home, now painted white with green trim, in the northern section of Hot Springs. Today, the house is privately owned.

In 1961, fifteen-year-old Bill took the family name of his stepfather, and became Bill Clinton. Bill Clinton was the Hot Springs High School delegate to Boys' State, and was then elected to be Arkansas' delegate to Boys' Nation in Washington, D. C. While there in 1963, he shook hands with President John F. Kennedy, and the moment was captured on film. His mother remembers that from that time on she knew that her son's future would be in politics.

Unfortunately, the Clinton household had its share of problems within the family. Roger Clinton, who is remembered as an essentially decent man, was plagued by alcoholism, which brought about violent periods in which he became physically abusive toward his wife. At the age of 14, Bill Clinton intervened on his mother's behalf, warning his stepfather never to harm his mother again, and consequently ended the violent episodes. Interestingly, Roger Clinton was never abusive toward either Bill or his younger half-brother, also named Roger.

When Bill Clinton was in tenth grade, he and his family moved to another home in Hot Springs, located at 213 Scully Street in the southern part of town. This home is a one-story brick structure on a small street, and is currently owned by the Houser family.

In 1964, Bill Clinton graduated from high school and attended Georgetown University in Washington, D.C. He graduated from Georgetown in 1968. The following year, he attended Oxford University in England as a Rhodes Scholar. He then returned to the United States to attend Yale Law School, where he met fellow student Hillary Rodham of Park Ridge, Illinois. Their relationship became a romance and the two were married in 1975.

In 1971, having already worked as an aide to Senator J. W. Fulbright of Arkansas while a student, Bill Clinton, who had earned his law degree, became active in a Connecticut senate campaign. In 1972, he was active in Senator George McGovern's unsuccessful presidential campaign, and later taught law at the University of Arkansas until 1976. In 1974, he lost a bid for Congress to incumbent Republican Representative John Paul Hammerschmidt.

In 1975, the Clintons bought a brick and stone home on California Street in Fayetteville, Arkansas, which they maintained during his successful race for attorney general of Arkansas in 1976. At this time, the Clintons also established a residence in Little Rock. In 1978, Bill Clinton was elected governor of Arkansas, thus becoming, at the age of 32, the youngest governor of any state in the nation at that time. The Clintons first moved into the governor's mansion in Little Rock at that point. On February 27, 1980, Chelsea Clinton was born, and later that year, Governor Clinton campaigned for election to a second two-year term. To his chagrin, he lost that re-election bid, but decided to remain in Little Rock to practice law. The Clintons bought a house at 816 Midland Avenue in the Pulaski Heights section of Little Rock, an eclectic, charming neighborhood high atop a hill west of town. The house was built in 1905 and is Victorian in appearance, with three bedrooms, a front porch, a lawn and garden and a carport. The house is comfortable and unpretentious, and is currently owned by Ray Whittier and his family.

In 1982, Bill Clinton won election as governor of Arkansas for a second time, and was re-elected to that post

President Clinton's first home in Hope, AR. This was the home of his maternal grandparents. It was restored and opened to the public in 1997. (Pre-restoration photo.)

President Clinton's second home in Hope, AR. He moved here after his mother married Roger Clinton.

every other year through 1990. The home in which President Clinton resided during his years as governor of Arkansas is a Georgian colonial mansion located on an eight-acre site formerly used by the Arkansas School for the Blind. Bricks from the school were used in the construction of the mansion, which is situated in the Quapaw Quarter of Little Rock. Construction was completed in 1950 at a cost of $197,000.00. The mansion's first occupants were Governor and Mrs. Sid McMath and their family. The main building is a two-story structure measuring 140 by 60 feet. Two cottages are linked to both sides of the main building by circular brick colonnades pierced with portholes. The west cottage is used by the governor's security force, and the east cottage is maintained for visiting state guests and their families. The property is accessible through an iron filigree gate, beyond which is a circular drive surrounding a tiered iron fountain, which was a gift from the Governor's Mansion Association, the five-member independent commission that oversees all changes and acquisitions concerning the mansion. Adorning the front entrance of the mansion is a colonnade with four columns. The Arkansas state seal is affixed to the top of the colonnade. In the back of the main building is a terrace running the length of the mansion. The patio furniture on the terrace was manufactured in Arkansas.

The foyer features marble flooring donated by the Batesville Marble Company. The chandelier is over two centuries old. It was brought from France in sections and then rechained in a process that lasted three months. Ascending to the second floor is a curving stairway made of rubbed walnut. This striking feature was added by Arkansas artisans in a recent renovation. At the center of the foyer is an antique rosewood table. The table rests on a richly patterned Oriental carpet.

The living room is furnished with Georgian colonial-style pieces. Here, the fireplace can be viewed from twin Chippendale sofas, between which is a Queen Anne mahogany table. The rare Kimmanshah Persian rug was donated by former Governor and Mrs. Winthrop Rockefeller. Above the fireplace mantel is Samuel F.B. Morse's portrait of Arkansas' first governor, James Miller. A second portrait, now hanging near the piano, once hung in a home in Scott, Arkansas. During the Civil War, a Union officer was so captivated by the subject of the portrait that he spared the house in Scott from the torch.

The dining room contains a Sheraton dining table fashioned in four sections, each of which stands on its own pillar and claw. Above the table hangs a Louis XVI chandelier adorned with a hand-blown bell. The chandelier was added to the mansion in the early 1970s. The room also holds 24 Chippendale side chairs with handmade needlepoint seats depicting seven periods in Arkansas history. The Hepplewhite sideboard, used to serve buffet to guests, is considered one of the finest antique pieces in the mansion. A Chippendale-style cabinet crafted in London houses a por-

tion of the mansion's silver service, which was originally given to the battleship *Arkansas* by the people of the state of Arkansas and then donated to the governor's mansion after the battleship was decommissioned. Included in the 62-piece silver service is a large punch bowl cast from 3,000 silver dollars donated by Arkansas school children.

East of the living room is the conference room, which is used by the Governor and his staff for meetings in a setting removed from the demands of the governor's office at the state capitol. The room features works of art on loan from the Arkansas Arts Center, including a large painting and other works made by Arkansans. The bookshelves hold books from Arkansas authors. Decorated with crewel draperies, the room is a colorful and cheerful setting for the conduct of state business.

The guest house to the east of the main building was completely renovated by Arkansas members of the American Society of Interior Designers. The setting is pleasant, and visitors to the mansion may enjoy the expansive lawns and gardens outside the mansion; including the herb, rose and vegetable gardens to which cuttings have been donated by garden clubs throughout Arkansas. The gardens are maintained by the mansion staff.

Proudly displayed in the mansion is its oldest item—a Grandfather clock made in 1770 by William Maddock of Waterford, Ireland. The clock was donated to the state by the family of the late Francis Cherry in remembrance of his service as Arkansas' 35th governor.

On October 3, 1990, Governor Clinton, having compiled a record including education reform, environmental initiatives, job development and other innovations in Arkansas state government, declared his candidacy for president of the United States; Senator Albert Gore, Jr., of Tennessee was selected as his running mate. During the ensuing primary and general election campaign, Governor Clinton presented a series of proposals for change, addressing economic, environmental and other national concerns. He faced two principal opponents, incumbent Republican President George Bush, and Texas billionaire H. Ross Perot, in the race for the presidency. Clinton defeated his opponents and, on November 3, 1992, was elected the forty-second president of the United States.

In 1996, the Clinton-Gore ticket was re-elected over Republican former Senate Majority Leader Bob Dole, Mr. Perot, and other opponents.

By visiting Hope, Hot Springs, and Little Rock, one can trace the life and development of a leader from his modest beginnings in a rural, middle class American town, to his growth in a popular American resort community, and then to his maturity as the political leader of a state. President Clinton's oldest friends remember him as a man of compassion who was always there for them, and believe that he wants to devote his talents to the service of others and will forget neither his humble origins nor the people who helped to shape him into the leader he has become.

THE WHITE HOUSE

1600 Pennsylvania Avenue
Washington, D.C.
(202) 456-7041
(202) 472-3669

Tours administered by the National Park Service.

Directions: The White House is located in the heart of Washington, D.C, near the Old Executive Office Building, across from Lafayette Park on Pennsylvania Avenue.

Open: Tuesday through Saturday, 10:00 a.m. to 12:00 p.m.; closed Sunday, Monday and some holidays.

Admission: Free.

Features: White House, President's Park (including trees associated with certain presidents), Rose Garden, Jacqueline Kennedy Garden, and Children's Garden. Handicapped accessible; handicapped visitors should go directly to the northeast gate on Pennsylvania Avenue, where wheelchairs are available. Visitors tour the ground and first floors of the house; the second and third floors are used by the presidential family and guests and are not open to the public.

Special Events: In April and October, garden tours are conducted on selected weekends. Candlelight tours of the White House are conducted during the Christmas season.

On Easter Monday, the traditional Easter Egg Roll takes place on the south lawn.

228

George Washington was the only president who never resided in the White House (as it is called today), but he was instrumental in choosing its location. On July 16, 1790, Congress passed the Residency Act, which empowered George Washington to select the precise location of a newly designed capital city somewhere along the banks of the Potomac River. After he made the selection, plans for the new "Federal City" were drawn by French engineer Pierre L'Enfant. He designed the capital city on the basis of two focal points: the Capitol and the President's House, which were symbols of the legislative and executive branches of government, respectively. At the suggestion of Thomas Jefferson, then secretary of state, the design for the structures of the two focal buildings was opened to a competition, which was announced on March 14, 1792 by the Commissioners for the District of Columbia. On July 17, 1792, James Hoban, an architect who was born and trained in Ireland, was declared the winner of the competition based on his design, which was modeled after the country houses of the British Isles. The cornerstone for the President's House was laid by the Commissioners for the District of Columbia and the Freemasons on October 13, 1792, and Mr. Hoban supervised the construction of the new residence of the chief executive.

Construction proceeded in 1793, using bricks fired at three kilns located in a brickyard on what is now the north lawn of the White House. The laborers for the project were housed in huts on what is now Lafayette Park, and stonemasons recruited from Edinburgh and slaves hired from their owners contributed to the construction effort. Materials included stone from the Aquia Creek quarry in Stafford County, Virginia, which was used for the foundations and exterior walls; wood from such places as North Carolina and Virginia, which was used for flooring, doors and frames; and lime for the mortar from the Frederick, Maryland region. By the end of George Washington's two terms as president, the walls of the new residence were in place and its roof was framed.

Construction continued as John Adams assumed office in 1797. Because the District of Columbia was still under construction, Philadelphia remained the United States capital for much of the Adams administration (New York City had been the first capital, but the capital of the young republic was moved to Philadelphia while George Washington was president). From 1797 to 1800, the windows of the new President's House were installed and the interior walls were plastered. On November 1, 1800, President John Adams became the house's first occupant, although the construction was not yet completed. On his second night in the President's House, President Adams, in a cold and unfinished chamber of the house, wrote to his wife (who had not yet arrived) the following words: "I pray heaven to bestow the best of Blessings on this House and all that shall hereafter inhabit it. May none but honest and wise men ever rule under this roof." These words, now carved on the mantel of the State Dining Room, are the motto of the White House.

Although President John Adams and Abigail Adams were already in residence at the President's House in late 1800 and early 1881, much work remained to complete the interior. Abigail Adams used the unfinished East Room as a place to hang the wash to dry. Because he was defeated for re-election in 1800, President Adams only spent a few short months as an occupant of the President's House. President Adams' successor, Thomas Jefferson, in keeping with his democratic beliefs, opened the President's House to all visitors, a practice which has been observed to this day. While Mr. Jefferson was president, the east and west terraces of the house were built.

President James Madison and his wife, Dolley Madison, became the next occupants of the President's House in 1809, and while they lived there the house became a place of fashionable entertainment for Washington society. The Madisons hired architect Benjamin Latrobe to design furniture and to decorate the oval room, and Latrobe-designed chairs and furnishings were placed in the President's House. But then the British captured Washington and set fire to the President's House on August 24, 1814, retaliating for the burning of public buildings in Canada by American forces. The fire destroyed the Latrobe pieces and, in fact, nothing remained of the house except its exterior sandstone walls and interior brickwork. The Madisons relocated to a place outside of Washington, then stayed on the second floor of Octagon House on New York Avenue in Washington, and then, from 1815 to the end of the Madison administration, lived in the corner house of "Seven Buildings" on Pennsylvania Avenue. The British forces had burned much of the capital city in 1814, and the "Seven Buildings" was the only structure between the White House and Georgetown to survive the 1814 fire.

Under the supervision of James Hoban, the President's House was rebuilt, and was ready to be occupied by President James Monroe, who had been staying at 2017 I Street in a house that he leased for his first few months as president while awaiting completion of the reconstruction work.

Many other significant changes and events have taken place at the official presidential residence over its nearly 200 years of existence. James Hoban, at an advanced age, was on hand to supervise the construction of the north portico of the President's House in 1824 (while President Monroe was in office) and the south portico in 1829 (the first year of the Jackson administration). Under President Andrew Jackson, the East Room was furnished and opened for public use, and in 1833, running water and a bathroom were installed at the property. In 1848, under President James K. Polk, gas lighting was installed. The first central and efficient heating system was installed in 1853 during the administration of President Franklin Pierce, and bathrooms and water closets on the second floor were improved. While President Pierce was in office, a glass conservatory was planned for the west terrace and was completed in 1857, while James Buchanan was president. While President Rutherford Hayes was in office (1877-1881), the conservatory was expanded with walks and benches added to the interior design, and was connected to the Executive Mansion (as it was known by that time) through the state dining room.

Over the years, the residence now known as the White House has been a place of both celebration and mourning. For example, in 1865, thousands of mourners passed by the coffin of slain President Abraham Lincoln, which was placed in the East Room, and on June 2, 1886, President Grover Cleveland, a bachelor when elected president, married Frances Folsom in the Blue Room. Although several weddings have been held at the official presidential residence, President Cleveland remains the only president to have married there.

Under President Benjamin Harrison, electric lights were added to the Executive Mansion in 1891, and other significant changes were made to the structure. When Theodore Roosevelt became president in 1901, he changed the official name of the structure to the name by which it had been popularly known even prior to the 1814 fire—the White House. He also learned that the house badly needed structural repairs and more space for the family and for the staff. Moreover, the interior was furnished in an unappealing mixture of styles. Congress appropriated the funding to both repair and refurnish the house, and to construct new presidential offices. The architectural firm of McKim, Mead and White was retained and began its work in June 1902. As part of the project, it replaced the old conservatories with the West Wing, an executive office building. The firm's work was completed by the end of the year. By 1909, when William Howard Taft became president, it was apparent that even more space was needed, and the West Wing was enlarged; among the rooms added was the Oval Office, which since that time has been the president's office. In 1913, during Woodrow Wilson's presidency, the first roses of the formal garden, now known as the Rose Garden, were planted just outside the Oval Office.

In 1927, while President Calvin Coolidge was in office, a third floor was added to the White House to provide more residential space. Two years later, a fire broke out in the West Wing on Christmas Eve, 1929, and President Herbert Hoover responded by leaving the dinner table to supervise the removal of papers from the Oval Office. While reconstruction of the West Wing was in progress, President Hoover first used the Lincoln Study (now the Lincoln Bedroom) as a temporary office and then used temporary working space in the State-War-Navy Building (today known as the Old Executive Office Building). The West Wing was enlarged yet again in 1934, under President Franklin Roosevelt. During World War II, the East Wing and an air raid shelter were constructed, and a movie theater was added in the east terrace. In 1948, President Harry S Truman had a balcony added to the south portico, but not long afterward, it was learned that the White House had serious structural problems due to weakened interior walls and support beams (some of which were timbers dating back to the 1817 restoration). The Truman family moved across the street to Blair-Lee

House for four years while renovation took place. The extensive repairs included gutting the interior, digging a new basement, laying a new foundation, and installing a steel framework. To avert the risk of a recurrence of the 1814 and 1929 fire problems, fireproofing was installed (and was supplemented by a fire-detection system in 1965, when President Lyndon Johnson was in office). In March 1952, the Trumans moved back to the White House, and President Truman gave the first tour of the "new" White House.

The administrations of President Truman's successors have endeavored to add to the White House collection of historic objects and artistic works. Continuing efforts have also been made to maintain and to preserve the White House, and a recent project involves the restoration of the exterior walls. This involved the stripping of 28 layers of paint and the repairing of the sandstone walls by expert stone carvers. The result is that the fine details on these walls, including carved garlands and roses, are restored to their original appearance.

Modern visitors to the White House begin their tour at the East Wing Entrance. Looking through windows in the ground floor corridor, visitors see the Jacqueline Kennedy Garden; both it and the Rose Garden, located by the West Wing, are used for bill signings and other formal ceremonies. The Jacqueline Kennedy Garden is ordinarily used for receptions and events associated with the first lady, while the Rose Garden is ordinarily used for ceremonies associated with the president. In 1971, the wedding of President Richard M. Nixon's daughter, Tricia Nixon, and Edward Cox took place in the Rose Garden. Outside on the White House grounds are trees planted by presidents, including an American elm planted by John Quincy Adams and a magnolia planted by Andrew Jackson.

Visitors enter the ground floor of the house to view the ceremonial rooms and other rooms routinely viewed by the public. Throughout the corridors and hallways of the ground and state floors of the White House hang portraits of the presidents and first ladies. Looking to the right, visitors see the Library. Its volumes are entirely written by American authors, and include biographies and works of fiction, history, and science. Federal period furnishings are seen here, as well as a chandelier that once belonged to the family of James Fenimore Cooper. Portraits painted by Charles Bird King in 1821 and 1822 depict five Indian leaders who visited President James Monroe. A Gilbert Stuart portrait of George Washington, circa 1805, hangs over the mantel. The paneling in the Library, the Vermeil Room and the China Room is made from the 1817 timbers salvaged from the 1948-52 reconstruction of the White House.

Across the hallway is the Vermeil (gilded silver) Room, in which a vermeil collection bequeathed to the White House in 1956 by Mrs. Margaret Thompson Biddle is displayed. Over the mantel hangs "Morning on the Seine," a gift to the White House in late 1963 by the family of President John F. Kennedy in his memory. Also in this room is a portrait of Eleanor Roosevelt by Douglas Chandor.

Moving up the hallway, visitors next come to the China Room, which was set aside by First Lady Edith Wilson to display china and glass pieces used by the presidents. The china pieces are housed in glass display cabinets. The portrait of Grace Coolidge visitors see in this room was painted in 1924 by Howard Chandler Christy. Mrs. Coolidge posed for the portrait because President Calvin Coolidge was too busy with events concerning the Teapot Dome Scandal to keep a scheduled appointment to sit for his portrait. The red dress worn by Mrs. Coolidge in the portrait determines the color scheme for this room, and is carried through by the velvet lined china cabinets and an English rug, circa 1850. Two early nineteenth-century chairs, known as "Martha Washington" or "lolling" chairs, flank the fireplace. The painting above the mantel, entitled *View on the Mississippi, Fifty-Seven Miles Below St. Anthony Falls, Minneapolis* was painted by Ferdinand Richard in 1858, the year Minnesota was admitted to the Union.

Proceeding up the hallway, visitors next come to the Diplomatic Reception Room. This room, one of three oval shaped rooms in the residence (the others are the Blue Room on the State Floor and the Yellow Oval Room on the second floor) was furnished in the manner of a Federal period parlor during President Dwight D. Eisenhower's presidency in 1960. At that time, the gold-and-white color scheme of the room was determined and such furnishings as a Pembroke table, sofa and armchairs, all of which are in the Hepplewhite style were placed in the room. The sofa is flanked by Sheridan-style card tables and there are also a pair of Sheridan-style settees and two matching chairs attributed to the Slover and Taylor workshop of New York. On the floor is an oval rug in the Aubusson style which was specially woven for this room; its border displays the emblems of the 50 states. (Due to wear and tear, the rug has been replaced twice, in 1971 and 1983.) A Regency chandelier was added to the room in 1971, while Richard M. Nixon was president. This room is used ceremonially by new ambassadors and their families, who enter the room directly through the South Grounds entrance to the White House to present their credentials to the president. President Franklin D. Roosevelt broadcast his famous "fireside chats" on the radio from this room. The wallpaper in this room, called "Scenic America," was first printed in 1834 by Jean Zuber et Cie in Rixheim, Alsace, France. It depicts Niagara Falls, New York Bay, West Point, Boston Harbor, and the Natural Bridge in Virginia.

The next room up the hallway is the Map Room, which was used by President Franklin Roosevelt as a situation room from which to follow the military events of World War II. In 1970, during Richard M. Nixon's presidency, the room was redecorated in the Chippendale style of the late eighteenth century, and now serves as a private meeting room for the president and the first lady. It contains several examples of "blockfront" furniture, an American adaptation of the Chippendale style in which the central of three vertical panels of a piece of furniture is recessed. A blockfront chest

made in Massachusetts circa 1760 and a blockfront slant-top desk from Rhode Island dating from between 1760 and 1765 is in this room. On a Philadelphia Chippendale desk in this room is a medicine chest that belonged to President James Madison which was taken from the White House by a British soldier in 1814 and was returned in 1939 by one of his descendants. Three landscape paintings by artists of the Hudson River School hang here: Jasper Cropsey's 1876 painting, *Autumn Landscape on the Hudson River*; William Hart's 1858 work, *Lake Among the Hills*; and Alvan Fisher's 1854 painting, *Tending Cows and Sheep*. The Persian rug in this room is a colorful Heriz, and the cut-glass chandelier seen here, which features rare star pendants, was made in England circa 1765.

Next, visitors proceed to the state floor, where they first view the East Room, the largest room in the White House. This room is used for ceremonies, receptions, press conferences, and other events requiring much space. Several weddings, including those of President Ulysses Grant's daughter Nellie, President Theodore Roosevelt's daughter Alice, and President Lyndon Johnson's daughter Lynda Bird, were held here. The bodies of seven presidents have lain in state here. The room was originally conceived by Mr. Hoban as a "public audience room," and its eighteenth-century classical style appearance today largely reflects the work of the McKim architectural firm during its 1902 restoration of the White House under President Theodore Roosevelt. The oak floor of Fontainebleau parquetry is notable, as are the three Bohemian cut-glass chandeliers. The wood paneling on the walls, painted white, includes eight relief insets illustrating Aesop's fables. Delicate plaster decorations adorn the ceiling. In keeping with the gold-and-white color scheme envisioned by Mrs. Theodore Roosevelt, gold damask draperies of French fabric were installed at the windows in 1983 during the presidency of Ronald Reagan. Normally, the room contains little furniture, but one piece normally on display here is a Steinway grand piano with gilt eagle supports and gilt stenciling by Dunbar Beck. The piano was designed by Eric Gugler and given to the White House by the manufacturer in 1938. Also here is a full-length portrait of George Washington which is a replica made by Gilbert Stuart of his original "Landsdowne" portrait. Except for a period after the 1814 fire, it has hung in the White House since 1814. Dolley Madison lingered during the 1814 White House fire to rescue the painting, ordering the canvas removed from its frame and taken away for safe keeping (time did not permit unscrewing the frame from the wall).

The next room on the tour is the Green Room, which was once used as President Thomas Jefferson's dining room. Today, it is a first floor parlor and is used for receptions. Most of the furnishings here were made by Duncan Phyfe in New York circa 1810. The green color scheme of the room began with President Jefferson, who wrote that the room included a "canvas floor cloth, painted Green," and was continued by President and Mrs. James Monroe, who decorated the room with green silks. Under President John Quincy

Adams, the name "Green Drawing Room" was used, and the room has remained the Green Room ever since that time. The room has been refurbished many times, most recently during the Nixon administration in 1971. Its walls were recovered with delicate watered-silk fabric originally selected by Mrs. John F. Kennedy in 1962, and its draperies are of striped beige, green and coral silk damask. The carpet is a Turkish Hereke of nineteenth-century design, and has a multi-colored pattern on a green field. A New York sofa table in front of a green, coral and white striped settee holds a silver Sheffield coffee urn that belonged to President John Adams and dates from circa 1785. It was presented to the White House in 1964 and an engraved, ribbon-hung ellipse above the spigot bears the initials "JAA"—John and Abigail Adams. The urn is flanked by matching silver French candlesticks purchased by James Madison from James Monroe in 1803. Portraits of these two presidents hang over the doors on the west wall here; the Madison portrait is by John Vanderlyn and the Monroe portrait is attributed to Samuel F. B. Morse. Other portraits here include Gilbert Stuart's portraits of John Quincy and Louisa Catherine Adams, painted in 1818 and 1821, respectively. George Martin's 1767 portrait of Benjamin Franklin hangs over the mantel, an 1858 George P.A. Healy portrait of President James K. Polk, and an 1895 Eastman Johnson portrait of President Benjamin Harrison also hang here.

The next room visitors see is the oval-shaped Blue Room, which is used by the president to greet guests. Its decor, in the French Empire style, was chosen by President Monroe in 1817, and it was completely renovated under President Nixon in 1972. The "blue room" tradition was originated by President Martin Van Buren, who redecorated the "oval saloon" in 1837. Today, seven of the French Bellange chairs and one settee selected by President Monroe are still in the room. The room also features an early nineteenth century French Empire gilt wood chandelier encircled by acanthus leaves. The wallpaper frieze, the cornice and the oval plaster ceiling medallion above the chandelier carry out this motif. The draperies, blue satin with handmade fringe and gold satin valances, were copied from an early nineteenth century French design. The oval rug, which displays an Oriental adaptation of a French design, was woven in Beijing, circa 1850. On the white marble mantel sits a Hannibal clock, one of the bronze-dore objects purchased for this room by President Monroe in 1817. Portraits hanging in the Blue Room include: an 1819 portrait of Andrew Jackson by John Wesley Jarvis; an 1800 Rembrandt Peale portrait of Thomas Jefferson (painted from life in Philadelphia while Mr. Jefferson was vice president); a 1793 portrait of John Adams by John Trumbull (added to the room in 1986); and an 1859 portrait of John Tyler by George P.A. Healy (considered to be the finest of a series of presidential portraits painted by Mr. Healy for the White House under a commission from Congress).

The Red Room, the next room on the White House tour, is one of four reception rooms in the White House. Presi-

dent John Adams used it as a breakfast room, and it was known as the "yellow drawing room" when Dolley Madison used it for her fashionable Wednesday night receptions. Mrs. Madison's portrait, painted by Gilbert Stuart in 1804, hangs in this room today. This room was also the place where Rutherford B. Hayes took the oath of office on March 3, 1877. The room was redecorated in 1971 under President Nixon, using the American Empire style chosen in 1962 during the Kennedy administration. The furnishings are of the 1810-1830 period, and include a mahogany secretary-bookcase and a mahogany sofa attributed to French-born cabinetmaker Charles-Honore Lannuier. The fabrics in the room were woven in the United States using French Empire designs. A neoclassical style white marble bust of President Martin Van Buren by Hiram Powers, for which the president posed in 1836, is displayed on a wall between the windows. Also in this room is a portrait of President Van Buren's daughter-in-law Angelica Singleton Van Buren, who acted as official hostess for the widower president at the President's House. This portrait was painted by Henry Inman in 1842. On the marble mantel, which is identical to the one in the Green Room, is a late eighteenth-century bronze-dore clock given to the White House by French President Vincent Auriol in 1952. The clock plays pastoral music on a miniature organ inside its gilded case. Hanging from the ceiling is a French Empire 36-light chandelier made of carved and gilded wood and dating from about 1805. Albert Bierstadt's *View of the Rocky Mountains*, signed and dated 1870, hangs above an 1825 Empire sofa.

The last room on the tour is the state dining room, which has a seating capacity of 140 and is used for state dinners and luncheons. It features English oak paneling dating from the 1902 renovation. The room was enlarged by the McKim firm in 1902. On display during tours here is a long mahogany dining table, which is surrounded by Queen Anne chairs. On the table are pieces from the gilt service purchased in France in 1817 for President Monroe. Suspended from the ceiling are two rococo revival candelabras from the Hayes administration. The soft green and brown rug was specially woven for this room in 1973 and resembles a seventeenth century Persian design. Above the mantel is George P. A. Healy's 1869 portrait of a contemplative President Abraham Lincoln, which was acquired by the president's son, Robert Todd Lincoln. Robert Todd Lincoln's widow bequeathed the portrait to the White House in 1939. Carved into the mantel is the White House motto, the words written by President Adams to his wife on his second night in the President's House in 1800.

On their way out of the White House, visitors walk through the Cross Hall, which extends between the state dining room and the East Room, on the state floor. On display in the Cross Hall are marble busts of American diplomat and poet Joel Barlow by Jean-Antoine Houdon and a bust of George Washington after Houdon. A French settee once owned by President Monroe is found below Aaron Shikler's 1970 portrait of John F. Kennedy, and Greta

Kempton's portrait of President Harry S Truman is also on the west end of the Cross Hall. On the east end of the Cross Hall are other presidential portraits: Lyndon Johnson by Elizabeth Shoumatoff, Richard Nixon by J. Anthony Wills, and Jimmy Carter by Herbert E. Abrams. The presidential seal is displayed above the Cross Hall entrance to the Blue Room.

Passing through the colonnade designed by architect James Hoban, visitors see the North Entrance Hall. Following in tradition, portraits of recent presidents hang here and in the Cross Hall. The east and west walls of the North Entrance Hall currently display portraits of Dwight D. Eisenhower and Gerald R. Ford. To the east is the main stairway, along which are portraits of Presidents Wilson, Harding, Franklin Roosevelt and William McKinley. A portrait of Herbert Hoover hangs above an American pier table on the stair landing. Before state dinners, the president greets guests of honor in the Yellow Oval Room on the third floor, then accompanies the guests down the main stairway to the East Room where the other guests are gathered. The North Entrance Hall is furnished with French Empire gilded furniture pieces used by President Monroe, as well as a French pier table and a pair of French settees with mahogany swan heads purchased by President Monroe in 1817.

Many rooms of the White House are used by the president and his family as living quarters or by the president and his staff as offices. These rooms are not included in the tour, and the family dining room, on the state floor, is one such room. On the third floor are: the East Sitting Hall, the Queens' Bedroom (named for its many royal guests), the Lincoln Bedroom, the Lincoln Sitting Room, the Treaty Room (the former Cabinet Room, where President Kennedy signed the Partial Nuclear Test Ban Treaty in 1963), the Center Hall, the Yellow Oval Room, the President's Dining Room, and the West Sitting Hall. The third floor also includes private residential space. The West Wing, where the President and his staff's offices are located, includes: the West Wing Reception Room, the Roosevelt Room (named in honor of Theodore Roosevelt and used for staff meetings and occasional press conferences), the Cabinet Room and the Oval Office.

The White House embodies the rich political, architectural and cultural traditions of the United States. But, like the nation whose chief executive resides there, it has evolved and changed over time, and will undoubtedly continue to be redecorated and enhanced to accommodate the changing needs of the president, his family, and the executive branch. There is so much to learn and to see while visiting the most famous house in America that repeated visits to the White House are warranted.

BIBLIOGRAPHY

Clark, Birge M., Memoirs About Mr. and Mrs Herbert Hoover, With Particular Emphasis on the Planning and Building of Their Home on San Juan Hill, Palo Alto, CA.

Dennis, Ruth, *The Homes of the Hoovers*, Herbert Hoover Presidential Library Association, Inc., West Branch, IA, 1986.

Hamke, Lorethea A., *All About William Henry Harrison*, Frances Vigo Chapter Daughters of the American Revolution, Vincennes, IN, 1985.

Hellman, Susan Holway, "Oak Hill: James Monroe's Loudon Seat," Thesis for the Degree of Master of Architectural History, School of Architecture, University of Virginia.

Kern, Ellyn R., *Where the American Presidents Lived*, Cottontail Publications, Indianapolis, IN, 1982.

Kochmann, Rachel M., *Presidents Birthplaces, Homes, and Burial Sites*, Hass Printing, Park Rapids, MN, 1989.

Krusen, Jessie Ball Thompson, *Tuckahoe Plantation*, Richmond, VA, 1975.

Whitney, David C., *The American Presidents*, Prentice Hall Press, NY, 1990.

PHOTO CREDITS

All photos by the authors unless otherwise indicated. 3: Mount Vernon Ladies' Association. 6: NPS photo by Thomas L. Davies. 8: NPS, Adams NHS, Richard Cheek. 24: Susan Holway Hellman. 27: SC Dept. of Parks, Recreation & Tourism. 32: NPS, ENP&MA. 37: Francis Vigo Chapter, DAR. 42: James K. Polk Memorial. 44: James K. Polk Memorial. 51: Thomas Noble, Fillmore Glen SP. 53: Aurora Historical Society. 60: Johnette Willa Myers. 65 (top): NPS, ENP&MA. 65 (bottom): Abraham Lincoln's Boyhood Home. 68: NPS photo by David Muench, Lincoln Boyhood NM, ENP&MA. 70: Lincoln's New Salem Enterprises. 72: NPS, Lincoln Home NHS. 80: Mr. & Mrs. John A. Ruthven. 82: Ulysses S. Grant NHS. 84: Bill Stover. 86: Illinois Historic Preservation Agency, Div. of Historic Sites, Photo by Jim Quick. 93: James A. Garfield NHS. 102: New York State Office of General Services. 111: Tim Belden, MB Operating Co. 115: NPS, ENP&MA. 135: Richland County Historic Preservation Commission. 137: Woodrow Wilson House, National Trust for Historic Preservation. 148: Vid Johnson. 151: National Society of Colonial Dames, State of Oregon. 154: Tom Fischer, photographer, Lou Henry Hoover House. 162: GA Dept. of Natural Resources, Parks & Historic Sites Div. 164: Lamar Lions Club. 166: Harry S Truman Library. 168: Harry S Truman Library. 171: Elizabeth Newland, The Little White House. 173: Milton Hinnant. 176: Dwight D. Eisenhower Library. 199: Gerald R. Ford Library. 201: Gerald R. Ford Library. 206: Jimmy Carter Library. 209: Phyllis B. Kandul. 211: Photo by Earl Krantz. 213: Ronald Reagan Home Preservation Foundation. 216: State of California Resources Agency, Dept. of Parks and Recreation. 220: The White House. 222: David Valdez, The White House. 224: The Governor's Mansion of Arkansas. 228: Bureau of Engraving and Printing.

ABOUT THE AUTHORS

NANCY DUFFIELD MYERS BENBOW is a teacher. She holds a Bachelor of Science degree from Wagner College in New York and a Master of Science degree from the City University of New York.

CHRISTOPHER H. BENBOW is an attorney. He earned a Bachelor of Arts degree from Hampshire College in Massachusetts and holds a Juris Doctor degree from New York Law School.